To Sarah
with all good wishes

The Abolition of Feudal Tenure in Scotland

For Lucy

The Abolition of Feudal Tenure in Scotland

Kenneth G C Reid, MA, LLB, WS, FRSE
Scottish Law Commissioner
Professor of Property Law, University of Edinburgh

Print on Demand Edition

Tottel
publishing

Published by
Tottel Publishing Ltd
Maxwelton House
41-43 Boltro Road
Haywards Heath
West Sussex
RH16 1BJ

Tottel Publishing Ltd
9-10 St Andrew Square
Edinburgh
EH2 2AF

ISBN 13: 978-1-84592-751-6
ISBN 10: 1-84592-751-6
© Kenneth G C Reid 2003
Formerly published by LexisNexis Butterworths

This edition reprinted by Tottel Publishing Ltd 2007

British Library Cataloguing-in-Publication Data.
A catalogue record for this book is available from the British Library.

Typeset by Phoenix Photosetting, Chatham, Kent
Printed and bound in Great Britain by
Marston Book Services, Abingdon, Oxfordshire

Preface

The feudal system of land tenure was introduced to Scotland in the twelfth century. Its abolition, on 28 November 2004, marks a profound change both in land law and in conveyancing practice. Abolition itself is achieved by the Abolition of Feudal Tenure etc (Scotland) Act 2000, while a new system of real burdens is inaugurated by the Title Conditions (Scotland) Act 2003. In describing the difficult transition from feudalism to post-feudalism, this book is concerned mainly with the 2000 Act, but something is also said of the 2003 Act.

For me these Acts have personal significance. Both originated with the Scottish Law Commission, and for several years they occupied most of my working life, and the working lives of others at the Commission. This book should not, however, be seen as an official guide. I am no longer on intimate terms with the legislation. The struggles and the doubts in developing the proposals, the occasional good ideas and the many bad ones, have faded from memory. What is left is a legislative text which requires to be interpreted and explained in the same way as any other. In attempting to do so I have tried to draw attention to the underlying policy objectives as well as to the interplay of, apparently disparate, provisions. It need hardly be said that the views expressed are entirely my own.

With some hesitation, and in the knowledge that experience will disclose their shortcomings, I have provided some styles and some suggested completions of the statutory forms. Prudent readers will consult the legislation as well as this book.

Kenneth G C Reid
22 June 2003

Contents

Table of Statutes

Table of Statutory Instruments

Table of Cases

Abbreviations

1974 Act
Land Tenure Reform (Scotland) Act 1974 (c 38)

2000 Act
Abolition of Feudal Tenure etc (Scotland) Act 2000 (asp 5)

2003 Act
Title Conditions (Scotland) Act 2003 (asp 9)

AFT(S)A 2000
Abolition of Feudal Tenure etc (Scotland) Act 2000 (asp 5)

Scottish Law Commission *Report on Abolition of the Feudal System*
Scottish Law Commission *Report on Abolition of the Feudal System*, Scot Law Com no 168 (1999; available on www.scotlawcom.gov.uk)

Scottish Law Commission *Report on Real Burdens*
Scottish Law Commission *Report on Real Burdens*, Scot Law Com no 181 (2000; available on www.scotlawcom.gov.uk)

TC(S)A 2003
Title Conditions (Scotland) Act 2003 (asp 9)

Glossary

Some terms of feudal law will not be familiar to all readers; and much new terminology is introduced by the legislation, particularly by the Title Conditions (Scotland) Act 2003. This glossary is a selective guide. The use of italics signifies that the word or phrase in question is defined elsewhere in the glossary.

Affirmative burden. A real burden comprising an obligation to do something: see the Title Conditions (Scotland) Act 2003, s 2(1)(a), (2)(a). An example would be an obligation to maintain the common parts in a tenement. Compare *negative burden*.

Allocated feuduty. A, previously *cumulo*, *feuduty* which has been formally divided among the *vassals* of the *feu*. Each vassal is liable only for that amount which has been allocated to his part of the feu.

Appointed day. Martinmas (28 November) 2004. This is the date set both for the abolition of the feudal system and for the introduction of the new regime for real burdens. See the Abolition of Feudal Tenure etc (Scotland) Act 2000, ss 71, 77 and TC(S)A 2003, ss 122(1), 129.

Apportioned feuduty. A *cumulo feuduty* which has been informally apportioned among the *vassals* of the *feu*. Compare *allocated feuduty*. Despite the apportionment, the feuduty can be claimed in full from any one vassal.

Benefited property. The land for the benefit of which a real burden or servitude is created: see TC(S)A 2003, s 1(2)(b). The more traditional term, used throughout the Abolition of Feudal Tenure etc (Scotland) Act 2000, is *dominant tenement*. After 28 November 2004 a *praedial real burden* is enforceable by the owner of the benefited property, and by any tenant, proper liferenter, or non-entitled spouse: see TC(S)A 2003, s 8.

Burdened property. The land burdened by a real burden or servitude: see TC(S)A 2003, s 1(2)(a). The more traditional term, used throughout the Abolition of Feudal Tenure etc (Scotland) Act 2000, is *servient tenement*. After 28 November 2004 a real burden is enforceable against the owner of the burdened property and, in the case of a *negative burden*, against any other person having use of that property: see TC(S)A 2003, s 9.

Co-feuars. A group of *feuars* (*vassals*) holding from the same superior and subject to the same or equivalent *feudal real burdens*.

Community burden. A real burden which regulates a group or 'community' of properties and which is mutually enforceable among the owners of those properties: see TC(S)A 2003, 25(1). Each property in the community is thus both a *burdened* and also a *benefited property*, and enforcement is reciprocal. Compare *neighbour burden*.

Compensation notice. A notice served under the Abolition of Feudal Tenure etc (Scotland) Act 2000 claiming compensation for the extinction of *feuduty* or of a *development value burden*. Compare *preservation notice*.

Conservation burden. A *personal real burden* held either by a conservation body or Scottish Ministers and which preserves the built or natural environment for the benefit of the public: see TC(S)A 2003, s 38(1).

Cumulo feuduty. The total *feuduty* for a *feu* in circumstances where the feu has been divided by *substitution* without the feuduty being *allocated*. Cumulo (or 'unallocated') feuduty can be claimed in full from any one *vassal*.

Development value burden. A *feudal real burden* which reserves development value and the imposition of which caused a significant reduction in the consideration for the feu: AFT(S)A 2000, s 33(1).

Dominant tenement. The land for the benefit of which a real burden or servitude is created. A synonym, preferred by the TC(S)A 2003, is *benefited property*.

Dominium. The Latin word for ownership.

Dominium directum. The feudal estate held by a *superior*. A synonym is *superiority*.

Dominium utile. The feudal estate held by the lowest *vassal* in a feudal chain.

Economic development burden. A *personal real burden* held either by a local authority or Scottish Ministers and which promotes economic development: see TC(S)A 2003, s 45(1).

Facility burden. A real burden which regulates the maintenance, management, reinstatement or use of facilities such as the common parts of a tenement, a common recreational area, a private road, private sewerage, or a boundary wall: see TC(S)A 2003, s 122(1), (3).

Feu. A feudal estate in land. The term usually refers to *dominium utile*.

Feuar. The person who holds feudal land, of a *superior*. A synonym is *vassal*.

Feudal real burden. A real burden created before 28 November 2004 in (i) a *grant in feu* (such as a feu disposition) or (ii) a deed of conditions registered in association with a grant in feu. All feudal real burdens are enforceable by the feudal *superior*. The *burdened property* is the *feu* held by the *vassal*. Some are also enforceable by *co-feuars*. Compare *non-feudal real burdens*.

Feuduty. The *reddendo* due by the *vassal* under feu farm tenure: a, usually small, sum of money payable twice a year at the term days of Whitsunday and Martinmas.

Grant in feu. The creation of a new feudal estate, by *subinfeudation*. Three deeds were available for this purpose: feu charter, feu disposition, and feu contract.

Grassum. Capital sum payable, usually for a *grant in feu*.

Health care burden. A *personal real burden* held either by a National Health Service trust or Scottish Ministers and which promotes the provision of facilities for health care: see TC(S)A 2003, s 46(1).

Manager burden. A real burden conferring power to manage a group of properties: see TC(S)A 2003, s 63(1). Almost always it is constituted as a *personal real burden*. Normally a manager burden has a fixed life of five years.

Maritime burden. A *personal real burden* held by the Crown in which the *burdened property* is the sea bed or foreshore: see TC(S)A 2003, s 44.

Negative burden. A real burden comprising an obligation not to do something, ie which restricts the use of the *burdened property*: see TC(S)A 2003, s 2(1)(b), (2)(b). An example would be a prohibition on use of the property for the purpose of any trade, business or profession. Compare *affirmative burden*.

Neighbour burden. A real burden in which the *benefited property* is itself free from the burden. Enforcement is therefore non-reciprocal: the owner of the benefited property can enforce against the owner of the *burdened property*, but not the other way around. Compare *community burden*. 'Neighbour burden' does not appear in the legislation.

Non-feudal real burden. A real burden created before 28 November 2004 in (i) a disposition or (ii) a deed of conditions registered in association with a disposition. As a type of *praedial real burden* a non-feudal burden must have a *benefited property* as well as a *burdened property*. Where a disposition is used, the benefited property is usually such land as was retained by the disponer. In the case of a deed of conditions it is typically the other properties which are subject to the same deed. Compare *feudal real burden*.

Over-feuduty. *Feuduty* due from a *superior* to his own superior.

Over-superior. The *superior* of a superior. Thus if C holds of B who holds of A, A is, from the point of view of C, the over-superior (B being the superior). From the point of view of A, C is the sub-vassal (B being the *vassal*).

Personal pre-emption burden. A right of pre-emption held as a *personal real burden*: see AFT(S)A 2000, s 18A(1).

Personal real burden. A real burden in favour of a person. Compare *praedial real burden*. In a personal real burden there is a *burdened property* but no *benefited property*. Eight types are recognised, but they are restricted in respect both of content and of permitted holder: see TC(S)A 2003, s 1(3). Examples include *conservation burdens* and *economic development burdens*.

Personal redemption burden. A right of redemption held as a *personal real burden*: see AFT(S)A 2000, s 18A(1).

Praedial real burden. A real burden in favour of another plot of land (or praedium). A praedial real burden thus requires a *benefited property* as well as a *burdened property*. Before 28 November 2004 real burdens were either *feudal* or *non-feudal*. A non-feudal real burden was praedial. On or after 28 November 2004 most real burdens are praedial (see TC(S)A 2003, s 1(1)) but a new category of *personal real burden* is also introduced. The term 'praedial real burden' does not appear in the legislation.

Preservation notice. A notice served and registered under the Abolition of Feudal Tenure etc (Scotland) Act 2000 and which has the effect of preserving a *feudal real burden*. Compare *compensation notice*.

Reddendo. The periodical payment, in money, services or in kind, due by a *vassal* to the *superior* in return for the *feu*. The standard reddendo is *feuduty*.

Rural housing burden. A right of pre-emption held by a rural housing body as a *personal real burden*: see TC(S)A 2003, s 43(1).

Separate tenement. Heritable property owned separately from the ownership of the ground. Of the limited examples recognised, some are corporeal (as for example minerals) and some incorporeal (as for example salmon fishings).

Service burden. A real burden on one property to supply a service, such as water or electricity, for another: see TC(S)A 2003, s 122(1).

Servient tenement. The land burdened by a real burden or servitude. A synonym, preferred by the TC(S)A 2003, is *burdened property*.

Subinfeudation. The creation of a new feudal estate by a *grant in feu*. Compare *substitution*. If B holds of A and then subfeus to C, the result is that C is the *vassal* of B, and B the vassal of A.

Subordinate real right. Any real right other than ownership (such real rights thus being 'subordinate' to the primary real right of ownership).

Substitution. An ordinary transfer of a *feu* such that the transferee substitutes in the feudal chain for the transferor. Compare *subinfeudation*. Substitution is effected by use of a disposition. Thus if B holds of A and then grants a disposition to C, the result is that C replaces B as the *vassal* of A.

Superior. The person of whom, in feudal tenure, land is held. Compare *vassal*.

Superiority. The feudal estate held by a *superior*. A synonym is *dominium directum*.

Title condition. Generic term for (i) real burdens; (ii) servitudes; (iii) conditions in long leases; and (iv) certain other conditions running with the land: see TC(S)A 2003, s 122(1). In effect it is the name given to those conditions that can be discharged by the Lands Tribunal. The equivalent term under the law in force before 28 November 2004 was 'land obligation'.

Vassal. The person who holds feudal land, of a *superior*. A synonym is *feuar*.

Chapter 1

The end of feudalism

THE FEUDAL SYSTEM OF LAND TENURE

Origins

1.1   The importance in European legal development of Roman law, canon law, and feudal law – of the three systems of learned law – needs hardly be stressed[1]. During the medieval period and beyond each constituted, in some sense, a *jus commune* (a common law) for much of Europe, with a common literature written in a common language. Thus the *Corpus Juris Civilis* and *Corpus Juris Canonici* of, respectively, Roman and canon law were matched by the *Libri Feudorum* (Books of the Feus), a twelfth-century compilation of Lombardic feudalism which was often included as an appendix to the *Corpus Juris Civilis*[2]. Like the *Corpus Juris Civilis* it came to be glossed by Accursius. Thomas Craig's *Jus Feudale* (c 1600), although much later, is a work in this tradition, and indeed is the only work by a Scottish jurist which can be considered as a *jus commune* text.

In Scotland feudalism arrived late by the standards of the rest of Europe[3]. It was brought to England by William the Conqueror in 1066 and spread north from there[4]. The oldest surviving grant in feu by a Scottish king dates from 1094[5]. By the end of the following century the grip of feudalism was reasonably secure, although several centuries would pass before the more remote parts of the kingdom succumbed. Even then, there were pockets of allodial (ie non-feudal) land remaining, especially in Orkney and Shetland which were ceded to Scotland by Norway only in the late fifteenth century and which even today retain the vestiges of udal (odal) law and of an allodial system of land law[6].

At first there was little to distinguish Scottish feudalism from the feudal system as it applied in England but over time the systems moved apart[7]. A key point of divergence was the statute *Quia Emptores* of 1290 which, by prohibiting subinfeudation in England, prevented a proliferation of feus. In Scotland, subinfeudation continued to be competent, and practised, right up to the time of the abolition of feudalism in 2004. In subinfeudation, indeed, lay the main utility of feudalism in the modern period.

1   See eg F Wieacker *A History of Private Law in Europe* (transl T Weir, 1995); O F Robinson, T
     D Fergus and W M Gordon *European Legal History* (3rd edn, 2000); J W Cairns 'Historical
     Introduction' in K Reid and R Zimmermann (eds) *A History of Private Law in Scotland* (2000)
     vol 1 pp 14 ff.
2   See eg Thomas Glyn Watkin *An Historical Introduction to Modern Civil Law* (1999) pp 89 ff.
     A translation of the *Libri Feudorum* is included at the end of the second volume of Lord
     Clyde's translation of Craig's *Jus Feudale*.
3   There is a rich historical literature on European feudalism. See for example M Bloch *Feudal
     Society* (transl L A Manyon, 1962); F L Ganshof *Feudalism* (3rd edn, trans P Grierson, 1964);
     S Reynolds *Fiefs and Vassals: the Medieval Evidence Reinterpreted* (1994). For Scotland see
     H L MacQueen *Common Law and Feudal Society in Medieval Scotland* (1993); H L
     MacQueen 'Tears of a Legal Historian: Scottish Feudalism and the Ius Commune' 2003 JR 1.
4   See eg A A M Duncan *Scotland: The Making of a Kingdom* (1975) pp 133 ff; M Lynch
     Scotland: A New History (1991) pp 55 ff.
5   It is reproduced in P Gouldesbrough *Formulary of Old Scots Legal Documents* (Stair Society
     vol 36, 1985) pp 158–9. The charter is by Duncan II in favour of the Monks of Durham.
6   Para 10.19. Other allodial land included certain property of the Church of Scotland. See further
     W M Gordon *Scottish Land Law* (2nd edn, 1999) ch 3.
7   For a stimulating account, see C D Farran *The Principles of Scots and English Land Law*
     (1958). C F Kolbert and N A M Mackay *History of Scots and English Land Law* (1977) is based
     on Farran's work.

Subinfeudation and substitution

1.2   As developed by the jurists of Continental Europe, feudalism was a system of
elegance, sophistication and complexity. Its intricate rules dominate the accounts of
land law given by the institutional writers in Scotland. For present purposes, however, feudal law can be reduced to a small number of key principles, familiar to
modern-day conveyancers[1].

The foundation principle is that land cannot be owned outright but must always be
held from (or 'of')[2] someone else. Ultimately, all titles derive from the Crown which,
in feudal theory, was the original owner of all land. Sometimes there is only one link
to the Crown, so that the person in possession is also the Crown vassal. Much more
commonly land is held of an intermediary, who in turn holds either of another intermediary or of the Crown itself. A person holding land is known as a 'vassal' or
'feuar', a person from whom the land is held as a 'superior'. And an intermediary is
both a vassal and a superior: the vassal of the person from whom the land is held and
the superior of the person who in turn holds the land from him.

This complex state of affairs is the product of subinfeudation[3]. Suppose that Andrew,
who holds directly of the Crown, wishes to sell land to Beth. The conveyancing may
be effected in one of two ways. If Andrew proceeds by substitution, the result is for
Beth to take his place as vassal of the Crown. In feudal terms, matters remain as they
were before, but with the substitution of one vassal for another. If, however, Andrew
proceeds by subinfeudation, a new feudal link is created and Beth becomes the vassal of Andrew, Andrew remaining in the feudal chain as the vassal of the Crown.

Substitution is achieved by the granting of a disposition. Subinfeudation requires a feu disposition, feu charter or feu contract. Relatively speaking, subinfeudation was always uncommon, and in modern times it has become increasingly rare. But every time it is resorted to the result is to create a new, and permanent, tenurial link, and hence further to complicate the relationship of vassal to the land.

<ol>
<li>Who will, it is hoped, forgive the elementary account which follows.</li>
<li>'Of' (the Latin preposition de) is more correct but can sound awkward in ordinary speech. It is used in the tenendas clause in grants of feu ('to be holden of me . . .').</li>
<li>See generally K G C Reid The Law of Property in Scotland (1996) (G L Gretton) paras 57–62.</li>
</ol>

Tenures and *reddendo*

1.3   Each subinfeudation imposes a new set of rights and obligations. The vassal has the right to use the land. In return he must make payment (*reddendo*) to the superior. The nature of the *reddendo* depends both on the type of tenure by which the land is to be held, and on what is stipulated for in the feu disposition or other grant in feu[1]. The only tenures to have survived into the twentieth century are feu farm and blench, with almost all land being held on the former. The *reddendo* in feu farm tenure is feuduty, a twice-yearly payment, originally often in kind but later converted into money. Blench tenure is, in effect, a free tenure, with only a notional payment to the superior, such as a penny Scots if asked only. A standard tenure of medieval feudalism was wardholding whose *reddendo* of hunting and hosting required of the vassal attendance, with his men, in the time of the King's wars.

For most of feudalism's long history the *reddendo*, a regular periodical payment, was supplemented by irregular payments on certain occurrences such as the transfer of the land, whether on sale or by inheritance. These 'casualties' varied with the type of tenure and could be of considerable value.

Under feudal law the right to natural (ie physical) possession is held only by the ultimate vassal. Thus if Andrew subfeus to Beth, the right to possess passes to Beth. But if Beth in turn subfeus to Colin, it is Colin who can possess, and Beth's role is confined to the receipt of *reddendo* from Colin and to the payment of *reddendo* to Andrew.

<ol>
<li>K G C Reid The Law of Property in Scotland (1996) (G L Gretton) paras 63 ff. See also A J van der Walt and D G Kleyn 'Duplex Dominium: The History and Significance of the Concept of Divided Ownership' in D P Visser (ed) Essays on the History of Law (1989) pp 213–60.</li>
</ol>

Dominium directum and *dominium utile*

1.4   The revival of Roman law in the eleventh and twelfth centuries prompted a re-examination of the theoretical basis of feudalism. One obvious difficulty was the location of ownership (*dominium*)[1]. Roman law taught that, in the normal case at least, ownership must be undivided, so that in respect of any one thing there can only be one right of ownership. But this rule could scarcely be applied to a feudal system in which the respective rights of superior and vassal were evenly balanced and where neither could be said to be an outright owner of the land. The result was a compromise. It was accepted, contrary to the teachings of Roman law, that ownership of feudal land was divided; but the quality of the ownership was not the same in each case. In terminology adopted from the *actio directa* and *actio utilis* of Roman law, it was said that the ultimate vassal held *dominium utile*, intermediate superiors *dominium directum*, and the Crown *dominium eminens*. Put together these fragmented rights amounted to full ownership of the land. Left separately they served as an explanation of a division of rights which was without parallel in the civil law.

These terms were adopted in Scotland[2], as elsewhere in Europe (although not in England), and they remain in use today. A common alternative to *dominium directum* is 'superiority'.

[1]   K G C Reid *The Law of Property in Scotland* (1996) (G L Gretton) paras 49–51.
[2]   Stair II.3.7, following Craig 1.9.9.

Later developments

1.5   Almost from the time of its introduction, feudalism in Scotland was in a state of gradual but continuous change. The long-term tendency was to move from a system of governance and control which happened to be founded on the ownership of land to a system which concerned the ownership of land alone. By the eighteenth century this process was substantially complete. A final date, if one is required, is 1746 when, following the rising by Bonnie Prince Charlie, legislation was passed which abolished the military tenure of wardholding and, substantially, the right of heritable jurisdiction[1]. From this point on most land was held on feu farm tenure, a holding which resembled nothing so much as a perpetual lease[2].

For some, these changes were evidence of the decline of a once vital institution. Already in 1600 Craig was complaining of the senility of feudalism (*feudorum senium*)[3]. By the 1820s, following the legislation just described, George Joseph Bell was able to tell his students at Edinburgh University that 'the feudal system is now abolished except as to the system of conveyancing formed upon it'[4].

The decline, if such it was, was accompanied by further reform[5]. In the middle years of the nineteenth century the system of feudal conveyancing was radically simplified. Symbolical delivery and instruments of sasine were dispensed with[6]. Charters by progress, other than charters of novodamus, were abolished, and with them the alternative manner of holding *a me vel de me*[7]. Feudal casualties were phased out from 1914 onwards[8], and even feuduty itself after 1974[9]. The result was a system largely divested of its medieval trappings. As George Gretton has observed[10]:

To the notary of the time of Charlemagne, to the author of the *Books of the Feus*, or even to Craig, the current Scottish system would appear not feudal but anti-feudal. Heritable proprietors are no longer bound to appear in arms at the summons of their superior, nor to attend his courts and to submit to his judgments in legal disputes, nor do unmarried owners find themselves faced with the choice either to accept the wife selected for them by their lord or to pay compensation if they are so ungrateful as to refuse. Properties may safely be offered for sale without fear of incurring the casualty of recognition, or even the casualty of composition, nor do law students have to master the casualties of relief, purpresture, non-entry, escheat, or disclamation. We complain that the law grows ever more complex, but sometimes we should recollect how much law has been consigned to a deserved and perpetual oblivion. Nonetheless, the Scottish system is still feudal, though most of the forms of feudalism have been abolished by statute, or have been abrogated by desuetude, and though the social and economic reality of feudalism has long since vanished.

1   Tenures Abolition Act 1746; Heritable Jurisdictions (Scotland) Act 1746.
2   Feu farm tenure was indeed often characterised as *emphyteusis*: see Craig I.9.19; Stair II.3.34; Erskine II.4.6.
3   Craig I.9.19.
4   G J Bell *Lectures on the Law of Scotland* p 164. This is a set of detailed notes in the possession of the writer which were taken of lectures delivered by Professor Bell between 26 October 1825 and 7 April 1826.
5   K G C Reid *The Law of Property in Scotland* (1996) (G L Gretton) para 113. And see para 1.17.
6   Infeftment Act 1845, s 1; Titles to Land (Scotland) Act 1858, s 1, later re-enacted as the Titles to Land Consolidation (Scotland) Act 1868, s 15. See further paras 1.22, 13.4.
7   Conveyancing (Scotland) Act 1874, s 4.
8   Feudal Casualties (Scotland) Act 1914.
9   Land Tenure Reform (Scotland) Act 1974, ss 1–7. See para 10.4.
10   K G C Reid *The Law of Property in Scotland* (1996) (G L Gretton) para 45.

Abolition

1.6   The feudal system was abolished in France as a result of the revolution of 1789. By the middle of the next century it had disappeared throughout Continental Europe[1]. In England feudalism was dismantled by Cromwell and further reformed in the 1920s so that the law today is feudal merely in the sense that land is still held from the Crown. In Scotland alone the feudal system has remained as an active system of land tenure. For this a number of reasons can be suggested. One is apathy or, to say the same thing more politely, lack of legislative opportunity. Another is a certain pride in the distinctiveness of Scots law; for if feudalism was not invented in Scotland, its continued presence there was a source of difference and, sometimes, of satisfaction. Feudalism too offered a measure of intellectual fulfilment, adding a veneer of scholasticism to the routine business of conveyancing, as well as a reassurance that the law remained, despite everything, a learned profession. To some extent it also made practical sense.

Thus feuduties were both a source of income for the superior and a convenience for a vassal who wished to pay for the land in stages and not all at once[2]; and the practice of imposing real burdens, which began in the 1790s and was in full flood by the 1820s, was a late, and novel, use of feudalism, and one which could not easily be replicated by other means. In itself this was an important reason for the preservation of the system at the very time when it was being abolished elsewhere[3].

In the course of its comprehensive review of conveyancing law and practice, published in 1966, the committee chaired by Professor J M Halliday recommended further modifications to the feudal system but not its abolition[4]. This approach, however, seemed over-cautious. Only three years later a white paper by the then Labour Government concluded that[5]:

> [T]he balance of argument is against perpetuation of the feudal system of land tenure . .The Government do not underrate the magnitude of the change which would be involved in adopting a new system. Nor do they imagine that the conversion to such a system and the working of the system itself would be free of difficulties. But, after careful consideration, they believe that it would be in the interests of Scotland and the Scottish people to abolish feudal tenure as a system of land-holding and to substitute a new system.

This conclusion was reinforced in a green paper published by the new Conservative administration in 1972[6]. The Land Tenure Reform (Scotland) Act of 1974 provided for the phasing out of feuduty, thus greatly assisting ultimate abolition. Yet the feudal system remained in place, and while the principle of abolition was widely accepted, the difficult question remained of how it was to be done. That question was finally taken up, some 20 years later, by the Scottish Law Commission.

[1] K G C Reid *The Law of Property in Scotland* (1996) (G L Gretton) para 45.
[2] Para 10.1.
[3] Paras 2.1–2.3.
[4] *Conveyancing Legislation and Practice* (Cmnd 3118, 1966) paras 38–57.
[5] Scottish Home and Health Department *Land Tenure in Scotland: A Plan for Reform* (Cmnd 4099, 1969) paras 21, 24.
[6] Scottish Home and Health Department *Land Tenure Reform in Scotland* (1972).

Abolition of Feudal Tenure etc (Scotland) Act 2000

1.7 By the time the Scottish Law Commission came to examine the question, the arguments in favour of feudal abolition were overwhelming[1]. As a result of the 1974 Act[2], feuduty had largely disappeared, following feudal casualties into the gloom of legal history. In the process the balance of interests between superior and vassal had been finally and irrevocably destroyed. The vassal was now the outright owner in everything but name; and in the absence of a *reddendo* for the feu, the superior's right was of little or no economic value. Indeed the fact that the cost of conveying a superiority was likely to exceed its value meant that superiorities were lapsing on death without being filled. The feudal system was falling in from above. Only real burdens remained of value, although, in a feudal context, with a tendency to be abused by superiors lacking a proper connection with the land other than a desire for the income generated by minutes of waiver[3]. By the end, the feudal system was like a ruined mansion in which only one room remained habitable. Rather than re-build the mansion, it was simpler to relocate the inhabitants.

The Scottish Law Commission's *Report on Abolition of the Feudal System*, complete with draft Bill, was published on 11 February 1999[4]. On 6 October 1999 the Bill, lightly revised, was introduced to the new Scottish Parliament. It completed its parliamentary progress on 3 May 2000, the fifth Bill to do so, and received Royal Assent on 9 June 2000[5]. A small number of provisions of the Abolition of Feudal Tenure etc (Scotland) Act 2000 came into force immediately, but the remainder of the Act comes into force in two stages[6]. Part 4, which allows superiors to preserve certain real burdens by service and registration of a notice, is in force from the autumn of 2003[7]. The day set for the abolition of the feudal system – referred to in the Act as the 'appointed day' – is Martinmas (28 November) 2004, when the rest of the Act comes into force[8]. The 2000 Act has since been amended in some important respects by the Title Conditions (Scotland) Act 2003[9], and is set out in that form in Appendix 1. It is with the 2000 Act as amended that this book is mainly concerned.

[1]   Scottish Law Commission *Report on Abolition of the Feudal System* paras 1.16–1.19.
[2]   Land Tenure Reform (Scotland) Act 1974, ss 4–6.
[3]   Para 2.3.
[4]   Scot Law Com no 168 (available on www.scotlawcom.gov.uk).
[5]   The lead committee at Stage 1 was the Justice and Home Affairs Committee, which heard oral evidence on 9 and 17 November 1999. The Committee's report was published in December 1999. The Stage 1 debate was on 15 December 1999. The Justice Committee reconsidered the Bill, at Stage 2, on 15, 21 and 29 March 2000. The Stage 3 debate, when the Bill was passed, was on 3 May 2000. The different stages are conveniently collected together in The Scottish Parliament *Passage of the Abolition of Feudal Tenure etc (Scotland) Bill 1999* (2001).
[6]   Abolition of Feudal Tenure etc (Scotland) Act 2000, s 77, as amended by the Title Conditions (Scotland) Act 2003, s 114(6), Sch 13, para 15.
[7]   At the time of writing the required order had not been made.
[8]   AFT(S)A 2000, s 71. At the time of writing the required order had not been made, but the date was announced by the Deputy First Minister during the Stage 1 debate on the Title Conditions Bill. See Scottish Parliament *Official Report* 21 November 2002 col 155.
[9]   TC(S)A 2003, ss 114, 128, Schs 13, 15.

EXTINCTION OF FEUDAL ESTATES

Abolition of the feudal system

1.8   The Abolition of Feudal Tenure etc (Scotland) Act 2000 begins with the words[1]:

The feudal system of land tenure, that is to say the entire system whereby land is held by a vassal on perpetual tenure from a superior is, on the appointed day, abolished.

This declamatory opening has attracted favourable comment[2] and is largely self-explanatory. The reference to 'the feudal system *of land tenure*' takes account of the fact that 'feudalism' is used pejoratively in popular speech to refer to all manner of antique rights and customs which have no connection with feudalism in the strict sense. They, of course, are unaffected by feudal abolition, as are aspects of feudalism – the House of Lords, for example – which are not tied to the system of land tenure[3].

[1]   Abolition of Feudal Tenure etc (Scotland) Act 2000, s 1.
[2]   As the Deputy First Minister said, 'Scotland has waited an awful long time to hear that sentence': see Scottish Parliament *Official Report* 15 December 1999 col 1543.
[3]   Scottish Law Commission *Report on Abolition of the Feudal System* paras 1.20, 1.21, 2.30.

From feudal ownership to outright ownership

1.9   On the appointed day *dominium utile* is upgraded to *dominium*, or in other words to outright ownership[1]. Law is thus brought into line with both economic reality and popular perception. In other respects the position of the (former) vassal is largely unchanged. Thus real rights which burdened the *dominium utile* before the appointed day – a standard security, for example, or a lease or servitude – will affect the new outright ownership after that day[2]. Only rights which depend on the feudal system – most notably feudal real burdens – are extinguished, although, as will be seen, with the possibility of preservation under Part 4 of the 2000 Act[3]. Further, the myriad restrictions on ownership of land imposed by common law and statute continue to affect post-feudal land in the same way as, previously, they affected land held on feudal tenure[4]. Outright ownership should not, therefore, be confused with unrestricted ownership. Indeed the restrictions on land are significantly increased by other legislation of the same Parliament, in particular by the Land Reform (Scotland) Act 2003 and the Agricultural Holdings (Scotland) Act 2003.

The conversion effected by the Act is directed at the right (*dominium utile*) and not at its holder, and the relationship of holder to right is intentionally unaffected. Thus a person who, immediately before the appointed day, was entitled under missives to the *dominium utile* of land has, on that day, the same entitlement in respect of outright ownership. Or the grantee of a disposition of land delivered before the appointed day but registered after it will become, on registration, the outright owner of the land.

[1]   Abolition of Feudal Tenure etc (Scotland) Act 2000, s 2(1): 'An estate of *dominium utile* of land shall, on the appointed day, cease to exist as a feudal estate but shall forthwith become the ownership of the land ...'
[2]   AFT(S)A 2000, s 2(1) continues: 'and, in so far as is consistent with the provisions of this Act, the land shall be subject to the same subordinate real rights and other encumbrances as was the

estate of *dominium utile*'. Subordinate real rights are real rights other than ownership: see K G
C Reid *The Law of Property in Scotland* (1996) para 6.

3   Para 1.17.
4   The main restrictions occupy almost 300 pages (pp 661–938) of W M Gordon *Scottish Land Law* (2nd edn 1999).

Abolition of superiorities

1.10   Feudal abolition presupposes the removal of superiorities and of superiors.
All superiorities, therefore, are abolished on the appointed day[1], including the paramount superiority of the Crown[2]. Subordinate real rights which burden a superiority
are, necessarily, extinguished to that extent but no further. Thus a standard security
over mixed estate (ie land held partly as *dominium directum* and partly as *dominium
utile*) is extinguished insofar as it burdens *dominium directum* but continues to burden the (now non-feudal) land which was previously held as *dominium utile*.

1   AFT(S)A 2000, s 2(2).
2   On the basis that the Act binds the Crown: see AFT(S)A 2000, s 58(1). For Crown rights, see
     paras 1.13–1.16.

Mixed estates

1.11   An owner who has feued some land but not all holds a mixture of *dominium
directum* and *dominium utile*. The same is true where land is feued under reservation
of minerals[1]. On the appointed day the result is for the *dominium utile* to be converted
into outright ownership and the *dominium directum* to be extinguished. It is then
important to be clear as to which part of the land was held on which basis. Usually
the issue will become a live one only on the first conveyance after the appointed day.
The 2000 Act amends the Land Registration (Scotland) Act 1979 so that, in Land
Register cases, the Keeper must refuse an application which relates in whole or in part
to an estate which has been abolished[2]. It will be for the applicant to carry out the
research necessary to convince the Keeper that no former superiority lands are
included within the application. In practice, the problem will arise mainly, or even
exclusively, on first registrations, for if land is already on the Land Register the problem of distinguishing *dominium utile* from superiority should already have been faced.

1   Para 8.4.
2   Land Registration (Scotland) Act 1979, s 4(2)(aa), inserted by the AFT(S)A 2000, s 3(a).

Removal of superiorities from the Land Register

1.12   Following feudal abolition, the Keeper is authorised to remove all superiorities from the Land Register, and without fear of a claim for indemnity[1]. In practice he
may not have the resources to do this quickly. It would, of course, be a straight-

forward matter to close a title sheet if it related to a superiority interest alone, but even here it will often be necessary to take account of a reservation of minerals which, if effective, would turn a superiority title into a mixed title. The title sheet would then remain open in respect of the minerals.

1   Land Registration (Scotland) Act 1979, ss 9(3B), 12(3)(cc), inserted by the AFT(S)A 2000, s 3(b), (c).

CROWN RIGHTS

Land already feued

1.13   To the extent that Crown land has already been feued the right of the Crown is reduced to that of feudal superior; and since the 2000 Act binds the Crown, the result on the appointed day is the abolition of the Crown's paramount superiority[1]. This idea proved controversial[2]. During the passage of the legislation it was argued on behalf of groups such as Land Reform Scotland and Scottish Environment Link that the paramount superiority amounted to a public interest in land and should be retained:[3]

> With all its flaws, the feudal system has one benefit; it means that all land is ultimately held in trust for the public through 'the Crown' – the 'Crown' meaning the government of Scotland. The 'Crown' protects the public interest – including issues like protection of the environment.

Arguments of this kind faced two obvious difficulties, however. One was that the Crown's superiority, like the superiorities of others, was a private right and not a public one. It was a right to feudal *reddendo* and not a right to control the use of land that had been feued. There was no legal basis for the assertion of public rights, and none had been asserted in the past.

The second difficulty was more fundamental. To retain the paramount superiority would be to retain the feudal system itself. It would be to replicate the position in England and Wales where all land is held from the Crown. A person would continue to hold *dominium utile* and not the land itself, and some at least of the complex infrastructure of feudalism, carefully dismantled by the Act, would require to be retained and re-enacted.

Having regard to these difficulties, and others, Parliament concluded that the paramount superiority should be abolished, and the Act so provides. For the avoidance of doubt the Act also provides for abolition of a possible second paramount superiority which, on one view[4], is held by the Prince and Steward of Scotland in respect of the Principality of Scotland (ie the hereditary lands of the Stewarts and the Earldom of Carrick and the Isles)[5].

1   Abolition of Feudal Tenure etc (Scotland) Act 2000, ss 2(2), 58(1).

2   The debate is summarised in the Justice and Home Affairs Committee's *Stage 1 Report on the Abolition of Feudal Tenure etc (Scotland) Bill* (1999) paras 12–17.

3   *Third Memorandum by Scottish Environment Link* para 5, reproduced in Annexe B p 40 to the Justice and Home Affairs Committee's *Stage 1 Report.*

4   5 *Stair Memorial Encyclopaedia* para 706.

5   AFT(S)A 2000, s 58(1).

Land unfeued

1.14 Crown land which is unfeued is allodial land, that is to say, land held outside the feudal system and without reference to a feudal superior. As such it is unaffected by feudal abolition. After the appointed day all land in Scotland will be allodial.

Crown land is unfeued either because it is not, of its nature, capable of alienation, such as the rights of use held for the public in relation to the foreshore and sea bed[1], or because, while alienable, it has not been alienated. Traditionally land and rights of the first kind are classified as *regalia majora*[2] and those of the second as *regalia minora*. Included among the latter are the sea bed within territorial waters[3], rights of salmon fishing not yet feued, and rights conferred on the Crown by statute such as the right to petroleum and natural gas[4].

1   The Scottish Law Commission has recommended that these be converted into rights held directly by the public, on the model of access rights under the Land Reform (Scotland) Act 2003, Pt 1. See *Report on Law of the Foreshore and Sea Bed* (Scot Law Com no 190, 2003; available on www.scotlawcom.gov.uk) paras 3.7, 3.8.

2   The right to *regalia majora* is expressly, if unnecessarily, preserved by the Act: see AFT(S)A 2000, s 58(2)(b)(ii).

3   The non-feudal nature of the Crown's ownership of the sea bed was confirmed in *Shetland Salmon Farmers Association v Crown Estate Commissioners* 1991 SLT 166.

4   Petroleum (Production) Act 1934, s 1.

Private land

1.15 *Dominium utile* of land held by the monarch in a personal capacity is treated by the Abolition of Feudal Tenure etc (Scotland) Act 2000 in the same way as dominium utile held by anyone else. On the appointed day it becomes outright ownership[1]. An incidental advantage is to end the awkwardness of land being held by the monarch in a personal capacity from itself in an official capacity – an awkwardness which required the comfort of a special statutory provision[2].

1   AFT(S)A 2000, s 2(1), discussed at para 1.9.

2   Conveyancing (Scotland) Act 1874, s 60. This provision is accordingly repealed by the AFT(S)A 2000, s 76(2), Sch 13.

Prerogative rights

1.16   In abolishing the Crown's superiority, the 2000 Act treats the Crown in the same way as anyone else; and, as with anyone else, other rights are unaffected. In the case of the Crown these include prerogative rights as sovereign or head of state. Nonetheless, in a spirit of caution, prerogative rights are expressly saved by the legislation[1]. These are said to include, non-exhaustively, any powers relating to peerages, dignities and other honours, and any powers relating to ownerless or unclaimed property[2]. Barony titles, however, are feudal in nature and are the subject of special provision, discussed later[3].

[1]   Abolition of Feudal Tenure etc (Scotland) Act 2000, s 58. See Scottish Law Commission *Report on Abolition of the Feudal System* para 2.25.
[2]   AFT(S)A 2000, s 58(2). On the latter, see *Lord Advocate v University of Aberdeen and Budge* 1963 SC 533.
[3]   AFT(S)A 2000, s 63. See paras 14.2–14.7.

SUPERIORS' RIGHTS

Feudal rights

1.17   Since the early eighteenth century superiors' rights have been progressively restricted or removed[1]. Personal services were abolished in 1715[2], prohibitions on alienation of the feu in 1746[3], prohibitions on subinfeudation and superiors' monopolies in respect of law agents in 1874[4], and feudal casualties in 1914[5]. Finally in 1974 provision was made for the phasing out of feudal *reddendo* – the vassal's rent for the feu which, in modern times, was usually restricted to the twice-yearly payment of small sums of money by way of feuduty. After 1974 no new feuduty could be imposed[6]. Yet a feu without *reddendo* was as meaningless as a lease without rent, and the phasing out of feuduty made almost inevitable the eventual abolition of the whole system. Insofar as superiors' rights had financial value, their loss in the past was compensated by an increase in feuduty, and when feuduty itself was extinguished the vassal was obliged to pay the capitalised value of the annual income which it generated. The Abolition of Feudal Tenure etc (Scotland) Act 2000 now completes this process of extinction and compensation by removing all remaining superiors' rights.

After 1974 only four types of right were left to superiors in their capacity as such. First, there was *dominium directum*, the very superiority right itself, reserved by implication from all grants in feu. Secondly, there were the remnants of a once elaborate system of feudal *reddendo*, now reduced to such feuduties as had not yet attracted the attention of the 1974 legislation. Thirdly, there were feudal real burdens, which had had the unexpected effect of reinvigorating feudalism during the nineteenth century. And finally there were reservations, mostly non-feudal in character[7].

The only feudal reservation of significance was sporting rights, that is, the right to use the feu for fishing and taking game, and even that was relatively uncommon.

The extinction of *dominium directum* has already been discussed[8]. On the appointed day all remaining feuduties are extinguished, but, as before, the former vassal must compensate the former superior by payment of the capitalised value[9]. By contrast, many feudal real burdens are preserved by one means or another, sometimes in favour of the former superior and sometimes in favour of neighbours. The complex rules are described in the next and following chapters. Except insofar as preserved, superiors' rights to enforce real burdens are extinguished on the appointed day[10]. Finally, sporting rights can also be preserved for the benefit of the former superior, by service and registration of a notice before the appointed day[11]. Otherwise they too are extinguished[12].

1   For an account of those rights, see Stair II.4; Bankton II.4; Erskine II.5; Hume, *Lectures* IV, 188 ff.
2   Highland Services Act 1715, ss 10–14; K G C Reid *The Law of Property in Scotland* (1996) (G L Gretton) paras 63 ff.
3   Tenures Abolition Act 1746, s 10.
4   Conveyancing (Scotland) Act 1874, s 22.
5   Feudal Casualties (Scotland) Act 1914.
6   Land Tenure Reform (Scotland) Act 1974, ss 1–7.
7   Para 1.20.
8   Para 1.10.
9   Chapter 10.
10   Abolition of Feudal Tenure etc (Scotland) Act 2000, s 17.
11   Paras 8.6–8.10.
12   AFT(S)A 2000, s 54.

Non-feudal rights

1.18   At one time all rights reserved in grants of feu were feudal in character, but in modern times it has been normal for feudal rights to co-exist with rights which might equally well be found in a disposition and which are non-feudal in character. Non-feudal rights do not depend on the feudal system of land tenure and in principle are unaffected by its abolition. Thus a superior who holds a non-feudal right before the appointed day will continue to hold that right even after the feudal system is abolished and he has ceased to be a superior.

Four broad classes of non-feudal right may be identified: ordinary real rights, reservations, trust rights, and contractual rights. Each is discussed below.

Ordinary real rights

1.19   A feu disposition might reserve to the granter an ordinary real right, for example a servitude, a non-feudal real burden, a proper liferent, or a pecuniary real burden[1]. Only the first is common.

Servitudes are used where the feu is being broken off from a larger estate and continuing rights over the feu are needed, for example for services or access. A well-ordered deed will nominate as the dominant tenement the land retained by the superior, or a part of that land; and even in the absence of express nomination the result is probably the same by legal implication[2]. As the retained land is *dominium utile* and not *dominium directum* it is unaffected, in respect of the servitude, by feudal abolition. Indeed it is doubtful whether a servitude could ever be created in favour of a bare superiority[3], but any such servitude as might exist would be extinguished, with the superiority, on the appointed day.

Occasionally there may be difficulties of classification. Any right which can be reserved as a servitude may also, in theory, be reserved as a (feudal) real burden[4]. Almost always, however, it is taken to be a servitude[5]. But that would not be so if the right falls outside the list of known servitudes[6], or if, the superior having failed to keep back land, there is no dominant tenement. Negative servitudes – relatively rare in practice – cause particular difficulty as being not readily distinguishable from real burdens. If there is doubt as to classification, it is safer to assume that the right is a (feudal) real burden rather than a servitude, and to take appropriate measures to ensure its survival.

Other real rights are rare in feu dispositions and merit only brief mention here. In theory a grant in feu might contain a non-feudal real burden, or in other words a burden which, like a servitude, is for the benefit of retained land and not the retained superiority[7]. Only express words could overturn the presumption that a burden in a grant in feu is for the benefit of the superiority[8], and in practice non-feudal real burdens are almost unknown[9].

A pecuniary real burden – despite its name – was a right in security rather than a title condition. It was created by reservation in a conveyance and was used, typically, to secure the purchase price in cases of sale on credit[10]. On one view, it ceased to be competent to create new pecuniary real burdens in 1970[11], but the position is put beyond doubt by the Title Conditions (Scotland) Act 2003[12]. Changing lending patterns meant that such burdens were rare in modern times, but any held by superiors will survive the appointed day[13].

---

[1]   Reversion, a fifth example, is discussed at para 1.23.

[2]   For a discussion, see D J Cusine and R R M Paisley *Servitudes and Rights of Way* (1998) para 2.35. This is the same rule as applies to non-feudal real burdens: see K G C Reid *The Law of Property in Scotland* (1996) para 403.

[3]   *Stewart v Steuart* (1877) 4 R 981; *Hemming v Duke of Athole* (1883) 11 R 93. For a discussion, see D J Cusine and R R M Paisley *Servitudes and Rights of Way* (1998) paras 1.06(1) and 2.10; Scottish Law Commission *Report on Abolition of the Feudal System* paras 6.17–6.21.

[4]   K G C Reid *The Law of Property in Scotland* (1996) para 391. The position is changed, after the appointed day, by the Title Conditions (Scotland) Act 2003 which, in ss 2, 79–81, draws a clear distinction between those rights which may be real burdens and those which may be servitudes. For an explanation, see Scottish Law Commission *Report on Real Burdens* paras 2.1–2.8.

[5]   In particular a right in the nature of a *positive* servitude would only in the most unusual circumstances be treated as a real burden.

6   For which see D J Cusine and R R M Paisley *Servitudes and Rights of Way* (1998) ch 3.

7   For the distinction between feudal and non-feudal real burdens, see para 2.2.

8   AFT(S)A 2000, s 48.

9   Para 2.6.

10   K G C Reid *The Law of Property in Scotland* (1996) para 375; Scottish Law Commission *Report on Abolition of the Feudal System* paras 6.13–6.15.

11   The argument turns on whether a pecuniary real burden can be characterised as a 'grant' of land to secure a debt, within the Conveyancing and Feudal Reform (Scotland) Act 1970, s 9(3).

12   Title Conditions (Scotland) Act 2003, s 117.

13   Subordinate real rights over the *dominium utile* are unaffected by feudal abolition: AFT(S)A 2000, s 2(1). See also Scottish Law Commission *Report on Abolition of the Feudal System* para 5.11.

Reservations

1.20   A reservation of minerals is almost standard in grants of feu. But it is non-feudal in character. The reservation elevates the minerals into a separate tenement, that is, into 'land' which can be held separately from ownership of the *solum*[1]. This means that in reserving minerals, the feu disposition is reserving *dominium utile* and not *dominium directum*; and, so far as the minerals are concerned, the granter and grantee are in a relationship of neighbours and not of superior and vassal. As *dominium utile*, the right to the minerals is undisturbed by feudal abolition. The position is the same in respect of a reservation of salmon fishings or other separate tenements. The subject is explored further in chapter 8.

1   For separate tenements, see K G C Reid *The Law of Property in Scotland* (1996) paras 207–212.

Trusts

1.21   Occasionally a grant in feu creates a trust. For example, a person might feu land to trustees for the purpose of building and maintaining a village hall. Trusts are unaffected by feudal abolition. From the viewpoint of the trustee/grantee, abolition affects the nature of the property but not the fiduciary manner in which it is held. *Dominium utile* held in trust before the appointed day becomes outright ownership after that day. But the trust remains[1]. Insofar, therefore, as a superior holds trust rights, whether as truster or as beneficiary, those rights survive feudal abolition.

1   Abolition of Feudal Tenure etc (Scotland) Act 2000, s 2(1) ('subject to the same ... other encumbrances as was the estate of *dominium utile*').

Contractual rights

1.22   A conveyance is a contract as well as a deed creating real rights, and its terms bind the original parties[1]. Feudal law, however, went further. The transfer of a feu was completed only by renewal of the investiture with the superior. Each new vassal, in other words, had to take feudal entry with the superior[2]. This involved a fresh grant by the superior on the same terms as the original. At one time this was by charter of resignation, following resignation of the feu by the outgoing vassal to the superior, but in later times transfers usually proceeded *a me vel de me*, by the alternative manner of holding, and were concluded by a charter of confirmation from the superior. In renewing the investiture, the charter of confirmation (or resignation) brought about a direct contractual relationship between superior and incoming vassal. Hence the conditions of the feu continued to be enforceable as a matter of contract even against successors. In 1874, however, actual entry with the superior was replaced by deemed entry. Charters of confirmation and resignation disappeared. Instead, the mere act of registering the disposition procured entry with the superior 'to the same effect as if such superior had granted a writ of confirmation according to the existing law and practice'[3]. Whether this virtual charter of confirmation had the same effect of creating contractual relations as before was doubtful, but never authoritatively decided[4]. The doubt is removed by the 2000 Act (as amended) which provides that, for the purposes of determining contractual enforceability, 'any enactment or rule of law whereby investiture is deemed renewed when the parties change shall be disregarded'[5]. There can be no question, therefore, of enforcement of feudal terms after the appointed day on the basis of a deemed contractual right.

The overall position may be summarised as follows. Feudal abolition does not affect rights held by the superior which are properly contractual in nature; and in principle all the terms of a grant in feu – including, for example, terms intended as real burdens[6] – are contractual in a question with the original grantee[7]. From those terms the legislation excepts only feuduty[8] and community burdens[9]. Hence if the original grantee is still in place on the appointed day, the other terms of the feu remain enforceable. Further, the enforcement rights are assignable, on general principles of contract law, so that a successor of the former superior may enforce against the original former vassal. But once the original grantee parts with the land, it seems that contractual liability comes to an end[10].

[1]   K G C Reid *The Law of Property in Scotland* (1996) para 392.
[2]   See also para 13.4.
[3]   Conveyancing (Scotland) Act 1874, s 4(2).
[4]   K G C Reid *The Law of Property in Scotland* (1996) para 393.
[5]   AFT(S)A 2000, s 75(2), inserted by the TC(S)A 2003, s 114(6), Sch 13, para 13.
[6]   Para 2.6.
[7]   Scottish Law Commission *Report on Abolition of the Feudal System* para 4.88.
[8]   AFT(S)A 2000, s 75(1). The exception is necessary to prevent continuing liability for feuduty even after the appointed day.
[9]   TC(S)A 2003, ss 61, 119(7). See para 2.6.
[10]   For it seems an implied term that the contract is only to last for so long as the grantee owns the land. See Scottish Law Commission *Report on Real Burdens* paras 3.40 and 3.41.

Reversions

1.23   Reversions merit special attention. A reversion is a right to reacquire property upon the purification of a condition or conditions[1]. For example, land might be feued on the basis that it is to revert to the superior[2] on ceasing to be used for a particular purpose. Where land is to revert at the option of the superior and on the payment of its value, the right is usually referred to as a redemption. Although the clause sometimes states otherwise, it is thought that a reversion cannot occur automatically but must always involve a re-conveyance on the part of the current owner[3].

It may be difficult to decide whether a particular form of words has the effect of creating a reversion. For example, it is not always easy to distinguish between (i) a clause conferring a right to reacquire land in the event of cessation of a particular use and (ii) a clause prohibiting all but the preferred use on pain of irritancy. The difference in legal effect, however, is clear enough[4]. The first is a reversion and the second a negative burden supported by irritancy; and following the abolition of feudal irritancy on 9 June 2000[5], a clause of the second type no longer results in the return of the land.

A reversion (or redemption) may take a number of legal forms. It might be no more than a contract, binding only the original parties. Or it might be constituted as a real burden, provided that it otherwise satisfies the rules for such rights[6]. A reversion can also be created as a self-standing real right, under the Reversion Act 1469 (c 3), although reversions of this kind ceased to be used, at the latest, in 1970 with the abolition of securities by way of *ex facie* absolute disposition[7]. Finally, statute provides for reversion in certain special circumstances, the best-known example being under s 2 of the School Sites Act 1841 in relation to land which was made available for schools and schoolhouses[8]. Since 1974 new reversions and redemptions have, for the most part, been restricted to 20 years[9].

Apart from (feudal) real burdens, the various methods of creating reversion are nonfeudal in character and will not be directly affected by feudal abolition. The Title Conditions (Scotland) Act 2003, however, disallows reversions as real burdens for the future[10], repeals the Reversion Act 1469[11], and converts reversions under the School Sites Act into a right to receive compensation or a conveyance, at the option of the education authority[12]. Except in relation to the last of these, the changes have no effect on existing reversions.

An existing reversion constituted as a feudal real burden will fall on the appointed day unless it is preserved either as a neighbour burden or (in the case of redemption) as a personal real burden, on principles discussed later[13]. Both require the service and registration of a notice before 28 November 2004.

[1] See generally, Scottish Law Commission *Report on Real Burdens* Pt 10.
[2] Reversions are, however, also found in non-feudal conveyancing.
[3] *Hamilton v Grampian Regional Council* 1996 GWD 5-277.
[4] For example, an obligation of the second type is, as a real burden, enforceable also by remedies other than irritancy.
[5] AFT(S)A 2000, s 53.
[6] It has, for example, been suggested, *obiter*, that a right of redemption could not be constituted as a real burden if the price payable was 'elusory': see *McElroy v Duke of Argyll* (1902) 4 F 885 at 889 per Lord Kyllachy. The difficulty with an elusory price, presumably, is that it is so prejudicial to the interests of the owner as to be repugnant with ownership: see TC(S)A 2003, s 3(6).

7   Conveyancing and Feudal Reform (Scotland) Act 1970, s 9(3).
8   On the School Sites Act, see Scottish Law Commission *Report on Real Burdens* paras 10.44–10.62.
9   Land Tenure Reform (Scotland) Act 1974, s 12.
10   TC(S)A 2003, s 3(5).
11   TC(S)A 2003, s 89.
12   TC(S)A 2003, s 86.
13   AFT(S)A 2000, s 17(1)(a). See chs 3 and 4.

SUPERIORS' OBLIGATIONS

Nature

1.24   In a feu there are also obligations on the superior, such as an obligation of warrandice, or to free and relieve the grantee of over-feuduties and public burdens. Both, as it happens, are implied[1], although warrandice is usually repeated expressly; but feus may also contain obligations which would not otherwise be implied, such as an obligation to construct an access road or to convey amenity ground to the trustees of a residents' association. Whether such obligations run with the superiority so as to be enforceable against successors is less clear. Warrandice, it has been held, does not transmit in this way[2], but an obligation to impose similar burdens in subsequent feus is probably transmissible[3]. No principles have been developed for determining which obligations do, and which do not, transmit, and indeed the legal basis of transmission is unclear[4].

1   The former at common law and the latter by the Land Registration (Scotland) Act 1979, s 16(3)(b).
2   *Stewart v Duke of Montrose* (1860) 22 D 755 at 803.
3   *Leith School Board v Rattray's Trs* 1918 SC 94.
4   K G C Reid *The Law of Property in Scotland* (1996) para 394.

Extinction, with exceptions

1.25   Superiors' obligations are extinguished on the appointed day, with two exceptions[1]. First, an obligation that is the counterpart of a real burden which itself survives feudal abolition will likewise survive and remain enforceable[2]. Thus if, before the appointed day, a superior could collect a service charge only if the money so collected was used for specified purposes, the right to collect will remain subject to the obligation in respect of use. Such counter-obligations are enforceable against the former superior or, if enforcement rights have passed elsewhere, against the person standing in his place. The notice procedure for preservation of burdens requires that the superior include details of counter-obligations, thus ensuring that their existence is patent from the Register[3]. A counter-obligation is parasitic on the principal burden, and will fall in the event that that burden is extinguished[4].

The second exception applies where the original superior is still in place on the appointed day. There is then continuing liability as a matter of contract, and the former vassal's correlative right is fully assignable[5]. It seems unlikely that this principle will be much invoked in practice.

Superior's obligations extinguished on the appointed day are not enforceable thereafter even in respect of prior breaches, except insofar as they relate to the payment of money or damages[6].

[1] Abolition of Feudal Tenure etc (Scotland) Act 2000, s 54(1).
[2] AFT(S)A 2000, s 25.
[3] See eg AFT(S)A 2000, ss 18(2)(e), 27(3)(e).
[4] AFT(S)A 2000, s 47.
[5] AFT(S)A 2000, s 75. This rule was discussed at para 1.22 in the context of obligations on the vassal.
[6] AFT(S)A 2000, s 54(2), (3). Parallel rules apply in relation to obligations of the vassal, and are discussed at para 2.13.

EUROPEAN CONVENTION ON HUMAN RIGHTS

1.26 An Act of the Scottish Parliament is not law to the extent that it breaches the European Convention on Human Rights[1]. In the case of the Abolition of Feudal Tenure etc (Scotland) Act 2000, the main risk is from the guarantee of property in article 1 of the First Protocol to the Convention. Whether article 1 is breached depends on the purpose and effect of the legislation.

The purpose of the legislation is to dismantle an archaic and potentially oppressive system of land tenure. This public benefit is achieved at the cost of extinguishing all superiorities, including the paramount superiority of the Crown. The value of a superiority lies in two elements: the right to collect feuduty and the right to enforce real burdens.

Full compensation is provided in respect of feuduty[2]. Indeed the 2000 Act can be seen merely as the last in a series of statutes, including the Feudal Casualties (Scotland) Act 1914 and the Land Tenure Reform (Scotland) Act 1974, which removed the financial rights of superiors in exchange for payment of compensation. Thus most of the compensation necessary for the abolition of superiorities was already paid before the 2000 Act was enacted.

The position of real burdens is more complex. Insofar as the superior has a praedial interest to enforce, he is able to save real burdens, whether by registration of a notice, by agreement with the vassal, or by application to the Lands Tribunal[3]. Insofar as there is no praedial interest, the superior's right is lost, usually without compensation[4]. In particular, no compensation is given for loss of the potential income stream from minutes of waiver, a stance which has been acknowledged as compatible with the ECHR[5]. Nonetheless limited compensation is payable in a case where a burden reserved development value and its imposition caused a substantial discount in the price[6]. It may be added that there is uncertainty as to whether a burden is enforceable at all in the absence of a praedial interest[7].

Barony titles, perhaps the only surviving aspect of the feudal system to carry significant value, are for that reason carefully preserved by the legislation[8].

The broad consensus of commentators is that the 2000 Act is compatible with the ECHR[9].

[1]   Scotland Act 1998, s 29(1), (2)(d).
[2]   Scottish Law Commission *Report on Abolition of the Feudal System* para 5.13. The rules are set out in ch 10.
[3]   See chs 3 and 4.
[4]   Scottish Law Commission *Report on Abolition of the Feudal System* paras 5.58–5.60.
[5]   *Strathclyde Joint Police Board v The Elderslie Estates Ltd* 2002 SLT (Lands Tr) 2. For a discussion, see K G C Reid and G L Gretton *Conveyancing 2001* (2002) pp 35–36; A J M Steven 'The Progress of Article 1 Protocol 1 in Scotland' (2002) 6 EdinLR 396.
[6]   See ch 9.
[7]   Para 4.7.
[8]   Scottish Law Commission *Report on Abolition of the Feudal System* para 2.40. See further paras 14.2–14.7.
[9]   C Ashton and V Finch *Human Rights and Scots Law* (2002) para 11.24; K Springham 'Property Law' in Lord Reed (ed) *A Practical Guide to Human Rights in Scotland* (2002) paras 7.40–7.42; G L Gretton 'The Protection of Property Rights' in A Boyle, C Himsworth, A Loux, and H MacQueen (eds) *Human Rights and Scots Law* (2002) pp 287–288; R Rennie in A Miller (ed) *Scottish Human Rights Service* para C8.011. For the view of the Scottish Law Commission, see *Report on Abolition of the Feudal System* paras 5.65–5.68.

FEUDAL ABOLITION AND PROPERTY LAW

1.27   For almost the whole period of its development, the law of property in Scotland has been subject to the competing influences of Roman law and feudal law. Moveable property was the province of Roman law, immoveable property, for the most part, of feudal law. In a well-known passage George Joseph Bell remarked that[1]:

> A double system of jurisprudence, in relation to the subjects of property, has thus arisen in Scotland, as in most European nations; – the one regulating Land and its accessories according to the spirit and arrangements of the feudal system; the other regulating the rights to Moveables according to the principles of Roman jurisprudence which prevailed before the establishment of feus.

One result was to obstruct development of a set of general principles which would be capable of application across the whole law of property.

Admittedly, the influence of Roman law even on land law was not negligible and tended to increase over time[2]. Subordinate real rights, for example, were divided between the feudal (security and proper liferent)[3] and the non-feudal (servitude and lease), while the introduction of the standard security in 1970 marked a shift to the non-feudal camp[4]. Nor was feudalism itself exempt from Roman influence: the re-characterisation of feudal rights as *dominium* was mentioned earlier[5]. Furthermore, as feudalism declined in importance, there was an increasing tendency to ignore it in practice and to treat the holder of the *dominium utile* as the 'true' owner. Where Roman principles collided with feudal, as for example in the case of the doctrine of accession[6], it was easier to apply the principle of Roman law than to grapple with complications posed by feudalism.

Nonetheless, right to the end the grip of feudalism remained surprisingly strong. Long after its dominance in legal practice had been lost, feudalism continued as the organising principle of conveyancing courses and textbooks. In its cause doctrines of property law were torn from their proper place and reassembled, often in mangled form, as an exposition of the clauses in the superior's charter. And the whole vocabulary of feudalism – antique, obscure and, to many, uninviting – permeated the language both of practice and of the law, obstructing the understanding, not only of those who avoided Scots conveyancing whenever they could, but even of those whose daily task was to work with it. To eliminate feudal concepts and terminology from the statute book has required the repeal of 45 entire Acts and innumerable provisions in other legislation[7].

With feudal abolition the 'double system' remarked on by Bell is replaced by a single, Romanistic, system. And for the first time Scotland will have a property law which is uniform, coherent, and functional[8].

---

1   Bell *Principles* s 636.
2   K Reid 'Property Law: Sources and Doctrine' in K Reid and R Zimmermann (eds) *A History of Private Law in Scotland* (2000) vol 1 pp 189–192.
3   For the treatment of proper liferent by the 2000 Act, see para 13.8.
4   Or so it must be supposed. The fact that the issue does not seem to have occurred to anyone is itself an indication of the decline in feudalism and feudal learning. See further Scottish Law Commission *Report on Abolition of the Feudal System* paras 7.38, 7.39.
5   Para 1.4.
6   K G C Reid *The Law of Property in Scotland* (1996) para 587.
7   AFT(S)A 2000, s 76(1), (2), Schs 12, 13. And see also Scottish Law Commission *Report on Abolition of the Feudal System* para 1.4
8   K G C Reid *The Law of Property in Scotland* (1996) para 1.

Chapter 2

Real burdens: towards the appointed day

Real burdens and feudalism

2.1   Real burdens were not much used before the 1820s, although their origins can be traced to the closing years of the previous century[1]; and it was not until 1840 that their validity was authoritatively established by the decision of the House of Lords in *Tailors of Aberdeen v Coutts*[2]. In the long history of feudalism, therefore, real burdens belong to the final phase, a modern invention imposed on an ancient, and increasingly rickety, structure[3]. Real burdens, moreover, are not primarily feudal in nature, and owe as much to servitudes as to feudalism itself[4]. In most European countries, indeed, servitudes do much of the work of real burdens and there is no separate class of obligations running with the land. In Scotland, however, servitudes did not seem up to the task of regulating the building boom of the Victorian age. Partly this was due to judicial reluctance to recognise new servitude types, appropriate to an industrial age. Partly also it was because servitudes could not impose affirmative obligations, such as an obligation to build or to maintain – a limitation which owed something to fidelity to Roman law, and something to the doctrinal awkwardness of admitting an affirmative obligation as a real right[5]. On this matter feudalism was less squeamish. Affirmative obligations on the vassal – to pay feuduty and casualties, to hunt and to host, to maintain a boat for the superior's use with six rowers and a steersman[6] – were of the very essence of the system of feudal tenure; and, not for the first time, it was feudalism which provided a means of escaping the rigidity of Roman law. In admitting affirmative obligations as real burdens – and so in allowing such obligations to run with the land – Scots law stands almost alone in modern Europe. Even in England, where servitudes (easements) were likewise supplemented by a second type of obligation, the freehold covenant, that covenant was, and is still, confined to negative obligations[7]. In England affirmative obligations could be imposed only under leasehold tenure. In Scotland the real burden allowed affirmative obligations to be combined with ownership.

[1]   K G C Reid *The Law of Property in Scotland* (1996) paras 375 ff; R Rodger *The Transformation of Edinburgh: Land, Property and Trust in the Nineteenth Century* (2001) chs 2 and 3.

[2]   (1840) 1 Rob 296.

3   K G C Reid '70 Years at One Blow: the Abolition of Feudal Land Tenure in Scotland' in P Jackson and D C Wilde (eds) *The Reform of Property Law* (1997); K G C Reid 'Vassals No More: feudalism and post-feudalism in Scotland' (2003) 11 European Review of Private Law 282.

4   K G C Reid *The Law of Property in Scotland* (1996) paras 380–3.

5   Hume Lectures III, 271.

6   *Duke of Argyle v Creditors of Tarbert* (1762) Mor 14495.

7   *Rhone v Stephens* [1994] 2 AC 310.

Feudal burdens and non-feudal (praedial) burdens

2.2   If real burdens are only partly feudal in origin, they are, equally, only partly feudal in use. In *Tailors of Aberdeen v Coutts*[1] the real burdens were contained in a disposition and not in a grant in feu; and from the very beginning non-feudal burdens were common. Real burdens, therefore, could be created in two different ways. In the first place, they could be created in a grant in feu (a feu disposition, feu charter, or feu contract)[2]. In that case they were enforceable by the granter, and the granter's successors as superior of the feu, against the grantee, and the grantee's successors as vassal. Alternatively, they could be created in an ordinary disposition. But in that case it was necessary to keep back some land to which enforcement rights could be attached[3]. For, in the absence of the relationship of superior and vassal, real burdens were viewed much in the same way as servitudes. That meant the need not only for a 'servient tenement' (the land disponed) but for a 'dominant tenement' as well (the land kept back, to which a right of enforcement could attach); and the burdens were then enforceable by the granter and successors as owner of the dominant tenement against the grantee and successors as owner of the servient tenement. Whereas, therefore, a feudal burden invoked the (metaphysical) relationship of superior and vassal, the non-feudal burden turned on the (basely physical) relationship of neighbour to neighbour. Like servitudes, non-feudal burdens benefited one property by the imposition of obligations on its neighbour.

Another name for non-feudal burdens is 'praedial real burdens', in recognition of the fact that there must be a *praedium* or benefited property. 'Praedial real burden' is likely to become the established term in the future as a means of distinguishing real burdens with benefited properties from those ('personal real burdens') without[4]. It is used freely in the present work.

'Dominant tenement' and 'servient tenement', the language of servitudes, are the terms used in the Abolition of Feudal Tenure etc (Scotland) Act 2000. The Title Conditions (Scotland) Act 2003, by contrast, employs the more modern, and less submissive, terminology of 'benefited property' and 'burdened property'. In this work, although primarily about the 2000 Act, the new terminology is used wherever possible.

Two complications should be mentioned at once. First, real burdens could also be created in a third deed, a deed of conditions[5]. But deeds of conditions were not conceived as an entirely independent means of creation. The original legislation, in

1874[6], allowed burdens to be effective only where the deed of conditions was incorporated by reference into a subsequence conveyance of the burdened property. After 1979 it became possible for burdens in deeds of conditions to be effective at once, on registration of the deed[7], but even then it seemed doubtful whether such deeds could be used without at least the prospect of a later conveyance[8]. For present purposes it is the later conveyance which is important, as determining the nature of the real burden. Thus where a deed of conditions was followed by a grant in feu, the burdens were feudal in character, and enforceable by the granter as superior. Where, however, an ordinary disposition was used, the burdens were praedial.

The second complication concerns enforcement rights. If A made an isolated grant in feu to B, any burdens in the grant were enforceable by A and A's successors against B and B's successors. If, however – as was common in practice – the feu to B was one of a number of grants in the same general location, and on much the same terms, the burdens might also be mutually enforceable amongst the various grantees (co-feuars)[9]. Such third-party rights are usually attributed, perhaps not very convincingly, to the doctrine of *jus quaesitum tertio*. In a well-drawn deed they would be conferred by express term, but even where this was not done the law would sometimes imply enforcement rights, although the rules are complex[10]. Insofar as feudal burdens are also enforceable by co-feuars – by neighbours, in other words – they take on a non-feudal character. For each feu is not only a burdened property (ie subject to the real burdens) but also a benefited property, carrying enforcement rights against the other feus. Such burdens are therefore hybrids, part feudal burdens (enforceable by the superior) and part non-feudal, or praedial, burdens (enforceable by neighbours).

1 (1840) 1 Rob 296.
2 Until 1858, when direct registration of conveyances first came to be allowed, the terms of the real burden required to be repeated in an instrument of sasine, and it was only the instrument that was registered.
3 Alternatively, the granter could, and can, nominate some land belonging to a third party as the benefited property, but this is virtually unknown in practice.
4 For personal real burdens, see TC(S)A 2003, s 1(3), and para 2.9 below. 'Praedial' is a familiar adjective in the context of servitudes: see eg Stair II.7.pr; Erskine II.9.5.
5 K G C Reid *The Law of Property in Scotland* (1996) para 388.
6 Conveyancing (Scotland) Act 1874, s 32.
7 Land Registration (Scotland) Act 1979, s 17.
8 For a discussion, see Scottish Law Commission Discussion Paper on Real Burdens (Scot Law Com DP no 106, 1998) paras 7.32–7.34.
9 'Feuar' and 'vassal' are inter-changeable terms. In general, this work follows the AFT(S)A 2000 in using 'vassal', but in the case of third-party rights of enforcement 'co-feuar' is the normal term.
10 K G C Reid *The Law of Property in Scotland* (1996) paras 399–402.

The challenge of feudal abolition

2.3 Without real burdens, it is doubtful if the feudal system would have survived for so long. For most of the twentieth century the opportunity to impose real burdens was the main reason for continuing to feu land. After 1974, when it ceased to be possible to impose feuduty[1], real burdens became the only reason. Thereafter feuing continued to be used by volume builders for housing estates, by local authorities in the sale of council houses under the right-to-buy legislation, by providers of owner-occupied sheltered housing, and in certain commercial contexts. Otherwise it was largely unknown.

For the project of feudal abolition, however, past use of real burdens was a greater problem than future demand. Perhaps as many as one half of all real burdens affecting land in Scotland is feudal in character. Of those, large numbers, admittedly, are obsolete or troublesome, and could be abolished without loss. But large numbers are also useful or, more than that, essential. Of particular importance are burdens regulating the maintenance and use of common parts of a building, or other shared facilities. Any scheme for feudal abolition would need to ensure their survival. Other types of burden which can also be argued to have a special claim for attention include burdens directed at conservation, or at economic development. But even beyond such special categories, there was a risk that feudal abolition would lead to the deregulation of land use on an apparently random basis and with unpredictable consequences. The position was made worse by the fact that non-feudal burdens would be unaffected by the proposed legislation, with the result that land subject to such burdens would continue to be regulated as before.

Two other factors in particular weighed with the Scottish Law Commission in its preparation of draft legislation[2]. One was the role of superiors. For superiors, real burdens were a means of controlling land which they no longer owned or, more commonly in modern times, a source of income for minutes of waiver. Neither use seemed acceptable. The collection of, sometimes large, amounts of money for waiving conditions of no conceivable benefit to the superior was no more than an abuse of a system which had fallen into decay and disrepute. In one modern case, for example, superiors sought £7,500 for a minute of waiver in respect of a condition in a 1936 feu charter, explaining that 'the premium ... will be based on 15 per cent of the net development gain, in accordance with standard practice'[3]. But sometimes enforcement might be worse than waiver itself. There could be no objection, of course, to enforcement for the benefit of neighbouring property owned by the superior. In such cases feudal burdens were functioning, in substance, as non-feudal burdens or servitudes[4]. But what was less acceptable was the superior in the role of a private planning authority, controlling the life opportunities of all those subject to the feudal burdens.

The other factor was the European Convention on Human Rights, and in particular the protection of 'possessions' guaranteed by article 1 of the First Protocol. This meant that, insofar as real burdens conferred a legitimate benefit[5] on superiors, either an opportunity should be given for their preservation or, alternatively, compensation should be payable[6].

---

[1]   Land Tenure Reform (Scotland) Act 1974, s 2.

[2]   Scottish Law Commission *Report on Abolition of the Feudal System* paras 4.16–4.19 and 5.65–5.68.

3   *Moran's Exrs v Shenstone Properties Ltd* 2001 Hous LR 124. In the event the burden was discharged by the Lands Tribunal without any compensation being awarded to the superiors. See also *Harris v Douglas* 1993 SLT (Lands Tr) 56.

4   And indeed ownership of neighbouring property was accepted, even for feudal burdens, as the main basis of interest to enforce. See K G C Reid *The Law of Property in Scotland* (1996) para 408.

5   The term 'legitimate benefit' is used by the Lands Tribunal in *Moran's Exrs v Shenstone Properties Ltd* 2001 Hous LR 124 at para 16–20.

6   For a discussion of the compatibility of the Abolition of Feudal Tenure etc (Scotland) Act 2000 with the ECHR, see para 1.26.

The statutory scheme

2.4   The eventual scheme favoured by the legislature is contained in Part 4 of the Abolition of Feudal Tenure etc (Scotland) Act 2000. Further, important, changes were made by the Title Conditions (Scotland) Act 2003, by way of amendment to the 2000 Act. For the most part, the scheme follows the recommendations of the Scottish Law Commission, although with some important differences. It is described in outline below, and in much greater detail in the chapters that follow. Inevitably, it is something of a compromise and, as a set of general provisions falling to be applied to innumerable particular cases, somewhat rough and ready. Usually it may be expected to work well enough. Sometimes, unavoidably, it will lead to results which are less satisfactory. No more could reasonably be expected from general legislation, operating in unyielding terrain.

Non-feudal (praedial) burdens

2.5   It is as well to begin with that which the 2000 Act does *not* cover. The 2000 Act has no effect on non-feudal (praedial) burdens. Nor does it affect feudal burdens to the extent that they are enforceable by those other than feudal superiors[1]. In that respect, as already mentioned, feudal burdens are themselves praedial in character; and so the (non-feudal) enforcement rights of neighbours are undisturbed. Thus even a feudal real burden will not be abolished on the appointed day if it is enforceable by neighbours as co-feuars. But the superior's enforcement rights will fall.

> *Example.* In 1970 a volume builder feus an estate of 100 houses. Common burdens are imposed under a deed of conditions. The deed provides for a right of enforcement by the owner of each house. Before the appointed day, therefore, the burdens are enforceable by (i) the volume builder as superior and (ii) the owners of each house. After the appointed day the house owners can still enforce, and the burdens remain in place as praedial real burdens. The superior's right, however, is lost.

The law of praedial real burdens is itself subjected to a fundamental overhaul by the Title Conditions Act, which also comes into force on the appointed day[2].

1   Abolition of Feudal Tenure etc (Scotland) Act 2000, s 17(1)(a).
2   Paras 2.12, 7.15–7.27, 13.15.

Abolition of superiors' rights

2.6   The abolition of superiors means the abolition of superiors' enforcement rights. In principle, therefore, superiors lose their rights to enforce real burdens on the appointed day (28 November 2004); and accordingly any real burden which was enforceable *only* by a superior is extinguished[1]. But this rule is subject to a number of important qualifications.

In the first place, the legislation gives superiors the opportunity to preserve enforcement rights in certain circumstances. Secondly, in relation to a limited class of burdens[2], superiors' rights are automatically preserved. Both exceptions are explored below[3].

Thirdly, a superior might, occasionally, hold a separate enforcement right in the capacity as neighbour or as holder of a personal real burden. If so, such rights are, on general principles, unaffected by feudal abolition[4].

> *Example.* A developer builds 10 houses. The development is made subject to a deed of conditions which is immediately effective on registration and which confers mutual enforcement rights on the owners of each house[5]. Thereafter the developer feus nine of the houses but retains one for his own use. In those circumstances the developer can enforce the burdens in the deed both as superior and also as owner of the tenth house. On the appointed day the former right will disappear but the latter will survive.

Another example, almost unknown in practice, would be where, in a feu disposition of land, the burden is declared enforceable by the superior in the capacity as owner of neighbouring land. An express declaration is needed: by contrast with the rule for non-feudal burdens[6], there is no implication that a burden is created for the benefit of such neighbouring land as is retained by the granter[7].

Fourthly, even where no enforcement right as a neighbour exists before the appointed day, one may be conferred on the former superior by the legislation. That topic too is explored below[8].

Finally, where, on the appointed day, the original vassal is still in place, the burdens remain enforceable by the former superior as a matter of contract[9]. This is because a grant in feu is itself a type of contract, giving the superior, in a question with the original vassal, a double entitlement to enforce its conditions[10]. Feudal abolition removes one of those entitlements (real burden) but leaves the other (contract) undisturbed[11]. There is one exception, introduced by the 2003 Act[12]. No contractual right is regarded as arising in the case of 'community burdens', that is to say, burdens imposed on four or more properties under a common scheme.

Example. In 2001 a developer builds and feus an estate of 100 houses. The entire estate is subject to uniform conditions set out in a deed of conditions. On the appointed day 60 of the houses remain owned by the original purchasers. On that day the former superior loses any right to enforce the conditions as superior; and as the conditions are community burdens, he also loses any right to enforce against the 60 original purchasers on the basis of contract. Hence the former superior cannot enforce the burdens.

In other cases, the contractual right survives the appointed day but disappears as soon as the original vassal parts with ownership. Like other contractual rights, the right to enforce can be assigned by the former superior to a third party[13].

1   AFT(S)A 2000, s 17(1).
2   Maritime burdens and management burdens.
3   Para 2.10.
4   AFT(S)A 2000, s 17(1)(b). This mentions only those personal real burdens that it was possible to create before the appointed day, ie conservation burdens, health care burdens, and economic development burdens.
5   A deed of conditions takes immediate effect unless, as is commonly done, the Land Registration (Scotland) Act 1979, s 17 is expressly excluded.
6   *J A Mactaggart & Co v Harrower* (1906) 8 F 1101.
7   The position is made clear, for the avoidance of doubt, by the AFT(S)A 2000, s 48.
8   Para 2.10.
9   AFT(S)A 2000, s 75. On one view, the taking of feudal entry by each successive vassal had the effect of placing the vassal in direct contractual relations with the superior – a view which is difficult to reconcile with the introduction of implied feudal entry by s 4(2) of the Conveyancing (Scotland) Act 1874. For a discussion, see K G C Reid *The Law of Property in Scotland* (1996) para 393. Any possible argument that a person who, on the appointed day, was a successor of the original vassal is in contractual relations with the superior is displaced by the new s 75(2), inserted by the TC(S)A 2003, s 102(6), Sch 12, para 13.
10 In the future, however, such contractual entitlement will cease to be a feature of real burdens. See TC(S)A 2003, s 56.
11 Para 1.22.
12 TC(S)A 2003, s 107(7).
13 Indeed it might be argued that any contractual right to enforce feuing conditions passed automatically in a disposition of the superiority by virtue of implied clause of assignation of writs. See Land Registration (Scotland) Act 1979, s 16(1), and G L Gretton and K G C Reid *Conveyancing* (2nd edn, 1999) para 11.18. In that case feuing conditions would remain enforceable on the appointed day provided that the original vassal was still in place, notwithstanding that the superiority had changed hands.

Feudal burdens: survival and extinction

2.7   A different perspective is to focus, not on the superior, but on the burdens themselves. Hybrid burdens – burdens which are part feudal and part non-feudal – will, as already noted, survive in relation to their non-feudal part. The position of wholly feudal burdens (or the feudal part of hybrid burdens) is more complex. Under the legislation, such burdens will quite often become non-feudal burdens, and so survive the appointed day. In some cases this requires the service and registration of a notice by the superior. In other cases conversion occurs automatically, by force of law, although the beneficiary is then rarely the superior. Equally, however, many feudal burdens will not be converted, but will be extinguished, with the feudal system itself, on the appointed day[1].

[1]   For a detailed account, see ch 7.

Community burdens and neighbour burdens

2.8   A preliminary classification of praedial real burdens helps in the understanding of the conversion process. Burdens can, of course, be classified in more than one way. A classification by nature of the obligation imposed would yield 'negative burdens' and 'affirmative burdens'. A classification by content of the obligation would yield 'maritime burdens', 'conservation burdens', 'facility burdens', 'service burdens', and many others. Much unfamiliar terminology of this kind is introduced by the Title Conditions (Scotland) Act 2003 but need not detain us here. For present purposes, the most useful classification is by type of enforcer. Until the appointed day this yielded two broad categories. Either the benefited property was itself subject to the same (or comparable) burdens, or it was free of the burdens altogether. In the first case burdens were generally imposed on a number of properties under a common plan, and were mutually enforceable among them, each property being at the same time both a benefited and a burdened property. Housing estates and tenements were typical examples. In the second case, the burden operated in a single direction only. The owner of the benefited property could enforce against the owner of the burdened, but the benefited property itself was free of the burdens. Typically this arose on subdivision: an owner selling off part of a garden, or a field, might impose burdens for the benefit of the part that was being retained. Burdens of the first type are called 'community burdens' by the Title Conditions Act[1]. A convenient name for burdens of the second type is 'neighbour burdens'[2].

[1]   TC(S)A 2003, s 25. Because Pt 2 of that Act provides for certain default rules which would be inappropriate in a tiny community, s 25 imposes as an additional definitional requirement that the community must comprise four or more units. But this refinement may be passed over for present purposes.
[2]   Scottish Law Commission *Report on Real Burdens* paras 1.9–1.11.

Personal real burdens

2.9   A third category of real burden is introduced by the Title Conditions Act: a burden which is conceived, not in favour of a benefited property, but of an individual[1]. Such a burden is 'real' only at the burdened end and not, as in the normal case, at the benefited end as well: hence the name 'personal real burden'. In one sense, of course, there is nothing unusual about a real right conceived in favour of a person. Most real rights – standard securities, liferents, and leases – are like this. But in the context of real burdens the idea, in Scotland at least[2], is a novelty. The introduction of personal real burdens is closely connected with feudal abolition. On one view of feudal law, it was possible to impose, and to enforce, burdens even where the superior owned no other land in the neighbourhood[3]. In function if not in form this was then a real burden in favour of a person. If this device was viewed, sometimes at least, as in the public interest, then something was lost by feudal abolition. Personal real burdens make up for the loss.

Naturally, if feudalism was not simply to be re-created under another name, it was necessary to restrict the circumstances in which personal real burdens were to be allowed. In its original version the 2000 Act admitted only two examples (conservation burdens and maritime burdens) but to this the 2003 Act has added a further six: economic development burdens, manager burdens, personal pre-emption burdens, personal redemption burdens, rural housing burdens, and health care burdens[4]. All are limited by subject matter, and a number by permitted holder as well. A conservation burden, for example, can be held only by a designated conservation body or by Scottish Ministers and must, as its name suggests, be concerned with conservation[5]. In addition, manager burdens are limited by duration, normally to five years[6].

1   TC(S)A 2003, s 1(3).
2   A number of other countries allow servitudes or covenants in favour of a person: see Scottish Law Commission *Report on Real Burdens* para 9.2.
3   The alternative view is that there would then be no interest to enforce. See K G C Reid *The Law of Property in Scotland* (1996) paras 407 and 408; K G C Reid and G L Gretton *Conveyancing 2001* (2002) pp 99–100. See also para 4.7.
4   Apart from manager burdens, the Scottish Law Commission did not favour extension of the list. See Pt 9 of its *Report on Real Burdens*.
5   TC(S)A 2003, s 38(1).
6   TC(S)A 2003, s 63(4), (5).

Conversion of feudal real burdens: the four principles

2.10   Although the detailed rules are complex, it is possible to discern four broad principles which govern the conversion of feudal burdens, on the appointed day, into non-feudal burdens. Three of the principles correspond to the three types of real burden (neighbour burden, community burden, and personal real burden) identified above. The fourth and final principle involves both neighbour and community burdens. Later in the book a separate chapter is devoted to each principle, but a summary may be helpful.

The *first principle* is that feudal burdens are converted into neighbour burdens if the superior serves and registers a preservation notice in the manner laid down by the legislation[1]. The notice nominates other land owned by the superior and which is to act as the new benefited property. It must be served and registered between the autumn of 2003, when the relevant provisions came into effect, and the appointed day (28 November 2004). On the appointed day the right to enforce then passes from the superiority to the benefited property, or in other words the feudal burden becomes a neighbour burden. The availability of this method of conversion is limited by the fact that the nominated land must usually contain a building used as a place of human habitation or resort and which lies with 100 metres of the feu.

The *second principle* is that feudal burdens are converted into personal real burdens of the appropriate type if the superior serves and registers a preservation notice in the manner laid down by the legislation[2]. On the appointed day the right to enforce then passes from the superiority to the (former) superior in person. Thereafter the right can usually be assigned, although with some restrictions. Only burdens which qualify, by subject matter and nature of the superior, as potential personal real burdens can be converted under this method. Sporting rights, that is, rights of fishing or game reserved to the superior, become separate legal tenements rather than real burdens, on analogy with the right of salmon fishing. A registered notice is required as usual[3]. Exceptionally, the conversion to maritime burdens and manager burdens occurs by force of law and without the need for a notice[4].

The *third principle* is that feudal burdens imposed on a group of related properties under a common plan are converted into community burdens on the appointed day[5]. The right to enforce then passes from the superior to the owners of each of the properties in the community[6]. The conversion occurs automatically and without the need for action on the part of the superior; and indeed the (former) superior takes no benefit unless he happens to own one of the properties in the community.

The *fourth principle,* likewise a case of automatic conversion, applies to those feudal burdens which qualify as facility burdens or service burdens[7]. A facility burden regulates the maintenance, management, reinstatement or use of a facility such as a shared part of a tenement building, or a shared recreational area, or a private road. A service burden relates to the provision of services, such as water or electricity, to another property[8]. On the appointed day the right to enforce passes from the superior to the owners of the properties which take benefit from the facility or, as the case may be, the service. Depending on the category of enforcers, the burdens are then community burdens or neighbour burdens, or even both.

The first two principles are mutually exclusive but the third and fourth are not. Thus a superior cannot register a preservation notice in respect of a neighbour burden, and then register a further notice, in respect of the same burden, for conversion to a conservation burden or other personal real burden[9]. But a preservation notice is competent in respect of burdens converted into community burdens and, if registered, would mean that the burdens were doubly enforceable – by the owners within the community, and by the (former) superior, outside the community, either as the owner of neighbouring property or as the holder of a personal real burden. Further, there is a substantial degree of overlap between the third and fourth principles, for facility burdens are often imposed on a common plan on a group of related properties[10]. In such a case each principle is likely to produce the same result, namely mutual enforceability within the community[11]; but insofar as different groups of enforcers are identified, both groups have enforcement rights. Where facility burdens are imposed otherwise than under a common plan, the result of the fourth principle is to create new neighbour burdens. This would occur, for example, in the case of a maintenance obligation imposed on the owner of a private road for the benefit of owners of neighbouring property who held a servitude right of way.

1   See further ch 3.
2   See further ch 4.
3   AFT(S)A 2000, s 65A. See further paras 8.6–8.10.
4   AFT(S)A 2000, s 60; TC(S)A 2003, s 63(9).
5   See further ch 5.
6   Sometimes, however, the owners of those properties already had enforcement rights, either because such rights were expressly conferred at the time when the burdens were first created, or because such rights were implied.
7   See further ch 6.
8   TC(S)A 2003, s 122.
9   AFT(S)A 2000, s 42(1). See further paras 11.3–11.6.
10 Scottish Law Commission *Report on Real Burdens* para 11.39.
11 Whichever principle is regarded as having operated, however, the burdens will have the status of a facility burden, which is significant in relation to discharge. For example the sunset rule (the rule that burdens may be extinguished after 100 years) does not apply to facility burdens. See TC(S)A 2003, s 20(3)(c).

Compensation: development value burdens

2.11   In the case of development value burdens, the entitlement of the superior is usually to compensation rather than to preservation. A development value burden is one reserving a share of the development value of land to the superior, the original consideration for the feu having been reduced accordingly. Sometimes such a burden can be preserved under one of the principles just described. But where this cannot be done, or is not done, the superior has the possibility of compensation. The rather complex rules are set out in chapter 9.

Validity as a real burden

2.12   In order to be eligible, under the legislation, for preservation or compensation, a feudal burden must itself be valid as a real burden. By no means all conditions in feu dispositions satisfy this test[1]. For example, a condition designed to achieve clawback by payment of a percentage of planning gain will usually fail as a real burden either because it has no proper connection with the burdened property and hence is not 'praedial'[2], or on the basis that the amount to be paid is not set out in the four corners of the deed[3].

The common law rules as to validity are now set out, in codified form, in the Title Conditions (Scotland) Act 2003. A real burden must relate in some way to the feu (the burdened property), typically by restricting its use or by imposing building or maintenance obligations on its owner. In addition, a condition which is to be preserved as a neighbour burden, under the first principle identified above, must confer benefit on the proposed benefited property. The burden, in short, must be praedial both at the burdened end and also at the benefited end.

Other restrictions affect both form and content[4]. The burden must be set out in full in the four corners of the deed[5], except that a maintenance or similar obligation can be apportioned by reference to the valuation roll or other public document[6]. A burden must not be contrary to public policy, for example by creating a monopoly[7]. Nor must the burden be so restrictive as to be repugnant with ownership[8]. For example, the provision typically found in sheltered housing by which owners are deprived of management rights is, probably, void as repugnant with ownership.

Usually a real burden comprises either an obligation to do something (termed an 'affirmative burden' by the 2003 Act) or an obligation not to do something (a 'negative burden')[9]. But it is probably competent for a real burden to confer a right to enter or make use of the burdened property, in imitation of a positive servitude, and conditions of this kind are occasionally found[10]. After the appointed day, real burdens are to be confined to affirmative and negative burdens[11], and rights to enter must be constituted as positive servitudes. This does not prevent a feudal burden which confers a right to enter from being preserved under the legislation; but, unless it is ancillary to an affirmative or negative burden (such as a right of entry to determine whether repairs are necessary or to carry out the repairs), a preserved right of entry is automatically converted into a positive servitude[12]. Preservation and conversion are simultaneous events, so that on the appointed day the feudal real burden is reborn as a positive servitude.

[1]   Scottish Law Commission *Report on Abolition of the Feudal System* para 5.12. And see paras 1.18–1.23.
[2]   Title Conditions (Scotland) Act 2003, s 3(1), (2). See also Scottish Law Commission *Report on Abolition of the Feudal System* para 5.23.
[3]   *Tailors of Aberdeen v Coutts* (1840) 1 Rob 296 at 340 per Lord Brougham. It will be noted that the TC(S)A 2003, s 5(1)(a) is confined to obligations to defray a cost.
[4]   K G C Reid *The Law of Property in Scotland* (1996) paras 391 and 392; Scottish Law Commission *Report on Real Burdens* Pt 2.
[5]   TC(S)A 2003, s 4(2)(a).
[6]   TC(S)A 2003, s 5(2). This provision, which may change the law, extends to burdens created before the appointed day.
[7]   TC(S)A 2003, s 3(6), (7).
[8]   TC(S)A 2003, s 3(6).
[9]   TC(S)A 2003, s 2.
[10] *B & C Group Management v Haren* (4 December 1992, unreported) Outer House.
[11] TC(S)A 2003, s 2.
[12] TC(S)A 2003, s 81.

Enforcement by superior before the appointed day

2.13   Superiors can enforce real burdens right up until the appointed day[1]. The remedy of irritancy, however, was abolished on 9 June 2000[2], and in its absence a suitable remedy may not always be available. A continuing breach is prevented by interdict, although any interdict will fall on the appointed day itself[3]. Affirmative obligations – an obligation to pay money, for example, or to erect a building – may likewise be enforced. The position is more difficult in respect of one-off breaches of negative burdens[4]. A typical example is the erection of a building in breach of a general obligation not to build. If the building was completed without complaint on the part of the superior, enforcement will usually be prevented by personal bar[5]. But even where this was not the case, there is a difficulty as to remedy. Courts are, for obvious reasons, reluctant to order demolition of a completed building[6]. But failing an order for demolition, and in the absence of irritancy, the superior's remedy is reduced to one of damages – always assuming that it is possible to show loss. In the absence of loss, there may be no remedy at all.

No real burden can be breached, in a question with a superior, on or after the appointed day; and the legislation makes clear that prior breaches too will no longer be enforceable (for otherwise the feudal system would live on)[7]. Any enforcement procedure in court on the appointed day is deemed abandoned, and most decrees previously obtained, including interdict, are treated as reduced or recalled. But a former superior is allowed to enforce any pre-existing right to recovery of damages or to the payment of money[8]. This means that even after the appointed day a former superior could recover, for example, unpaid arrears of service charge.

Sometimes a person will lose enforcement rights as a superior only to reacquire them, on the appointed day and simultaneously, on some other basis, for example as the owner of neighbouring property. In that case it seems doubtful that the person could enforce in respect of breaches before the appointed day, that is to say, before acquiring the new right of enforcement[9]. A continuing breach would, of course, be in a different position. Any interdict already obtained by the person as superior would fall on the appointed day, on the rule already mentioned, but a fresh interdict could be obtained in the new capacity of post-feudal enforcer.

1   But not, generally, beyond: see the Abolition of Feudal Tenure etc (Scotland) Act 2000, s 17(2)(a).

2   AFT(S)A 2000, s 53. By s 77(1) this provision came into force on Royal Assent. Section 53 contains certain transitional rules for current proceedings, but these do not seem to have been used.

3   AFT(S)A 2000, s 17(2)(c).

4   A negative burden is 'an obligation to refrain from doing something': see the Title Conditions (Scotland) Act 2003, s 2.

5   K G C Reid *The Law of Property in Scotland* (1996) paras 427–8.

6   K G C Reid *The Law of Property in Scotland* (1996) para 423.

7   AFT(S)A 2000, s 17(2).

8   AFT(S)A 2000, s 17(3)(b).

9   And see TC(S)A 2003, s 57(3).

Chapter 3

Preservation as neighbour burdens

INTRODUCTION

The procedure in outline

3.1　Feudal burdens can be preserved as neighbour burdens[1] if the superior owns – that is to say, has the *dominium utile* of – suitable other land in the vicinity of the feu[2]. The end result, on completion of the relevant procedure, is for the other land to become the benefited property in the burdens. This means that on the appointed day the right to enforce passes from the superiority, now defunct, to that land. In the language of the Abolition of Feudal Tenure etc (Scotland) Act 2000, the burden is 'reallotted'. Normally land is eligible for this purpose only if it contains a permanent building which lies within 100 metres of the feu and is in use as a place of human habitation or resort.

The procedure must be both commenced and, except in the case of an application to the Lands Tribunal, completed during the period beginning in the autumn of 2003 and ending on 27 November 2004[3]. Normally it involves the service and registration of a preservation notice in accordance with s 18 of the 2000 Act[4]. If, however, the superior's property is not within 100 metres, s 18 cannot be used and it is necessary to seek agreement with the vassal under s 19[5], failing which, to apply to the Lands Tribunal under s 20[6]. These latter sections did not appear in the draft Bill prepared by the Scottish Law Commission but were added by the Scottish Executive prior to the Bill's introduction to Parliament[7]. Further aspects of preservation notices are considered in chapter 11.

1　For neighbour burdens, see para 2.8.
2　Abolition of Feudal Tenure etc (Scotland) Act 2000, ss 18–20. In cases where the 100-metres rule does not apply, there is no formal requirement that the land be in the neighbourhood of the feu; but without reasonable proximity there would be no interest to enforce.
3　Normally registration must take place 'before the appointed day'. For the exceptional case where registration is wrongly refused, see the AFT(S)A 2000, s 45, discussed at para 11.16. See generally, on preservation, Scott Wortley 'Preserving Feudal Burdens as Praedial Real Burdens: Reallotment under the Abolition of Feudal Tenure etc (Scotland) Act 2000' (2003) 71 SLG 73.
4　Paras 3.4–3.16.
5　Paras 3.17–3.23.

7   The Scottish Law Commission considered, but in the end rejected, the idea that a superior who failed the 100-metres test should nonetheless have a second opportunity, by means of the Lands Tribunal, to save the burdens. See *Report on Abolition of the Feudal System* paras 4.40–4.45.

Excluded burdens

3.2   The only burden type formally excluded from ss 18–20 of the Abolition of Feudal Tenure Act is sporting rights[1]. Instead the superior must use the special procedure, described later[2], for conversion into separate tenements. But in two other cases ss 18–20, although formally competent, are in practice of no value.

One is for manager burdens (burdens reserving to the superior the right to act as, or to appoint, the manager of a development)[3]. Such burdens, if recent, are preserved automatically but for a limited period only[4]. They are not further preserved by the use of s 18.

The other is for community burdens in circumstances where, unusually, the potential benefited property is itself part of the community. Here a s 18 notice confers no advantage, for under the Title Conditions Act the burdens, already enforceable as community burdens, cannot be additionally enforced as neighbour burdens[5]. Instead the former superior must take his luck as an ordinary member of the community, and has no power to prevent variation or discharge occurring under the normal rules for community burdens[6].

> *Example.* A developer builds 100 houses. Before the appointed day 98 have been feued. The development is subject to common burdens under a deed of conditions which does not exclude the Land Registration (Scotland) Act 1979, s 17. Under the 2000 Act, a s 18 notice is registered in favour of the remaining two houses in relation to such of the other houses as lie within 100 metres. After the appointed day the burdens are community burdens, mutually enforceable in terms of s 53 of the 2003 Act[7]. Consequently the developer (and its successors as owners of the two houses) can enforce against the other houses only as such community burdens. If, however, s 17 of the 1979 Act had been excluded, the developer could enforce as neighbour burdens for as long as the two houses were not subject to the common burdens.

The rule operates in a slightly different way for sheltered or retirement housing. In developments of this kind the superior often reserves a unit as accommodation for the warden or for some other special use; and typically the unit is not subject to the community burdens that affect the rest of the development. Nonetheless, the 2003 Act treats the unit as part of the 'community' and hence as carrying a right of enforcement[8]. One effect, on the principle just discussed, is to remove any advantage to the superior which might otherwise have arisen from making that unit the subject of a s 18 notice[9].

1   Abolition of Feudal Tenure etc (Scotland) Act 2000, s 49 (definition of 'real burden'). In view of this definition it is not clear why sporting rights are excluded from s 18(7)(b)(i).

2   Paras 8.6–8.10.

3   The AFT(S)A 2000, s 18(6A) provides that registration shall not be effective to preserve any right to enforce a manager burden. There is no equivalent rule where the superior proceeds under ss 19 or 20.

4   Title Conditions (Scotland) Act 2003, s 63(10). See para 4.27.

5   TC(S)A 2003, s 62(2).

6   Para 7.21.

7   For which see paras 5.7–5.12.

8   TC(S)A 2003, ss 25(2), 26(2)(b), 54(1).

9   Scottish Law Commission *Report on Real Burdens* para 11.66. The Law Commission's legislative solution was different, but with similar effect.

Evaluating preservation

3.3   The 100-metres rule relieves superiors of what might otherwise have been a difficult choice in respect of preservation. For many feus lie outside a 100-metre radius of a superior's building and so, with minor exceptions, are automatically disqualified from s 18 of the Abolition of Feudal Tenure Act. In practice this is likely to mean that the burdens are abandoned except in those cases, probably few in number, where their importance justifies a Lands Tribunal application and offers reasonable prospects of success. But even within the 100-metre radius superiors will sometimes – perhaps quite often – be hesitant in invoking s 18. For before s 18 can be used it is necessary to check through chartularies or other collections of titles to identify the qualifying feus and burdens. A separate notice is needed for each feu[1], which must then be served on the vassal and registered against both the feu and the new benefited property. The cost of registration is £25[2], or £50 if the notice requires to be registered in both the Land Register and the Register of Sasines[3], and to this must be added the cost of employing a solicitor or other person to conduct the initial research and prepare the notices. Whether this trouble and expense can be justified will depend on the nature of the burdens. Some, on reflection, will turn out to be of little value to the superior's land and hardly worth saving, even assuming that interest to enforce could be shown. Other burdens are valuable but will be preserved in any event on other grounds, most notably as facility burdens[4]. No s 18 notice is then required. Still others are elderly and hence subject – or soon to be subject – to the sunset rule, which, after the appointed day, will allow the unilateral extinction of burdens of more than 100 years old[5]. It will also be borne in mind that neighbour burdens are in a less favourable position than the feudal burdens from which they are derived in respect that the remedy of irritancy is not available[6], and that interest to enforce is not presumed but falls to be proved[7]. Given the new statutory definition of interest[8], the latter may prove to be a significant hurdle.

None of these factors should, or probably will, deter superiors where the burdens are genuinely of value and importance. The standard case is likely to be the urban subdivision, where part of a house or garden was feued subject to burdens for the benefit of the part retained. By contrast, in large rural estates the superior may conclude that there is little merit in preserving the burdens for those feus which happen to lie within 100 metres if the same burdens cannot be preserved in respect of any other feu.

1   Abolition of Feudal Tenure etc (Scotland) Act 2000, s 42(2), (3).
2   Fees in the Registers of Scotland Order 1995, SI 1995/1945, Schedule, Pt III, para 2.
3   Ie because the title to one of the properties (eg the benefited property) is still in the Register of Sasines, while the title to the other is in the Land Register.
4   For facility burdens, see ch 7.
5   Title Conditions (Scotland) Act 2003, ss 20–24, discussed in para 7.22.
6   AFT(S)A 2000, s 53; TC(S)A 2003, s 67.
7   AFT(S)A 2000, s 24; TC(S)A 2003, s 8.
8   TC(S)A 2003, s 8(3). The standard test is that, 'in the circumstances of any case, failure to comply with the real burden is resulting in, or will result in, material detriment to the value or enjoyment of the person's ownership of, or right in, the benefited property'.

SECTION 18 NOTICE

Title to preserve

3.4   A person has title to preserve feudal burdens under s 18 of the Abolition of Feudal Tenure Act if the person (i) is the superior of the feu in respect of which the burdens are imposed and (ii) as such is able to enforce those burdens[1]. 'Superior' includes over-superior[2].

As respects (i) there is no requirement that the person be infeft provided that he 'has right' to the superiority and so would be able to complete title by notice of title or equivalent procedure in the Land Register[3]. If, as occasionally happens, there is more than one uninfeft superior, only the most recent such superior can use s 18[4].

> *Example.* Alan is superior. On his death Brian confirms as executor. Brian executes a docket transfer in favour of Alan's widow, Carol. Carol does not complete title. There are thus two uninfeft superiors (Brian and Carol), but only Carol, as the more recent of the two, is able to use s 18.

Similarly, if there is both an infeft superior and a later uninfeft superior – as where the superiority has been disponed but the disponee has not registered the disposition – the uninfeft superior, as the more recent, is the person entitled to use s 18.

If, as often, land has been subfeued more than once, there is likely to be more than one set of burdens and more than one superior. In that case, each superior has title to enforce only his 'own' burdens, and hence can use s 18 only in respect of those.

> *Example.* In 1960 Douglas feus land to Elspeth imposing real burdens. In 1970 Elspeth subfeus to George imposing burdens. In 1980 George further subfeus

to Helen imposing burdens. There are thus three sets of burdens and three superiors – or, more correctly, an immediate superior (George), and two over-superiors (Douglas and Elspeth). Each can use s 18 in respect of his or her 'own' burdens but not in respect of the other burdens. Thus Douglas (or his successor as superior) can preserve the 1960 burdens, Elspeth (or successor) the 1970 burdens, and George (or successor) the 1980 burdens. But Douglas cannot register a s 18 notice in respect of the 1970 or 1980 burdens.

In theory title to enforce might not be enough, for s 18(1) requires that the burdens are 'enforceable' by the superior, and enforcement requires interest as well as title. But for all practical purposes a superior who satisfies the 100-metres rules may be taken to have sufficient interest to enforce[5].

1   Abolition of Feudal Tenure etc (Scotland) Act 2000, s 18(1). The words 'would be so enforceable were the person in question to complete title to the *dominium directum*' are in acknowledgement of the rule that, as the law currently stands, only a person who is infeft can enforce a real burden. See K G C Reid *The Law of Property in Scotland* (1996) para 397.
2   AFT(S)A 2000, s 49.
3   AFT(S)A 2000, s 49. The expression 'has right' used in the definition of 'superior' picks up the usage in the Conveyancing (Scotland) Act 1924, ss 3, 4. A person who 'has right' can expede and register a notice of title under the 1924 Act, s 4 or, in Land Register cases, can procure direct registration under the Land Registration (Scotland) Act 1979, s 3(6).
4   AFT(S)A 2000, s 49.
5   For superiors, interest to enforce is generally (or perhaps always) conferred by ownership of neighbouring land. See K G C Reid *The Law of Property in Scotland* (1996) para 408. For interest in cases where the 100-metres rule does not apply, see para 3.8 below. Interest to enforce is used, in effect, as the criterion for preservation by the Lands Tribunal under s 20: see para 3.30.

Qualifying burdens

3.5   Not all conditions in grants in feu are real burdens[1]. Only those that are will qualify for conversion under s 18 of the Abolition of Feudal Tenure Act. In addition, as already mentioned, sporting rights are excluded from s 18 and must be preserved instead under s 65A[2] of the 2000 Act. The fact that a burden will survive feudal abolition on some other ground – as a community burden, for example, or as a facility burden – is not of itself a barrier to the use of s 18; but if the superior will gain enforcement rights by the other route, no purpose is likely to be served by using s 18.

> *Example.* Laura feus part of her garden to Malcolm, imposing an obligation to erect and maintain a boundary wall. On the appointed day the obligation will survive as a facility burden under s 51 of the Title Conditions (Scotland) Act 2003, and as such will be enforceable by Laura as the owner of land 'to which the facility is (and is intended to be) of benefit'. No purpose is served by registering a notice under s 18.

If a notice has already been registered to convert the burden into a personal real burden[3], a s 18 notice cannot be used in respect of the same burden unless the earlier notice is discharged[4].

[1]   Paras 1.18–1.23, 2.12.
[2]   AFT(S)A 2000, s 49 (definition of 'real burden'). For s 65A, see paras 8.6–8.10.
[3]   For personal real burdens, see ch 4.
[4]   AFT(S)A 2000, s 42(1), discussed at paras 11.3–11.6.

Qualifying land

3.6   The superior must own other land suitable for nomination as the benefited property[1]. If this is not already the case, either the superior must acquire such land or, more likely in practice, a neighbour must acquire the superiority. However, a neighbour who already has (non-feudal) enforcement rights in respect of the burdens will retain those after the appointed day and has nothing to gain from acquiring the superiority[2].

A title to both the superiority and the land is required only for the period of execution and registration of the notice. Once the notice is duly registered, the land or superiority, or both, can be sold. But s 18(6) of the Abolition of Feudal Tenure Act requires that the burdens be still enforceable by the superior immediately before the appointed day, and if the superior owns no land in the neighbourhood (whether the nominated property or some other property) it is arguable that the burdens are unenforceable for lack of interest[3].

In order to qualify as the replacement benefited property (or 'dominant tenement' in the terminology of the 2000 Act), the land must satisfy either the 100-metres rule or one of the alternatives to that rule. Both are discussed below. In addition the land must, as already mentioned, be owned by the superior. Except in the unusual case of allodial land (such as udal land), a superior 'owns' in the required sense only by having *dominium utile*, although actual infeftment is not insisted on[4]. In cases where there is no infeftment the notice must, in effect, deduce title[5]. The title to the land must match precisely the title to the superiority[6]. Thus if the superiors are the trustees of the tenth duke, and the proposed land is owned by the eleventh duke, the requirement is not complied with and s 18 cannot be used, or at least not without some preliminary conveyancing, either of the superiority or of the land. Similarly, if Andrew is the sole superior but the land is owned by common by Andrew and Beth, the requirements of s 18 are not satisfied.

There is no requirement that the land be in Scotland, and in the case of a feu on the border with England it would be competent to nominate land on the English side[7].

Where the superior owns two or more qualifying areas, only one may be nominated for the purposes of s 18[8]. The idea is that a single superiority is to be replaced by a single plot of land. But there is no restriction as to size and, provided the 100-metres rule (or equivalent) can be satisfied, it would be open to the superior to nominate either the whole estate retained by him or her or, if preferred, a part only. From the superior's point of view, the former will generally be safer. It is difficult to predict the future pattern of land sales and the superior will not wish to be left in 20 years' time with the part of the estate to which enforcement rights do not attach. The converse risk, of undue proliferation of enforcement rights, is largely avoided by s 12 of the Title Conditions Act which provides that, except where the conveyance otherwise provides, a plot of land broken off from the benefited property after the appointed day will cease to carry enforcement rights.

The same land may be used in respect of any number of feus, but a separate notice is required in each case[9].

[1]   Abolition of Feudal Tenure etc (Scotland) Act 2000, s 18(1).
[2]   AFT(S)A 2000, s 17(1)(b).
[3]   K G C Reid *The Law of Property in Scotland* (1996) para 408.
[4]   Section 18(1) requires only that the superior 'has right'.
[5]   AFT(S)A 2000, Sch 5, note 5.
[6]   By s 18(1) the superior must have right to the 'sole *dominium utile*'.
[7]   This is presupposed by the AFT(S)A 2000, s 42(5).
[8]   A s 18 notice can be registered only in respect of one plot of land, and a second such notice is prevented by s 42(1).
[9]   Para 3.13.

100-metres rule

3.7   Normally the land being nominated must comply with the 100-metres rule[1]. The rule is intended is to prevent the indiscriminate preservation of burdens in circumstances where there is unlikely to be an interest to enforce. For even without such an interest, a burden on the Register has a nuisance value sufficient to generate income for minutes of waiver and hence to keep alive one of the abuses which feudal abolition was designed to bring to an end[2].

The 100-metres rule imposes three conditions: (i) the land must contain a permanent building; (ii) the building must lie within 100 metres of the feu; and (iii) the building must be in use wholly or mainly as a place of human habitation or resort.

The first of these is straightforward. A proper building is required, generally with foundations. A mobile home, for example, would not qualify, or a portacabin. Land which is unbuilt on is, of course, excluded.

The second condition requires measurement from 'some point' of the building and not from the land itself. Thus the mere fact that the land itself is within 100-metres is of no assistance. The measurement runs on a horizontal plane from the outer edge of the building to the nearest boundary of the feu, and differences in level are disregarded[3]. Thus if the ground slopes upwards from the feu, so that the building is on a hill, the measurement is made on the assumption that both building and feu are on the same level. And if the feu is a flat in a tenement, all other flats in the building are treated as on the same level.

The final condition may sometimes give rise to greater difficulty, although most cases will be clear enough. Thus a house or office or restaurant is a place of human habitation or resort, and qualifies without question; and stables or a grain store are neither a place of human habitation nor, except incidentally, a place of human resort[4]. The effect of the words 'wholly or mainly' in the statutory formula is that incidental use is disregarded.

The 100-metres rule requires each feu to be viewed separately. Thus if the rule is complied with in respect of four feus but not of the remaining forty-seven, a s 18 notice can be used only in respect of the four feus. A feu which has been divided and is in separate ownership is treated as two different feus, each of which must separately satisfy the 100-metres rule[5].

The relevant time for compliance with the rule is the period of execution and registration of the notice[6]. Once the notice is registered, it does not matter that the building is demolished or put to a non-qualifying use.

The 100-metres rule excited some controversy during the passage of the legislation[7] and was reconsidered by the Scottish Executive in the context of the Title Conditions (Scotland) Act 2003 when the decision was made that it should be retained[8]. As with any fixed-distance rule, it is arbitrary to some degree, and will exclude some burdens where there is interest to enforce while including others where interest is absent. For the former at least there is the possibility of an application to the Lands Tribunal under s 20 of the 2000 Act[9]. Although the rule has been criticised on the basis that 100 metres has a different effect as between town and country, the rule was devised mainly with rural areas in mind. In a town or city it will be relatively rare for a superior to own neighbouring property, and usually such property will be immediately adjacent. Rural superiors, by contrast, often own extensive tracts of land which, in the absence of a distance restriction, would be freely available for the purposes of s 18.

[1]   Abolition of Feudal Tenure etc (Scotland) Act 2000, s 18(1),(7)(a).
[2]   Scottish Law Commission *Report on Abolition of the Feudal System* paras 4.33 and 4.34.
[3]   Scottish Law Commission *Report on Abolition of the Feudal System* para 4.35.
[4]   Scottish Law Commission *Report on Abolition of the Feudal System* para 4.34.
[5]   AFT(S)A 2000, s 42(2). The expression '*dominium utile* of land' picks up the opening words of s 18(1).
[6]   AFT(S)A 2000, s 18(1). The only requirement at the time of the appointed day is that the burden remain enforceable: see s 18(6), discussed at para 3.15.
[7]   Scottish Parliament *Official Report* 3 May 2000 cols 235–42.
[8]   Scottish Parliament *Official Report* 21 November 2002 col 156.
[9]   Paras 3.24–3.34.

Alternatives to 100-metres rule

3.8   In four cases the 100-metres rule is dispensed with, and with it the requirement that the nominated land contain a building[1]. This is because the burdens covered by these cases are not, by their nature, concerned with amenity, or at least with the amenity of buildings[2]. Nonetheless, unless the nominated land is reasonably close by, it is unlikely to confer an interest to enforce, either before the appointed day or thereafter; and a failure on the first count will usually prevent the use of s 18 of the 2000 Act altogether[3].

The four cases are described below.

1   Abolition of Feudal Tenure etc (Scotland) Act 2000, s 18(7)(b), (c).
2   Scottish Law Commission *Report on Abolition of the Feudal System* paras 4.37–4.39.
3   If there is no such interest before the appointed day, the burden is not 'enforceable' as required by s 18(1)(a). See further para 3.15. But in theory the requisite interest might be created by land belonging to the superior other than that nominated for the purposes of s 18.

Case (1): rights of entry/use

3.9   Where a grant in feu reserved a right of access or other right of intermittent use, the proper legal classification is usually servitude rather than real burden; and, as already noted[1], servitudes are unaffected by feudal abolition. If, however, the right does not qualify as a servitude – usually because it is not one of the 'known' servitudes recognised by Scots law[2] – it can probably be reconceptualised as a real burden[3]. Maintenance burdens, for example, might include a right of entry for the superior for the purposes of inspecting the feu and, in the event of the vassal's default, of carrying out repairs. In that particular case the right will survive the appointed day as part of a facility burden[4]. A freestanding right would require a notice under s 18 of the 2000 Act. The 100-metres rule does not then apply[5]. Examples are likely to be rare, particularly in view of the fact that, as already mentioned, sporting rights fall to be saved under s 65A[6].

After the appointed day it will not usually be possible for rights of this kind to be constituted as real burdens[7]. Instead they must be constituted as positive servitudes, and the fixed list of known servitudes is abandoned in respect of servitudes created by registration[8]. Indeed any right of entry or use preserved under s 18 will automatically become a servitude on the appointed day[9].

1   Para 1.19.
2   As to which see D J Cusine and R R M Paisley *Servitudes and Rights of Way* (1998) ch 3.
3   *B & C Group Management v Haren* (4 December 1992, unreported) Outer House, discussed in K G C Reid *The Law of Property in Scotland* (1996) para 391. A right to enter the surface to work minerals is not, however, a real burden but rather an integral part of a reservation (or grant) of minerals. See para 8.5.
4   See ch 6.
5   Abolition of Feudal Tenure etc (Scotland) Act 2000, s 18(7)(b)(i).
6   They are excluded from s 18 by s 49 (definition of 'real burden'). See, for the s 65A procedure, paras 8.6–8.10.
7   Title Conditions (Scotland) Act 2003, s 2. But there is an exception for rights which are ancillary to standard real burdens (as in the example given in the text of a right of entry to carry out repairs).

8   TC(S)A 2003, s 76. See further Scottish Law Commission *Report on Real Burdens* paras 2.1–2.8 and 12.22–12.24.

9   TC(S)A 2003, s 81. As s 81(2)(a) makes clear, the burden must first be saved under s 18 of the AFT(S)A 2000 or by virtue of some other provision. Section 81 does not apply to rights 'to enter, or otherwise make use of, property' for a purpose ancillary to a maintenance or other 'normal' real burden, and such rights remain real burdens. The right of entry for repairs mentioned earlier would be an example of such an 'ancillary burden' (see the TC(S)A 2003, s 2(4) for the terminology).

Case (2): pre-emptions and redemptions

3.10   A right of pre-emption is a right of first refusal in the event that the vassal wishes to sell. A right of redemption is a right of repurchase, whether at the option of the superior, at some fixed point in time, or on the occurrence of a future event. Both pre-emptions and redemptions may be preserved under s 18, assuming a suitable benefited property can be found, and the 100-metres rule does not apply[1]; but since both may also be preserved, without a benefited property, as personal real burdens[2], it seems unlikely that s 18 will be much used for this purpose.

1   Abolition of Feudal Tenure etc (Scotland) Act 2000, s 18(7)(b)(ii).
2   AFT(S)A 2000, s 18A, discussed at paras 4.21–4.23.

Case (3): burdens for the benefit of minerals

3.11   Typically, the minerals under a feu are reserved to the superior – a reservation which, as *dominium utile*, will survive the appointed day[1]. And occasionally burdens imposed on the feu were imposed for the benefit of the mineral estate itself. An example might be a restriction or prohibition on building, owing to the risk of subsidence. Where 'it is apparent from the terms of the real burden that it was created for the benefit of' a mineral estate, a s 18 notice can nominate that estate without regard to the 100-metres rule[2]. Once again, usage is expected to be light[3].

It is important to distinguish conditions of the kind just mentioned from conditions forming an integral part of the minerals reservation. Common examples include an obligation on the superior to pay compensation for subsidence, or a right to work the minerals, including, sometimes, a right to work from the surface. Such rights and obligations, being neither real burdens nor feudal in character, are unaffected by feudal abolition[4].

1   See further para 8.4.
2   Abolition of Feudal Tenure etc (Scotland) Act 2000, s 18(7)(c)(i).
3   For a discussion, see Robert Rennie *Minerals and the Law of Scotland* (2001) pp 15–18.
4   Para 8.5.

Case (4): burdens for the benefit of salmon fishings

3.12   A similar rule applies in respect of burdens imposed for the benefit of the separate tenement of salmon fishing[1]; and once again it is necessary to distinguish such burdens from conditions which form part of the content of the separate tenement itself and which are therefore unaffected by feudal abolition[2]. A qualifying burden, it may be assumed, would usually restrict the use of the river to facilitate the exercise of the fishing right. Where s 18 of the 2000 Act is used, the separate tenement of salmon fishings – which is treated as 'land' under Scottish property law[3] – is nominated as the benefited property, and the 100-metres rule does not apply. Ownership by superiors of salmon fishings is far less common than ownership of minerals.

In principle, s 18 can be used on the same basis for other incorporeal separate tenements, such as the right to mussels or oysters[4], but such rights are rare, and burdens imposed in association with them are actually, or practically, unknown.

[1]   Abolition of Feudal Tenure etc (Scotland) Act 2000, s 18(7)(c)(ii).
[2]   K G C Reid *The Law of Property in Scotland* (1996) paras 327–330.
[3]   Para 8.1.
[4]   For the incorporeal separate tenements, see K G C Reid *The Law of Property in Scotland* (1996) paras 209–212. Sporting rights are not currently separate tenements, but those saved under s 65A of the 2000 Act will acquire this status: see s 65A(5).

Preparation and registration of notice

3.13   Section 18 of the Abolition of Feudal Tenure Act requires the preparation, service, execution and registration of a notice. The notice must follow the form provided in Schedule 5 to the 2000 Act, although minor deviations are permitted[1]. The statutory form provides for[2]:

- the name and address of the superior;
- a conveyancing description both of the feu[3] and of the nominated land;
- a statement as to which of the 100-metres rule or permitted alternatives has been satisfied;
- a list of the real burden or burdens, either in full text or by reference to the deed by which they were imposed;
- details of that deed, including the date and place of registration;
- a list of any obligations on the superior which are the counterpart of the real burden or burdens[4];
- an account of the title to the superiority by reference to the Registers including, in a case where the superior is uninfeft, a list of the midcouples;
- an account of the superior's title to the nominated land, in the same form; and
- details of service on the vassal.

A style of completed notice is set out in Appendix 3 to this book.

The same notice can be used for more than one burden[5]. Thus a superior who is seeking to save all the burdens on a particular feu need only use a single notice. But a separate notice is required for each feu, partly because, as already mentioned[6], the 100-metres rule must be satisfied separately for each feu[7].

The notice must be served on the vassal before execution, thus ensuring that the details of service – to be added to the notice after service – are covered by the superior's signature and oath[8]. Service is effected by sending by post a copy of the notice and of the explanatory note provided in Schedule 5. Service is more fully discussed in chapter 11[9]. The notice is then completed by entering the details of service[10], and by signature before a notary public, the superior having sworn or affirmed that to the best of his knowledge or belief all the information contained in the notice is true[11]. The notary must also sign[12]. Swearing or affirming a statement that is known to be false or is believed not to be true is an offence under the False Oaths (Scotland) Act 1933. Normally the oath must be given by the superior personally and not, for example, through a solicitor; but a company or other juristic person is represented by a person authorised to sign documents on its behalf[13], and a person without legal capacity by an appropriate person[14]. An oath outside Scotland may be given before any person duly authorised by the country in question to administer oaths or receive affirmations[15]. If the superiority is held as common or joint property, each superior must separately swear or affirm, and sign the notice[16]. The position of trustees is discussed below[17].

The final step is to register the notice, in the Land Register or Register of Sasines. Section 18 requires registration against both the feu (the burdened property) and also the nominated land (the benefited property)[18]. This follows the new rules, in operation after the appointed day, for the creation of real burdens[19], and is intended to ensure that burdens are fully transparent from the Registers, and in particular that owners of the benefited property have notice of their right to enforce. The Keeper is directed to cross-refer to the entries, so that, for example, the title sheet of the benefited property will identify the burdened property[20]. No warrant of registration is needed in respect of registration in the Register of Sasines.[21] If one of the properties is already in the Land Register but the other still in the Register of Sasines, registration will be needed in both Registers. The fee for registration is £25 if the notice is to be registered in one Register and £50 if it is to be registered in both[22]. Neither stamp duty nor its replacement, stamp duty land tax, is payable[23].

---

[1]   Abolition of Feudal Tenure etc (Scotland) Act 2000, s 18(1).

[2]   AFT(S)A 2000, s 18(2), Sch 5.

[3]   Or, at the superior's option, part only of the feu. See AFT(S)A 2000, s 18(2)(b). In that case only the part described will be subject to the burden after the appointed day.

[4]   For superiors' obligations, see paras 1.24, 1.25.

[5]   AFT(S)A 2000, s 42(4)(a).

[6]   Para 3.7.

[7]   AFT(S)A 2000, s 42(3). Where the land originally feued has been divided and is in separate ownership, each separate part is treated as a separate feu for this purpose: see s 42(2).

[8]   AFT(S)A 2000, s 41(3).

9   Paras 11.7, 11.8.
10   AFT(S)A 2000, s 41(4).
11   AFT(S)A 2000, s 18(4).
12   AFT(S)A 2000, Sch 5, note 7.
13   See generally the Requirements of Writing (Scotland) Act 1995, Sch 2.
14   AFT(S)A 2000, s 18(5).
15   AFT(S)A 2000, s 49 (definition of 'notary public').
16   This is because the obligations in s 18 are placed on 'the superior', and the singular includes the plural.
17   Para 3.14.
18   AFT(S)A 2000, s 18(1), (3).
19   Title Conditions (Scotland) Act 2003, s 4(5).
20   And vice versa: see Land Registration (Scotland) Act 1979, s 6(1)(e), (ee), as amended by the TC(S)A 2003, s 112(2).
21   AFT(S)A 2000, s 41(2).
22   Fees in the Registers of Scotland Order 1995, SI 1995/1945, Schedule, Pt III, para 2.
23   Paras 11.9–11.11.

Trustees as superiors

3.14   In a case where the superiors are trustees, compliance with s 18 of the Abolition of Feudal Tenure Act may require greater thought and care. The correct method of proceeding depends on the state of the title to the superiority. There are three possibilities: either (i) all of the trustees are infeft or (ii) none of them is infeft or (iii) some are infeft and some are uninfeft.

If all the trustees are infeft, there is no difficulty. Each is a superior, and each must swear or affirm, and sign, the s 18 notice.

If all the trustees are uninfeft, the position is much the same, the only difference being that the notice must list the midcouples linking the trustees to the person last infeft[1]. This is required even in a case where the superiority is on the Land Register.

If, finally, some trustees are infeft and some uninfeft, the position is more complex. Typically this result has come about because of the assumption of new trustees without registering the deed of assumption and conveyance; and, equally typically, the deed of assumption conveys the trust property, not only to the new trustees but also to such of the existing trustees as are to continue. The result is that the existing trustees are, or may be, infeft (on their original title) but are also simultaneously uninfeft (by virtue of being grantees of the deed of assumption and conveyance). The effect of the 2000 Act is that the 'superiors' are the most recent holders of that title, or in other words the (uninfeft) grantees of the deed of assumption and conveyance[2]. The fact, therefore, that some trustees are infeft is disregarded, and the s 18 notice is completed on the basis that everyone is uninfeft.

1   Abolition of Feudal Tenure etc (Scotland) Act 2000, Sch 5, note 5.
2   AFT(S)A 2000, s 49 (definition of 'superior').

The appointed day: a further condition

3.15 For the most part, the relevant time for satisfaction of the conditions laid down by s 18 of the 2000 Act is the execution and registration of the notice rather than the appointed day itself[1]. In particular, the effectiveness of a notice is not impaired if, after the date of registration, the superior parts with the superiority or with the nominated land, or if the building ceases to be a place of human habitation or resort. But one condition is tied to the appointed day itself. Conversion under s 18 requires that the feudal burden continues to be enforceable by the superior 'immediately before the appointed day'[2].

There are two reasons why this might turn out not to be so. One is that the burden has come to be extinguished, whether by minute of waiver by the superior, by order of the Lands Tribunal, by negative prescription, or on some other ground[3].

The other is that, while the burden remains, the superior has lost any interest to enforce. Although the position is not clear beyond doubt[4], it seems likely that, at least in the ordinary case, interest to enforce requires ownership of other land in the neighbourhood[5]; and typically this will be the land now nominated as the benefited property. Hence if, after registration of the notice, either land or superiority is sold, the person holding the superiority may no longer hold any land which is capable of giving rise to interest to enforce. In that case, it is arguable that the burden is no longer 'enforceable' as required by the 2000 Act.

[1] Abolition of Feudal Tenure etc (Scotland) Act 2000, s 18(1).
[2] AFT(S)A 2000, s 18(6).
[3] For extinction of real burdens, see K G C Reid *The Law of Property in Scotland* (1996) paras 426–438.
[4] Scottish Law Commission *Report on Abolition of the Feudal System* para 5.22.
[5] K G C Reid *The Law of Property in Scotland* (1996) paras 407–08. And see para 4.7 below.

Effect of conversion

3.16 Assuming a notice under s 18 of the 2000 Act to have been validly drawn up and registered, and the feudal burden to be still enforceable, the result on the appointed day is for the feudal burden to be converted into a neighbour burden[1]. The burdened property remains the (former) feu, as before, but now upgraded from *dominium utile* to outright ownership, while the benefited property is the land nominated in the notice. Thus instead of the burden being enforceable by the superior against the vassal, it is now enforceable by the owner (or occupier) of the benefited property against the owner (or occupier) of the burdened property. And in principle there is no difference between a neighbour burden created in this way, by conversion of a feudal burden, and a neighbour burden newly created, or created before the appointed day by ordinary disposition and without reference to the feudal system. The right to enforce is subject to any counter-obligation previously enforceable against the superior[2].

¹   Abolition of Feudal Tenure etc (Scotland) Act 2000, s 18(6). For neighbour burdens, see para 2.8.
²   And, it seems, whether listed in the notice or not. See AFT(S)A 2000, s 25. For counter-obligations, see para 1.25.

SECTION 19 AGREEMENT

Scope

3.17   Feudal burdens can also be converted into neighbour burdens by agreement, made under s 19 of the Abolition of Feudal Tenure Act. This, however, is likely to be a last resort, used only where s 18 is unavailable, typically because the 100-metres rule is not satisfied. The fact that the consent of the vassal is needed (unlike with s 18) is a major disadvantage and may require the persuasive force of money. A marginal advantage of the s 19 procedure is that the burdens can be modified (though not augmented)[1].

Section 19 is necessary at all only because of the doubt as to whether deeds of conditions can be used as self-standing deeds rather than, as envisaged by the original legislative provision[2], as a deed granted in association with a conveyance[3]. The legal effect is not in any event identical. A deed of conditions would create new real burdens, to replace those lost by feudal abolition. A s 19 agreement[4] preserves the existing burdens and reallots the right to enforce. In view of the doubts concerning deeds of conditions, a prudent superior will opt for s 19.

¹   Abolition of Feudal Tenure etc (Scotland) Act 2000, s 19(1).
²   Conveyancing (Scotland) Act 1874, s 32.
³   For a discussion, see Scottish Law Commission *Discussion Paper on Real Burdens* (Scot Law Com DP no 106, 1998) paras 7.32–7.34, and *Report on Real Burdens* para 3.13. The doubt is not, however, shared by the official *Explanatory Notes* para 82.
⁴   Not, of course, to be confused with an agreement under the Land Registration (Scotland) Act 1979, s 19 in respect of common boundaries.

Requirements

3.18   The rules as to the superior's title and qualifying burdens are the same as for s 18[1]. And as with s 18 there must also be qualifying land – land in the neighbourhood owned by the superior and to which enforcement rights can be reallotted[2]. There is no requirement that the 100-metres rule (or an alternative to that rule) be complied with; but unless the land is reasonably close the burden is likely to fail in the future for lack of interest to enforce[3].

A s 19 agreement is entered into by the superior and the vassal. Neither need be infeft, nor need the superior be infeft in the land being nominated as the benefited property[4]. In the absence of infeftment a clause of deduction of title is generally needed[5]. The gist of a s 19 agreement is that, on the appointed day, the nominated land is to become the new benefited property in the real burden.

1   Paras 3.4, 3.5.
2   Para 3.6.
3   Title Conditions (Scotland) Act 2003, s 17.
4   Abolition of Feudal Tenure etc (Scotland) Act 2000, ss 19(1), 49 (definition of 'superior'). The rules for superior and vassal are not absolutely identical. As already seen (para 3.4), if more than one person has right to the superiority, only the last such person qualifies. But it seems that *any* person who has right to the feu can enter into a s 19 agreement ('the person who has right to the feu') so that, if there is more than one, the superior has a choice.
5   AFT(S)A 2000, s 19(6), Sch 6, note 4. The, rather complex, rules here are explored more fully in para 3.20.

Content

3.19   Section 19 of the Abolition of Feudal Tenure Act lays down rules as to content but not as to form. An agreement must contain[1]:

- a statement that it is made under s 19;
- the name and address both of the superior and of the vassal;
- a conveyancing description both of the feu[2] and of the nominated land;
- a list of the real burden or burdens, either in full text or by reference to the deed by which they were imposed;
- details of that deed, including the date and place of registration;
- a list of any obligations on the superior which are the counterpart of the real burden or burdens[3];
- a list of the proposed modifications, if any, to the real burdens or counter-obligations;
- an account of the title to the superiority by reference to the Registers including, in a case where the superior is uninfeft, a list of the midcouples; and
- an account of the superior's title to the nominated land, in the same form.

The agreement may be drafted to cover some or all of the real burdens enforceable by the superior against the vassal[4]; but, if only for practical reasons[5], a separate agreement is needed in respect of each feu. Both parties must sign[6].

1   Abolition of Feudal Tenure etc (Scotland) Act 2000, s 19(3), (6).
2   Or, at the superior's option, part only of the feu. See AFT(S)A 2000, s 19(2)(b). In that case only the part described will be subject to the burden after the appointed day.
3   For superiors' obligations, see paras 1.24, 1.25.
4   AFT(S)A 2000, s 42(4)(b).
5   There is, however, no equivalent of s 42(3) in respect of s 19 agreements.
6   Requirements of Writing (Scotland) Act 1995, ss 1(2)(b) and 2.

Form

3.20   In the absence of a statutory form, the following is offered as a possible style. Naturally, however, there are many other ways in which a s 19 agreement could be drafted. The statutory requirements suggest a form halfway between a notice and a conventional deed.

Style of s 19 Agreement

(1) This Agreement is made under section 19 of the Abolition of Feudal Tenure etc (Scotland) Act 2000 between the Superior and the Vassal of the Servient Tenement.

(2) The Superior is AB (*address*).

(3) The Vassal is CD (*address*).

(4) The Servient Tenement is ALL and WHOLE (*description*).

(5) The Nominated Property is ALL and WHOLE (*description*).

(6) The Superior's title to the *dominium directum* of the Servient Tenement is constituted by Disposition by EF in favour of the Superior dated (*date*) and recorded in the Division of the General Register of Sasines for the County of (*county*) on (*date*)[1].

[(7) The *dominium utile* of the Servient Tenement was last vested in GH (*address*), whose title thereto is recorded in the Division of the General Register of Sasines for the Country of (*county*) on (*date*) and from whom the Vassal acquired right by (*midcouples*)[2].]

(8) The Superior's title to the *dominium utile* of the Nominated Property is registered under Title Number (*number*)[3].

(9) The Real Burdens, which were constituted by Feu Disposition by JK in favour of LM dated (*date*) and recorded in the Division of the General Register of Sasines for the County of (*county*) on (*date*), are (*give terms of burdens or import the terms by reference to the deed by which they were constituted*)[4].

[(10) As modified by this Agreement, the Real Burdens are to be (*give terms of real burdens as so modified*)][5].

[(11) The Counter-Obligations, which were constituted by the said Feu Disposition by JK in favour of LM dated and recorded as aforesaid, are (*give terms of any counter-obligations on the superior or import the terms by reference to the deed by which they were constituted*)[6].]

[(12) As modified by this Agreement, the Counter-Obligations are to be (*give terms of counter-obligations as so modified*)][7].

(13) The Superior and the Vassal hereby nominate the Nominated Property as a dominant tenement in relation to the Real Burdens[8] insofar as they affect the Servient Tenement: IN WITNESS WHEREOF

---

[1] This presupposes both infeftment and a Sasine title. For other cases, see the Abolition of Feudal Tenure etc (Scotland) Act 2000, Sch 6, note 4. If the superior is uninfeft, deduction of title is needed even in Land Register cases. Thus for example: 'The *dominium directum* of the Servient Tenement was last vested in GH (*address*), whose title thereto is registered in the Land Register under Title Number (*number*) on (*date*) and from whom the Superior acquired right by (*list midcouples*)'.

2   Insert only where (i) the title to the *dominium utile* remains on the Register of Sasines *and* (ii) the vassal is uninfeft. See AFT(S)A 2000, s 19(6). In other cases there is no requirement that the vassal set out his title.
3   This presupposes both infeftment and a Land Register title. For other cases, see the AFT(S)A 2000, Sch 6, note 4. If the superior is uninfeft, deduction of title is needed even in Land Register cases. Thus for example: 'The *dominium utile* of the Nominated Property was last vested in GH (*address*), whose title thereto is registered in the Land Register under Title Number (*number*) on (*date*) and from whom the Superior acquired right by (*list midcouples*)'.
4   AFT(S)A 2000, Sch 6, note 3.
5   The parties are free to modify the existing burdens: see AFT(S)A 2000, s 19(1).
6   AFT(S)A 2000, Sch 6, note 3.
7   The parties are free to modify the existing counter-obligations: see AFT(S)A 2000, s 19(1).
8   Add 'as modified' in a case where the burdens have been modified by the Agreement.

Registration

3.21   A s 19 agreement must be executed and registered before the appointed day (28 November 2004)[1]. Otherwise the superior's rights will be lost on the appointed day. Even after that day, however, the burdens could be revived by agreement, for the doubt surrounding deeds of conditions[2] is removed by the Title Conditions Act, which allows real burdens to be created in any deed that is appropriately worded and executed by the owner of the burdened property (ie the former vassal)[3]. But there would then be a gap period beginning with the appointed day and ending with the registration of the deed during which the burdens would not be enforceable.

As with a s 18 notice, a s 19 agreement must be registered against both the burdened and the benefited property (ie, in the words of the style, the servient tenement and the nominated property)[4]. A warrant of registration is needed in respect of registration in the Register of Sasines[5]. If one of the properties is already in the Land Register but the other still in the Register of Sasines, registration will be needed in both Registers. The fee is £25 for registration in one register and £50 for registration in both[6]. It is arguable that stamp duty of £5 is payable[7].

1   Abolition of Feudal Tenure etc (Scotland) Act 2000, s 19(1).
2   Para 3.17.
3   Title Conditions (Scotland) Act 2003, s 4.
4   AFT(S)A 2000, s 19(4).
5   The AFT(S)A 2000, s 41(2) removes the need for a warrant of registration for notices but not for a s 19 agreement.
6   Fees in the Registers of Scotland Order 1995, SI 1995/1945, Schedule, Pt III, para 2.
7   Para 11.10. For the position as to stamp duty land tax, see para 11.11.

Effect of conversion

3.22   Assuming an agreement under s 19 to have been validly drawn up and registered, and the feudal burden to be still enforceable[1], the result on the appointed day is for the feudal burden to be converted into a neighbour burden[2]. The burdened property remains the (former) feu, as before, while the benefited property is the land nominated in the agreement and not, as previously, the feudal superiority. The right to enforce is subject to any counter-obligation previously enforceable against the superior[3].

[1]   See, on this topic, para 3.15 above.
[2]   AFT(S)A 2000, s 19(5).
[3]   And, it seems, whether listed in the agreement or not. See AFT(S)A 2000, s 25.

Preliminary notice

3.23   Section 19 of the Abolition of Feudal Tenure Act also provides for a preliminary notice by the superior in which the vassal is invited to enter into a s 19 agreement[1]. Unlike other notices provided for by the 2000 Act, a notice under s 19 cannot be registered. The notice indeed is not mandatory, and an agreement without a notice is perfectly effective[2]. In practice a letter or a telephone call might seem a less aggressive prelude to negotiations with the vassal.

An application to the Lands Tribunal, however, requires that the superior should first have attempted to reach agreement under s 19[3]; and a s 19 notice is convenient, and on one view mandatory, evidence of such a failed attempt. In practice, therefore, a s 19 notice should be sent in any case where the prospects of agreement look poor.

As with other notices under the 2000 Act, the requirements of a s 19 notice are strictly prescribed. Thus the notice must contain[4]:

- the name and address both of the superior and of the vassal;
- a description both of the feu[5] and of the nominated land[6];
- a list of the real burden or burdens, either in full text or by reference to the deed by which they were imposed;
- details of that deed, including the date and place of registration;
- a list of any obligations on the superior which are the counterpart of the real burden or burdens;
- a list of the proposed modifications, if any, to the real burdens or counter-obligations;
- an account of the title to the superiority by reference to the Registers including, in a case where the superior is uninfeft, a list of the midcouples;
- an account of the superior's title to the nominated land, in the same form; and
- details of service on the vassal.

A style of completed notice is set out in Appendix 3 to this book.

The notice is served on the vassal by post or delivery[7], and then signed by the superior. There is no requirement for an oath, and a notary public is not needed. Although no specific provision is made, it may be assumed that the notice should be accompanied by the explanatory note set out in Schedule 6 to the 2000 Act[8].

1   Abolition of Feudal Tenure etc (Scotland) Act 2000, s 19(1)(a).
.2   Section 19(5) requires only that paras (b) and (c) of subsection (1) are satisfied.
3   AFT(S)A 2000, s 20(1), (2), discussed at para 3.26 below.
4   AFT(S)A 2000, s 19(2), Sch 6.
5   Or part only of the feu: see AFT(S)A 2000, s 19(2)(b).
6   As the notice is not registered, however, the legislation does not insist on a full conveyancing
     description. A postal address, for example, would usually be sufficient.
7   AFT(S)A 2000, Sch 6, note 5. By contrast, other notices must normally be sent by post: see
     s 41(3).
8   Compare the AFT(S)A 2000, s 41(3) (which does not apply to s 19 notices). Note 5 to Schedule
     6 requires only service of 'a copy of the notice'. Of course it is possible to argue that the
     explanatory note is part of the notice.

SECTION 20 APPLICATION

Eligibility

3.24   As has been seen, a s 18 notice may be used if and only if the 100-metres rule
(or an equivalent) is satisfied[1]. For other cases the legislation proposes two alternatives. One, just discussed, is to reach agreement under s 19 of the Abolition of Feudal
Tenure Act. The other is to seek reallotment by order of the Lands Tribunal under s
20 of the 2000 Act.

In order to be eligible for an application under s 20 the superior must satisfy all the
requirements of s 18 other than the 100-metres rule (or equivalent)[2]. In particular,
there must be a valid real burden; the burden must be enforceable by the superior;
and the superior must own other land in the vicinity which is capable of acting as a
replacement benefited property. Infeftment is not required, either in the superiority or
in the other land.

1   Paras 3.7–3.12.
2   See generally paras 3.4–3.6.

Procedure in outline

3.25   A s 20 application involves three separate stages. First, the superior attempts
to reach agreement with the vassal under s 19. Secondly, and following the failure of
such an attempt, the superior makes an application to the Lands Tribunal. Finally, the
superior draws up, serves, and registers a blocking notice[1], that is to say, a notice
which blocks the extinction of rights which would otherwise be brought about, on the
appointed day, by s 17(1) of the Abolition of Feudal Tenure Act. All stages are
mandatory. Thus a Tribunal application cannot be made without a prior attempt to
reach agreement[2]; and the Tribunal cannot exercise its statutory powers unless a
notice has first been registered[3].

These stages are now considered in more detail.

1 The name, however, is not used in the Abolition of Feudal Tenure etc (Scotland) Act 2000.
2 AFT(S)A 2000, s 20(1).
3 AFT(S)A 2000, s 20(7).

Stage (1): attempted agreement

3.26 An initial attempt must be made to reach agreement under s 19 of the 2000 Act[1]. If successful, a s 19 agreement is executed and registered and nothing further is required. If the attempt fails, an application may then be made to the Lands Tribunal under s 20. The application narrates the failed attempt[2] and should demonstrate a certain amount of patience and perseverance on the part of the superior. At the least the vassal must have been given a reasonable opportunity to respond to the superior's approach, whether that approach was made by a s 19 notice[3] or in some less formal manner. A cautious view would be that a s 19 notice is mandatory[4].

1 Abolition of Feudal Tenure etc (Scotland) Act 2000, s 20(1). For s 19 agreements, see paras 3.17–3.23.
2 AFT(S)A 2000, s 20(2).
3 For which see para 3.23.
4 The issue turns on the proper meaning to be given to the words '*in pursuance of* section 19 of this Act' in the AFT(S)A 2000, s 20(1). There is no suggestion in the official *Explanatory Notes* paras 91, 93, 94 that a s 19 notice is mandatory. On the other hand it is difficult to see why detailed provision was made for a notice if the same effect could be achieved informally.

Stage (2): Tribunal application

3.27 The Tribunal application can be made at any time between the commencement of s 20 (autumn 2003) and the appointed day itself (28 November 2004)[1]. But in practice an application could not be made immediately on commencement as the superior must first seek agreement under s 19 (which itself commences only on the same day as s 20). Following the application, the Tribunal must give notice to the vassal and may give notice to others[2].

1 Abolition of Feudal Tenure etc (Scotland) Act 2000, s 20(1).
2 AFT(S)A 2000, s 21(1). As ever in Part 4 of the 2000 Act the word 'vassal' is not used but rather 'any person who has right to the feu'. In the case of an executry, or if the property is being sold, more than one person might qualify. The method of advertisement is to be prescribed by Scottish Ministers, but this had not been done at the time of writing.

Stage (3): blocking notice

3.28 Once an application has been made, the superior has 42 days in which to draft, serve, execute and register a blocking notice[1]. Its effect is to disapply s 17(1) of the 2000 Act, thus ensuring that burdens which are the subject of a Tribunal applica-tion are not swept away on the appointed day[2]. Such a blocking device is unnecessary for those applications which are dealt with before the appointed day, but the require-ment of a notice is a universal one.

The 42-day period can be extended by the Lands Tribunal on cause shown[3], and indeed it is not clear what purpose is served by any time limit, beyond a general requirement that registration occur before the appointed day (ie before the extinctive event which is to be blocked)[4]. As it is, s 20, as amended by the Title Conditions (Scotland) Act 2003, now seems to allow for the possibility of registration *after* the appointed day[5]. This would occur if, for example, the Tribunal application were made 7 days before the appointed day and the notice registered 41 days later. The legal result is then not entirely certain. In the absence of a registered notice the supe-rior's rights would be extinguished on the appointed day only, presumably, to revive on registration of the notice. And it is possible to argue that the revival would then be retrospective, drawing back to the appointed day.

[1]   Abolition of Feudal Tenure etc (Scotland) Act 2000, s 20(3)(a).
[2]   AFT(S)A 2000, s 20(3).
[3]   AFT(S)A 2000, s 20(3)(b).
[4]   This would then be the same as the rule for other notices.
[5]   As originally enacted, s 20(1) required that the initial application be made within a period to be prescribed (and which was intended to finish some time before the appointed day).

Blocking notice: preparation and registration

3.29   The blocking notice is modelled closely on a s 18 notice. The statutory form, in Schedule 7 to the 2000 Act, provides for:

- the name and address of the superior;
- a conveyancing description both of the feu[1] and of the nominated land;
- a list of the real burden or burdens, either in full text or by reference to the deed by which they were imposed;
- details of that deed, including the date and place of registration;
- a list of any obligations on the superior which are the counterpart of the real bur-den or burdens[2];
- an account of the title to the superiority by reference to the Registers including, in a case where the superior is uninfeft, a list of the midcouples;
- an account of the superior's title to the nominated land, in the same form;
- a description, as given in the Lands Tribunal application, of the attempt to reach agreement under s 19; and
- details of service on the vassal.

A style of completed notice is set out in Appendix 3 to this book.

The notice is served, before execution[3], by sending a copy by post together with the explanatory note provided in Schedule 7. Service is more fully discussed in chapter

11[4]. The notice is then completed by entering the details of service[5], and by signature before a notary public, the superior having sworn or affirmed that to the best of his knowledge or belief all the information contained in the notice is true[6]. The notary must also sign[7]. Swearing or affirming a statement that is known to be false or is believed not to be true is an offence under the False Oaths (Scotland) Act 1933. Normally the oath must be given by the superior personally and not, for example, through a solicitor; but a company or other juristic person is represented by a person authorised to sign documents on its behalf[8], and a person without legal capacity by an appropriate person[9]. An oath outside Scotland may be given before any person duly authorised by the country in question to administer oaths or receive affirmations[10]. If the superiority is held as common or joint property, each superior must separately swear or affirm, and sign the notice[11].

The final step is to register the notice, in the Land Register or Register of Sasines, against both the feu (the burdened property) and also the nominated land (the benefited property)[12]. No warrant of registration is needed in respect of registration in the Register of Sasines[13]. If one of the properties is already in the Land Register but the other still in the Register of Sasines, registration will be needed in both Registers. The fee is £25 for registration in one register and £50 for registration in both[14]. Neither stamp duty nor its successor, stamp duty land tax, is payable[15].

[1]   Or, at the superior's option, part only of the feu. See the Abolition of Feudal Tenure etc (Scotland) Act 2000, s 20(4)(b). In that case only the part described will be subject to the burden after the appointed day.

[2]   For superiors' obligations, see paras 1.24, 1.25.

[3]   AFT(S)A 2000, s 41(3).

[4]   Paras 11.7, 11.8.

[5]   AFT(S)A 2000, s 41(4).

[6]   AFT(S)A 2000, s 20(15).

[7]   AFT(S)A 2000, Sch 7, note 7.

[8]   See generally the Requirements of Writing (Scotland) Act 1995, Sch 2.

[9]   AFT(S)A 2000, s 20(16).

[10] AFT(S)A 2000, s 49 (definition of 'notary public').

[11] This is because the obligations in s 20(15) are placed on 'the superior', and the singular includes the plural. For the special position of trustees, see para 3.14.

[12] AFT(S)A 2000, s 20(3), (5).

[13] AFT(S)A 2000, s 41(2).

[14] Fees in the Registers of Scotland Order 1995, SI 1995/1945, Schedule, Pt III, para 2.

[15] Paras 11.9–11.11.

Disposal by Lands Tribunal

3.30   The vassal has always a right to oppose an application made under s 20 of the 2000 Act[1]. So too has anyone else – a tenant for example[2] – who is affected by the burden or by its proposed reallotment[3]. A person who opposes an application may have to meet his own costs, at least if unsuccessful, but is not liable for those of the applicant unless the person's actings were vexatious or frivolous[4].

In considering an application the Tribunal must decide whether, if the burden were to be extinguished and not preserved, there would be material detriment to the value or enjoyment of the superior's ownership of the nominated land. If so, the application may (but not must) be granted[5]. The test is a deliberate echo of the rule for interest to enforce in the Title Conditions Act[6]: for superiors with an interest to enforce should, in principle, be able to preserve the burden. How the test will be interpreted remains to be seen, and little or no guidance can be found in existing case law on interest[7]. Further, whereas interest to enforce in the narrow sense is of relevance only in the context of a particular breach[8], the Tribunal must consider in more general terms whether, on a range of possible breaches, interest is or is not likely to arise. To put the matter another way, the Tribunal is concerned, not with the effect of a specific breach, but with the effect of extinction of the burden and hence extinction of the possibility of preventing all future, and unknowable, breaches.

At the time of the application, enforcement rights attach to the superiority and not to the nominated land. Nonetheless the test presupposes that the burden must *already* contribute to the value and enjoyment of the superior's ownership of that land, and that extinction would lead to significant loss ('material detriment'). Sometimes that loss might be measurable by a decline in value, on the basis that the property is worth more with the burden than without it. But more usually the applicant will found on the other part of the test, that the enjoyment of the property would be materially affected by extinction. This, needless to say, is a matter on which views will differ, although the test seems to be objective in character and would not be satisfied merely by the idiosyncratic preferences of the current applicant.

If the application is granted the Tribunal must itself, and 'forthwith', extract the order and register it against both properties. The cost of registration is met by the applicant[9]. Unusually, there is no appeal against the Tribunal's decision[10].

The Tribunal's order may modify the burden (or a counter-obligation to the burden)[11], and sometimes this may be the only basis on which the application will be granted. It would presumably be open to the parties, or either of them, to propose an appropriate modification, typically to the effect of weakening the burden. The Tribunal, however, is able to act of its own accord and without the consent of either party[12].

---

[1]   Whether or not the application has been intimated to him or her (as it ought to have been): see the Abolition of Feudal Tenure etc (Scotland) Act 2000, s 21(2).

[2]   Arguably tenants of the benefited property are affected by at least some categories of real burden. See K G C Reid *The Law of Property in Scotland* (1996) para 413. For the future, the position is made clear by the Title Conditions (Scotland) Act 2003, s 9.

[3]   AFT(S)A 2000, s 21(2). It is not clear that a person could be affected by the reallotment without also being affected by the burden itself. Oddly, s 21(2) goes on to confer a discretion on the Tribunal to hear any person who 'appears to it' to be affected by the burden or its reallotment, implying that there is a distinction between (i) a person who *is* so affected (and therefore can be heard as of right) and (ii) a person who is *not* so affected but nonetheless is considered by the Tribunal, wrongly, to be so affected (and therefore can be heard in the exercise of the Tribunal's discretion).

4   AFT(S)A 2000, s 20(13).

5   AFT(S)A 2000, s 20(7).

6   TC(S)A 2003, s 8(3)(a). This test was introduced to the Abolition of Feudal Tenure etc (Scotland) Act 2000 only by amendment by the TC(S)A 2003, s 114(6), Sch 13, para 4(b). The original version of s 20(7) of the 2000 Act required 'substantial loss or disadvantage to the applicant as owner (taking him to be such) of the dominant tenement', a test which in turn copies one of the grounds for which compensation can be awarded by the Lands Tribunal following variation or discharge: see the Conveyancing and Feudal Reform (Scotland) Act 1970, s 2(4)(i). In fact, the two tests are broadly similar in character and effect.

7   Scottish Law Commission *Report on Real Burdens* para 4.17.

8   Scottish Law Commission *Report on Real Burdens* para 4.16. Section 8(3)(a) of the Title Conditions (Scotland) Act 2003 begins with the words 'in the circumstances of any case'.

9   AFT(S)A 2000, s 20(11).

10   Tribunal and Inquiries Act 1992, s 11(1), (2)(b), as inserted by AFT(S)A 2000, s 22; AFT(S)A 2000, s 20(10).

11   AFT(S)A 2000, s 20(9).

12   Compare Conveyancing and Feudal Reform (Scotland) Act 1970, s 2(5), which requires the consent of the burdened owner.

Position on the appointed day

3.31   The position on the appointed day depends on how far the procedure has progressed. There are three possibilities. Either (i) the application has been granted or (ii) it has been refused or (iii) the application is still pending. These possibilities are now considered in turn.

Application granted

3.32   If, by the appointed day, the application has been granted, and the extract order duly registered by the Lands Tribunal, the position is much the same as under a s 18 notice. So long as the burden remained enforceable by the superior (or a successor of the superior) up to the appointed day, it is converted on that day into a neighbour burden in which the burdened property is the feu and the benefited property the land nominated in the Tribunal application[1]. As usual, the right to enforce is subject to any counter-obligation previously enforceable against the superior[2].

1   Abolition of Feudal Tenure etc (Scotland) Act 2000, s 20(8)(a)(i).

2   AFT(S)A 2000, s 25.

Application refused

3.33   If, conversely, the application has been refused, the intention was presumably that the burden should then be extinguished on the appointed day; and indeed that was the effect of s 20 of the 2000 Act as originally enacted[1]. However, in its amended form, s 20 treats an application refused in the same way as an application still pending[2]. This means that the burden survives the appointed day until such time as the 'transitional period' (described in the next paragraph) is brought to an end by statutory instrument[3]. Assuming this to be an error in the legislation, it is possible that it will be corrected under the amending power reserved in the 2003 Act[4].

1   Abolition of Feudal Tenure etc (Scotland) Act 2000, s 20(5), (7)(b), (11).
2   It was amended by the Title Conditions (Scotland) Act 2003, s 128, Sch 15.
3   AFT(S)A 2000, s 20(5), (6).
4   TC(S)A 2003, s 128(4), (5) (a so-called 'Henry VIII clause'). The text of the final paragraph of the explanatory note in the AFT(S)A 2000, Sch 7, suggests that this is indeed an error.

Application still pending

3.34   If, finally, the application to the Lands Tribunal is still pending, the burden survives the appointed day, owing to the blocking notice, and for a transitional period is converted into a neighbour burden[1]. In other words, the position is initially as if the application had already been granted by the Tribunal. The transitional period begins on the appointed day and ends on either (i) the day on which a Tribunal order granting the application is registered or (ii) such other day as is specified by order by Scottish Ministers[2]. The latter will put a final date on the life of a blocking notice. Once it is reached, the transitional period ends, and with it the converted neighbour burden[3]. If, however, a Tribunal order granting the application is registered first, the temporary conversion to a neighbour burden is made permanent[4].

Where a burden is extinguished, the usual provisions govern enforcement in respect of a past breach[5].

1   Abolition of Feudal Tenure etc (Scotland) Act 2000, s 20(5).
2   AFT(S)A 2000, s 20(6).
3   This may probably be taken by implication from the fact that the transitional period – and hence the effect of s 20(5) – has ended. But the legislation is not as clear as might have been wished.
4   AFT(S)A 2000, s 20(8)(a)(ii).
5   AFT(S)A 2000, s 17(2), (3), as applied by s 20(12). See further para 2.13.

Chapter 4

Preservation as personal real burdens

INTRODUCTION

The procedure in outline

4.1 Mention was made earlier of the new juridical category of personal real burden[1]. Eight such burdens are recognised: conservation burdens, economic development burdens, health care burdens, personal pre-emption burdens, rural housing burdens, personal redemption burdens, manager burdens, and maritime burdens[2]. Once Part 3 of the Title Conditions (Scotland) Act 2003 is in force – expected to be in the autumn of 2003[3] – it will be possible to create such burdens of new in the limited circumstances in which they are allowed[4]. In addition, a feudal real burden which mimics a personal real burden may be preserved as a personal burden of the appropriate type[5]. Thus conversion into personal real burdens provides a further means of preserving feudal real burdens. That is the subject of the present chapter.

The conversion procedure must both be commenced and completed during the period beginning in the autumn of 2003 and ending on 27 November 2004[6]. Normally this involves the superior serving and registering a preservation notice in statutory form. In the case of two personal real burdens, however (maritime burdens and manager burdens), conversion occurs automatically on the appointed day without the need for action on the part of the superior.

A burden which has already been the subject of a preservation notice or agreement for conversion into a neighbour burden[7] cannot be the subject of a second notice for conversion into a personal real burden unless the earlier notice or agreement is discharged[8]. This, and further aspects of preservation notices, are considered more fully in chapter 11.

[1]   Para 2.9.
[2]   Title Conditions (Scotland) Act 2003, s 1(3).
[3]   TC(S)A 2003, s 129(4).
[4]   However, personal pre-emption burdens and personal redemption burdens cannot be created of new but will exist only as converted feudal burdens.
[5]   Abolition of Feudal Tenure etc (Scotland) Act 2000, Pt 4.

⁶   Normally registration must take place 'before the appointed day'. For the exceptional case where registration is wrongly refused, see s 45 of the AFT(S)A 2000, discussed at para 11.16. At the time of writing no order had yet been made bringing the relevant provisions into force.
⁷   For which see ch 3.
⁸   AFT(S)A 2000, s 42(1).

Effect of conversion

4.2   Assuming the relevant procedure to have been properly complied with, a feudal real burden escapes extinction by being converted, on the appointed day, into a personal real burden of the appropriate type. Thus a feudal burden concerned with conservation may be converted into a conservation burden; and a burden which promotes economic development and in which the superior is a local authority or Scottish Ministers may be converted into an economic development burden. The trappings of feudalism fall away, but otherwise little is changed. As before, the burden is personally enforceable by its holder – the, now former, feudal superior (or, in some cases, by a nominee of that superior); and, as before, interest to enforce is presumed[1]. Most, but not all, personal real burdens are transferable, although now by assignation rather than, as formerly, by disposition (ie of the superiority)[2]. Like praedial real burdens, personal real burdens are governed by the new code set out in the Title Conditions Act[3].

¹   Title Conditions (Scotland) Act 2003, s 47. By contrast, there is no presumption of interest in respect of converted neighbour burdens: see the Abolition of Feudal Tenure etc (Scotland) Act 2000, s 24.
²   The following personal real burdens are transferable: personal pre-emption burdens, personal redemption burdens (AFT(S)A 2000, s 18A(7)), conservation burdens (TC(S)A 2003, s 39), rural housing burdens (TC(S)A 2003, s 43(10)), and manager burdens (TC(S)A 2003, s 63(3)). Transfer is by assignation, for which see TC(S)A 2003, ss 39 and 41. Where the class of holder is limited (as with eg conservation burdens), assignation must be to another person of the same class. The other personal real burdens may not be assigned: see TC(S)A 2003, ss 44(2), 45(4)(b), 46(4)(b).
³   Summarised at paras 7.15 ff.

Evaluation

4.3   Some of the drawbacks which affect conversion into neighbour burdens affect, equally, conversion into personal real burdens[1]. Thus before the procedure can be activated it will be necessary to check through chartularies or other collections of titles to identify qualifying feus and burdens. Deciding whether a burden qualifies as, say, a conservation burden may often be a skilled task, and sometimes a controversial one. A separate notice is needed for each feu[2], and must be served on the vassal and registered. The cost of registration is £25[3], to which must be added the cost of employing a solicitor or other person to conduct the initial research and prepare the notices. In some, perhaps many, cases the effort may not seem worthwhile. Burdens exceeding, or even approaching, 100 years in age are vulnerable to unilateral extinction under the sunset rule[4]. A personal pre-emption burden entitles its holder to one offer only[5], while a personal redemption burden created after 1 September 1974 has a total lifespan of 20 years counting from its first appearance as a feudal burden[6].

Nonetheless, the position is in some respects more favourable than in conversion to neighbour burdens. As there is no benefited property, a notice need be registered only once and not twice. Once conversion is complete, interest to enforce is presumed, thus avoiding the need to surmount what may sometimes be a significant hurdle[7]; and indeed it is difficult to think of circumstances in which the presumption will be overcome. Above all, the legislation on personal real burdens is narrower, and more carefully targeted. It would not be surprising if, relatively speaking, it turns out to be the more widely used.

[1]   Para 3.3.
[2]   Abolition of Feudal Tenure etc (Scotland) Act 2000, s 42(2), (3).
[3]   Fees in the Registers of Scotland Order 1995, SI 1995/1945, Schedule, Pt III, para 2.
[4]   Title Conditions (Scotland) Act 2003, ss 20–24, discussed in para 7.22.
[5]   TC(S)A 2003, ss 82, 84. This repeats in different language the rule previously contained in the Conveyancing (Scotland) Act 1938, s 9.
[6]   Land Tenure Reform (Scotland) Act 1974, s 12.
[7]   TC(S)A 2003, s 47. For praedial real burdens, the rule is set out in s 8(1), (3).

PRESERVATION AS CONSERVATION BURDENS

Qualifying burdens

4.4   Conservation burdens were introduced, by the Title Conditions Act[1], to assist the work of conservation trusts and other similar bodies. The fact that no benefited property is needed allows, for example, a conservation body to restore a building and sell it and yet still impose burdens which would preserve its historical features. In developing the idea of conservation burdens the Scottish Law Commission was influenced by the Uniform Conservation Easement Act of 1981 which has been adopted by a number of jurisdictions in the United States[2].

An existing feudal burden may be converted into a conservation burden if both (i) it qualifies as to content and (ii) the preservation of such a burden is in the public interest[3]. These criteria are discussed below.

[1]   Title Conditions (Scotland) Act 2003, ss 38–42.
[2]   Scottish Law Commission *Discussion Paper on Real Burdens* (Scot Law Com DP no 106) paras 2.56–2.59.
[3]   Abolition of Feudal Tenure etc (Scotland) Act 2000, ss 27, 27A.

The first criterion: content

4.5   A feudal burden qualifies as to content if, in respect of the land on which it is imposed, it has the purpose of preserving or protecting

  (i)   the architectural or historical characteristics of that land; or
  (ii)   any other special characteristic of the land (including, without prejudice to the generality of this paragraph, a special characteristic derived from the flora, fauna or general appearance of the land)[1].

'Land' includes buildings and other like structures[2], and the provision is aimed at both the built and the natural environment.

Whether, in any particular case, the definition is satisfied depends largely on the nature of the land or building. Thus the mere fact that the obligation is one not to build, or not to alter, does not of itself make the burden eligible for conversion. For obligations of this kind are commonplace in, for example, volume housing estates or rural feus. Rather, the building or land must itself have some special feature which justifies conservation. In the case of a building there must be particular architectural or historical merit. In the case of undeveloped land, there must be distinctive flora or fauna, or some other cogent reason why this land, above others, should be preserved in its present state.

1   Abolition of Feudal Tenure etc (Scotland) Act 2000, s 27(2). The definition for newly created conservation burdens is the same: see the Title Conditions (Scotland) Act 2003, s 38(1).
2   The Scotland Act 1998 (Transitory and Transitional Provisions) (Publication and Interpretation etc of Acts of the Scottish Parliament) Order 1999, SI 1999/2379, art 6(2), Sch 2.

The second criterion: public benefit

4.6   The survival of the feudal burden must also confer public benefit[1]. This has two aspects, at least. In the first place, the burden must, in context, be sufficiently important that palpable benefit will result from its preservation – and hence from the preservation of that at which the burden is directed. Trivial burdens, or those concerning undistinguished land or buildings, would fail this test. This reinforces a point which also arises from the first criterion (content) and was discussed above. Secondly, the benefit from survival must fall, wholly or mainly, on the public at large rather than on the particular superior. Conversion to a conservation burden cannot be used to safeguard future income from minutes of waiver; and the thing conserved must have some degree of public significance.

1   Abolition of Feudal Tenure etc (Scotland) Act 2000, ss 27(1), 27A(1). Contrast praedial real burdens, which must be for the benefit of the benefited property: Title Conditions (Scotland) Act 2003, s 3(3). According to the official *Explanatory Notes* para 121, 'The words "for the benefit of the public" are intended to ensure that the preservation of conservation burdens in the future must be in the public interest'. It may be noted that for *new* conservation burdens, it

is the burdens themselves, and not their preservation, which is to be for the benefit of the public: see TC(S)A 2003, s 38(1). This more direct means of expression could not be used in the AFT(S)A 2000 because the initial purpose of a feudal burden might have been unconnected with the public interest.

Title to preserve

4.7 Only the superior can take the steps necessary to preserve feudal burdens as conservation burdens. More precisely, a person has title to preserve such burdens if he (i) is the superior of the feu in respect of which the burdens are imposed and (ii) as such is able to enforce those burdens[1]. 'Superior' includes over-superior[2].

As respects (i) there is no requirement that the person be infeft provided that he 'has right' to the superiority and so would be able to complete title by notice of title or equivalent procedure in the Land Register[3]. If, as occasionally, there is more than one uninfeft superior, only the most recent such superior is eligible[4]. Or if there is both an infeft superior and a later uninfeft superior – as where the superiority has been disponed but the disponee has not registered the disposition – the uninfeft superior, as the more recent, is the person entitled to seek preservation. Where land has been subfeued more than once, there is likely to be more than one set of burdens and more than one 'superior'; and in that case, each superior has title to enforce only his 'own' burdens, and hence can use the preservation procedure only in respect of those burdens[5].

As respects (ii), a person who is superior will always have title to enforce the burdens but may not have interest. Traditionally, a superior was thought to have interest in all or most burdens on the feu, partly because the feu was security for the payment of feuduty and partly because of the contingent possibility that the feu might revert on irritancy. Now, however, that irritancy has been abolished and most feuduties redeemed[6], it is arguable that interest can be demonstrated only by ownership (*dominium utile*) of other land in the vicinity[7]. If that is correct, superiors will sometimes have no interest to enforce[8]. But this argument should not be pressed too hard. For interest to enforce is presumed unless the contrary can be shown[9], there are no reported cases in which the presumption has been successfully overturned[10], and superiors are unlikely to be deterred from preserving burdens by what they may see as theoretical concerns as to lack of interest.

1   Abolition of Feudal Tenure etc (Scotland) Act 2000, ss 27(1), 27A(1). The words 'would have that right were it or they to complete title to the *dominium directum*' are in acknowledgement of the rule that, as the law currently stands, only a person who is infeft can enforce a real burden. See K G C Reid *The Law of Property in Scotland* (1996) para 397.
2   AFT(S)A 2000, s 49.
3   AFT(S)A 2000, s 49. The expression 'has right' used in the definition of 'superior' picks up the usage in the Conveyancing (Scotland) Act 1924, ss 3, 4. A person who 'has right' can expede and register a notice of title under the 1924 Act, s 4 or, in Land Register cases, can procure direct registration under the Land Registration (Scotland) Act 1979, s 3(6).

⁴   AFT(S)A 2000, s 49. For an example, see para 3.4.
⁵   For an example, see para 3.4.
⁶   By virtue of, respectively, the AFT(S)A 2000, s 53 (in force since 9 June 2000) and the Land Tenure Reform (Scotland) Act 1974, ss 4–6.
⁷   K G C Reid *The Law of Property in Scotland* (1996) para 408; K G C Reid and G L Gretton *Conveyancing 2001* (2002) pp 99–100.
⁸   If, as often, there is a right of pre-emption, the superior retains a contingent right to return of the feu. But in such a case he must usually pay its value, and hence has no interest in seeing that value enhanced.
⁹   K G C Reid *The Law of Property in Scotland* (1996) para 408.
¹⁰   K G C Reid *The Law of Property in Scotland* (1996) para 430.

Conservation bodies and Scottish Ministers

4.8   Conservation burdens can be held only by Scottish Ministers or by conservation bodies[1]. By 'Scottish Ministers' is meant the (ministerial) members of the Scottish Executive acting collectively[2]. A 'conservation body' is one which is included in a list to be prescribed for that purpose by Scottish Ministers[3]. Bodies may be added to or removed from the list[4]. In the case of a trust, the conservation body is the trustees[5].

This rule has obvious implications for the process of conversion. If the superior is either a conservation body or Scottish Ministers there is of course no difficulty. But if the superior is not qualified to hold a conservation burden, it is necessary to nominate someone else who is. The 2000 Act lays down the procedure[6]. The superior must seek out, and obtain the consent of, an appropriate conservation body (or Scottish Ministers). Once consent is obtained, the superior formally nominates the body by naming it in the s 27A notice, which is signed by the body and then served and registered in the manner described below. On the appointed day the right to enforce the burden passes from the superior to the nominated body[7].

¹   Title Conditions (Scotland) Act 2003, s 38(1).
²   Scotland Act 1998, s 44(2). Property, including superiorities, may be held by Scottish Ministers by that name, and if so belongs to the Scottish Ministers for the time being: see SA 1998, s 59(1), (2).
³   Abolition of Feudal Tenure etc (Scotland) Act 2000, s 49. The power to prescribe conservation bodies is contained in the TC(S)A 2003, s 38(4). The list will be reproduced in K G C Reid and G L Gretton *Conveyancing 2003* (forthcoming, 2004).
⁴   TC(S)A 2003, s 38(4), (7).
⁵   TC(S)A 2003, s 38(6).
⁶   AFT(S)A 2000, s 27A, inserted by the TC(S)A 2003, s 114(3).
⁷   AFT(S)A 2000, s 28A, inserted by the TC(S)A 2003, s 114(4).

Preparation and registration of notice

4.9   In order for preservation to take place the superior must, before the appointed day, prepare, serve, execute, and register a notice in the required form[1]. If the superior is itself a conservation body or Scottish Ministers the form is as laid down in s 27 of and Schedule 8 to the Abolition of Feudal Tenure Act. Otherwise matters are regulated by s 27A and Schedule 8A. The only difference between a notice under s 27 and one under s 27A is that the latter must nominate a conservation body (or Scottish Ministers) and carry the additional signature of that body, and for present purposes the two may be treated together.

The statutory form, from which minor deviations are permitted[2], provides for:

- the name and address of the superior[3];
- in the case of a s 27A notice only, the name and address of the body nominated as the holder of the conservation burden;
- a statement that either the superior (s 27 notice) or the nominee (s 27A notice) is a conservation body or Scottish Ministers, giving details, in the former case, of the statutory instrument which lists the body;
- a conveyancing description of the feu[4];
- a list of the real burden or burdens, either in full text or by reference to the deed by which they were imposed;
- details of that deed, including the date and place of registration;
- a list of any obligations on the superior which are the counterpart of the real burden or burdens[5];
- an account of the title to the superiority by reference to the Registers including, in a case where the superior is uninfeft, a list of the midcouples;
- details of service on the vassal.

A style of completed notice is set out in Appendix 4 to this book.

The same notice can be used for more than one burden[6], but a separate notice is needed for each feu[7]. The superior signs after service but the nominee (in the case of a s 27A notice) before[8]. In each case a witness must also sign, and the normal rules of attestation should be complied with[9]. With some other notices under the 2000 Act, the superior must swear or affirm before a notary public and, except where otherwise permitted, sign in person[10]. But since no oath is needed for notices under ss 27 and 27A, there seems no reason of legal policy why the superior (or nominee) should sign personally. Under the general law a requirement that a person must sign is met by the signature of an agent acting on that person's behalf[11]. No doubt the path of caution would be for the superior (or nominee) to sign personally except where this is obviously impossible, as for example where the superior is a juristic person or under a legal disability[12]. But it is thought that a signature by a solicitor or other agent on behalf of the superior would be sufficient in all cases. If the superiority is held as common or joint property, each superior must separately sign or have someone sign on his behalf[13].

Service is effected by sending by post a copy of the notice and of the explanatory note provided in Schedule 8 or, as the case may be, in Schedule 8A to the 2000 Act. Service is more fully discussed in chapter 11[14]. After signature by the superior and a witness, the process is completed by registration in the Land Register or Register of Sasines. In the case of the former, the Keeper is directed to identify in the entry the holder of the burden[15]. No warrant of registration is needed in respect of registration in the Register of Sasines[16]. The fee for registration of notices is £25[17]. Neither stamp duty nor its successor, stamp duty land tax, is payable[18].

[1]   Abolition of Feudal Tenure etc (Scotland) Act 2000, ss 27, 27A.
[2]   AFT(S)A 2000, ss 27(1), 27A(1).
[3]   In the case of a s 27A notice, there is no express requirement that the address be given, although this will usually be necessary if the superior is to be identifiable.
[4]   Or, at the superior's option, part only of the feu. See AFT(S)A 2000, ss 27(3)(c), 27A(3)(b). In that case only the part described will be subject to the burden after the appointed day.
[5]   For superiors' obligations, see paras 1.24, 1.25.
[6]   AFT(S)A 2000, s 42(4)(a).
[7]   AFT(S)A 2000, s 42(3). Where the land originally feued has been divided and is in separate ownership, each separate part is treated as a separate feu for this purpose: see s 42(2).
[8]   AFT(S)A 2000, s 41(3) (superior), Sch 8A, note 8 (nominee). Scottish Ministers sign through any member of the Scottish Executive: see the Scotland Act 1998, s 59(4). It may be noted that whereas the rule for the superior is contained in a statutory provision, the rule for the nominee rests on a note which, like all such notes, is declared to 'have no legal effect'. Such differential treatment can also be found in some other places in the 2000 Act.
[9]   Requirements of Writing (Scotland) Act 1995, s 3. Under s 6 probativity is generally a requirement of registrability, at least in the Register of Sasines.
[10]   See eg AFT(S)A 2000, s 18(4), (5).
[11]   K G C Reid *Requirements of Writing (Scotland) Act 1995* (1995) p 30. It is true that at least two forms in the AFT(S)A 2000 (in Schs 5B and 5C) expressly state that the signature is to be 'on behalf of superior', but in both cases the superior is a juristic person and could not sign personally.
[12]   The two cases mentioned in AFT(S)A 2000, s 18(5) and similar places.
[13]   This is because the obligations in ss 27 and 27A are placed on 'the superior', and the singular includes the plural. For the position of trustees, see para 3.14.
[14]   Paras 11.7, 11.8.
[15]   Land Registration (Scotland) Act 1979, s 6(1)(e), amended by the Title Conditions (Scotland) Act 2003, s 112(2).
[16]   AFT(S)A 2000, s 41(2).
[17]   Fees in the Registers of Scotland Order 1995, SI 1995/1945, Schedule, Pt III, para 2.
[18]   Paras 11.9–11.11.

Effect of conversion

4.10   Assuming the notice to have been validly drawn up and registered, and the feudal real burden to be still enforceable[1], the result on the appointed day is for the feudal burden to be converted into a conservation burden.[2] Its holder is the (former) superior or, in the case of a notice under s 27A of the 2000 Act, the body nominated in the notice. Matters are largely unaffected by a change in the identity of superior between the date of registration and the appointed day. In the case of a s 27 notice, however, it is the new superior who takes the benefit of the conservation burden; and if that superior is neither a conservation body nor Scottish Ministers, the notice falls and the burden is lost on the appointed day[3].

The right to enforce is subject to any counter-obligation previously enforceable against the superior[4].

1   See, on this topic, para 3.15.
2   Abolition of Feudal Tenure etc (Scotland) Act 2000, ss 28(1), 28A.
3   AFT(S)A 2000, s 28(2).
4   And, it seems, whether listed in the agreement or not. See AFT(S)A 2000, ss 28(1)(a), 28A(a).

PRESERVATION AS ECONOMIC DEVELOPMENT BURDENS

Qualifying burdens

4.11   Economic development burdens, an innovation of the Title Conditions Act[1], are an approximate equivalent of the statutory facility which, for many years now, has allowed Scottish Enterprise and Highlands and Islands Enterprise to regulate or restrict the use of land by agreement[2]. The idea is that local authorities and Scottish Ministers (ie the Scottish Executive)[3] should be able to sell land outright and yet at the same time to impose as a personal real burden an obligation which has the general effect of promoting economic development. Alternatively an existing owner might choose to create such a burden in favour of a local authority or Scottish Ministers, for example as a condition of receiving a grant.

An existing feudal burden may be converted into an economic development burden if both (i) it qualifies as to content and (ii) the superior is either a local authority or Scottish Ministers[4]. These criteria are discussed below.

1   Title Conditions (Scotland) Act 2003, s 45.
2   The current provision is the Enterprise and New Towns (Scotland) Act 1990, s 32, now amended by the TC(S)A 2003, s 113. For an explanation of the amendments, see Scottish Law Commission *Report on Real Burdens* para 9.38. Section 32 agreements are not, however, real burdens, and so are not subject eg to the rules for variation and discharge set out in the 2003 Act.
3   Scotland Act 1998, s 44(2).
4   Abolition of Feudal Tenure etc (Scotland) Act 2000, s 18B, inserted by the TC(S)A 2003, s 114(2).

The first criterion: content

4.12   A feudal burden qualifies as to content if the burden was 'imposed for the purpose of promoting economic development'[1]. With affirmative burdens, such as an obligation to build a factory, the position may often be clear and straightforward. But a negative burden – one restricting the use to which the feu is put – is more likely to inhibit economic development than to promote it, and would usually fail to qualify[2]. Doubtless, however, there will be exceptions, particularly where the wider background is taken into account. For example, a restriction might be the counterpart of a reduced price, or of a public grant. In that case it is arguable that economic development is promoted. Further, there is no requirement – as there is with conservation burdens[3] – that the statutory formula should apply to the actual land that is being burdened. It is enough if economic development is promoted in the round[4]. And it is easy to imagine how a restriction on one feu might have the effect of promoting the economic development of another, especially if the owners of the first are prohibited from engaging in the very economic activity which is being carried out on the second.

By statutory concession, an economic development burden created of new under the Title Conditions Act may comprise an obligation to pay a sum of money, for example by way of clawback of planning gain[5]. It is doubtful whether the same could ever be true of an economic development burden by conversion, for as a matter of general law a real burden must confer praedial benefit, or in other words must benefit the superior as owner and not merely in a personal capacity[6]. This means that a feudal obligation which amounted to payment of a debt could not usually be a real burden[7], and so could not be converted into an economic development burden.

[1]   Abolition of Feudal Tenure etc (Scotland) Act 2000, s 18B(1).
[2]   See the Title Conditions (Scotland) Act 2003, s 2 for the terminology 'negative burden' and 'affirmative burden'.
[3]   See para 4.5.
[4]   Thus Mr Jim Wallace MSP, the Deputy First Minister: 'Local authorities will be able to create economic development burdens in circumstances in which they wish to sell land with a view to encouraging economic development *within their area*'. See Scottish Parliament *Official Report* Justice 1 Committee, 20 December 2002, col 4355.
[5]   TC(S)A 2003, s 45(3).
[6]   K G C Reid *The Law of Property in Scotland* (1996) para 391; Scottish Law Commission *Report on Real Burdens* paras 2.9–2.18. While the rule is carried forward into the new law (by the TC(S)A 2003, s 3(3)) it must be assumed that this requirement is overriden, in the case of new economic development burdens, by s 45(3).
[7]   Scottish Law Commission *Report on Abolition of the Feudal System* para 5.23.

The second criterion: type of superior

4.13   Since economic development burdens may only be held by local authorities or by Scottish Ministers, it is a condition of conversion to such a burden that the superior is likewise a local authority or Scottish Ministers[1]. By contrast with the position for conservation burdens[2], there is no facility for a non-qualifying superior to nominate a body that would qualify in its place. It is not, however, required that the qualifying body granted the original feu or was otherwise responsible for the creation of the burdens

Some further rules, familiar from other notices under the 2000 Act, also apply[3]. Thus the burden must be 'enforceable' by the superior, signifying the need for interest as well as title[4]. But the superior need not be infeft, a rule of considerable help both to local authorities and to Scottish Ministers; and if there are two uninfeft superiors, or one infeft and one uninfeft, the qualifying superior is the last in time[5]. 'Superior' includes over-superior[6].

[1] Abolition of Feudal Tenure etc (Scotland) Act 2000, s 18B(1). A 'local authority' is a council constituted under the Local Government etc (Scotland) Act 1994, s 2: see AFT(S)A 2000, s 49. By 'Scottish Ministers' is meant the members of the Scottish Executive acting collectively: see the Scotland Act 1998, s 44(2).
[2] See para 4.8.
[3] A fuller treatment is given in para 4.7.
[4] AFT(S)A 2000, s 18B(1).
[5] AFT(S)A 2000, s 49. For an example, see para 3.4
[6] AFT(S)A 2000, s 49.

Preparation and registration of notice

4.14 A feudal burden is preserved as an economic development burden by the preparation, service, execution and registration by the superior, before the appointed day, of a notice in the form laid down in s 18B(2) of and Schedule 5B to the Abolition of Feudal Tenure Act. This provides for:

- the name and address of the local authority or, as the case may be, the name 'Scottish Ministers';
- a conveyancing description of the feu[1];
- a list of the real burden or burdens, either in full text or by reference to the deed by which they were imposed;
- details of that deed, including the date and place of registration;
- a statement that the burden was imposed for the purpose of promoting economic development and a justification of the statement;
- a list of any obligations on the superior which are the counterpart of the real burden or burdens[2];
- an account of the title to the superiority by reference to the Registers including, in a case where the superior is uninfeft, a list of the midcouples;
- details of service on the vassal.

A style of completed notice is set out in Appendix 4 to this book. Minor deviations are permitted[3].

The same notice can be used for more than one burden[4], but a separate notice is needed for each feu[5]. Once completed, the notice is served, by post, together with a copy of the explanatory note provided in Schedule 5B to the 2000 Act. Service is more fully discussed in chapter 11[6]. The local authority or Scottish Ministers then sign, without a requirement of witnesses or a notary public. Under the general law a local authority signs through its proper officer, and it seems desirable to make the notice probative by sealing or by the signature of a witness, if only to avoid possible difficulties on registration[7]. Scottish Ministers sign through a member of the Scottish Executive[8].

After signature the process is completed by registration in the Land Register or Register of Sasines. In the case of the former, the Keeper is directed to identify in the entry the holder of the burden[9]. No warrant of registration is needed in respect of registration in the Register of Sasines[10]. The fee for registration of notices is £25[11]. Neither stamp duty nor its successor, stamp duty land tax, is payable[12].

[1]   Or, at the superior's option, part only of the feu. See the Abolition of Feudal Tenure etc (Scotland) Act 2000, s 18B(2)(b). In that case only the part described will be subject to the burden after the appointed day.

[2]   For superiors' obligations, see paras 1.24, 1.25.

[3]   AFT(S)A 2000, s 18B(1).

[4]   AFT(S)A 2000, s 42(4)(a).

[5]   AFT(S)A 2000, s 42(3). Where the land originally feued has been divided and is in separate ownership, each part is treated as a separate feu for this purpose: see s 42(2).

[6]   Paras 11.7, 11.8.

[7]   Requirements of Writing (Scotland) Act 1995, Sch 2, para 4. An improbative deed cannot be registered in the Register of Sasines except by express statutory rule: see 1995 Act, s 6.

[8]   Scotland Act 1998, s 59(4). The Scottish Executive comprises the First Minister, such other Ministers as the First Minister may appoint, the Lord Advocate, and the Solicitor General for Scotland. Collectively they are known as the 'Scottish Ministers': see the Scotland Act 1998, s 44(1), (2).

[9]   Land Registration (Scotland) Act 1979, s 6(1)(e), amended by the Title Conditions (Scotland) Act 2003, s 112(2).

[10]   AFT(S)A 2000, s 41(2).

[11]   Fees in the Registers of Scotland Order 1995, SI 1995/1945, Schedule, Pt III, para 2.

[12]   Paras 11.9–11.11.

Effect of conversion

4.15   If, having registered a notice, the local authority or Scottish Ministers then dispose of the superiority, the notice falls[1]. The same is true if the burden itself ceases to be enforceable, whether on account of a minute of waiver or for some other reason[2]. Otherwise the result of registration is that on the appointed day the feudal burden becomes an economic development burden, enforceable, as before, by the local authority or by Scottish Ministers[3]. The right to enforce is subject to any counter-obligation which was previously enforceable[4].

[1]   The reference to successors found in other provisions is absent from s 18B(3) of the Abolition of Feudal Tenure etc (Scotland) Act 2000.

[2]   AFT(S)A 2000, s 18B(3).

[3]   AFT(S)A 2000, s 18B(3).

[4]   AFT(S)A 2000, s 18B(4). By contrast with some other conversion processes, however, it seems that the holder is affected only by those counter-obligations actually listed in the notice.

PRESERVATION AS HEALTH CARE BURDENS

Qualifying burdens

4.16   The purpose of health care burdens, another innovation of the Title Conditions Act[1], is to allow National Health Service trusts or Scottish Ministers (in their role as property holders for health boards) both to sell land and yet at the same time to restrict its future use to health care purposes[2]. A standard example would be the sale of land for the construction of a hospital or accommodation for medical staff. A health care burden would both formalise the obligation on the acquirer and also ensure that it ran with the land.

An existing feudal real burden may be converted into a health care burden if both (i) it qualifies as to content and (ii) the superior is either an NHS trust or Scottish Ministers[3]. These criteria are discussed below.

[1] Title Conditions (Scotland) Act 2003, s 46.
[2] Thus Mr Jim Wallace, the Deputy First Minister (Scottish Parliament *Official Report* 26 February 2003 col 18694): 'National health service trusts will be able to create health care burdens in circumstances where they wish to sell land while ensuring that that land continues to be used for the purposes of health care.'
[3] Abolition of Feudal Tenure etc (Scotland) Act 2000, s 18C, inserted by the TC(S)A 2003, s 114(2).

The first criterion: content

4.17 A feudal burden qualifies as to content if it was 'imposed for the purpose of promoting the provision of facilities for health care'[1], including facilities ancillary to such care, as for example accommodation for medical staff[2]. A straightforward example is where land was feued subject to an obligation to build a particular medical facility, or under a restriction limiting future use to medical purposes. A less obvious case is where, by restricting some use of the feu, the burden promotes the use for medical purposes, not of the feu itself[3], but of adjoining land retained by the superior. It is possible to go further and argue that *any* burden imposed by an NHS trust (or predecessor body) which had the potential to generate income, typically in respect of minutes of waiver, must qualify for conversion, on the basis that the income would itself then be used for the promotion of health care facilities. But this allows too great a separation between burden and ultimate purpose, and such burdens seem unlikely to fall within the statutory rule.

By statutory concession, a health care burden created of new under the Title Conditions Act may comprise an obligation to pay a sum of money, for example by way of clawback of planning gain[4]. It is doubtful whether the same could ever be true of a health care burden by conversion, for as a matter of general law a real burden must confer praedial benefit, or in other words must benefit the superior as owner and not merely in a personal capacity[5]. This means that a feudal obligation which amounted to payment of a debt could not usually be a real burden[6], and so could not be converted into a health care burden.

[1] Abolition of Feudal Tenure etc (Scotland) Act 2000, s 18C(1).
[2] AFT(S)A 2000, s 18C(5).
[3] For, by contrast with conservation burdens (for which see para 4.5), there is no requirement that it is the feu that should be affected by the statutory purpose.

4   Title Conditions (Scotland) Act 2003, s 46(3).
5   K G C Reid *The Law of Property in Scotland* (1996) para 391; Scottish Law Commission *Report on Real Burdens* paras 2.9–2.18. While the rule is carried forward into the new law (by the TC(S)A 2003, s 3(3)) it must be assumed that this requirement is overriden, in the case of new health care burdens, by s 46(3).
6   Scottish Law Commission *Report on Abolition of the Feudal System* para 5.23.

The second criterion: type of superior

4.18   Since health care burdens may only be held by NHS trusts or by Scottish Ministers, it is a condition of conversion to such a burden that the superior is likewise an NHS trust or Scottish Ministers[1]. By contrast with the position for conservation burdens[2], there is no facility for a non-qualifying superior to nominate a body that would qualify in its place. It is not, however, required that the qualifying body granted the original feu or was otherwise responsible for the creation of the burdens.

Some further rules, familiar from other notices under the 2000 Act, also apply[3]. Thus the burden must be 'enforceable' by the superior, signifying the need for interest as well as title[4]. But the superior need not be infeft, a rule of considerable help both to NHS trusts and to Scottish Ministers; and if there are two uninfeft superiors, or one infeft and one uninfeft, the qualifying superior is the last in time[5]. 'Superior' includes over-superior[6].

1   Abolition of Feudal Tenure etc (Scotland) Act 2000, s 18C(1). For NHS trusts, see the National Health Service (Scotland) Act 1978, s 12A, inserted by the National Health Service and Community Care Act 1990, s 31. By 'Scottish Ministers' is meant the members of the Scottish Executive acting collectively: see the Scotland Act 1998, s 44(2).
2   See para 4.8.
3   A fuller treatment is given in para 4.7.
4   AFT(S)A 2000, s 18C(1).
5   AFT(S)A 2000, s 49. For an example, see para 3.4
6   AFT(S)A 2000, s 49.

Preparation and registration of notice

4.19   A feudal burden is preserved as a health care burden by the preparation, service, execution and registration by the superior, before the appointed day, of a notice in the form laid down in s 18C(2) of and Schedule 5C to the Abolition of Feudal Tenure Act. This provides for:

* the name and address of the NHS trust or, as the case may be, the name 'Scottish Ministers';
* a conveyancing description of the feu[1];
* a list of the real burden or burdens, either in full text or by reference to the deed by which they were imposed;

- details of that deed, including the date and place of registration;
- a statement that the burden was imposed to promote the provision of facilities for health care and a justification of the statement;
- a list of any obligations on the superior which are the counterpart of the real burden or burdens[2];
- an account of the title to the superiority by reference to the Registers including, in a case where the superior is uninfeft, a list of the midcouples;
- details of service on the vassal.

A style of completed notice is set out in Appendix 4 to this book. Minor deviations are permitted[3].

The same notice can be used for more than one burden[4], but a separate notice is needed for each feu[5]. Once completed, the notice is served, by post, together with a copy of the explanatory note provided in Schedule 5C to the 2000 Act. Service is more fully discussed in chapter 11[6]. The NHS trust or Scottish Ministers then sign, without a requirement of witnesses or a notary public. Under the general law, an NHS trust signs through a director or some other person suitably authorised[7], while Scottish Ministers sign through a member of the Scottish Executive[8].

After signature the process is completed by registration in the Land Register or Register of Sasines. In the case of the former, the Keeper is directed to identify in the entry the holder of the burden[9]. No warrant of registration is needed in respect of registration in the Register of Sasines[10]. The fee for registration of notices is £25[11]. Neither stamp duty nor its successor, stamp duty land tax, is payable[12].

---

[1] Or, at the superior's option, part only of the feu. See the Abolition of Feudal Tenure etc (Scotland) Act 2000, s 18C(2)(b). In that case only the part described will be subject to the burden after the appointed day.

[2] For superiors' obligations, see paras 1.24, 1.25.

[3] AFT(S)A 2000, s 18C(1).

[4] AFT(S)A 2000, s 42(4)(a).

[5] AFT(S)A 2000, s 42(3). Where the land originally feued has been divided and is in separate ownership, each part is treated as a separate feu for this purpose: see s 42(2).

[6] Paras 11.7, 11.8.

[7] National Health Service Trusts (Membership and Procedure) (Scotland) Regulations 1991, SI 1991/535, reg 15(1). It is thought that the AFT(S)A 2000, Sch 5C is not an 'enactment ... relating to the authentication of documents under the law of Scotland' so that the more onerous rules in reg 15(2) do not apply.

[8] Scotland Act 1998, s 59(4). The Scottish Executive comprises the First Minister, such other Ministers as the First Minister may appoint, the Lord Advocate, and the Solicitor General for Scotland. Collectively they are known as 'Scottish Ministers': see SA 1998, s 44(1), (2).

[9] Land Registration (Scotland) Act 1979, s 6(1)(e), amended by the Title Conditions (Scotland) Act 2003, s 112(2).

[10] AFT(S)A 2000, s 41(2).

[11] Fees in the Registers of Scotland Order 1995, SI 1995/1945, Schedule, Pt III, para 2.

[12] Paras 11.9–11.11.

Effect of conversion

4.20   If, having registered a notice, the NHS trust or Scottish Ministers then dispose of the superiority, the notice falls[1]. The same is true if the burden itself ceases to be enforceable, whether on account of a minute of waiver or for some other reason[2]. Otherwise the result of registration is that on the appointed day the feudal burden becomes a health care burden, enforceable, as before, by the NHS trust or by Scottish Ministers[3]. The right to enforce is subject to any counter-obligation which was previously enforceable[4].

[1]   The reference to successors found in other provisions is absent from s 18C(3) of the Abolition of Feudal Tenure etc (Scotland) Act 2000.
[2]   AFT(S)A 2000, s 18C(3).
[3]   AFT(S)A 2000, s 18C(3).
[4]   AFT(S)A 2000, s 18C(4). By contrast with some other conversion processes, it seems that the holder is affected only by those counter-obligations actually listed in the notice.

PRESERVATION AS PERSONAL PRE-EMPTION BURDENS

Neighbour burdens or personal real burdens?

4.21   If other land is owned in the vicinity of the feu, a superior can save a right of pre-emption as an ordinary neighbour burden, by registration of a notice under s 18 of the Abolition of Feudal Tenure Act. Unusually, there is no need to comply with the 100-metres rule[1]. But whether suitable land is owned or not[2], s 18A of the 2000 Act gives the alternative of preservation as a type of personal real burden, known as a personal pre-emption burden[3]; and as the procedure is simpler and the result more flexible, it seems likely that this course will be preferred by most superiors. An obvious advantage is to allow the superior to dispose of the neighbouring land, whether now or after the appointed day, while at the same time retaining the benefit of the right of pre-emption.

Rights of pre-emption are common in grants in feu, but are brought to an end on the first occasion that the property is offered back to the superior, even if met by a refusal. For this reason many – perhaps most – pre-emptions found in titles today are already extinguished[4]. They are not revived by registration of a notice. Indeed such a notice would be incompetent, for the pre-emption requires to be 'enforceable' by the superior[5]. Unfortunately, the extinction of a pre-emption is not usually traceable from the Registers, and the pre-emption is likely to remain as an apparent burden on the property. Even if the pre-emption has genuinely survived, however, the superior will be conscious of the fact that it will be extinguished on the first offer (which might occur before the appointed day)[6] and, unless seriously interested in reacquiring the feu, may well conclude that the trouble and expense of preservation cannot be justified.

1   Abolition of Feudal Tenure etc (Scotland) Act 2000, s 18(7)(b)(ii), discussed at para 3.10.
2   If there is no land at all, it is arguable that the pre-emption is unenforceable through lack of
     interest. See para 4.7.
3   AFT(S)A 2000, s 18A, inserted by the Title Conditions (Scotland) Act 2003, s 114(2).
4   Conveyancing (Scotland) Act 1938, s 9. For difficulties in the operation of this provision, see
     Scottish Law Commission *Report on Real Burdens* para 10.36.
5   AFT(S)A 2000, ss 18(1), 18A(1).
6   The rule is now reformulated in TC(S)A 2003, ss 82–84.

Section 18A notice

4.22   A feudal pre-emption is preserved as a personal pre-emption burden by registration of a notice under s 18A of the 2000 Act before the appointed day. The notice
runs in the name of the superior, who must serve and sign it prior to registration.
'Superior' includes over-superior[1]. The superior is excused infeftment; and if there
are two uninfeft superiors, or one infeft and one uninfeft, the qualifying superior is
the last in time[2].

The statutory form of notice provides for[3]:

- the name and address of the superior;
- a conveyancing description of the feu[4];
- the terms of the right of pre-emption, either in full or by reference to the deed by
  which it was imposed;
- details of that deed, including the date and place of registration;
- a list of any obligations on the superior which are the counterpart of the pre-emption[5];
- an account of the title to the superiority by reference to the Registers including,
  in a case where the superior is uninfeft, a list of the midcouples;
- details of service on the vassal.

A style of completed notice is set out in Appendix 4 to this book. Minor deviations
are permitted[6].

A separate notice is needed for each feu[7]. Once completed, the notice is served, by
post, together with a copy of the explanatory note provided in Schedule 5A to the
2000 Act. Service is more fully discussed in chapter 11[8]. The notice is then completed by entering the details of service[9], and by signature before a notary public, the
superior having sworn or affirmed that to the best of his knowledge or belief all the
information contained in the notice is true[10]. The notary must also sign[11]. Swearing or
affirming a statement that is known to be false or is believed not to be true is an
offence under the False Oaths (Scotland) Act 1933. Normally the oath must be given
by the superior personally and not, for example, through a solicitor; but a company
or other juristic person is represented by a person authorised to sign documents on its
behalf[12], and a person without legal capacity by an appropriate person[13]. An oath outside Scotland may be given before any person duly authorised by the country in

question to administer oaths or receive affirmations[14]. If the superiority is held as common or joint property, each superior must separately swear or affirm, and sign the notice[15].

After signature the process is completed by registration in the Land Register or Register of Sasines. In the case of the former, the Keeper is directed to identify in the entry the holder of the burden[16]. No warrant of registration is needed in respect of registration in the Register of Sasines[17]. The fee for registration of notices is £25[18]. Neither stamp duty nor its successor, stamp duty land tax, is payable[19].

[1]   Abolition of Feudal Tenure etc (Scotland) Act 2000, s 49.
[2]   AFT(S)A 2000, s 49. For an example, see para 3.4
[3]   AFT(S)A 2000, s 18A(2), Sch 5A.
[4]   Or, at the superior's option, part only of the feu. See AFT(S)A 2000, s 18A(2)(b). In that case only the part described will be subject to the burden after the appointed day.
[5]   For superiors' obligations, see paras 1.24, 1.25.
[6]   AFT(S)A 2000, s 18A(1).
[7]   AFT(S)A 2000, s 42(3). Where the land originally feued has been divided and is in separate ownership, each part is treated as a separate feu for this purpose: see s 42(2).
[8]   Paras 11.7, 11.8.
[9]   AFT(S)A 2000, s 41(4).
[10] AFT(S)A 2000, s 18A(3).
[11] AFT(S)A 2000, Sch 5A, note 6.
[12] See generally the Requirements of Writing (Scotland) Act 1995, Sch 2.
[13] AFT(S)A 2000, s 18A(4).
[14] AFT(S)A 2000, s 49 (definition of 'notary public').
[15] This is because the obligations in s 18A are placed on 'the superior', and the singular includes the plural. For the position of trustees, see para 3.14.
[16] Land Registration (Scotland) Act 1979, s 6(1)(e), amended by the Title Conditions (Scotland) Act 2003, s 112(2).
[17] AFT(S)A 2000, s 41(2).
[18] Fees in the Registers of Scotland Order 1995, SI 1995/1945, Schedule, Pt III, para 2.
[19] Paras 11.9–11.11.

Effect of conversion

4.23   Assuming the notice to have been validly drawn up and registered, and the feudal real burden to be still enforceable[1], the result on the appointed day is for the feudal pre-emption to be converted into a personal pre-emption burden[2]. Its holder is the (former) superior or, if the superiority has changed hands since registration of the notice, that person's successor. The right to enforce is subject to any counter-obligation previously enforceable against the superior[3]. A special rule is mentioned in the next section.

[1]   See, on this topic, para 3.15.
[2]   Abolition of Feudal Tenure etc (Scotland) Act 2000, s 18A(5).
[3]   If listed in the notice: see AFT(S)A 2000, s 18A(6).

PRESERVATION AS RURAL HOUSING BURDENS

New personal rights of pre-emption

4.24 While existing feudal pre-emptions can be preserved as personal pre-emption burdens, as just seen, no provision is made in the Title Conditions Act for the creation of such burdens of new. Accordingly, a right of pre-emption after the appointed day may be constituted only as a praedial real burden, in favour of a benefited property[1]. There is one exception. The 2003 Act empowers Scottish Ministers to designate as 'rural housing bodies' bodies whose function is or includes the provision of housing on rural land or of rural land for housing[2]. The initial list was still awaited at the time of writing[3]. Uniquely, a personal right of pre-emption, known as a rural housing burden, can then be created in favour of a designated rural housing body[4]. The purpose, it was said in Parliament, is so that bodies selling land 'in the interests of providing local community housing at affordable prices should be allowed to control the subsequent sale of the land by creating a burden over the property'[5]. An important privilege of such burdens, as compared to other pre-emptions, is that they are not extinguished by the first offer but last until such time as the pre-emption is exercised[6].

[1] See the Title Conditions (Scotland) Act 2003, s 3(5). Until the appointed day, however, it would be possible to feu land imposing a pre-emption and then to convert the right into a personal pre-emption burden by registering a s 18A notice.

[2] TC(S)A 2003, s 43(5), (6).

[3] The list will be reproduced in K G C Reid and G L Gretton *Conveyancing 2003* (forthcoming, 2004). The list can be augmented or reduced: see TC(S)A 2003, s 43(5), (8).

[4] TC(S)A 2003, s 43(1).

[5] By Jim Wallace MSP, the Deputy First Minister. See Scottish Parliament *Official Report* 26 February 2003 col 18691.

[6] TC(S)A 2003, ss 83(1), 84(1).

Personal pre-emption burdens as rural housing burdens

4.25 If a feudal pre-emption is preserved as a personal pre-emption burden by a superior which is a designated rural housing body, the resulting personal pre-emption burden is treated as a rural housing burden[1]. In effect, the feudal burden is preserved as a rural housing burden – something which thus can only be achieved indirectly, by a notice under s 18A of the Abolition of Feudal Tenure Act. The result is the same if, later on, a personal pre-emption burden comes to be acquired by a rural housing body, even if the holder on the appointed day was not such a body. An unexpected consequence is that a right of pre-emption which, before the appointed day, would have been extinguished by a single offer is now elevated by feudal abolition into a right in perpetuity.

[1] Title Conditions (Scotland) Act 2003, s 122(1) (definition of 'rural housing burden').

PRESERVATION AS PERSONAL REDEMPTION BURDENS

4.26   A right of redemption is a right to repurchase the feu, whether at the superior's option, at some fixed point in time, or on the occurrence of a future event[1]. Under the 2000 Act feudal redemptions are treated in the same way as feudal preemptions, and may equally be preserved by a notice under s 18A[2]. The details were given earlier and need not be repeated[3]. On the appointed day the feudal redemption becomes a personal real burden known as a personal redemption burden[4]. Its duration then depends on the date on which the right of redemption was originally constituted. If the redemption was constituted by a deed executed after 1 September 1974 the burden is limited to 20 years from the date of constitution, as under the present law[5]. One which was constituted earlier is perpetual[6].

1   Scottish Law Commission *Report on Real Burdens* para 10.3.
2   Abolition of Feudal Tenure etc (Scotland) Act 2000, s 18A, Sch 5A.
3   Paras 4.22, 4.23.
4   AFT(S)A 2000, s 18A(5).
5   Land Tenure Reform (Scotland) Act 1974, s 12.
6   Title Conditions (Scotland) Act 2003, s 7.

PRESERVATION AS MANAGER BURDENS

4.27   A real burden which reserves to the superior the power to manage a development personally, or to nominate the factor or manager of such a development, is called a 'manager burden' by the Title Conditions Act[1]. Typically, the superior is a developer who wishes to retain a power of management until such time as all the units have been sold; but management powers are also commonly reserved in the case of sheltered or retirement housing, and then generally on a permanent basis[2].

Manager burdens are treated both favourably and unfavourably by the Title Conditions Act. The favourable treatment is that they survive feudal abolition automatically, without any action being required of the superior[3]. Indeed it is not possible to preserve such a burden by a s 18 notice[4]. In effect the feudal burden is preserved as a personal real burden[5]. The unfavourable treatment is that the manager burden is then limited as to time[6]. The normal period is five years after registration of the deed in which the burden was originally created, but this is reduced to three years in the case of sheltered or retirement housing and extended to thirty years for sales of council houses under the right-to-buy legislation. The relevant provision came into force on 4 April 2003 and has already operated to extinguish many such burdens[7]. The result is that no feudal burden will survive to be preserved as a manager burden, in the ordinary case at least, unless the deed in which it was created was registered after 28 November 1998 (ie within five years of the appointed day). And in most cases the subsequent encounter with the post-feudal world is likely to be brief.

1 Title Conditions (Scotland) Act 2003, s 63(1). Note that, unlike other personal real burdens, the term 'manager burden' is correct even before feudal abolition. This is because, in principle, a manager burden is not confined to personal real burdens but is capable of encompassing both feudal burdens and also praedial real burdens.
2 For a discussion, see Scottish Law Commission *Report on Real Burdens* paras 2.29–2.39.
3 TC(S)A 2003, s 63(9).
4 Abolition of Feudal Tenure etc (Scotland) Act 2000, s 18(6A), discussed at para 3.2.
5 Although not in terms. A manager burden is listed as one of the personal real burdens in the TC(S)A 2003, s 1(3).
6 TC(S)A 2003, s 63(4)–(7).
7 TC(S)A 2003, s 129(3).

PRESERVATION AS MARITIME BURDENS

4.28 Almost always, the sea bed in Scotland is owned by the Crown, but substantial sections of foreshore are in private ownership. Where ownership (*dominium utile*) of the foreshore or sea bed is subject to real burdens enforceable by the Crown as superior – in practice because the title originated with a Crown grant – the burdens survive feudal abolition as 'maritime burdens'[1]. A maritime burden is a type of personal real burden[2]. No action by the Crown is needed, partly in recognition of the public importance of such burdens, but also because, owing to their limited nature, maritime burdens will be obvious from even the most cursory examination of title. The Keeper is placed under a statutory duty, beginning ten years after the appointed day, to acknowledge the burdens as maritime burdens on the title sheet of the relevant section of sea bed or foreshore[3].

The Crown's right to enforce a maritime burden is subject to any counter-obligation by which it was bound prior to the appointed day[4].

1 Abolition of Feudal Tenure etc (Scotland) Act 2000, s 60. See also Scottish Law Commission *Report on Abolition of the Feudal System* para 4.51.
2 See further the Title Conditions (Scotland) Act 2003, s 44.
3 TC(S)A 2003, s 58.
4 AFT(S)A 2000, s 60(1)(a). For counter-obligations, see para 1.25.

Chapter 5

Preservation as community burdens

INTRODUCTION

Automatic preservation

5.1   Feudal real burdens imposed under a common scheme are preserved, on the appointed day, as community burdens. A 'community burden' is one which regulates a group or 'community' of properties and which is mutually enforceable by the owners within that community[1]. The rule just described was not part of the original scheme for feudal abolition, and the relevant provisions are set out in ss 52–54 of the Title Conditions (Scotland) Act 2003 and not in the Abolition of Feudal Tenure etc (Scotland) Act 2000[2]. They come into force on the appointed day (28 November 2004)[3].

Preservation under this rule occurs automatically, without the need for action on the part of the superior. Indeed only rarely is the superior a beneficiary. The end result is for the burdens to be mutually enforceable among the owners of the properties affected by the common scheme (ie the former feus). If, as quite often, that was already the position – if, in other words, co-feuars held enforcement rights, either expressly or by implication – the rule serves merely to reinforce the status quo. But in a case where only the superior could previously enforce, preservation operates, in effect, by taking the right from the superior and giving it to the (former) co-feuars[4].

By contrast to some other methods of preservation no entry is made on the Register, but the Keeper may, and after ten years must, enter on the Land Register a statement that the burdens remain in force by virtue of the statutory provision in question[5].

---

1   Title Conditions (Scotland) Act 2003, s 25(1). See further para 2.8.
2   The Scottish Law Commission was opposed to the idea that superiors' rights should be handed over to neighbours, except in the special case of tenements. This was mainly because of the difficulty of obtaining waivers. See *Report on Real Burdens* paras 11.57–11.60.
3   TC(S)A 2003, s 129(2).
4   That, however, is a figure of speech. More accurately (i) the right of the superior is extinguished and (ii) rights are created of new in the (former) co-feuars.
5   TC(S)A 2003, s 58. See para 8.12.

Meaning of 'common scheme'

5.2   'Common scheme' is not defined in the Title Conditions Act, but its meaning is familiar from the case law on implied rights to enforce real burdens[1]. Three defining characteristics may be identified.

In the first place, for burdens to be imposed under a common scheme two properties at least must be subject to the burdens. Typically there are many more, as for example in a tenement or a housing estate[2], for community burdens presuppose a 'community'[3]. This need not have been so at the time when the burdens were first created, however. So for example if Anne feus a hectare of land to Brian imposing real burdens, and Brian later divides the land into six plots selling each of them, the end result is that six plots are subject to the burdens. But initially only one plot (the original hectare) was so subject. Given that circumstances may change, as the example shows, it is important to know at what point of time the requirement of a community must be satisfied. Generally the answer under the 2003 Act is on the appointed day, although some specialities affect rights arising under s 53.

Secondly, the burdens affecting the properties must be identical or substantially similar, or at least in some sense equivalent[4]. In mixed developments there is often equivalence rather than uniformity. For example, in a deed of conditions affecting a development comprising flats, town houses and villas, some burdens might be common to the development as a whole while others might apply only to particular housing types. In such a case the special burdens on the flats are different from, but equivalent to, the special burdens on the town houses or villas, and the whole amounts to a common scheme. The same is likely to be true of a development which mixes commercial and residential units. Occasionally, however, the burdens affecting units of one type may be so different from those affecting units of the other as to suggest two common schemes and not one[5].

Finally, the burdens must probably come from a common source. The common law indeed required a common author, but the 2003 Act does not go so far[6]. It does not therefore matter that the burdens on the earlier units were imposed by A Limited and those on the later units by B Limited, provided there is something to connect the two (typically that B Limited acquired the residue of the site from A Limited). Conversely, it is difficult to say that burdens were imposed under a common scheme when imposed by half a dozen different superiors with no apparent connection beyond the fact of being represented by the same solicitor armed with the same bank of styles.

As will be seen, the main provision (s 53) adds a fourth requirement, that the properties be 'related' in some way to one another[7].

[1]   A J McDonald, 'The Enforcement of Title Conditions by Neighbouring Proprietors' in D J Cusine (ed) *A Scots Conveyancing Miscellany: Essays in Honour of Professor J M Halliday* (1987) pp 16 ff; K G C Reid *The Law of Property in Scotland* (1996) paras 399ff; Scottish Law Commission *Report on Real Burdens* para 11.6.

² Strictly the burdens cannot be community burdens unless there are at least four properties: see the Title Conditions (Scotland) Act 2003, s 25(1)(a). But this requirement is added only for the purposes of the rules on majority decision-making in Pt 2 of the Act, and it has no bearing on the reallocation of enforcement rights. In this chapter the term 'community burdens' is used without regard to the number of properties affected by the common scheme burdens.

³ For 'community', see TC(S)A 2003, s 26(2)(a).

⁴ For equivalence, see *Botanic Gardens Picture House Ltd v Adamson* 1924 SC 549 at 563 per Lord President Clyde; *Lees v North East Fife District Council* 1987 SLT 769.

⁵ Or even three. Thus (i) burdens affecting units of type A; (ii) burdens affecting units of type B; and (iii) burdens affecting units of both types.

⁶ Scottish Law Commission *Report on Real Burdens* para 11.52.

⁷ Para 5.7.

The law before the appointed day

5.3 Under the pre-2004 law the rules of enforcement were anything but uniform. Thus burdens imposed by a superior on a community of properties (such as a housing estate) under a common scheme might, depending on the circumstances, be enforceable[1]:

(i) by the superior alone;

(ii) by the superior and, by virtue of rights expressly conferred in the deed, by the owners of some of the properties in the community;

(iii) by the superior and, by virtue of rights expressly conferred in the deed, by the owners of all of the properties in the community;

(iv) by the superior and, by virtue of implied enforcement rights, by the owners of some of the properties in the community; or

(v) by the superior and, by virtue of implied enforcement rights, by the owners of all of the properties in the community[2].

Insofar as the burdens were enforceable by the owners of *all* the properties they were community burdens already (although the usage is anachronistic).

If non-feudal (praedial) burdens are taken into account, the analysis would be much the same, subject to the omission of superiors. But with non-feudal burdens it is surprisingly common to find that, due usually to some conveyancing accident, there are no enforcement rights at all[3].

The Acts of 2000 and 2003 retain the burdens themselves but, for the most part, sweep away such enforcement rights as currently exist. Superiors' rights, of course, fall on the appointed day[4]. So too do the rights of owners arising by implication[5]. Only rights which were expressly conferred remain unaffected. In place of the rights which are to be lost, the 2003 Act provides new rights by application of the rules set out in the next paragraph. These are to apply to all communities affected by common scheme burdens[6]; and since the new rules are more generous than those that they replace, the overall result is a substantial expansion of enforcement rights. Superiors apart, all those who held rights before the appointed day will retain those rights after that day (albeit often in a statutory form); but many new rights are created in addition. It is above all the new rights, replacing those formerly held by superiors, that ensure the survival of common scheme burdens after the appointed day.

1   The list that follows is not exhaustive. For example, there might be a housing estate in which the owners of some houses had enforcement rights by virtue of an express provision, the owners of other houses had enforcement rights by implication, and the owners of still others had no enforcement rights at all.

2   For implied enforcement rights, see K G C Reid *The Law of Property in Scotland* (1996) paras 399–402.

3   See para 5.11. Hence the Title Conditions (Scotland) Act 2003, s 57(2), which is intended to allow the rescue of burdens which, due to the absence of a benefited property (ie enforcement rights), were never 'imposed' in the first place.

4   Abolition of Feudal Tenure etc (Scotland) Act 2000, s 17(1).

5   At least in common scheme cases. See TC(S)A 2003, ss 49, 50(1), (6).

6   In principle even to those with *express* enforcement rights; but in practice the new rules are likely merely to repeat that which is already in the deed.

Three rules

5.4   The principle that common scheme burdens are preserved, on the appointed day, as community burdens may be broken up into three, rather complex, rules, corresponding to three separate provisions of the Title Conditions (Scotland) Act 2003[1].

The *rule in s 53* is that burdens imposed on a common scheme on a group of related properties are, from the appointed day, mutually enforceable by the owners of each property[2]. They become, in other words, community burdens in respect of which the group of related properties forms the community.

The *rule in s 52* is that where burdens are imposed on a common scheme on a group of properties (whether 'related' or not) and, in respect of any given property, the conditions mentioned below are satisfied, then so far as that property is concerned, the owners of the other properties in the group have rights of enforcement[3]. Assuming that the conditions are met by all or most of the properties in the group, the result is a set of community burdens in which the group forms the community. There are two conditions, one positive and one negative. The positive condition is that the title to the property should contain notice of the existence of the common scheme. The negative condition is that nothing in the title should suggest an absence of mutual enforcement rights.

The *rule in s 54* applies only to sheltered or retirement housing and is intended to take account of the common practice whereby a property is held back by the developer, typically as a warden's flat, and so is not itself subject to the burdens which affect the remaining properties. The rule is that where burdens are imposed on a common scheme on all the properties in a sheltered housing development, or on all bar a special property such as a warden's flat, rights of enforcement are conferred on the owners of all the properties (including the special property)[4]. The burdens then become community burdens, regulating the community of sheltered housing.

1   In para 7.3 these are given as rules (ii)–(iv).
2   See further paras 5.7–5.12.
3   See further paras 5.13–5.17.
4   See further paras 5.18, 5.19.

Evaluation

5.5   Of these three rules, that derived from s 53 of the 2003 Act is overwhelmingly the most important. Section 52 is merely residual in nature, designed to capture further cases of implied enforcement rights existing under the present law and which might not be covered by s 53. Section 54 extends the normal principles, as set out in s 53, to deal with a particular circumstance. Each rule is considered more fully below.

The rules overlap, not only with one another but also with the rules, considered in the next chapter, on facility burdens and service burdens[1]. Or to put the matter another way, the same set of burdens may qualify for the application of more than one rule. In theory the proper method of proceeding is then to apply each rule in turn and to accumulate the results; but it is rarely necessary to do so in practice except in relation to facility and service burdens, a subject which may be postponed until the next chapter[2]. So far as the rules on common scheme burdens are concerned, matters are in practice largely straightforward. If the properties form a sheltered housing development, s 54 applies. In any other case s 53 should be applied in the first instance, and it is only if (or to the extent that) the properties are not 'related' that it is necessary to have regard to s 52. As will be seen, most properties subject to a common scheme are in fact 'related' in the sense required by the Title Conditions Act.

The three rules, and those on facility and service burdens, apply to all real burdens created before the appointed day and not merely to those created by or in association with grants in feu. The underlying purpose is to achieve uniform rules of enforcement for housing estates, tenements, and other communities, regardless of the provenance of the burdens[3]. But in relation to real burdens originating in the feudal system the rules have the important additional purpose of reallocating the rights formerly held by superiors.

1   This, of course, is deliberate, indeed unavoidable. For burdens as they appear in deeds do not fall into neat, mutually exclusive, categories. See Scottish Law Commission *Report on Real Burdens* para 11.71.
2   Para 6.4.
3   Thus Jim Wallace MSP, the Deputy First Minister (Scottish Parliament *Official Report* Justice 1 Committee, 10 December 2002 col 4371): the purpose of s 53 'is to ensure that amenity burdens in all housing estates or tenements should be mutually enforceable by the owners of houses in the estate or of flats in a tenement. They would become community burdens ... A large majority of respondents to the consultation on the Bill were in favour of such amenity burdens being treated in the same way, irrespective of whether rights had been granted expressly to owners in the original deeds or whether they had arisen by implication under existing law.'

Three exceptions

5.6 Victorian building charters are much taken up with roads and sewers. Fortunately, these unattractively detailed provisions are usually irrelevant in modern times because responsibility for maintenance has been assumed by the local authority. They are not preserved by the Title Conditions Act, either as community burdens (the subject of the present chapter) or as facility burdens (the subject of the next), except in a case where the road, sewer or other facility remains a matter for private maintenance[1]. Thus the principle of preservation as community burdens does not extend to such real burdens.

Nor does it extend to a right of pre-emption, redemption or reversion[2]. Such a right, by its nature, can only properly be held by a single person[3]. The Abolition of Feudal Tenure Act allows pre-emptions or redemptions held by a superior to be preserved either as neighbour burdens or as personal pre-emption or redemption burdens by registration of an appropriate notice[4]. But if they are not so preserved, they are not re-allotted to the (former) co-feuars by ss 52–54 of the 2003 Act and will fall on the appointed day.

There is also a third exception. Usually under ss 52–54 there is an automatic conferral of enforcement rights on the owners of all properties within the community. But this principle is not to operate so as to revive a right of enforcement waived or otherwise lost before the appointed day[5]. Some examples may help[6].

> *Example 1.* In 1985 a developer feus 100 houses subject to uniform real burdens set out in a deed of conditions. Express enforcement rights are conferred on the co-feuars. In 2001 the owner of house 41 grants a minute of waiver with respect to a burden insofar as affecting house 42. *Result*: The right waived by the owner of house 41 does not revive on the appointed day.

> *Example 2.* The same, except that the minute of waiver is granted by the superior. *Result*: Since the waiver was granted by the superior, its effect after the appointed day is neutral. The co-feuars' rights are unaffected by the minute of waiver and survive the appointed day[7]. The superior's rights are lost on the appointed day.

> *Example 3.* The same except that only the superior has enforcement rights. *Result*: The minute of waiver extinguishes the burden in respect of house 42. It cannot therefore revive on the appointed day.

---

1   Title Conditions (Scotland) Act 2003, s 122(2). See Scottish Law Commission *Report on Abolition of the Feudal System* para 4.82. In principle they will also survive where they are subject to express enforcement rights, although they should presumably be omitted from the Land Register on the basis that they are no longer 'subsisting': see Land Registration (Scotland) Act 1979, s 6(1)(e).
2   TC(S)A 2003, ss 52(3), 53(3), 54(6).
3   Scottish Law Commission *Report on Real Burdens* para 10.32.
4   Para 4.21.

5   TC(S)A 2003, s 57(1).
6   Only the first is an example of TC(S)A 2003, s 57(1).
7   They survive because they are non-feudal in nature and so are unaffected by feudal abolition. See para 2.5. But note that the same effect is also achieved by the TC(S)A 2003, s 53, discussed below.

SECTION 53: RELATED PROPERTIES

The rule in summary

5.7   The first rule, by far the most important of the three, is set out in s 53 of the Title Conditions (Scotland) Act 2003. Three conditions must be satisfied. First, real burdens must be imposed on a common scheme. Secondly, the properties on which they are imposed must be 'related'. And thirdly, in respect of at least one of the properties, the deed by which the burdens are imposed must have been registered before the appointed day. There is no further requirement, as there is under the pre-2004 law[1], that the deed imposing the burdens give notice of the common scheme. In effect, the requirement that the properties be 'related' replaces the former requirement of notice.

The meaning of 'common scheme' has already been considered[2]. The other conditions are discussed below.

Assuming these conditions to be satisfied, s 53 provides that, on and after the appointed day, all the properties in question are benefited properties in the real burdens. And since, by definition, the properties are subject to the burdens and so are already burdened properties, the effect of s 53 is to create community burdens – burdens in which each property is both a benefited property and a burdened property[3]. To put the matter another way, the burdens become mutually enforceable within the community which is constituted by the related properties.

Section 53 applies to all real burdens which fulfil the stipulated conditions, and not merely to those created in, or in association with, grants in feu. Thus the purpose of the provision goes beyond the preservation of feudal burdens from extinction.

1   And therefore under the Title Conditions (Scotland) Act 2003, s 52, discussed at paras 5.13–5.17 below. 'Pre-2004' because s 53 does not come into force until 28 November 2004.
2   Para 5.2.
3   TC(S)A 2003, s 25(1).

Meaning of 'related properties'

5.8   Section 53(2) of the Title Conditions Act gives a non-exhaustive list of circumstances in which properties might be said to be 'related'. From this it may be taken that properties are 'related' either because of their physical connection or proximity or, less conclusively, because they are treated as a single community by the deed or deeds in which the burdens are imposed[1].

The first will often be clear. Flats in a tenement are related to one another[2]. So too are houses in a housing estate or units in a commercial development. Conversely, there is no sufficient relation between scattered properties feued off on an occasional basis by a landed estate[3]. A shared facility – garden ground, for example, or car parking area – tends to indicate that the properties are related[4]. So, which will often come to the same thing, is property owned in common[5]. A shared maintenance obligation – a facility burden, in other words – is another indicator[6].

The second factor more or less turns on the existence of a deed of conditions[7]. For a deed of conditions both suggests that properties are related – for why otherwise would they be treated together? – and also, for the most part, marks out the limit of the community. Take, for example, a development comprising three blocks of flats. Within each block the flats are related, as already mentioned. But if a single deed of conditions applies to all three, this points to a 'relatedness' applying across the blocks as well as within them. The matter is put beyond doubt if a facility is shared by all three blocks.

[1]   Note that a second definition of 'related properties' appears in the Title Conditions (Scotland) Act 2003, s 66, but for the purposes of the use of that expression in ss 63–65 (manager burdens).

[2]   TC(S)A 2003, s 53(2)(d).

[3]   Thus in introducing the provision Jim Wallace MSP, the Deputy First Minister, stated that 'houses on a typical housing estate would be related properties' but not 'scattered properties in rural areas': see Scottish Parliament *Official Report*, Justice 1 Committee, 10 December 2002 col 4372.

[4]   TC(S)A 2003, s 53(2)(a)(i).

[5]   TC(S)A 2003, s 53(2)(b).

[6]   TC(S)A 2003, s 53(2)(a)(ii).

[7]   TC(S)A 2003, s 53(2)(c).

Registration before the appointed day

5.9   In principle ss 52–54 of the Title Conditions (Scotland) Act 2003[1] are confined to burdens created before the appointed day. For such burdens they rationalise and replace the common law rules of implied enforcement rights. But for burdens created on or after 28 November 2004 the possibility of implied rights is withdrawn altogether, and the constitutive deed must both nominate, and be registered against, the benefited property or properties[2].

To this principle, s 53 is, however, a partial exception. Provided that one related property, at least, was burdened by a deed registered before the appointed day, it does not matter that the other such properties are burdened by later deeds. Relatively speaking, that would of course be unusual. Typically all the related properties in a community will have been burdened long before the appointed day. But this flexibility allowed by s 53 is directed at two situations in particular.

One, concerning the sale of council houses, is considered in the next paragraph. The other is the uncompleted development. For example:

> *Example.* A developer registers a deed of conditions in March 2004. Section 17 of the Land Registration (Scotland) Act 1979 – which would otherwise make the burdens immediately enforceable – is excluded, as often in practice[3]. No provision is made as to enforcement rights. The development site comprises 100 units. By 28 November 2004 60 units have been disponed[4] but 40 remain. A different provision of the Title Conditions Act[5] allows the developer to burden the remaining units by reference to the deed of conditions, notwithstanding its non-compliance with the new rules for the creation of real burdens[6]. And as the remaining units are sold, the effect of s 53 is that each becomes part of the community of related properties, and each gains enforcement rights in respect of the units previously sold.

[1] Ie the three rules on preservation as community burdens.
[2] Title Conditions (Scotland) Act 2003, s 4.
[3] If, however, s 17 of the 1979 Act were not excluded, the burdens would be immediately enforceable and hence created, in respect of all 100 units, before the appointed day. In such a case the deed by which the burdens are 'imposed' within the meaning of ss 52–54 would be the deed of conditions and not, as in the example, the individual break-off conveyances.
[4] Whether by grant in feu or ordinary disposition.
[5] TC(S)A 2003, s 6.
[6] Ie due to a failure to nominate the benefited properties.

Council house sales

5.10 Various conveyancing devices were open to councils in the sale of houses under the right-to-buy legislation[1]. One was to register in advance for each group of houses a deed of conditions containing common burdens and rights of enforcement. As and when a house was sold, it would then take both the burden and the benefit provided for in the deed. On the whole, however, council house sales were not undertaken in this way. Instead the typical pattern was for houses to be feued subject to individually listed burdens which were enforceable only by the council as superior. The abolition of the feudal system threatens this arrangement. All enforcement rights held by the council will be lost, except to the extent that they are saved as neighbour burdens under s 18 of the Abolition of Feudal Tenure Act or as facility burdens under s 56 of the Title Conditions Act[2]. And in the absence of alternative rights held by neighbours, the remaining burdens are at risk of extinction. The position is complicated by the fact that councils (or their successors as social landlords) retain many houses which continue to be subject to a right to buy.

Section 53 of the 2003 Act is intended to provide a measure of relief, depending on the factual situation. Thus in respect of any given group of houses, the position at the appointed day will be that either one or more houses has already been sold or that none has been sold.

In the second case, unusual in practice, there is of course no difficulty. When the first house comes to be sold, the council can register a deed of conditions over the whole group, thus ensuring mutual rights of enforcement.

In the first case the effect of s 53 is to provide the possibility of a rolling community. Suppose, for example, that by the appointed day seven of the twelve houses in a group have been sold, each by feu disposition and subject to common burdens. At that stage the conditions of s 53 are satisfied with respect to the seven houses in question[3], so that there is a community of seven, with mutual rights of enforcement. The burdens, no longer enforceable by the council, are enforceable by the owners of the houses instead; and thus they survive feudal abolition.

Thereafter the community can grow, in one of two ways. Incremental growth is achieved by the gradual sale of the remaining houses. As a house is sold, subject to the same burdens, so it joins, and swells, the existing community. The owner of the new house can enforce the burdens against the houses previously sold[4]; and in exchange the owners of the latter can enforce against the owner of the former.

Alternatively the council could register a deed of conditions imposing identical (or equivalent) burdens on those houses that remain unsold. Immediately all twelve houses would be part of the community[5], and the council's right of enforcement restored, not as superior, but as owner of the unsold houses. It would last for as long as the council retained ownership of a house[6]. Section 53 allows for the registration of a deed of conditions at any time, after the appointed day as well as before[7]; and councils may wish to wait and determine by experience whether enforcement rights are really needed before incurring the expense of a programme of mass registration. A deed of conditions registered after the appointed day would, of course, be governed by the new law and in particular would need to nominate the benefited properties (in practice in our example either the five houses now being burdened, or all twelve in the group)[8]. But whatever was stated in the deed on this matter, the effect of s 53 would be for all twelve houses to be benefited properties.

1   Currently the Housing (Scotland) Act 1987, Pt III.
2   See, respectively, paras 3.4–3.16 and 6.1–6.5.
3   Ie there are (i) common scheme burdens (ii) imposed on related properties (iii) by at least one deed registered before the appointed day.
4   In terms of the Title Conditions (Scotland) Act 2003, s 53(1) it does not matter that the burdens imposed on the newly sold house were 'not by virtue of a deed registered before the appointed day'.
5   On the assumption that all twelve are truly 'related' within the meaning of s 53.
6   See, for the possible right to manage the community by virtue of a manager burden, para 4.27.
7   At Stage 1 of the parliamentary passage of the Title Conditions (Scotland) Act 2003, doubts were expressed as to whether a deed of conditions could be used to impose burdens other than in association with a sale. The issue is touched on at para 3.17 above. Given, however, that councils are under a statutory obligation to sell the houses, and that the burdens are being

imposed, at least in part, to regulate the houses once sold, there does not seem any real doubt as to the competency of a deed of conditions. See Justice 1 Committee *Stage 1 Report on Title Conditions (Scotland) Bill* (SP Paper 687, 2002) paras 117, 118. The supposed difficulty does not affected deeds of conditions registered after the appointed day because of the rule of the new law that real burdens can be created in a deed of any kind: see TC(S)A 2003, s 4(1), (2).

8   TC(S)A 2003, s 4. A disadvantage of nominating all twelve would be the expense of registering the deed against the seven houses already sold.

Effect: changes in enforcement rights

5.11   If the conditions for its application are duly satisfied, s 53 of the Title Conditions Act operates to make each related property, already a burdened property, a benefited property as well. In other words it creates, or reaffirms, the status of the burdens as community burdens. The extent to which this alters existing rights depends on the position before the appointed day[1].

If, before the appointed day, the burdens were enforceable by the superior alone, enforcement by neighbours replaces enforcement by the superior. The superior's right is lost, by feudal abolition[2], and those within the community acquire enforcement rights of new by virtue of s 53.

Quite often, however, the burdens were enforceable *both* by the superior and also by neighbours (co-feuars). In that case the overall result is for the superior's right to be extinguished and for those of the neighbours to remain. But the manner in which this is achieved depends on whether the neighbours' rights originally arose by express grant or by implication. Express rights are unaffected by the legislation; and while in principle s 53 applies even to a case of express rights, its effect is usually to duplicate the result already achieved by the constitutive deed[3]. Implied rights, by contrast, are extinguished on the appointed day[4] but then re-created by s 53.

The final possibility does not affect feudal burdens at all and is mentioned only for the sake of completeness. Where burdens were imposed under a common scheme by disposition, or by a deed of conditions granted in association with dispositions, doubts may arise as to whether enforcement rights exist at all, at least if the deed is silent on the subject. For there is no superior, as with feudal burdens; and, depending on the circumstances, it may not be possible to imply enforcement rights in co-disponees[5]. Section 53 avoids these difficulties by conferring enforcement rights in all cases. Sometimes, and depending on the proper analysis of the pre-2004 law, the effect is to breathe life into burdens originally stillborn.

Section 53 can be, and has been, criticised as providing over-generously for enforcement, with predictable difficulties further down the line for obtaining minutes of waiver[6]. Certainly it goes far beyond anything contemplated by the Scottish Law Commission[7]. Nonetheless, in an area where there are no perfect solutions, s 53 is not without merit. It treats like burdens alike, regardless of provenance or history. It avoids the complexities, the unresolved debates, and the scope for conveyancing accidents which characterised the pre-2004 law. And, on the view that existing burdens are, on the whole, worth preserving – a view that, admittedly, not everyone would accept – it ensures that the dismantling of feudal law does not dismantle also the existing regulation of housing estates, tenements, and other communities.

1   As to which see para 5.3.
2   Abolition of Feudal Tenure etc (Scotland) Act 2000, s 17(1).
3   For express rights, too, are generally to the effect that everyone in the community has title to enforce.
4   Title Conditions (Scotland) Act 2003, s 49(1).
5   For a discussion, see K G C Reid *The Law of Property in Scotland* (1996) para 404.
6   The criticisms are summarised in Justice 1 Committee *Stage 1 Report on Title Conditions (Scotland) Bill* (SP Paper 687, 2002) paras 152–158.
7   The Scottish Law Commission would have applied the principle of s 53 only to tenements, as a group of properties which are unequivocally related. For other properties the existing rules of implied rights would have survived (as under s 52) but only for those within four metres of the burdened property in question. The overall approach was thus more to cut down than to increase implied enforcement rights. See Scottish Law Commission *Report on Real Burdens* paras 11.43–11.67.

Enforcement before the appointed day

5.12   No right conferred by s 53 of the 2003 Act allows enforcement in respect of a breach occurring before the appointed day, the rights conferred being prospective only[1]. For those with enforcement rights both before and after the appointed day – whether on the same or on a different ground – this rule is of theoretical interest only. But in a case where the superior alone could enforce before the appointed day and neighbours alone thereafter, it is necessary to have regard to title to sue. Once the appointed day has passed, (former) superiors are usually barred from pursuing even a breach which occurred before that day[2]; but provided that the breach is continuous in nature it would then found an action on the part of neighbours who had acquired rights under s 53.

1   Title Conditions (Scotland) Act 2003, s 57(3).
2   Abolition of Feudal Tenure etc (Scotland) Act 2000, s 17(2), (3), discussed at para 2.13.

SECTION 52: UNRELATED PROPERTIES

Scope

5.13   Section 53 of the Title Conditions Act covers those common scheme cases where the properties are 'related'. But under the law in force before 2004 enforcement rights might be implied even for unrelated properties[1]. Section 52 ensures the survival of such rights by the simple device of re-enacting the common law[2]. The result is a complex and uninviting provision, reflecting faithfully the twists and turns of a case law which was often ignored in practice. Fortunately it will be needed only infrequently.

So far as feudal abolition is concerned, s 52 is neutral in effect. Unlike s 53, which, in one aspect, preserves feudal burdens as community burdens by the creation of new rights of enforcement, s 52 does no more than confirm the status quo. So if, before the appointed day, common burdens on a group of unrelated properties were enforceable both by the superior and also, by implication, by neighbours as co-feuars, the burdens after that day will continue to be enforceable by neighbours (only). But if the burdens were previously enforceable by the superior alone, no new rights are created by s 52 and the burdens will perish, with the feudal system itself, on the appointed day[3].

1   For the pre-2004 law, see K G C Reid *The Law of Property in Scotland* (1996) paras 399–403.
2   Thus Jim Wallace MSP, the Deputy First Minister (Scottish Parliament *Official Report*, Justice 1 Committee, 10 December 2002 col 4371): 'The purpose of amendment 109 [ie s 52 in its present form] is to restate the common law on who has implied rights to enforce. Setting that out in statute will ensure that no one who has implied rights at present will lose them.'
3   If the properties had been 'related' the burdens would have been rescued by s 53.

The rule in summary

5.14   Like s 53, s 52 of the 2003 Act presupposes the imposition of real burdens, feudal or non-feudal, on a common scheme[1]. But thereafter its focus is on individual properties rather than on the community as a whole.

Whether enforcement rights can be implied *in relation to a given property* depends, under s 52, on the deed – either a conveyance or a deed of conditions – in which the burdens for that property are set out[2], and in particular on whether its wording satisfies the two conditions set out in the following paragraphs[3]. Assuming the conditions to be satisfied, the burdens, in relation to that property, are enforceable by the owners of such other properties as are also subject to the common scheme. And if the conditions are satisfied in relation to other properties also – which is by no means always the case – the result is mutual enforceability or, in other words, community burdens[4].

If a single deed contains the burdens for all the properties, the position can be established reasonably quickly. That would be so where a deed of conditions had been used, although the very use of such a deed is usually sufficient to bring in s 53[5]. It would be the case also where a single area, conveyed subject to real burdens, had later been subdivided[6]. Otherwise the burdens will be contained in separate deeds each one of which must be examined if the overall position is to be ascertained[7]. Before they can be read, of course, such deeds must first be found; and the very fact that the properties are not 'related' increases the difficulty of tracking them down. In such cases the task of investigation is likely to be time-consuming, expensive and, it may be, inconclusive[8].

¹   For the meaning of 'common scheme', see para 5.2.
²   The deed in which the burdens are set out may not be the same as that by which they are
    imposed. Thus burdens are imposed if they are set out in a grant in feu or in a deed of condi-
    tions which does not exclude the Land Registration (Scotland) Act 1979, s 17. But burdens set
    out in a deed of conditions in which s 17 is excluded are imposed only by the later conveyance
    in which the deed of conditions is incorporated in accordance with the Conveyancing
    (Scotland) Act 1874, s 32. In the latter case s 52 allows recourse to both deeds.
³   Paras 5.15. and 5.16 below. A third condition, that the burdens derive from a common author,
    is not insisted on by s 52, the only respect in which it innovates on the common law. See
    Scottish Law Commission *Report on Real Burdens* para 11.52. But without at least a common
    source of burdens, it is doubtful whether they could be said to be imposed on a common
    scheme. See para 5.2.
⁴   For community burdens, see the Title Conditions (Scotland) Act 2003, s 25(1), and para 2.8.
⁵   TC(S)A 2003, s 53(2)(c). See para 5.8.
⁶   This is the second of the two situations distinguished by Lord Watson, in a famous passage, in
    Hislop v MacRitchie's Trs (1881) 8 R (HL) 95 at 103.
⁷   This is the first of Lord Watson's two situations.
⁸   Scottish Law Commission *Report on Real Burdens* para 11.23. The difficulty was largely
    avoided by the Law Commission's proposal (paras 11.48–11.56), in the event not adopted,
    which restricted enforcement rights to properties lying within four metres.

The first condition: notice

5.15   In terms of s 52 of the Title Conditions (Scotland) Act 2003, two conditions
must be satisfied by the deed in which, in relation to the property in question, the burdens are set out¹. The first is that the deed must give notice that the burdens are part
of a common scheme applying to other properties². In this way the owner is warned
of – and in the traditional analysis is deemed to have given consent to – the existence
of enforcement rights in neighbours.

If the deed sets out the burdens not only for that property but for the other properties
as well, the condition is plainly satisfied. For merely by reading the description in the
deed the owner knows of, and can identify, the other properties³.

Matters are more difficult if the deed is restricted to the property in question, and in
practice the requirement of notice may then not be satisfied. Traditionally, two methods of giving notice are recognised, and there may possibly be others. One is where
there is an obligation on the granter to include identical or equivalent burdens in subsequent grants from the same estate⁴, for '[t]here could be no reason for putting the
superior under such an obligation, unless the vassal was to enforce the conditions
agreed to be inserted'⁵.

The other recognised method is by making reference to a common feuing scheme or
plan⁶. 'Plan' is not used here in the sense of a map⁷, although in many cases a map
will, of course, exist. What is required, rather, is an indication in the deed that the
property being conveyed is part of a larger and uniform development, that the uniformity will be policed by real burdens such as the ones in the grantee's title, and
therefore, by implication, that the burdens are to be enforceable by the co-grantees

among themselves. There is uncertainty as to how specific the reference to a plan need be. Clearly, it is sufficient if the deed discloses the existence of a formal plan or scheme and indicates that common conditions are to be in every property[8]. Equally clearly it is insufficient if a plan is referred to only for the purposes of identifying the property[9]. But between these two cases lies considerable scope for argument and uncertainty[10].

[1] Including, if different, the conveyance by which, by incorporation of the earlier deed, the burdens are actually imposed. See the Title Conditions (Scotland) Act 2003, s 52(1).
[2] TC(S)A 2003, s 52(1): 'expressly refers to the common scheme or is so worded that the existence of the common scheme is to be implied'.
[3] '[A] subfeuar or disponee acquiring a building lot, subject to a particular condition, with notice in his titles that the common author, whether his immediate or over-superior, has imposed that condition upon the whole area of which his lot formed a part, must be taken as consenting that the condition shall be for mutual behoof of all the feuars or disponees within the area, and that all who have interest shall have a title to enforce it': *Hislop v MacRitchie's Trs* (1881) 8 R (HL) 95 at 104 per Lord Watson. See further eg *Low v Scottish Amicable Building Society* 1940 SLT 295.
[4] Eg *McGibbon v Rankin* (1871) 9 M 423.
[5] *Johnston v The Walker Trs* (1897) 24 R 1061 at 1075 per Lord McLaren.
[6] *Hislop v MacRitchie's Trs* (1881) 8 R (HL) 95 at 98 per Lord Selborne LC.
[7] *Botanic Gardens Picture House Ltd v Adamson* 1924 SC 549 at 563 per Lord President Clyde.
[8] *Main v Lord Doune* 1972 SLT (Lands Tr) 14.
[9] *Murray's Trs v St Margaret's Convent Trs* (1906) 8 F 1109 affd 1907 SC (HL) 8.
[10] See eg *Johnston v The Walker Trs* (1897) 24 R 1061.

The second condition: absence of contra-indicators

5.16 The second condition is negative in character. Following the common law, no rights are implied under s 52 of the 2003 Act if their existence is inconsistent with some other provision of the deed[1]. The standard example, specifically mentioned in s 52, is the reservation of a right in the granter to vary or waive the burdens[2]. Another example, in a case where the community has arisen only by subdivision of the property originally conveyed, is a prohibition of such subdivision[3].

[1] Title Conditions (Scotland) Act 2003, s 52(2): enforcement rights are conferred 'only in so far as no provision to the contrary is impliedly ... or expressly made in the deed'.
[2] *Thomson v Alley and Maclellan* (1883) 10 R 433; *Walker and Dick v Park* (1888) 15 R 477; *Turner v Hamilton* (1890) 17 R 494. See also A J McDonald 'The Enforcement of Title Conditions by Neighbouring Proprietors' in D J Cusine (ed) *A Scots Conveyancing Miscellany: Essays in Honour of Professor J M Halliday* (1987) pp 22–24. The existence of such a right was often enough to prevent implied rights arising under deeds of conditions – an obstacle now removed by recourse to s 53.
[3] *Girls School Co Ltd v Buchanan* 1958 SLT (N) 2.

Registration before the appointed day

5.17 Section 52 of the 2003 Act is confined to deeds registered before the appointed day[1]. For burdens created after that day the benefited property must always be nominated, and there can be no question of enforcement rights arising by implication[2].

Example. Before the appointed day A Ltd convey 15 properties over a 10-year period subject to identical real burdens set out in each conveyance. The properties are not 'related' within s 53 but each conveyance complies with s 52. Accordingly, the burdens are community burdens. After the appointed day A Ltd convey a 16th property subject to identical conditions. As required under the new law the conveyance nominates as the benefited properties the 15 properties already conveyed. *Result:* While the 15 properties are benefited properties with respect to the 16th, the 16th is excluded from the operation of s 52[3] and so cannot form the benefited property in relation to the 15 properties previously conveyed. Hence the 16th property is not a part of the community, and its burdens are not community burdens[4].

[1]   Title Conditions (Scotland) Act 2003, s 52(1).
[2]   TC(S)A 2003, ss 4, 49(1). Section 53, however, forms a partial exception: see paras 5.9, 5.10.
[3]   Because the conveyance of that property is not a deed 'so registered', ie registered before the appointed day.
[4]   See TC(S)A 2003, s 25(1). The 16th property is a burdened property but not a benefited property.

SECTION 54: SHELTERED HOUSING

The problem of the unburdened property

5.18   The principal rule, in s 53 of the Title Conditions Act[1], is directed at communities where all the properties are burdened but none, or not all, are benefited. Thus the shortfall being provided for is at the benefited end and not at the burdened. But occasionally a shortfall may exist at the burdened end also. In sheltered housing, in particular, the developer may hold back one or two properties from sale so that they can be used for some special purpose such as accommodation for a warden or for visitors; and, not having been conveyed, such properties are usually exempt from the real burdens affecting the rest of the development[2]. Section 54 of the 2003 Act is intended to solve the problem of the unburdened property in sheltered and retirement housing[3].

The provision is straightforward. Where a property in a sheltered housing development is 'used in some special way', the fact that it is unburdened is disregarded; and the effect of s 54 is that all the properties in the development, including the special property, become benefited properties. Thus the burdens are mutually enforceable throughout the development. Furthermore it is provided that the special property is part of the 'community' in the legal sense, overriding the principle that a community consists only of properties which are both burdened and benefited[4]. This means, for example, that the special property is included for the purposes of voting for repairs, or of calculating majorities for variation or discharge of burdens[5].

As with s 52 (but not s 53), s 54 applies only to deeds registered before the appointed day[6]; and the effect of the deeds must have been to burden the whole development, other than any special property. That would exclude a development which was in the process of being sold at the appointed day[7].

1   Paras 5.7–5.12.
2   This is because the deed of conditions usually excludes the Land Registration (Scotland) Act 1979, s 17.
3   Title Conditions (Scotland) Act 2003, s 54(3) defines 'sheltered or retirement housing development' as 'a group of dwelling-houses which, having regard to their design, size and other features, are particularly suitable for occupation by elderly people (or by people who are disabled or infirm or in some other way vulnerable) and which, for the purposes of such occupation, are provided with facilities substantially different from those of ordinary dwelling-houses'. The Bill on introduction referred only to 'sheltered housing', and 'retirement housing' was added in response to the argument, strongly made, that retirement housing is distinct from sheltered housing. See eg Scottish Parliament *Official Report,* Justice 1 Committee, 17 December 2002 cols 4384 ff. The issue is of only presentational importance, however, as the definition just quoted encompasses both.
4   TC(S)A 2003, s 26(2). Similarly, the burdens are community burdens despite the fact that one of the properties is unburdened: see s 25(2).
5   See generally the TC(S)A 2003, Pt 2.
6   TC(S)A 2003, s 54(1).
7   Although such a development would be subject to s 53, provided that one at least of the deeds was registered before the appointed day. See paras 5.9, 5.10.

Interaction with feudal abolition

5.19   Most sheltered housing developments are feued, with the developer/superior retaining extensive powers of management and enforcement. The powers of management – characterised by the Title Conditions Act as 'manager burdens' – are extinguished three years after the deed of conditions was registered, by virtue of a provision which came into force on 4 April 2003[1]. Thereafter it is for the residents to manage the development by themselves, although the existing manager can continue to act unless or until replaced[2].

The right to enforce real burdens as superior is retained until the appointed day but not beyond[3]. On that day, as has been seen, new enforcement rights are created by s 54 in favour of the residents in the development, insofar as they did not exist already, and those powers extend to the superior in its capacity as owner of the warden's accommodation or other special property[4]. No additional enforcement rights can be acquired by the superior by virtue of a notice under s 18 of the Abolition of Feudal Tenure Act[5].

1   Title Conditions (Scotland) Act 2003, s 63(4)–(6). See para 4.27.
2   TC(S)A 2003, s 65. A new manager can normally be appointed by a simple majority under the TC(S)A 2003, s 28.
3   Abolition of Feudal Tenure etc (Scotland) Act 2000, s 17(1).
4   Scottish Law Commission *Report on Real Burdens* para 11.66.
5   TC(S)A 2003, s 62(2). See para 3.2.

Chapter 6

Preservation as facility or service burdens

FACILITY BURDENS

Meaning of 'facility burden'

6.1 Feudal real burdens which qualify as 'facility burdens' are automatically preserved on the appointed day. This rule, which originated in the Abolition of Feudal Tenure etc (Scotland) Act 2000[1], was re-enacted by s 56 of the Title Conditions (Scotland) Act 2003 for all real burdens including those which are non-feudal in origin[2]. The burden must be created by a deed registered before the appointed day. By contrast to some other methods of preservation no entry is made on the Register, but the Keeper may, and after ten years must, enter on the Land Register a statement that the burdens remain in force by virtue of the statutory provision in question[3].

A 'facility burden' is a real burden which regulates the maintenance, management, reinstatement or use of facilities such as the roof or other common parts of a tenement, a common recreational area, a private road, private sewerage, or a boundary wall[4]. As these examples show, a facility is usually something that is shared, but s 56 would also apply to a facility sited on one property for the sole benefit of another – for example a stairway leading to an upper flat.

[1] Abolition of Feudal Tenure etc (Scotland) Act 2000, s 23, repealed by the Title Conditions (Scotland) Act 2003, s 128, Sch 15.
[2] Burdens are included even if originally stillborn due to the lack of a benefited property – a difficulty which affects non-feudal burdens only (for in feudal burdens there is always a superior with enforcement rights). See TC(S)A 2003, s 57(2).
[3] TC(S)A 2003, s 58. See para 7.12.
[4] TC(S)A 2003, s 122(1), (3). The examples given in the text are all mentioned in the definition.

Effect

6.2 Section 56 of the Title Conditions Act does not preserve superiors' rights as such. On the appointed day facility burdens become enforceable by the owners of any property to which the facility is, and is intended to be, of benefit; or in other words the properties in question become the benefited properties[1]. Depending on the circumstances that may, or may not, confer rights on a former superior. Thus maintenance obligations concerning the common parts of a tenement become enforceable by the owners of all flats in the tenement; burdens concerning private roads by those who, as owners of property, have a right to use the road; and burdens concerning a garden wall by the owners of the property on either side. The requirement that the facility must not only benefit the property in question but be 'intended to be' of such benefit is designed to exclude the merely adventitious, and the expression reappears in the definition of 'facility burden' itself[2]. The Scottish Law Commission gives the example of a garage on a neighbour's ground which protects from the prevailing wind and a view of the municipal waste ground but nonetheless could not be said to have been 'intended to constitute a facility of benefit to other land'[3].

Naturally, a facility cannot benefit from itself; and to cover the possibility that a person owns the facility without at the same time owning other property which takes benefit from it, s 56 includes the facility as a second category of benefited property[4]. The extension will rarely be needed. Often the facility is owned in common as a pertinent of the properties which benefit from it, and even where it is in sole ownership (as for example the roof of a tenement at common law) the owner is usually a beneficiary of the facility in some other capacity (as for example the owner of the upper flat). Nonetheless it is possible to think of cases where this would not be so. One is where a developer sells all the houses in a residential development but retains the recreational ground, perhaps with the ultimate intention of conveying it to a management company. Invariably the obligation to maintain the ground – the facility burden, in other words – is imposed on the houses. The effect of s 56 is that the benefited properties are not only houses (as benefiting from the ground) but also the ground itself, with the result that the burden can be enforced by the developer.

Section 56 is prospective in effect and confers no right of enforcement in relation to breaches occurring before the appointed day[5]. Nor, usually, can a former superior found on such a breach once the appointed day has arrived[6]. A continuous breach, however, is in a different position and could be litigated by a person acquiring rights under s 56.

1   Title Conditions (Scotland) Act 2003, s 56(1)(a).
2   TC(S)A 2003, s 122(1).
3   Scottish Law Commission *Report on Real Burdens* para 11.34.
4   TC(S)A 2003, s 56(1)(a)(ii).
5   TC(S)A 2003, s 57(3).
6   Para 2.13.

Community burdens, neighbour burdens, and combined burdens

6.3   Section 56 of the 2003 Act is phrased in the singular but will usually operate in the plural, for maintenance liabilities tend to be exacted from more than one property. To the extent that those bound by the burden coincide with those on whom enforcement rights are now to be conferred – to the extent, in other words, that the burdened properties are also the (new) benefited properties – the result is a community burden[1]. That indeed is likely to be the typical product of s 56, as for example where a maintenance obligation is imposed on all the flats in a tenement, or on all the houses in an estate. Less commonly, the result will be neighbour burdens[2]. For example, an obligation to maintain a boundary wall imposed solely on one property would be transformed by s 56 into a neighbour burden for the benefit of the other. Finally, but much more rarely, the result of s 56 might be a combined burden – a facility burden that in respect of some benefited properties was a community burden and in respect of others was a neighbour burden[3].

> *Example.* Six properties are served by a private road. The road is owned by the owner of the first property. The remaining five properties have a servitude right of access over it, but also an obligation, constituted as a real burden, to maintain it. Since the road is a facility of benefit to all six properties, all are benefited properties in terms of s 56. In respect of the five properties which are also subject to the burden, the burden is a community burden, with the result that maintenance, variation and discharge are regulated by a decision of the majority[4]. But in respect of the first property the burden is a neighbour burden and may be enforced according to its terms.

[1]   For community burdens, see the Title Conditions (Scotland) Act 2003, s 25(1) and para 2.8.
[2]   For neighbour burdens, see para 2.8.
[3]   For combined burdens, see the TC(S)A 2003, s 62.
[4]   Ie under the TC(S)A 2003, Pt 2.

Duplication of other rules

6.4   To the extent that s 56 produces community burdens it largely duplicates the work of ss 52–54 of the 2003 Act, which also operate automatically[1]. Indeed s 53, the widest of these provisions, makes recourse to s 56 unnecessary in many cases[2]. That is generally true of maintenance obligations imposed on the flats of a tenement or the houses in an estate. For in practice the facility burden is only one of a series of common scheme burdens governed by s 53 and there is no reason for separating it out and seeking the same result from a different provision. Indeed insofar as the two provisions might produce different results, s 53 is likely to be the broader in scope[3].

Section 56 remains of significance, however, in two situations. One is where the properties are not 'related' so that s 53 cannot apply and recourse must be had to s 52[4]. Here s 56 will sometimes apply where s 52 does not, for example because of absence of notice in the titles; and even where s 52 has the potential to apply, it will often be easier to invoke s 56.

The other situation is where s 56 produces a combined burden, for to the extent that there is a neighbour burden there is no duplication of s 53.

1   Para 5.5.
2   See generally, for s 53 of the 2003 Act, paras 5.7–5.12.
3   This is because the 'community' is likely to be wider than the class of properties which take benefit from the facility. Take for example the case of an estate comprising three blocks of flats. The deed of conditions imposes (i) separate maintenance burdens on each block and (ii) other burdens which affect the whole estate. The effect of s 53 is for burdens of both classes to be enforceable by everyone on the estate. The effect of s 56 is for the burdens of class (i) to be enforceable, in relation to each block, only by the owners within that block.
4   See generally, for s 52, paras 5.13–5.17.

Three exceptions

6.5   The automatic preservation of burdens is not to apply to spent burdens concerned with roads, sewage or other facilities. Accordingly there is excluded from the definition of 'facility burden' any obligation to maintain or reinstate which has been assumed by a local or other public authority[1]. Manager burdens are also excluded[2]. They survive by virtue of a separate provision[3].

Facility burdens are rarely the subject of minutes of waiver, but a right of enforcement which was waived or otherwise extinguished before the appointed day is not revived by s 56 of the Title Conditions Act[4].

1   Title Conditions (Scotland) Act 2003, s 122(2). The exclusion equally affects ss 52–54: see para 5.6.
2   TC(S)A 2003, s 56(2). This avoids the possible argument, if s 56 were to apply, that the appointment of the manager needed the unanimous agreement of all the owners.
3   TC(S)A 2003, s 63, discussed at para 4.27.
4   TC(S)A 2003, s 57(1). For a discussion see para 5.6.

SERVICE BURDENS

6.6   Feudal real burdens which qualify as 'service burdens' are automatically preserved on the appointed day. As with facility burdens, the governing provision is s 56 of the Title Conditions (Scotland) Act 2003, and many of the same rules apply[1].

A 'service burden' is a burden on one property to supply services to another, for example water or electricity[2]. Service burdens are uncommon in practice.

The superior's right of enforcement is lost, as such, on the appointed day[3], but in its place s 56 nominates as a benefited property the property to which the services are provided[4]. The result, usually, is to convert a feudal burden into a neighbour burden.

1   Paras 6.1–6.5. They are not repeated here. Note in particular that the Title Conditions (Scotland) Act 2003, s 57 applies to service burdens.
2   TC(S)A 2003, s 122(1).
3   Abolition of Feudal Tenure etc (Scotland) Act 2000, s 17(1).
4   TC(S)A 2003, s 56(1)(b).

Chapter 7

Real burdens: on and after the appointed day

INTRODUCTION

7.1   The means by which feudal burdens might be preserved were considered in the previous chapters. In this chapter, and at the risk of some repetition, the material is drawn together by considering the position of real burdens on and after the appointed day. On the appointed day many real burdens are abolished but most will survive. Two questions then arise. Which burdens survive? And, following the removal of superiors, by whom are they to be enforced? The answers are that real burdens survive if they are the subject of one of the special rules already described, and summarised in numbered form below; and that they are enforceable by those for whose benefit the special rules operate. Conversely, burdens which are not subject to any of the rules are extinguished on the appointed day.

Three further points should be made. First, some of the rules apply not only to feudal burdens (burdens originally imposed in, or in association with, a grant in feu) but also to non-feudal burdens (burdens originally imposed in, or in association with, a disposition)[1]. This is because the Title Conditions (Scotland) Act 2003 re-writes the rules on implied enforcement rights as they apply to real burdens generally[2]. The result is that such rights are significantly extended.

Secondly, the rules overlap to some extent. For example, feudal burdens which qualify under rule (i) will usually qualify under rule (ii) as well. The same might be said of rules (ii) and (iv). Rule (v) often, but not always, overlaps with rule (ii). The legislative technique is deliberate[3]. Insofar as the rules identify the same enforcers – as is often the case – the overlap is neutral in effect. Insofar as they identify different enforcers, the effect is cumulative, so that both groups so identified have enforcement rights. The intended result is that no person who needs enforcement rights is left out.

Finally, the rules, with one limited exception[4], apply only to burdens imposed before the appointed day. They are transitional in nature, and burdens imposed on or after the appointed day are unaffected.

---

[1]   Para 2.2.
[2]   Title Conditions (Scotland) Act 2003, Pt 4.

3   Scottish Law Commission *Report on Real Burdens* para 11.71.
4   The TCS(S)A 2003, s 53 (rule (ii) below) applies to burdens imposed after the appointed day provided that they were imposed before that day on at least one of the properties within the group.

RULES APPLYING TO ALL REAL BURDENS

Burdens subject to express enforcement rights

7.2   Quite often there are express enforcement rights. For example, if a house is divided into two flats and the lower flat sold, the burdens imposed in the disposition of the lower flat are often declared to be enforceable by the granter and successors as owner of the upper flat. Or if burdens are imposed by deed of conditions on a common scheme, enforcement rights may be conferred on the owners of each affected property. Express enforcement rights are unaffected by the legislation[1], with the result that burdens subject to express rights continue to be enforceable after the appointed day in the same manner as they were before. The rule therefore is that

> (i)   *Burdens expressly declared to be enforceable by the owners of a particular property or properties continue to be enforceable by such owners.*

There is one exception. Burdens expressed as being enforceable by the superior cease to be so enforceable, there being no superiors after the appointed day[2]. In fact superiors' rights were usually left to implication rather than being expressed in the deed.

[1]   This proposition is not expressly vouched by the legislation but arises by necessary implication, eg from the Abolition of Feudal Tenure etc (Scotland) Act 2000, s 17(1)(b).
[2]   AFT(S)A 2000, s 17(1)(a).

Burdens imposed under a common scheme

7.3   A 'common scheme' arises where the same, or broadly similar, burdens are imposed on two or more properties[1]. Three transitional rules then apply, although most cases will be covered by the first. Almost always the effect is to create community burdens[2].

> (ii)   *Burdens imposed on related properties under a common scheme survive and are mutually enforceable by the owners of each of the properties*[3].

This covers, for example, burdens imposed, typically by a deed of conditions, on a housing estate or block of flats. In a case where the burdens were previously enforceable only by the superior, the effect of the rule is to transfer enforcement rights from superior to neighbours.

    (iii)   *Burdens imposed on all units in a sheltered or retirement housing development (or all units other than the warden's flat or other unit used in a special way) under a common scheme survive and are mutually enforceable by the owners of each of the units (including the warden's flat or other special unit)*[4].

A special rule for sheltered and retirement housing was made necessary by the fact that the warden's flat is not usually subject to the burdens and so would not, but for this rule, acquire enforcement rights.

    (iv)   *Burdens imposed under a common scheme survive and are mutually enforceable by the owners of the affected properties if the deed (or deeds) creating the burdens*

        (a)   *gives notice that a common scheme exists, and*
        (b)   *contains nothing to exclude mutual enforceability*[5].

This residual rule repeats, more or less, the law of implied enforcement rights as it was before the appointed day, thus ensuring that no rights previously held by neighbours are lost. The standard example of a provision which is taken as excluding mutual enforceability (within rule (iv)(b)) is a reservation by the superior or other granter of a right to vary. Naturally, most cases covered by rule (iv) are also covered by rule (ii), and with the same result in respect of identification of enforcers. But rule (iv) is necessary for the case where the properties are not 'related', as for example with a ribbon development of feus carved out, over time, from a rural estate. However, co-feuars who were without enforcement rights will not qualify under rule (iv), and the burdens will be extinguished on the appointed day.

[1]   Para 5.2.
[2]   For community burdens, see para 2.8.
[3]   Title Conditions (Scotland) Act 2003, s 53. See paras 5.7–5.12.
[4]   TC(S)A 2003, s 54. See paras 5.18, 5.19.
[5]   TC(S)A 2003, s 52. See paras 5.13–5.17.

Facility burdens

7.4   A facility burden is a real burden which regulates the maintenance, management, reinstatement or use of shared facilities. Typical examples include maintenance burdens within tenements and housing estates, or obligations to maintain boundary walls or private roads[1]. All facility burdens survive the appointed day. The rule is that:

    (v)   *Facility burdens survive and are enforceable by the owners of any property to which the facility is of benefit and by the owners of the facility itself*[2].

Many facility burdens are imposed on related properties under a common scheme and will also be preserved, with identical results, by rule (ii).

1   Title Conditions (Scotland) Act 2003, s 122.
2   TC(S)A 2003, s 56(1). See paras 6.1–6.5.

Service burdens

7.5   A service burden is a real burden which relates to the provision of services – water or electricity, for example – to another property or properties[1]. Unlike facility burdens, service burdens are uncommon; but like facility burdens they will survive the appointed day. The rule is that

> *(vi)   Service burdens survive and are enforceable by the owners of any property to which the services are to be provided[2].*

1   Title Conditions (Scotland) Act 2003, s 122(1).
2   TC(S)A 2003, s 56(2). See para 6.6.

Manager burdens

7.6   Especially in housing estates and other developments, a real burden may make provision for the appointment of the developer, or some other person, as manager. The Title Conditions (Scotland) Act 2003 restricts the life of such 'manager burdens' to five years in the normal case, but the period is thirty years for burdens imposed by social landlords under the right-to-buy legislation, and only three years in the case of sheltered or retirement housing[1]. Manager burdens are unaffected by the appointed day as such[2]. Thus a manager burden imposed by a deed of conditions registered on 1 June 1999 would, in the normal case, expire on 1 June 2004, a few months before the appointed day; but a burden imposed on 1 June 2003, whether in favour of a superior or otherwise, will survive until 1 June 2008 notwithstanding the abolition of the feudal system. The survival is automatic and no action need be taken by the superior or developer. The rule therefore is that

> *(vii)   Manager burdens are unaffected by the appointed day but are extinguished –*
>
> > *(a)   in the case of a sale under the right-to-buy legislation, thirty years*
> >
> > *(b)   in the case of sheltered or retirement housing, three years, and*
> >
> > *(c)   in any other case, five years*
>
> *after the registration of the constitutive deed[3].*

1   Title Conditions (Scotland) Act 2003, s 63. By s 63(4)(c) a manager burden is also extinguished if, for a period of 90 continuous days, the person holding the burden does not own one of the properties in the development.
2   TC(S)A 2003, s 63(10).
3   TC(S)A 2003, s 63. See para 4.27.

RULES APPLYING ONLY TO FEUDAL BURDENS

Neighbour burdens by registration

7.7   Under the rules which apply exclusively to feudal burdens, preservation is normally achieved only by the service and registration of a notice before the appointed day. Depending on the circumstances, feudal burdens can be preserved either as neighbour burdens or as personal real burdens[1]. So far as the former are concerned, the rule is that

> (viii)   *Feudal burdens survive and are enforceable by the owners of the property nominated for that purpose provided that there is registered before the appointed day –*
>
> > (a)   *a notice under s 18 of the Abolition of Feudal Tenure etc (Scotland) Act 2000;*
> > (b)   *an agreement under s 19 of the 2000 Act; or*
> > (c)   *a notice or an order of the Lands Tribunal under s 20 of the 2000 Act[2].*

[1]   For terminology, see paras 2.8, 2.9.
[2]   See generally ch 3.

Personal real burdens by registration

7.8   Feudal burdens can also be preserved as one of the new personal real burdens, in the limited circumstances in which these are available. The rule is that:

> (ix)   *Feudal burdens survive and are enforceable by the person or body nominated for that purpose provided that there is registered before the appointed day –*
>
> > (a)   *a notice under s 18A of the Abolition of Feudal Tenure etc (Scotland) Act 2000 (personal pre-emption and redemption burdens);*
> > (b)   *a notice under s 18B of the 2000 Act (economic development burdens);*
> > (c)   *a notice under s 18C of the 2000 Act (health care burdens); or*
> > (d)   *a notice under ss 27 or 27A of the 2000 Act (conservation burdens)[1].*

It should be added that by a notice under s 65A of the 2000 Act a reservation of sporting rights is converted, not into a personal real burden, but into a separate tenement in land, analogous to a right of salmon fishing[2].

[1]   See generally ch 4.
[2]   Paras 8.6–8.10.

Maritime burdens

7.9   The Crown is exempted from the need to register a notice in respect of maritime burdens, which survive by force of statute. A maritime burden is a real burden held by the Crown as superior in respect of the sea bed or foreshore. The rule is that:

>   (x)   *Maritime burdens continue to be enforceable by the Crown[1].*

[1]   Abolition of Feudal Tenure etc (Scotland) Act 2000, s 60. See para 4.28.

RULES APPLYING ONLY TO NON-FEUDAL BURDENS

Neighbour burdens subject to implied enforcement rights

7.10   Under the law before the appointed day, implied enforcement rights could arise in two different ways[1]. One, already mentioned[2], was where burdens were imposed under a common scheme. The other, restricted to non-feudal burdens[3], was where land was subdivided. More precisely, the rule was that if one part was sold and the other part retained, there was an implication that burdens imposed in the disposition of first part were enforceable by the owners of the second (retained) part[4]. In the vocabulary of the new legislation, the first (common scheme) case resulted in community burdens and the second (subdivision) in neighbour burdens. The Title Conditions (Scotland) Act 2003 extinguishes all existing implied rights to enforce, but makes a distinction between common scheme cases and subdivision cases[5]. So far as the former are concerned, the existing rules of implied rights are replaced, on the appointed day, by new rules (ii)–(iv) above. The effect is to expand the incidence of implied rights. The position for subdivision cases is different. Existing implied rights are not extinguished on the appointed day itself but ten years later, on 28 November 2014[6]. They are not replaced. But such rights can be preserved by the service and registration of a notice on or after the appointed day but before 28 November 2014[7]. The notice identifies the benefited property and explains the basis on which enforcement rights arise. On 28 November 2014 all other implied rights arising on subdivision are extinguished, and with them the real burdens by virtue of which they are enforced. The rule therefore is that:

>   (xi)   *Non-feudal burdens enforceable as neighbour burdens by virtue of an implied right to enforce survive the appointed day but are extinguished on 28 November 2014 unless, before that date, they are preserved by registration of a notice.*

[1]   K G C Reid *The Law of Property in Scotland* (1996) paras 399–404.
[2]   Para 7.3.
[3]   Abolition of Feudal Tenure etc (Scotland) Act 2000, s 48.
[4]   *J A Mactaggart & Co v Harrower* (1906) 8 F 1101. For possible difficulties, see *Marsden v Craighelen Lawn Tennis and Squash Club* 1999 GWD 37-1820, discussed in K G C Reid and G L Gretton *Conveyancing 1999* (2000) pp 59–61.

5   Title Conditions (Scotland) Act 2003, s 49.
6   TC(S)A 2003, s 49(1).
7   TC(S)A 2003, s 50. See further Scottish Law Commission *Report on Real Burdens* paras
     11.72–11.79. A fuller discussion is beyond the scope of this book.

IDENTIFYING SURVIVING BURDENS

Cleansing of the Register

7.11 The Keeper is at liberty to cleanse the Land Register of burdens extinguished by feudal abolition[1]; but he cannot be made to do so until the end of a period to be prescribed by Scottish Ministers and which the Scottish Law Commission recommended should be five years[2]. Inevitably the process will be a slow one. Once the prescribed period is at an end, the Keeper will be open to applications for the removal of spent burdens. This can be done under the rectification procedure[3], but in most cases a request for removal seems likely to accompany an ordinary application for registration following an acquisition of the burdened property. Indeed it may become a routine matter for the first such application after expiry of the prescribed period to list the real burdens said to be extinguished on the appointed day and to request their removal. The Keeper will then require to be satisfied, whether by argument or by evidence, that the burdens were not preserved under one or another of the rules set out above.

Whether the Keeper will also remove burdens of his own accord remains to be seen. Once the prescribed period has expired, he is bound to consider the issue at least in relation to first registrations, for only subsisting real burdens may be included in the title sheet[4].

If a burden is removed in error, it may not be reinstated if, as usual, that would be to the prejudice of a proprietor in possession[5]. But this is subject to the usual exceptions where rectification against a proprietor in possession is allowed[6].

1   The legislation makes clear that removal of spent burdens is not to be treated as prejudicing a
     proprietor in possession, nor as allowing a claim for indemnity. See Land Registration
     (Scotland) Act 1979, ss 9(3B) and 12(3)(cc), inserted by the Abolition of Feudal Tenure etc
     (Scotland) Act 2000, s 3. It is, however, difficult to see how there could be prejudice, or a claim
     for indemnity, in respect of the removal of something which is already, for other reasons, extinguished.
2   AFT(S)A 2000, s 46(1). See Scottish Law Commission *Report on Abolition of the Feudal
     System* para 4.24. The reason given by the Commission for the transitional period – that under
     the proposed legislation on title conditions those holding implied rights to enforce burdens
     (including feudal burdens) would have five years to register their rights – has not come to pass
     in the Title Conditions (Scotland) Act 2003. Registration in respect of implied rights is required
     only for non-feudal burdens, and the period allowed for registration is ten years and not five.
     See TC(S)A 2003, s 50. A corresponding provision (s 51) allows the Keeper the same period of
     ten years before he is required to accept applications for the removal of burdens on the basis
     that implied rights have been extinguished. For a discussion, see Scottish Law Commission
     Report on Real Burdens para 11.83.

³   Land Registration (Scotland) Act 1979, s 9; Land Registration (Scotland) Rules 1980, SI 1980/1413, r 20.
⁴   LR(S)A 1979, s 6(1)(e). Until the prescribed period expires the Keeper is at liberty to include spent burdens on the title sheet on first registration: see AFT(S)A 2000, s 46(2).
⁵   LR(S)A 1979, s 9(3C), inserted by the AFT(S)A 2000, s 3(b).
⁶   LR(S)A 1979, s 9(3)(a).

Noting survival and enforceability

7.12   The Register may mark survival as well as extinction. If survival occurs automatically[1], without registration of a notice, the Keeper is empowered to enter a statement, by reference to the relevant statutory provision, that the burdens remain in force[2]. So where, for example, burdens were imposed on related properties under a common scheme, the Keeper can note on the title sheet that they subsist by virtue of s 53 of the Title Conditions Act. That example invokes rule (ii), but the same principle applies in respect also of rules (iii), (iv), (v), (vi) and (x). Ten years after the appointed day the power turns into a duty and the Keeper is bound to enter the statement in question, but only 'where satisfied that a real burden subsists' by virtue of one of the rules. It is unclear whether the Keeper will act of his own accord or whether, as the legislation seems to permit, he will await applications supported by sufficient evidence.

Normally the statement is entered on the title sheet of the burdened property alone, although in the case of community burdens – the typical product of the rules in question – the burdened and benefited properties are one and the same. If, however, the Keeper has sufficient information, he must give details of the benefited property and enter a corresponding statement on its title sheet[3].

The power and duty just discussed are useful for another reason also. After the appointed day all new real burdens must list the benefited property as well as the burdened and must be registered under both[4]. Notices preserving feudal burdens (under rules (viii) and (ix)) are subject to similar rules[5]. Following the appointed day, therefore, the only burdens in respect of which this information is not readily available are those preserved by force of law. An expansive exercise of the Keeper's new power will do much to bring those burdens into line.

¹   Except in the case of rule (vii) (manager burdens).
²   Title Conditions (Scotland) Act 2003, s 58.
³   An equivalent rule operates in cases involving preservation notices: see Land Registration (Scotland) Act 1979, s 6(1)(e), (ee), amended by the TC(S)A 2003, s 112.
⁴   TC(S)A 2003, s 4(1), (2)(c)(ii), (5).
⁵   See eg para 3.13.

Transformation of the Register

7.13   It follows from what has been said that, over time, the Land Register will be transformed. Feudal burdens which were not preserved will disappear. So too, quite often, will real burdens more than 100 years old, extinguished by the sunset rule, described below[1]. The burdens remaining on the Register will tend to be relatively modern and of obvious continuing utility. Often they will be registered against the benefited property as well as the burdened property. Even more often it will be clear from the Register where enforcement rights lie.

[1] Para 7.22.

Distinguishing spent burdens from live burdens

7.14 The transformation of the Register is a matter for the future. Until then the question of which burdens survived feudal abolition and which did not will often be a pressing one. And since the Keeper may in practice need persuasion to remove burdens in the latter class, some ready means is required of identifying the burdens in question.

The difficulties here, although considerable, should not be overstated. The first step is to determine which burdens affecting a particular property were feudal and which non-feudal. Non-feudal burdens are unaffected by feudal abolition and need not be considered further[1].

The second, and final, step is to decide whether any of the rules outlined above might apply. If none applies, the feudal burdens were extinguished on the appointed day.

Two of the rules (rules (viii) and (ix)) require registration of a notice before the appointed day, and so present no difficulty. Another rule (rule (i)) turns on express enforcement rights which, equally, are patent from the Register. Three rules apply only where burdens are imposed under a common scheme. Of those, one (rule (iv)) requires that the deed give notice of the existence of the scheme, a second (rule (iii)) applies only in the case of sheltered or retirement housing, while the third (rule (ii)) requires a group of related properties, a requirement which in most cases will be obvious. The remaining rules depend on nothing more than the content of the burden. These are facility burdens (rule (v)), service burdens (rule (vi)), manager burdens (rule (vii)), and maritime burdens (rule (x))

A rule of thumb may also be helpful. Roughly speaking, feudal burdens are extinguished on the appointed day if either they are one-off burdens imposed on one feu only, or they are imposed on a number of feus on a common plan but the feus are insufficiently related for the purposes of rule (ii). Conversely, feudal burdens survive if there are express enforcement rights, if they are imposed on a common plan on a housing estate, block of flats or other related properties, if they concern the maintenance and management of common facilities such as the common parts in a tenement or a boundary wall, or if they are the subject of a registered notice.

[1] Para 2.5. However, as has been seen (para 7.10), one class of non-feudal burdens is extinguished ten years after the appointed day unless a notice of preservation is registered.

ENFORCEMENT

General

7.15   A feudal burden which survives the appointed day does so either as a praedial real burden or as one of the new personal real burdens. In either case it is governed by the same rules as other burdens, that is to say, as burdens created before the appointed day but by non-feudal means and burdens created on or after the appointed day[1]. Those rules, comprehensively reformed and restated by the Title Conditions Act, are beyond the scope of the present work[2]. Only a brief summary can be given here.

[1]   The only exception is in interpretation. See para 7.18.
[2]   A detailed account of the Bill which, to a large extent, became the Title Conditions (Scotland) Act 2003 will be found in Scottish Law Commission *Report on Real Burdens.*

Title and interest

7.16   In order to enforce a real burden there must be both title and interest[1]. In the ordinary case, title comes from ownership of a benefited property. Completion of title by registration is not required[2]. As well as owners, the 2003 Act extends enforcement rights to tenants of a benefited property, and to proper liferenters and non-entitled spouses[3]. If a benefited property is divided, enforcement rights are lost to the part disponed unless the split-off disposition provides otherwise; but this rule does not apply to community burdens or to facility burdens[4].

By contrast with the rule for superiors, interest to enforce is not presumed but must be demonstrated[5]. A person has interest if, in the circumstances that have arisen, failure to comply with the burden will result in material detriment to the value or enjoyment of the person's ownership or other right[6].

Special rules apply to personal real burdens[7]. Only the holder of the burden may enforce. Some personal real burdens can be assigned, allowing the identity of the holder to change over time[8]. There is no requirement that title be completed[9]. Interest to enforce is presumed and is not likely to be at issue in practice[10].

[1]   Title Conditions (Scotland) Act 2003, s 8(1).
[2]   TC(S)A 2003, s 123(1).
[3]   TC(S)A 2003, s 8(2). But only owners can enforce rights of pre-emption and redemption. See s 8(4).
[4]   TC(S)A 2003, s 12.
[5]   Abolition of Feudal Tenure etc (Scotland) Act 2000, s 24.
[6]   TC(S)A 2003, s 8(3).
[7]   TC(S)A 2003, s 8(1), (6).
[8]   The assignable burdens are personal pre-emption burdens, personal redemption burdens, conservation burdens, rural housing burdens, and manager burdens: see AFT(S)A 2000, s 18B(7)

and TC(S)A 2003, ss 39, 43(10), 63(3). The others cannot be assigned: see TC(S)A 2003, ss 44(2), 45(4)(b), 46(4)(b).
9   TC(S)A 2003, s 40.
10   TC(S)A 2003, s 47.

Person against whom enforcement may be made

7.17   All real burdens are enforceable against the owner of the burdened property[1]. In addition, negative burdens (ie burdens imposing a restriction) are enforceable against tenants and other persons having use of the property. There is a special rule for where property changes hands at a time when an affirmative burden (ie an obligation to do something, such as pay money) is outstanding. Both the outgoing and incoming owners are liable, jointly and severally; but, except insofar as is otherwise agreed (eg in missives), an incoming owner who is made to pay can recover from the outgoing owner[2].

1   Title Conditions (Scotland) Act 2003, s 9.
2   TC(S)A 2003, s 10.

Interpretation

7.18   In the past real burdens have tended to be interpreted in a manner that is over-strict with the result, sometimes, that the burden is treated as void or fails to achieve the effect which was intended[1]. In future real burdens (including those created before the appointed day) are to be construed 'in the same manner as other provisions of deeds which relate to land and are intended for registration'[2]. The effect is to bring real burdens into line with, for example, servitudes, leases, and standard securities[3].

A special difficulty is the survival of feudal terminology in formerly feudal burdens. The Abolition of Feudal Tenure Act provides a set of translation rules, so that, for example, '*dominium utile*' is to be construed as a reference to ownership, and 'feuing' to disponing[4]. These apply, not only to the deeds in which the burdens were created, but also to any entry made on the Land Register, or in a land or charge certificate, as a result of such a deed.

The most important word is 'superior'. In real burdens references to superiors might occur, for example, in the context of informal waiver ('no building shall be erected without the consent of us and our successors as superiors') or, much more rarely, in the context of an obligation on the superior which is the counterpart of the obligation on the vassal (for example, obliging the superior to use money collected under a maintenance obligation to carry out certain works). Usually the translation rules require 'superior' to be read as meaning the new, non-feudal enforcer[5]. So where, for example, a feudal burden is converted into a neighbour burden[6], any reference to 'superior' becomes a reference to the owner of the new benefited property. Indeed arguably the result is the same even if the word 'superior' is missing: so long as the burden made clear, by whatever words, that the right or obligation affected the person holding the superiority, that right or obligation will pass to the new enforcer. The idea is to replicate after the appointed day the rights and obligations held before that day. And often there will be continuity of personnel, for the owner of the (new) benefited property is generally the same person as the (former) superior.

In one case the word 'superior' is disregarded rather than translated[7]. A feudal burden which survives only as a community burden[8] does not, except adventitiously, confer enforcement rights on the former superior; and it would be awkward to translate 'superior' as the numerous neighbours who now stand in his place. Instead the word is treated as excised.

> *Example.* In 1995 Property Developers Ltd feu 100 houses. The development is subject to a deed of conditions. One of its terms is that no alterations are to be made without the consent of Property Developers as superiors[9]. After the appointed day, the burdens become community burdens under s 53 of the Title Conditions Act. Accordingly the reference to superiors' consent falls, and the burden is re-cast as an unqualified prohibition on alterations.

It will be seen that the result of the example, a common one in practice, is to increase the burden on the owners of the houses. Before the appointed day, the (informal) consent of the superior would have been enough to allow an alteration to proceed, and that would be so even if the deed of conditions had conferred enforcement rights on co-feuars[10]. Now a formal discharge is needed, and therefore a much larger number of consents[11]. If that result seems unsatisfactory, it would also have been unsatisfactory to allow a former superior, now without enforcement rights, to continue to control a development by means of informal waivers[12]. It is a sound principle of the new law of real burdens that only a holder of the burden is empowered to waive compliance[13].

The exception for community burdens, just described, does not apply to the extent that the burdens are also facility burdens[14]. This is because facility burdens occasionally imposed a counter-obligation on the superior, and those who succeed to the superiors' enforcement rights should succeed also to the counter-obligation.

[1]   K G C Reid *The Law of Property in Scotland* (1996) paras 415–422. For recent examples, see *Heritage Fisheries Ltd v Duke of Roxburghe* 2000 SLT 800; *Grampian Joint Police Board v Pearson* 2001 SC 772.
[2]   Title Conditions (Scotland) Act 2003, s 14.
[3]   Scottish Law Commission *Report on Real Burdens* paras 4.61–4.67.
[4]   Abolition of Feudal Tenure etc (Scotland) Act 2000, s 73.
[5]   AFT(S)A 2000, s 73(2).
[6]   Under s 18 of the AFT(S)A 2000. See ch 3.
[7]   AFT(S)A 2000, s 73(2).
[8]   Whether under s 53 of the TC(S)A 2003 or because the burden is already is a community burden due to the existence of express co-feuars' rights. See ch 5.

9   The result would be the same if the consent was to be given by Property Developers personally rather than *qua* superiors. See AFT(S)A 2000, s 73(2A).
10   K G C Reid and G L Gretton *Conveyancing 2001* (2002) pp 89–90.
11   But not the consent of the owners of all 100 houses. See para 7.21.
12   In introducing s 73(2A) of the AFT(S)A 2000 (by means of the TC(S)A 2003, s 114(6) and Sch 12 para 13(c)), the Deputy First Minister explained that it would 'ensure that former feudal superiors who lose their ability to enforce burdens on the appointed day will also lose their ability to give that kind of consent'. See Scottish Parliament *Official Report*, Justice 1 Committee, 10 December 2002 col 4359.
13   TC(S)A 2003, s 3(9).
14   The TC(S)A 2003, s 56 is among the provisions listed in s 73(2) of the AFT(S)A 2000.

Remedies

7.19   The right of a superior to irritate the feu was abolished more than four years before the appointed day, on 9 June 2000[1]. This was accompanied by transitional arrangements which seem not to have been needed and which may now be taken as spent. Whether irritancy was also competent in respect of non-feudal burdens was never entirely clear[2], but the remedy, assuming it to have existed, was abolished on 4 April 2003[3]. In all other respects, the remedies available for enforcement of real burdens are unchanged. In particular enforcement can be by interdict, by implement, by action for payment, and by a claim for damages[4].

1   Abolition of Feudal Tenure etc (Scotland) Act 2000, s 53.
2   K G C Reid *The Law of Property in Scotland* (1996) para 424.
3   Title Conditions (Scotland) Act 2003, ss 67, 129(3).
4   K G C Reid *The Law of Property in Scotland* (1996) para 423.

EXTINCTION

Minute of waiver

7.20   The ordinary minute of waiver continues to be available after the appointed day, and the Title Conditions Act makes clear what was previously in doubt, namely that a completed title is not necessary in order to grant such a deed[1]. In Sasine cases it will then be necessary to deduce title[2]. The fact that tenants and others can now enforce burdens[3] has no bearing on minutes of waiver which, as before, need be granted only by the owner.

A convenient feature of the feudal system was that a minute of waiver might require only one signature. Admittedly, the superior would exact a price in return[4]; but the whole transaction could usually be carried out quickly and painlessly. No doubt superiors' waivers were relied on more than was entirely proper. There was a natural tendency to overlook co-feuars' rights, and hence the fact that, where such rights existed, a waiver from the superior was of little value. But, for better or for worse, many transactions were settled on the basis of a deed signed by the superior alone. This convenient device is not available after the appointed day. Instead it is necessary to focus much more carefully than in the past on the location of enforcement rights. The effect of the 2003 Act is that in most cases the answer will be readily discoverable – as under the present law it might not have been. But quite often, at least to conveyancers[5], the answer will be unwelcome. In particular, if the property is part of a housing estate or other development, the effect of s 53 is usually to confer enforcement rights on everyone in the estate. At this point any idea of a minute of waiver has to be abandoned.

1   Title Conditions (Scotland) Act 2003, ss 15, 123(1).
2   TC(S)A 2003, s 60(1).
3   Para 7.16.
4   And sometimes, of course, the superior's monopoly position was abused. See Scottish Law Commission *Report on Abolition of the Feudal System* paras 4.16–4.18.
5   There are, of course, other points of view. A person seeking to stop a neighbour from carrying out a building project will be grateful for the opportunity of preventing it.

Variation or discharge of community burdens

7.21   Partly to meet the difficulty just mentioned, the 2003 Act introduces no fewer than four additional methods of variation or discharge which are available only for community burdens. These are for registration, against the properties affected, of a deed granted by:

- the owners of a majority of units[1] in the community[2];
- the manager, if duly authorised to do so (whether in the constitutive deed or by a majority of owners under s 27(1)(b))[3];
- such owners as may be specified in the constitutive deed[4]; or
- the owners of the affected unit (or units) together with the owners of all other units in the community within four metres[5] (discounting roads less than twenty metres wide)[6].

'Variation' includes the imposition of new community burdens[7]. It will be seen that these methods depart, on one view radically, from the principle of variation and discharge by the owners of *all* of the benefited properties.

The method chosen in any particular case is likely to depend both on the size of the community and on whether the discharge is for one unit only or for all (or most) of the units. Most discharges are in respect of only a single unit. In that case the easiest method will usually be the final one (four-metre discharge), as requiring the smallest number of signatories. Only if the community is small are the other methods likely to be attractive. The four-metre rule matches the rules of neighbour notification for the purposes of planning permission[8], and it may be that the two processes could be combined. The four-metre discharge is not, however, available for facility burdens or in one or two other cases[9].

If the discharge is for all units, one of the other methods is likely to be selected, and often only the first will in practice be available. Here again much depends on the size of the community. In an estate of 20 or even 30 houses, obtaining the signatures of a majority of owners may be a reasonable proposition. For much larger numbers the task is likely to be unachievable.

Obtaining the necessary signatures is not the only step. Those who have not signed stand to lose rights without consent. Therefore they must be informed, and given the opportunity to object[10]. Usually this involves sending a copy of the executed deed together with a notice and explanatory note in statutory form. In the case, however, of a four-metre discharge it is sufficient to fix a notice to the affected property and to an appropriate lamp post or posts – presumably on the basis that those most directly affected have already indicated their consent by signature[11]. Once notice has been given, any owner who did not sign may apply to the Lands Tribunal within eight weeks for preservation, unvaried, of the burden insofar as constituted against the units whose owners (or all of whose owners) did not sign. The application proceeds in much the same way as an ordinary Lands Tribunal case except that the applicant is the benefited owner and not the burdened[12].

Although in theory the deed can be registered at once, it would not then vary or discharge the burdens in respect of the properties whose owners have not signed. In practice, therefore, there is a delay of eight weeks to allow for applications to the Lands Tribunal. Assuming that none is received the Tribunal will endorse the deed with a statement to that effect[13]. In addition the grantee (or one of them) must swear or affirm before a notary public, with an appropriate endorsement on the deed, that intimation duly took place and as to the date when the eight-week period expired[14]. The deed is then ready for registration, and on registration the burdens are duly discharged, or varied.

The procedure is, necessarily, cumbersome and slow. It will be useful for relatively small communities, or in relation to discharges for single units. Even then it is likely to take several months, to involve, possibly significant, expense, and to run the risk of neighbours who refuse to sign or cannot readily be traced. But in the context, for example, of building operations which also require planning permission, the additional hurdle of a four-metre discharge may not seem unacceptably onerous.

1   'Unit' is defined in the Title Conditions (Scotland) Act 2003, s 122(1) as 'any land which is designed to be held in separate ownership (whether it is so held or not)'. In a housing estate each house is a unit.
2   TC(S)A 2003, s 33(2)(a).
3   TC(S)A 2003, s 33(2)(b).
4   TC(S)A 2003, s 33(1)(a).
5   TC(S)A 2003 ss 32, 35(1).
6   TC(S)A 2003, ss 35, 125
7   TC(S)A 2003, s 33(1), 122(1).
8   For a discussion, see Scottish Law Commission *Report on Real Burdens* paras 11.50, 11.51.

⁹   Service burdens and in sheltered or retirement housing. See TC(S)A 2003, s 35(1)(b).
¹⁰   TC(S)A 2003, ss 34, 36, 37(1).
¹¹   TC(S)A 2003, s 36(2). If there are no lamp posts, it is permissible to intimate by newspaper advertisement.
¹²   TC(S)A 2003, ss 90(1)(c), 97, 98.
¹³   TC(S)A 2003, ss 34(4), 37(2), (3).
¹⁴   TC(S)A 2003, ss 34(4), 37(4).

Sunset rule

7.22   If burdens are more than 100 years old, there is a faster and simpler proce-dure. Furthermore, it is not confined to community burdens, although facility burdens and some other burden types are excluded[1]. It resembles the four-metre dis-charge described above, except that the privilege of those owners within the four-metre zone is merely to receive an individual copy of the notice proposing the termination of the burdens.

In outline the procedure is as follows[2]. The owner of the burdened property – or any other person, such as a tenant, against whom the burden is enforceable – draws up a notice of termination in statutory form. A single notice can be used for any number of burdens[3], thus allowing all burdens of more than 100 years to be extinguished in one operation. The notice is sent to the owners of all benefited properties within four metres[4]. In respect of other benefited properties it is sufficient to fix a notice on the burdened property and on an appropriate lamp post or posts. Benefited owners then have a minimum period of eight weeks to object by applying to the Lands Tribunal for renewal of the burden[5]. If no application is made (or if it does not extend to all the burdens, or all the benefited properties), the notice is endorsed with a certificate by the Tribunal and may then be registered. On registration the burden is extinguished (subject to the outcome of any Tribunal application) – or, in the metaphor of the name by which the rule has come to be known, the sun sets on the burden.

¹   Title Conditions (Scotland) Act 2003, s 20(3). The others include conservation burdens, mar-itime burdens, and service burdens.
²   TC(S)A 2003, ss 20–24.
³   TC(S)A 2003, s 20(6).
⁴   Disregarding roads less than 20 metres wide: see TC(S)A 2003, s 125.
⁵   TC(S)A 2003, s 90(1)(b)(i).

Variation or discharge by the Lands Tribunal

7.23   The familiar jurisdiction of the Lands Tribunal remains in place after the appointed day, subject to some changes designed to streamline and speed up the pro-cedure[1]. In particular, if an application is unopposed, the Tribunal is no longer required to consider its merits but must grant the application[2]. A person wishing to oppose an application must now pay a fee[3], and may be liable for expenses if unsuccessful[4]. The grounds on which an application may be granted, in opposed cases, are reconfigured and extended, but with only limited change in substance[5]. The Tribunal is given a new jurisdiction to pronounce on the validity of real burdens, and on their enforceability and construction[6].

[1]   See generally the Title Conditions (Scotland) Act 2003, Pt 9. The current legislation, which is being replaced, is contained in the Conveyancing and Feudal Reform (Scotland) Act 1970, ss 1, 2.
[2]   TC(S)A 2003, s 97. This applies only to real burdens, and even then excludes facility burdens, service burdens, and community burdens in sheltered or retirement housing.
[3]   TC(S)A 2003, s 96(2).
[4]   TC(S)A 2003, s 103.
[5]   TC(S)A 2003, s 100.
[6]   TC(S)A 2003, s 90(1)(a)(ii).

Compulsory purchase

7.24   It is usually assumed that compulsory purchase extinguishes all real burdens and servitudes, although the authorities are rather unclear[1]. The 2003 Act removes the doubt. After the appointed day all real burdens and servitudes are extinguished on registration of a conveyance which follows a compulsory purchase order, except insofar as the conveyance or order otherwise provides[2]. The rule does not insist on the use of a so-called statutory conveyance[3] but applies even in the case of ordinary dispositions; and indeed there seems little point in using statutory conveyances in the future.

A slightly different rule applies to acquisitions by agreement, in the shadow of the statutory powers[4]. Here the acquiring authority must first give notice – typically by advertisement or by fixing a notice to the property and an appropriate lamp post – to the owners of any benefited property. There is then a period of not less then 21 days during which such an owner can apply to the Lands Tribunal for renewal of the condition[5]. The procedure is much as already described in the context of the sunset rule and the discharge of community burdens. Assuming that no application is received, a certificate to that effect is endorsed on the conveyance by the Lands Tribunal. Following registration all real burdens and servitudes are then extinguished.

[1]   Scottish Law Commission *Report on Real Burdens* para 13.14.
[2]   Title Conditions (Scotland) Act 2003, s 106.
[3]   Ie a conveyance in the form of the Lands Clauses Consolidation (Scotland) Act 1845, Sch A.
[4]   TC(S)A 2003, s 107.
[5]   TC(S)A 2003, ss 90(1)(b)(ii), 107(5).

Negative prescription

7.25   On one view, negative prescription did not apply at all to feudal burdens, although the position was controversial[1]. After the appointed day, all real burdens are subject to negative prescription, and the period is reduced from 20 years to 5[2]. In effect, this means that any breach which is more than 5 years old ceases to be challengeable and can be disregarded. Normally the 5 years is to run from the date of the breach, but for breaches occurring before the appointed day the 5 years runs from that day[3]. The usual rules about interruption of prescription apply. Once the prescriptive period has run the burden is extinguished, but only to the extent of the breach. Thus for example if, in breach of an obligation not to build, a garage is erected, the burden is, at the end of 5 years, extinguished with respect to the garage but not otherwise. Further buildings would be unlawful.

[1]   W M Gordon *Scottish Land Law* (2nd edn, 1999) para 22–82; K G C Reid *The Law of Property in Scotland* (1996) para 431.
[2]   Title Conditions (Scotland) Act 2003, s 18.
[3]   TC(S)A 2003, s 18(5), (7). The former 20-year period can also be used, so that a breach which occurred 17 years before the appointed day would be extinguished 3 years (and not 5 years) after that day.

Acquiescence

7.26   The rules of acquiescence are restated and clarified by the 2003 Act, and are likely to be resorted to much more frequently than in the past[1]. The relevant provision applies wherever a real burden is breached in such a way that material expenditure is incurred, the benefit of which would be substantially lost if the burden were now to be enforced. In practice this will usually involve cases of unauthorised alterations. The burden is extinguished to the extent of the breach if either the owner of the benefited property consented to the work, however informally, or where all those with enforcement rights (which might include tenants and other occupiers) either consented or failed to object within the period ending 12 weeks after the work was substantially completed (or a shorter period if that is reasonable)[2]. The work must be sufficiently obvious that the enforcers knew, or ought to have known, of it. For the purposes of the provision a person with a title to enforce but, in the context of the particular breach, no interest is disregarded[3]. Once the 12-week period has expired, there is a presumption, unless the contrary can be shown, that no objection was indeed made and hence that the burden was duly extinguished[4].

[1]   Title Conditions (Scotland) Act 2003, s 16. It is assumed, however, that the common law of acquiescence survives to the extent that it is not replaced.
[2]   The ground of failure to object does not, however, apply to conservation burdens, economic development burdens, or health care burdens.
[3]   For absence of interest to enforce, see s 17 discussed below.
[4]   TC(S)A 2003, s 16(2).

Absence of interest to enforce

7.27   It sometimes happens that a particular breach is too slight, or remote, for anyone to have an interest to enforce. In that case, the burden is immediately extinguished to the extent of the breach[1].

[1]   Title Conditions (Scotland) Act 2003, s 17.

Chapter 8

Minerals, sporting rights, and other reservations

SEPARATE TENEMENTS

Salmon fishings and other regalian rights

8.1   Historically, certain rights over land were considered as so valuable or prestigious that they were reserved from Crown grants by implication[1]. Most prominent of all was the right of salmon fishing, while others included the right to gather mussels or oysters and the right of port and ferry. Further rights were added by statute. The Royal Mines Act 1424, still in force and not disturbed by the Abolition of Feudal Tenure etc (Scotland) Act 2000, reserved mines of gold and silver. Modern legislation reserves petroleum and natural gas[2].

Rights reserved in this way could nonetheless be feued if the Crown chose to do so. They were, in other words, *inter regalia minora* and not *inter regalia majora*[3]. Sometimes, therefore, the Crown grantee would receive the regalian right as well, although for that to happen express words were needed. Just as commonly, the Crown feued the right to a third party, separately from the land, or retained the right as part of its patrimony. By an Act of 1592 the person with *dominium utile* of the surface is always entitled to a feu of mines of gold and silver subject to payment of one tenth of the value of all metal mined[4]. The payment is a royalty rather than a feuduty or perpetual feudal payment and is expressly saved by the 2000 Act[5].

The idea that mere (incorporeal) rights could be feued is perhaps a strange one, although one to which lawyers in Scotland have long been accustomed. In effect, regalian rights are treated as 'land' and can be dealt with in exactly the same way as other land. Some regalian rights, however, are corporeal, for example mines of gold and silver. The Scottish Law Commission considered, but in the end rejected, the idea of converting incorporeal rights into personal servitudes[6] as part of the abolition of the feudal system.

The overall effect of Crown feuing policy is that the surface of land might be held by one person, and a regalian right in respect of the same land by another. Thus in Scotland a person who owns a stretch of river might, or might not, hold the right to fish for salmon there. Equally the right to fish might be held by someone else.

1   K G C Reid *The Law of Property in Scotland* (1996) paras 207–211; W M Gordon *Scottish Land Law* (2nd edn, 1999) ch 10.
2   Petroleum (Production) Act 1934, s 1.
3   See further W M Gordon *Scottish Land Law* (2nd edn, 1999) paras 27–06, 27–07. Property held as *regalia majora* is inalienable.
4   Mines and Metals Act 1592 (c 31). After the appointed day the entitlement is to a disposition and not to a grant in feu, a change which necessitated amendments couched in the language of the sixteenth century. Thus for example for the words 'saidis fewis' there is now substituted 'disposition of the saidis mynis', and for 'four witnesses' there is substituted 'ane witness'. See the Abolition of Feudal Tenure etc (Scotland) Act 2000, s 76(1), Sch 12, para 1.
5   AFT(S)A 2000, s 61. See Scottish Law Commission *Report on Abolition of the Feudal System* para 3.56.
6   Scottish Law Commission *Report on Abolition of the Feudal System* paras 7.16–7.18.

Legal and conventional separate tenements

8.2   A regalian right is an example of a 'separate tenement'. Heritable property is a separate tenement if it is owned separately from the surface of the land. It is helpful to distinguish between property which is always considered as separate from the surface ('legal' separate tenements) and property which is normally included in ownership of the surface but which the law allows to be held separately if the appropriate conveyancing arrangements are made ('conventional' separate tenements)[1]. Regalian rights are the main type of legal separate tenement, the only other examples being coal, which is reserved to the Coal Authority[2], and teinds, now obsolete, and abolished by the Abolition of Feudal Tenure Act[3]. Minerals and tenement flats are the main examples of conventional separate tenements, and the law is slow to admit other examples although the precise position is unclear[4]. Minerals are considered more fully in the next section. Except in relation to salmon fishing, sporting rights cannot be held as separate tenements, a rule which caused some difficulty in preparing the legislation on feudal abolition[5].

1   K G C Reid *The Law of Property in Scotland* (1996) paras 207–209.
2   Coal Industry Act 1994, s 7(3).
3   Abolition of Feudal Tenure etc (Scotland) Act 2000, s 56, discussed at para 10.20. Teinds were the right of the church to a tenth part of the land and industry of the laity, long since converted into a monetary equivalent. See Scottish Law Commission *Report on Abolition of the Feudal System* para 3.51, and more generally W M Gordon *Scottish Land Law* (2nd edn, 1999) paras 10–50 ff.
4   K G C Reid *The Law of Property in Scotland* (1996) para 212; W M Gordon *Scottish Land Law* (2nd edn, 1999) para 6–01.
5   For sporting rights, see paras 8.6–8.10.

Effect of feudal abolition

8.3   As a separate tenement is itself 'land' held under feudal tenure, it is treated by the 2000 Act in exactly the same way as other land. Thus the person who holds *dominium utile* of, say, minerals or salmon fishings becomes, on the appointed day, its outright owner[1]. All superiority interests are extinguished[2]. Regalian rights which were unfeued and thus still held by the Crown remain allodial property, as before[3]. After the appointed day a Crown grant of salmon fishings can still be made, but only by disposition and not by grant in feu[4].

A separate tenement can be nominated as the benefited property for real burdens under s 18 of the 2000 Act and is generally exempted from the 100-metres rule[5].

[1]   Abolition of Feudal Tenure etc (Scotland) Act 2000, s 2(1). See further para 1.9.
[2]   AFT(S)A 2000, s 2(2).
[3]   Scottish Law Commission *Report on Abolition of the Feudal System* para 2.22. And see para 1.14 above.
[4]   AFT(S)A 2000, s 59.
[5]   AFT(S)A 2000, s 18(7)(c), discussed at paras 3.11, 3.12.

MINERALS

Reservations

8.4   Minerals are a conventional separate tenement[1]. In reserving minerals, therefore – as standardly occurs in grants in feu – a superior is reserving 'land' itself and not merely a right to work a commodity which belongs to someone else[2]. Furthermore, the reservation is of *dominium utile* and not of *dominium directum*. From the superior's perspective, therefore, the result is mixed estate. So far as concerns the surface of the land, the superior has *dominium directum* and the vassal *dominium utile*. But in respect of the minerals there is no right in the vassal (the minerals being reserved) and the superior has *dominium utile*. Thus parties who stand in the relationship of superior and vassal in respect of the surface stand in the relationship of vassal and vassal – of neighbours in other words – in respect of the minerals. It is only where the minerals are *not* reserved that the right of the superior is reduced to that of *dominium directum*.

Dominium utile of minerals is not lost by feudal abolition, any more than *dominium utile* of any other kind. On the contrary, it is upgraded to outright ownership[3]. For practical purposes, this relieves a superior of the need to take any action ahead of the appointed day. If minerals are reserved, the reservation will survive automatically, leaving the former superior as owner of the minerals. If minerals are not reserved, the *dominium directum* will be extinguished along with the *dominium directum* of the surface, and cannot be preserved[4].

It would, however, be rash to assume that a clause reserving minerals is indicative of a proper title[5]. Quite often the minerals had already been reserved higher up the feudal chain, the current reservation serving merely to make the position clear to the grantee and hence to prevent a claim in warrandice[6]. So for example if A, having *dominium utile* of both the minerals and the surface, feus to B reserving the minerals, and B later feus to C also reserving the minerals, the title to the minerals is in A and not in B. For this reason, among others, there will often be difficulty in disentangling minerals from a title which is otherwise superiority alone. In principle such a title will survive the appointed day in respect of the minerals, but in cases involving the Land Register it may be necessary to persuade the Keeper that the reservation of minerals was effective to create a title.

1   Para 8.2.
2   *Graham v Duke of Hamilton* (1871) 9 M (HL) 98. See further K G C Reid *The Law of Property in Scotland* (1996) para 212.
3   Abolition of Feudal Tenure etc (Scotland) Act 2000, s 2(1), discussed at para 1.9. See further Scottish Law Commission *Report on Abolition of the Feudal System* para 6.4; R Rennie *Minerals and the Law of Scotland* (2001) pp 13–14.
4   AFT(S)A 2000, s 2(2).
5   *Registration of Title Practice Book* (2nd edn, 2000) para 6.91.
6   In warrandice only the content of the dispositive clause is guaranteed. Hence a reservation of minerals has the effect of removing any guarantee. See K G C Reid *The Law of Property in Scotland* (1996) para 703.

Conditions

8.5   Under the general law the separate tenement of minerals includes, of its nature, certain rights and obligations. In particular there is a right to work the minerals, although not from the surface, as well as an obligation of support and a further obligation to pay damages in the event that support is withdrawn[1]. In practice these rights and obligations are usually repeated, often with modifications, in the clause reserving the minerals. If so they will appear, in Land Register cases, in the burdens section of the title sheet of the feu[2]. Nonetheless the conditions are not real burdens on the feu – an extrinsic qualification of a right which was granted – but are rather part of the very content of the reservation of minerals[3]. Thus they do not fall under the rules for preservation of real burdens set out in the preceding chapters. Nor indeed are they feudal in character, being obligations due by one estate of *dominium utile* to another estate of *dominium utile*, and hence unaffected by feudal abolition[4]. From the superior's point of view this means that conditions governing a reservation of minerals will survive the appointed day, with the reservation itself, without the need for further action. From the vassal's point of view it means that feudal abolition will not relieve the property of what may sometimes be onerous conditions.

The conditions just described should be distinguished from ordinary real burdens, contained, in practice, in a different part of the feu disposition or charter, but which nonetheless might benefit the reserved mineral estate. An example would be a burden requiring plans and specifications of any building within a certain distance of known workings or mine shafts to be approved of by the superior[5]. Such burdens will fall on feudal abolition in the usual way unless preserved, whether as neighbour burdens or in some other manner[6]. The 100-metres rule does not apply in relation to preservation for the benefit of a mineral estate[7].

1   See generally R Rennie *Minerals and the Law of Scotland* (2001) ch 4.
2   *Registration of Title Practice Book* (2nd edn, 2000) para 6.96.
3   K G C Reid *The Law of Property in Scotland* (1996) para 266. Apart from anything else, insofar as the conditions are obligations on the mineral estate, they do not fulfil the rules of constitution of real burdens which would require that they were contained in a conveyance of that estate.
4   Scottish Law Commission *Report on Abolition of the Feudal System* para 6.5; R Rennie *Minerals and the Law of Scotland* (2001) p 15.
5   R Rennie *Minerals and the Law of Scotland* (2001) p 15.
6   Abolition of Feudal Tenure etc (Scotland) Act 2000, s 17(1).
7   AFT(S)A 2000, s 18(7)(c), discussed at para 3.11.

SPORTING RIGHTS

Juridical nature

8.6   A right to fish for salmon, at least if exclusive in nature, is a (legal) separate tenement and so will survive feudal abolition of its own accord[1]. But other sporting rights which may be reserved to superiors – typically rights to take freshwater fish or game – are in a different position. Such rights, it is settled, are not separate tenements, whether legal or conventional[2]. Nor, probably, are they servitudes[3]. The most plausible approach is to treat them as real burdens, although the case law is sparse and no definitive choice could be said to have been made[4]. Insofar as they are real burdens, sporting rights are thought to be *non-exclusive* in character, so that the relevant right, while exercisable by the superior, can be exercised by the vassal as well[5]. Whether an *exclusive* right to game or fishing is a valid reservation at all, and if so on what ground, is open to question and may yet have to be litigated[6].

Sporting rights do not survive feudal abolition unless some step is taken for their preservation[7]. As originally enacted, the Abolition of Feudal Tenure etc (Scotland) Act 2000 allowed for the preservation of sporting rights as neighbour burdens under s 18[8]. This, however, presupposed both that the rights were real burdens, and also that the superior owned suitable land in the neighbourhood which could act as a benefited property. The Title Conditions (Scotland) Act 2003 has now liberalised the position. A new s 65A is inserted into the 2000 Act, allowing preservation of sporting rights as a separate tenement[9]. At the same time the use of s 18 is withdrawn, before the provision came into force[10].

1   Para 8.3.
2   *Earl of Galloway v Duke of Bedford* (1902) 4 F 851; *Beckett v Bisset* 1921 2 SLT 33.
3   D J Cusine and R R M Paisley *Servitudes and Rights of Way* (1998) paras 3.08, 3.63.
4   Scottish Law Commission *Report on Abolition of the Feudal System* para 6.32.
5   *Beckett v Bisset* 1921 2 SLT 33.

⁶   For a comprehensive review of the authorities, see Scottish Law Commission *Report on Abolition of the Feudal System* paras 6.25–6.29.
⁷   Abolition of Feudal Tenure etc (Scotland) Act 2000, s 54(1), amended by the Title Conditions (Scotland) Act 2003, s 114(6), Sch 13, para 11(a)(ii). Even though sporting rights are usually real burdens, they are not extinguished by s 17(1) because the definition of 'real burden' in s 49 is altered by the TC(S)A 2003, s 114(6), Sch 13, para 10(e) so as to exclude sporting rights.
⁸   The 100-metres rule, however, did not apply: see the AFT(S)A 2000, s 18(7)(b)(i).
⁹   TC(S)A 2003, s 114(5).
¹⁰   AFT(S)A 2000, s 49, amended by the TC(S)A 2003, s 114(6), Sch 13, para 10(e) (definition of 'real burden').

Preservation as separate tenements

8.7   Section 65A of the 2000 Act allows the preservation of sporting rights as separate tenements. The choice of juridical category is of interest. The underlying objective was to allow preservation without a benefited property. Normally that would have meant preservation as a member of the new category of personal real burdens[1]. But a sporting right comprises a right to enter and make use of the burdened property, and so, after the appointed day, could be constituted only as a servitude and not as a real burden[2]. One possible response would have been to create a second new category, of personal servitude, but that could hardly have been done without the enactment of rules as to creation, transfer, discharge and other matters, a degree of effort not justified by the small number of sporting rights which are likely to be preserved. In the end the choice was to use the existing device of separate tenements, and to treat sporting rights in much the same way as salmon fishings. A precedent of sorts can be found in the legislation which allows leases of freshwater fishing[3].

If preserved under s 65A, a sporting right becomes, on the appointed day, a conventional separate tenement. As such it commands its own title sheet in the Land Register[4], is immune from negative prescription[5], and is transferred by disposition and not by assignation[6]. In short it is 'land' and not a mere burden on the land of others. Unlike salmon fishings, however, a sporting right is neither regalian in character nor a legal separate tenement. One practical result is that in conveyances of the former feu it will be necessary to exclude the right – assumed otherwise to be conveyed – if a claim in warrandice is to be avoided[7]. A further difference is that sporting rights are not necessarily, or perhaps at all, exclusive in nature.

¹   For which see generally ch 4 above.
²   Title Conditions (Scotland) Act 2003, s 2.
³   See now the Salmon and Freshwater Fisheries (Consolidation) (Scotland) Act 2003, s 66. And see also *Palmer v Brown* 1989 SLT 128.
⁴   A rule which has to be teased out of the Land Registration (Scotland) Act 1979. Thus by s 5(1)(a) the Keeper completes first registration of an interest in land which is not a heritable security, liferent or incorporeal heritable right by making up a new title sheet for it. The definition of 'incorporeal heritable right' in s 28(1) then excludes both salmon fishings and now, by amendment (TC(S)A 2003, s 128(1), Sch 14, para 7(7)(a)), sporting rights. The effect is to bring sporting rights within s 5(1)(a).

⁵   As a 'real right of ownership in land': see the Prescription and Limitation (Scotland) Act 1973, Sch 3(a).

⁶   K G C Reid *The Law of Property in Scotland* (1996) para 208.

⁷   This is because warrandice warrants the land as described in the deed, and land is taken to include all conventional legal tenements (such as minerals) unless the contrary is stated. See K G C Reid *The Law of Property in Scotland* (1996) para 703. The difficulty disappears in the case of land registered in the Land Register, because the reference to the title number has the effect of incorporating any reservations.

Qualifying reservations

8.8   A reservation qualifies for preservation as a separate tenement if it is a right of fishing or game, and if it is enforceable by the superior[1]. As already mentioned, there is room for argument as to whether an exclusive right can be treated as so enforceable[2]. On the other hand, the Keeper is relieved of any duty to determine enforceability, and in practice notices will probably be accepted for registration even in respect of exclusive rights[3].

In principle s 65A of the 2000 Act can be used for salmon as well as for freshwater fishing, although in the normal case there would be nothing to be gained as salmon fishings are already separate tenements and so unaffected by feudal abolition. In perhaps only one case this would not be so. If A feus salmon fishings to B but reserves a non-exclusive right to fish, the right reserved to A, as the law currently stands, would be a real burden and not a separate tenement. Thus B's right would survive feudal abolition but A's would not unless preserved under s 65A[4].

Only a superior can activate s 65A. 'Superior' presumably includes over-superior. There is probably no requirement that the superior be infeft[5].

¹   Abolition of Feudal Tenure etc (Scotland) Act 2000, s 65A(1), (9).

²   Para 8.6.

³   AFT(S)A 2000, s 43(2)(a), as applied by s 65A(11). But the Keeper must still determine whether, in compliance with s 65A(1), the 'feudal estate of *dominium utile* of land is subject to sporting rights' in the first place, and it is arguable that this requirement might not be met in respect of an exclusive right. For a similar point in relation to real burdens, see para 11.15.

⁴   AFT(S)A 2000, s 54(1).

⁵   That may be implicit in s 65A(1). A difficulty is that the definition of 'superior' in s 49 of the 2000 Act (which allows uninfeft superiors, and, where necessary, provides a ranking) applies only for the purposes of Pt 4 (ss 17–49) of the 2000 Act and so does not extend to s 65A. It may be assumed, however, that a court would seek to apply the same rules to notices under s 65A as to notices under Pt 4.

Preparation and registration of notice

8.9   Sporting rights are preserved as separate tenements by the preparation, service, execution and registration by the superior, before the appointed day, of a notice in the form laid down in s 65A(2) of and Schedule 11A to the Abolition of Feudal Tenure Act. This provides for:

- the name and address of the superior;
- a conveyancing description of the feu[1];
- a description of the sporting rights, either in full or by reference to the deed by which they were reserved;
- details of that deed, including the date and place of registration;
- a list of any obligations on the superior which are the counterpart of the sporting rights[2];
- an account of the title to the superiority by reference to the Registers including, in a case where the superior is uninfeft, a list of the midcouples;
- details of service on the vassal.

This follows closely the form of the other notices under the 2000 Act[3]. Minor deviations are permitted[4]. Unlike other notices, it appears that the same notice may be used in respect of more than one feu (including the subdivided parts of a formerly single feu)[5].

Once completed, the notice is served, by post, together with a copy of the explanatory note provided in Schedule 11A[6]. The notice is then completed by entering the details of service[7], and by signature before a notary public, the superior having sworn or affirmed that to the best of his knowledge or belief all the information contained in the notice is true[8]. The notary must also sign[9]. Swearing or affirming a statement that is known to be false or is believed not to be true is an offence under the False Oaths (Scotland) Act 1933. Normally the oath must be given by the superior personally and not, for example, through a solicitor; but a company or other juristic person is represented by a person authorised to sign documents on its behalf[10], and a person without legal capacity by an appropriate person[11]. An oath outside Scotland may be given before any person duly authorised by the country in question to administer oaths or receive affirmations[12]. If the superiority is held as common or joint property, each superior must separately swear or affirm, and sign the notice[13].

The final step is to register the notice in the Land Register or Register of Sasines. No warrant of registration is needed in respect of registration in the Register of Sasines[14]. The fee for registration of notices is £25[15]. Neither stamp duty nor its successor, stamp duty land tax, is payable[16].

---

[1]   Or, at the superior's option, part only of the feu. See the Abolition of Feudal Tenure etc (Scotland) Act 2000, s 65A(2)(b). In that case only the part described will be subject to sporting rights after the appointed day.

[2]   For superiors' obligations, see paras 1.24, 1.25.

[3]   For styles of completed notices, see Appendices 3 and 4.

[4]   AFT(S)A 2000, s 65A(1).

[5]   This is because, perhaps due to an oversight, the AFT(S)A 2000, s 42(3) is not applied to s 65A notices (although s 65A(7) is a precise equivalent of s 42(2)).

[6]   AFT(S)A 2000, s 41(3), applied by s 65A(10). See further paras 11.7, 11.8.

[7]   AFT(S)A 2000, s 41(4), applied by s 65A(10).

8 AFT(S)A 2000, s 18(4), applied by s 65A(3).
9 AFT(S)A 2000, Sch 11A, note 6.
10 See generally the Requirements of Writing (Scotland) Act 1995, Sch 2.
11 AFT(S)A 2000, s 18(5), applied by s 65A(4).
12 AFT(S)A 2000, s 49 (definition of 'notary public').
13 This is because the obligations in s 65A are placed on 'the superior', and the singular includes the plural. For the position of trustees, see para 3.14.
14 AFT(S)A 2000, s 41(2).
15 Fees in the Registers of Scotland Order 1995, SI 1995/1945, Schedule, Pt III, para 2.
16 Paras 11.9–11.11.

Effect of preservation

8.10 Assuming the sporting rights to be still enforceable immediately before the appointed day, they are converted on that day into a separate tenement in land[1]. If the person who registered the notice has since disposed of the superiority, the separate tenement is held by his successor as superior. A person who was infeft in the superiority is, presumably, treated as having a completed title to the separate tenement. If the superiority was on the Land Register, it is arguable that the Keeper should give effect to the conversion by closing the superiority title sheet and opening a new title sheet for the sporting rights[2]. Otherwise a title sheet must await a transfer of the sporting rights for value, and first registration[3].

It is expressly, and probably unnecessarily, provided that no greater or more exclusive sporting rights are conferred than existed immediately before the appointed day[4]. The rights are subject to any counter-obligation which was formerly enforceable against the superior[5].

1 Abolition of Feudal Tenure etc (Scotland) Act 2000, s 65A(6).
2 Land Registration (Scotland) Act 1979, s 9(3B). The moratorium allowed by the AFT(S)A 2000, s 46 does not apply to sporting rights.
3 LR(S)A 1979, s 2(1).
4 AFT(S)A 2000, s 65A(6).
5 Whether included in the notice (as they ought to have been) or not. See the AFT(S)A 2000, s 65A(8), which also applies s 47 to the effect that, on extinction of the sporting rights, there is likewise extinction of any counter-obligations.

Chapter 9

Compensation (1): development value burdens

INTRODUCTION

The availability of compensation

9.1 Where, under the law in force before the appointed day, a real burden is varied or discharged by the Lands Tribunal, there is a power to award compensation to the superior or other benefited proprietor[1]. Compensation is available in respect of any substantial loss or disadvantage to the proprietor as benefited proprietor, or alternatively to make up for any discount in the price paid for the original grant due to the imposition of the burden. In applying the first of these grounds, the Lands Tribunal has refused to award compensation merely for loss of income from minutes of waiver[2], an approach which has been held to be compatible with the European Convention on Human Rights[3].

The Abolition of Feudal Tenure etc (Scotland) Act 2000 builds on the existing compensation regime. The first ground (substantial loss or disadvantage as benefited proprietor) presupposes ownership of land in the neighbourhood which would be materially affected by loss of the burden[4]. Under the 2000 Act a superior who owns such land is usually able to preserve the burden as a neighbour burden, by a notice under s 18 where the 100-metres rule is satisfied, and by an application to the Lands Tribunal under s 20 where it is not[5]. There is therefore no need for compensation[6].

The second ground (discounted price) is, however, preserved in the context of the reservation of development value. Thus compensation is available under the 2000 Act where a real burden reserved to the superior the development value of the land and where, in exchange, the price payable for the feu was significantly discounted or no price was paid at all[7]. The justification is plain enough. Assuming such a burden to be still enforceable, its extinction on the appointed day would upset the original arrangement between the parties. On the one hand, the release of development value would give a windfall benefit to the vassal which neither party had anticipated. And on the other, the superior would receive a poor return on the investment represented by the original discount. The compensation provisions for 'development value burdens' are designed to redress the balance between the parties.

1   Conveyancing and Feudal Reform (Scotland) Act 1970, s 1(4). The provision is re-enacted by the Title Conditions (Scotland) Act 2003, s 90(6), (7).
2   Sir Crispin Agnew of Lochnaw *Variation and Discharge of Land Obligations* (1999) paras 7–18 to 7–21.
3   *Strathclyde Joint Police Board v The Elderslie Estates Ltd* 2002 SLT (Lands Tr) 2.
4   Agnew of Lochnaw *Variation and Discharge of Land Obligations* para 7–11.
5   See ch 3 above.
6   Scottish Law Commission *Report on Abolition of the Feudal System* paras 5.58–5.60.
7   Abolition of Feudal Tenure etc (Scotland) Act 2000, s 33.

The procedure in outline

9.2   A right to claim compensation does not arise automatically but must be reserved by the superior by service and registration of a notice under s 33 of the Abolition of Feudal Tenure Act between the autumn of 2003, when the relevant provisions came into force, and the appointed day (28 November 2004)[1]. Typically, compensation is being claimed because the burden cannot be preserved; but if the burden is eligible for preservation as a neighbour burden or personal real burden, the superior must choose between preservation and compensation. He cannot have both. Thus the very presence on the register of a preservation notice prevents the registration, in respect of the same burden, of a notice under s 33[2].

A s 33 notice neither preserves the burden after feudal abolition nor, necessarily, confers a right to compensation. On the appointed day the burden is extinguished, at least in respect of the superior's rights[3]. But in one sense it lives on, as a kind of phantom, and must be complied with on pain of compensation. Thus for as long as the 'burden', on the hypothesis that it still exists, is complied with, there is no entitlement to compensation; and if the 'burden' is complied with for the first 20 years after the appointed day, no compensation is due at all. But in the event that the vassal – now owner – does something in the first 20 years which breaches the phantom burden, a right to compensation arises at once[4]. There can of course be no question of preventing the 'breach', the burden having been extinguished. The owner is free to do as he pleases. But, following a 'breach', the former superior has three years in which to serve a second notice, under s 35 of the 2000 Act, in which a claim for compensation is made. In the event of disagreement as to amount, the matter is referred to the Lands Tribunal[5].

It will be seen that compensation may involve up to three distinct stages. First, the superior must serve and register a s 33 notice before the appointed day. Secondly, and in the event of a 'breach' during the following 20 years, he must serve a s 35 notice within three years claiming compensation. And finally there may be a hearing by the Lands Tribunal to determine the amount due.

1   Paras 9.8–9.11. Late registration is, however, allowed if the initial application was wrongly refused. See the Abolition of Feudal Tenure etc (Scotland) Act 2000, s 45, discussed at para 11.16.

² AFT(S)A 2000, s 42(1). But an earlier notice can be discharged: see paras 11.5, 11.6.
³ AFT(S)A 2000, s 17(1). Others, however, may have enforcement rights, in which case the burden would survive in a question with them: see para 2.5.
⁴ AFT(S)A 2000, s 35(1), (2). See paras 9.12–9.14.
⁵ AFT(S)A 2000, s 44(2). See para 9.19.

Evaluation

9.3 As will shortly be seen[1], most burdens are not development value burdens and so do not qualify for compensation. But even if compensation is available in principle, it will be necessary to decide whether the trouble and expense of a s 33 notice, and potentially of further procedural steps, are worth the likely gain. Here three factors in particular may be relevant.

One is the probability of a breach of the phantom burden within the 20 years allowed for the purposes of compensation. In a settled residential area, for example, there may be little or no prospect of a breach which would release development value and so allow a claim. The planning position may be stable, and hostile to development. Conversely, a more fluid planning environment may, over a 20-year period, hold out the possibility of development gain.

A second factor is the age of the burden. Compensation cannot exceed the original discount in price, and it is not clear that an allowance will be made for inflation[2]. If not, even a substantial discount given in, say, 1914, would be worth little in the depreciated currency of today.

Finally, there is the question of entitlement to compensation arising in some other way. In a question between the original parties a grant of feu is contractual, and the contract is not disturbed by the abolition of the feudal system[3]. Even after the appointed day, therefore, conditions of the feu will remain perfectly valid and enforceable for as long as the original grantee remains in place. Quite often, indeed, the documentation is more elaborate. In a commercial sale, the quest for clawback is likely to involve a detailed minute of agreement, often secured by a standard security. If a real burden is used at all, it is merely as a third line of defence[4]. The fact that development gain can be recovered in some other way is usually fatal to a claim under the 2000 Act[5]. The former superior is expected to enforce the contract or the standard security[6]. Only if both prove unsatisfactory is a claim for compensation under s 35 likely to succeed.

¹ Paras 9.4–9.7.
² Para 9.17.
³ Abolition of Feudal Tenure etc (Scotland) Act 2000, s 75. See para 1.22.
⁴ Scottish Law Commission *Report on Real Burdens* paras 9.30–9.37.
⁵ AFT(S)A 2000, s 37(3)(a). See Scottish Law Commision *Report on Abolition of the Feudal System* para 5.47.
⁶ Under the original Bill produced by the Scottish Law Commission (cl 28(2)), the existence of a heritable security prevented even the registration of the initial notice.

QUALIFYING BURDENS

Three criteria

9.4   A burden potentially qualifies for compensation if three conditions are met[1]. The burden must reserve development value to the superior. Its imposition must have produced a substantial discount in price, or no price must have been paid. And the burden must be enforceable by the superior, both at the time of registration of the notice under s 33 of the 2000 Act and later, just before the appointed day. These conditions are considered more fully below. Their combined effect is to restrict compensation to 'development value burdens' – to burdens which reserve development value in exchange for a reduction in the price. Ordinary burdens of the kind routinely found in deeds of conditions or estate feus are not development value burdens in this sense[2]. An example of a transaction within the scope of the provisions is where land is given, or sold cheaply, for some community purpose such as a village hall, and a real burden is added to police the use, the superior being willing to feu the land at that price only for that use. In the event that, later, the acquirers wish to develop the land – for housing, say, or for some commercial purpose – they must negotiate a minute of waiver with the superior, and in practice at a premium which represents the development value[3].

[1]   Abolition of Feudal Tenure etc (Scotland) Act 2000, s 33(1).
[2]   Scottish Law Commission *Report on Abolition of the Feudal System* para 5.21.
[3]   Scottish Law Commission *Report on Abolition of the Feudal System* paras 5.14–5.18. And see the explanatory note in the AFT(S)A 2000, Sch 9.

The first criterion: reservation of development value

9.5   A burden qualifies for compensation, on extinction, only if it reserved to the superior the benefit, wholly or in part, of any development value of the land[1]. By 'development value' is meant any significant increase in value arising from the land becoming free to be used in some way not permitted under the grant in feu[2]. Reservation of development value might be done directly, as where the burden is a right of redemption, at a modest price, in the event that the land ceases to be used for a stipulated purpose[3]. More commonly, it is done indirectly, by confining permitted use within a narrow compass and so ensuring that further development requires a waiver from the superior. The statutory wording suggests an objective test, but in most cases the reservation of development value is likely to have been intentional and acknowledged, on both sides. If the land has no development potential, there can, naturally, be no question of a development value burden. The fact that, since 1970, burdens can be varied or discharged by the Lands Tribunal makes them less secure and, accordingly, less likely to be used as the principal means of reserving development value[4].

The legislation envisages a single burden, which stands out from other, 'ordinary' burdens in the title, and a superior who claims that more than one burden qualifies as a development value burden must, in a s 33 notice, account separately for each[5].

1. Abolition of Feudal Tenure etc (Scotland) Act 2000, s 33(1)(a).
2. AFT(S)A 2000, s 33(5).
3. If, however, the price is so small as to be 'elusory', the redemption may not be enforceable as a real burden. See *McElroy v Duke of Argyll* (1902) 4 F 885 at 889 per Lord Kyllachy.
4. Scottish Law Commission *Report on Abolition of the Feudal System* para 5.19. On the other hand, compensation might be awarded under the Conveyancing and Feudal Reform (Scotland) Act 1970, s 1(4).
5. AFT(S)A 2000, Sch 9, notes 3, 4 and 7.

The second criterion: donation or discounted price

9.6   The land must have been donated, or sold at a discounted price[1]. The discount can be seen as the vassal's 'price' for the development gain, or alternatively the development gain as a second instalment of the sale price due to the superior.

In feudal law an out-and-out donation means a grant in blench tenure[2]. In a case involving discount rather than donation, the discount must be attributable to the development value burden, so that, but for the burden, a higher price would have been paid. 'Price' for this purpose means feuduty, grassum or both. The effect of the burden must have been that the price was 'significantly lower'. Only the burden is of relevance. Whether, in a more general sense, account was taken of development potential in fixing the price is a different question and not one which requires to be answered for the purposes of s 33 of the 2000 Act.

The amount of discount must be quantified in the s 33 notice, at least 'to the best of the superior's knowledge and belief'[3]. Often the task will be far from straightforward[4]. If the feu is elderly, an investigation of historical prices seems unavoidable. The simplest approach may be to compare the feu with other feus granted by the same superior at the same time. An actual figure must be given in the notice and, if more than one development value burden is claimed, a separate figure for each burden[5]. If the reduction was in feuduty rather than in grassum, the appropriate figure is arrived at by capitalising the annual discount[6]. This can be done conveniently and, one imagines, safely by reference to the current price of two and one half per cent Consolidated Stock[7].

Naturally the figure given in the s 33 notice must be arrived at with care. Since it marks the outer limit of the compensation which the superior is likely to receive[8], it should not be set too low. But if set too high it may provoke a challenge at the time when compensation comes to be claimed. Further, the superior is required to swear or affirm that the information in the notice is true, and an inflated figure might attract penalties under the False Oaths (Scotland) Act 1933[9].

1. Abolition of Feudal Tenure etc (Scotland) Act 2000, s 33(1)(b).
2. In blench tenure only a nominal *reddendo* is due.
3. AFT(S)A 2000, s 33(2)(e).

4   Sir Crispin Agnew of Lochnaw *Variation and Discharge of Land Obligations* (1999) para 7–22 ('often a difficult, if not impossible, task').

5   AFT(S)A 2000, Sch 9, note 7.

6   *Manz v Butter's Trs* 1973 SLT (Lands Tr) 2; *Gorrie and Banks Ltd v Musselburgh Town Council* 1974 SLT (Lands Tr) 5.

7   Sir Crispin Agnew of Lochnaw *Variation and Discharge of Land Obligations* (1999) para 7–25. This is the basis of capitalisation used elsewhere in the 2000 Act. See AFT(S)A 2000, s 9(1).

8   AFT(S)A 2000, s 37(2), discussed at para 9.17 below. But the figure may possibly be adjusted for inflation.

9   AFT(S)A 2000, s 33(3).

The third criterion: current enforceability

9.7   As with other notices under the Abolition of Feudal Tenure Act, an essential prerequisite is that the burden is valid[1], and enforceable by the superior. Enforceability is required both at the time when the s 33 notice is served and registered, and also immediately before the appointed day itself[2]. If, between these two dates, the superiority is disponed, the requirement is that the burden be enforceable by the new superior and not by the (former) superior in whose favour compensation was reserved[3].

Not all conditions directed at development value will be valid as real burdens. In particular, an obligation to pay money if the feu is put to a particular use is likely to fail for lack of praedial benefit[4]. A condition should restrict use rather than require the payment of money. Assuming the burden to be valid, it is enforceable only if the superior has the requisite interest. It is arguable that interest requires the superior to own other land which takes benefit from the burden, but the position is uncertain[5].

1   Para 2.12.

2   Abolition of Feudal Tenure etc (Scotland) Act 2000, ss 33(1)(a), 35(2)(a).

3   AFT(S)A 2000, s 35(1), (2) contrasts 'any person who has ... a reserved right to claim compensation' with 'the superior'.

4   K G C Reid *The Law of Property in Scotland* (1996) para 391. See Scottish Law Commission *Report on Abolition of the Feudal System* para 5.23. The praedial rule is re-enacted by the Title Conditions (Scotland) Act 2003, s 3(1), (2). Another possible ground of objection, for monetary obligations, is that the amount due is not to be found within the four corners of the deed: see *Tailors of Aberdeen v Coutts* (1840) 1 Rob 296 at 340 per Lord Brougham.

5   Para 4.7.

RESERVING A CLAIM: SECTION 33 NOTICE

Title

9.8   Only the superior can reserve a claim to compensation[1]. Infeftment is not required, and if there is more than one uninfeft superior, or both an infeft and uninfeft superior, it is the last to acquire the right who is able to register a s 33 notice[2]. 'Superior' includes oversuperior, but a superior can only register in respect of a burden which he is entitled to enforce[3].

1   Abolition of Feudal Tenure etc (Scotland) Act 2000, s 33(1).
2   AFT(S)A 2000, s 49.
3   Para 3.4.

Preparation and registration of notice

9.9   The right to claim compensation is reserved by service, execution and registration, before the appointed day, of a notice in the form set out in Schedule 9 to the 2000 Act. The notice gives warning to a purchaser or other person coming to deal with the land that the burden will, in some sense, continue after the appointed day, and that a 'breach' will attract a claim for compensation.

The statutory form of notice provides for[1]:

- the name and address of the superior;
- a conveyancing description of the feu;
- the terms of the development value burden, either in full or by reference to the deed by which it was imposed;
- details of that deed, including the date and place of registration;
- a statement that the burden reserves development value, together with any supporting information;
- an account of the title to the superiority by reference to the Registers including, in a case where the superior is uninfeft, a list of the midcouples;
- a statement of the amount by which the consideration was reduced because of the imposition of the burden[2];
- details of service on the vassal.

A style of completed notice is set out in Appendix 5 to this book. Minor deviations are permitted[3].

Usually there will be only one development value burden, but the same notice can be used for two or more such burdens provided they are numbered and listed separately[4]. A separate notice is needed for each feu[5]. Once completed, the notice is served, by post, together with a copy of the explanatory note provided in Schedule 9[6]. The notice is then completed by entering the details of service[7], and by signature before a notary public, the superior having sworn or affirmed that to the best of his knowledge or belief all the information contained in the notice is true[8]. The notary must also sign[9]. Swearing or affirming a statement that is known to be false or is believed not to be true is an offence under the False Oaths (Scotland) Act 1933. Normally the oath must be given by the superior personally and not, for example, through a solicitor; but a company or other juristic person is represented by a person authorised to sign documents on its behalf[10], and a person without legal capacity by an appropriate person[11]. An oath outside Scotland may be given before any person duly authorised by the country in question to administer oaths or receive affirmations[12]. If the superiority is held as common or joint property, each superior must separately swear or affirm, and sign the notice[13].

After signature the process is completed by registration in the Land Register or Register of Sasines. No warrant of registration is needed in respect of registration in the Register of Sasines[14]. The registration fee is £25[15]. No stamp duty or stamp duty land tax is payable[16].

[1]   Abolition of Feudal Tenure etc (Scotland) Act 2000, s 33(2), Sch 9.
[2]   See para 9.6 above.
[3]   AFT(S)A 2000, s 33(1).
[4]   AFT(S)A 2000, s 42(4)(a), Sch 9, note 3.
[5]   AFT(S)A 2000, s 42(3). Where the land originally feued has been divided and is in separate ownership, each separate part is treated as a separate feu for this purpose: see s 42(2).
[6]   For service, see further paras 11.7, 11.8.
[7]   AFT(S)A 2000, s 41(4).
[8]   AFT(S)A 2000, s 33(3).
[9]   AFT(S)A 2000, Sch 9, note 9.
[10]   See generally the Requirements of Writing (Scotland) Act 1995, Sch 2.
[11]   AFT(S)A 2000, s 33(4).
[12]   AFT(S)A 2000, s 49 (definition of 'notary public').
[13]   This is because the obligations in s 33 are placed on 'the superior', and the singular includes the plural. For the position of trustees, see para 3.14.
[14]   AFT(S)A 2000, s 41(2).
[15]   Fees in the Registers of Scotland Order 1995, SI 1995/1945, Schedule, Pt III, para 2.
[16]   Paras 11.9–11.11.

Removal of notice

9.10   Since a s 33 notice neither preserves the burden in question nor, of itself, entitles anyone to compensation, the vassal, or any successor of the vassal as owner, may be content to leave matters as they are. The notice will expire automatically on 28 November 2024, at the end of the 20-year period[1]. If, in the meantime, there is no development in a manner which would 'breach' the 'burden', the notice can in practice be disregarded. The owner is in much the same position as if the Lands Tribunal had already discharged the burden but the question of compensation remained open. That is plainly an advance on the position before the appointed day.

The situation may not always seem so favourable, however. Development may in fact be in contemplation. Or a sale may be in prospect which is at risk from the existence of the notice. The owner's thoughts may then turn to the removal of the notice. Here there are two possibilities. One is to approach the former superior for a restriction or discharge of the notice – in effect for a minute of waiver of a phantom burden. It may be assumed that, as with minutes of waiver proper, a charge will be made. A statutory form of discharge is provided[2]. The other option is to challenge the notice on its merits in the Lands Tribunal[3]. For example, it might be possible to show that the burden was unenforceable all along, that no discount had ever been given, or that the notice failed for some other reason, whether substantive or procedural. The burden of proving any disputed question of fact lies with the former superior[4]. In particular it would be for the superior to demonstrate the existence and the extent of the discount claimed by the notice.

[1]   Abolition of Feudal Tenure etc (Scotland) Act 2000, s 35(2)(c)(ii).
[2]   AFT(S)A 2000, s 40, Sch 11. See para 11.6 for a style.
[3]   AFT(S)A 2000, s 44(1). See para 11.19. In a case where the notice was obviously inept, the Keeper might possibly be persuaded, in Land Register cases, to rectify the Register by deleting the notice. See para 11.18.
[4]   AFT(S)A 2000, s 44(3).

Assignation

9.11   Once a s 33 notice is registered, the right to claim compensation is severed from the superiority itself. It is then no more than a contingent, and personal, debt, with a value in the market place. As such it is freely assignable[1]. This means that if the superiority is sold, the right to compensation would not pass with it in the absence of express assignation. And the right is of course unaffected by the extinction of the superiority on the appointed day.

A style of assignation is provided by the 2000 Act[2]:

Style of assignation of s 33 notice

I, [AB], (*designation*), in consideration of (*price*)[3] paid to me by CD, (*designation*), hereby assign to the said CD the right to claim compensation reserved by a notice dated (*date*) and registered in the Land Register of Scotland on (*date*) against the subjects in title number (*number*) [*or* recorded in the Register of Sasines for (*county*) on (*date*) under (*fiche and frame*)]: IN WITNESS WHEREOF

Additional wording is needed where, as permitted[4], the assignation is in respect of a percentage only of any future claim[5]. The assignation is completed by registration, although an assignee can assign in turn without first completing title provided that a clause of deduction of title is included in the assignation[6]. A warrant of registration is needed for registration in the Register of Sasines up to the appointed day but not thereafter[7].

[1]   Abolition of Feudal Tenure etc (Scotland) Act 2000, s 34. The Scottish Law Commission had recommended that it should not be assignable, '[i]n order to discourage the development of a market in reserved claims, which might in turn encourage the registration of false or speculative notices'. See *Report on Abolition of the Feudal System* para 5.35.

2   AFT(S)A 2000, s 40, Sch 11.
3   The statutory style does not refer to consideration, but in practice a price will often be payable.
4   AFT(S)A 2000, s 40(a).
5   The following additional words are needed: 'but only to the extent of (*percentage*) of each claim which may come to be made'.
6   AFT(S)A 2000, Sch 11.
7   That is the normal rule for deeds: see the Titles to Land Consolidation (Scotland) Act 1868, s 141 (repealed on the appointed day by the AFT(S)A 2000, s 76, Sch 13) for the position before the appointed day, and the AFT(S)A 2000, s 5 for the position thereafter. Section 41(2), which exempts certain notices from warrants of registration even before the appointed day, applies to s 33 notices but not to their assignation.

MAKING A CLAIM: SECTION 35 NOTICE

Extinction of superior's rights

9.12   Since compensation is paid for loss of enforcement rights, a necessary pre-condition of any claim is that the superior's right to enforce should have been duly extinguished[1]. No claim, therefore, can be made before the appointed day[2]. Nor, under the Abolition of Feudal Tenure Act, could a claim be made if the superior's right survived that day[3]. In practice, however, such survival seems improbable, or even impossible. Certainly the superior's right could not have been reallotted to other property, or preserved in the form of a personal real burden, because, like compensation itself, each requires the registration of a notice, and two notices in respect of the same burden and feu are not permitted under the 2000 Act[4]. In a small number of cases a superior might retain, or obtain, enforcement rights on some other basis. For example, the superior might happen to own, or acquire, neighbouring property which carried an independent right of enforcement in respect of the same real burden; or he might own a 'related property' on which enforcement rights are conferred by s 53 of the Title Conditions (Scotland) Act 2003. But his right to enforce would then be as a neighbour and not as feudal superior. Nor, by contrast with reallotment, could the new right be said to have derived from the old. Rather the right would have an independent source not attributable to the superior's former position under the feudal system.

What is true of the former superior is even more obviously true of an assignee of the right reserved by a s 33 notice. An assignee is merely a creditor in a commercial debt. Ownership of a benefited property in respect of the same burden would be both coincidental and irrelevant.

1   If the superior was the only enforcer, that would mean the extinction of the burden as a whole.
2   Abolition of Feudal Tenure etc (Scotland) Act 2000, s 17(1).
3   AFT(S)A 2000, s 35(2)(b).
4   AFT(S)A 2000, s 42(1), discussed at paras 11.3–11.6.

'Breach' of the 'burden'

9.13   The right reserved by a s 33 notice is contingent in nature, the contingency being that, during the period which ends on 28 November 2024, there is an occurrence which, but for the burden becoming unenforceable on the appointed day, would be a breach of the burden[1]. In other words, the trigger for compensation is that the phantom 'burden' is 'breached'[2]. The 'breach' need not be by the *owner* of the 'burdened' property, for negative burdens[3] bind every user of the property[4]. So if the offending shopping centre is built by a tenant and not by the landlord, the 'burden' is 'breached' all the same, and compensation is due. The debt, however, is then that of the landlord[5], a factor which may need to be taken into account in the granting of leases.

If the breach occurred before the appointed day and not after, there is usually no right to compensation. The position indeed is largely self-regulating. Thus if the breach were of an affirmative burden[6], either the superior would enforce or he would not enforce. In the first case the breach is cured, or compensated by an award of damages, in the second the superior does not deserve another chance. The position is much the same in respect of negative burdens. An indolent superior will do nothing, and deserves neither sympathy nor compensation. An active superior will interdict the breach, putting an end to it for the time being. The interdict, of course, falls on the appointed day, leaving open the possibility of a new 'breach' in the future[7]; but any new 'breach' would, by definition, be after the appointed day and so would attract a claim for compensation under s 35.

A breach might occur too close to the appointed day to leave the superior with a proper chance of enforcement. For that reason, s 35 allows compensation to be claimed for breaches occurring up to five years before the appointed day[8]. Thus the total period in respect of which claims may be made begins on 28 November 1999 and ends on 27 November 2024.

[1]   The reasons for selecting a 20-year period are given in Scottish Law Commission *Report on Abolition of the Feudal System* para 5.37.
[2]   Abolition of Feudal Tenure etc (Scotland) Act 2000, s 35(2)(c)(ii).
[3]   Ie burdens in the form of restrictions: see the Title Conditions (Scotland) Act 2003, s 2(1)(b), (2)(b).
[4]   TC(S)A 2003, s 9(2).
[5]   Para 9.14.
[6]   Ie burdens in the form of an obligation to do something: see TC(S)A 2003, s 2(1)(a), (2)(a).
[7]   AFT(S)A 2000, s 17(2)(c), discussed at para 2.13.
[8]   AFT(S)A 2000, s 35(2)(c)(i).

Making a claim

9.14   If a 'burden' is 'breached' a claim for compensation may be made at once, and must be made not later than three years after the 'breach' or, in the case of a breach occurring before the appointed day, three years after that day[1]. For this purpose a continuing 'breach', such as an unauthorised use, is taken to occur on the day when it first happens[2]. A claim for compensation is also subject to the long negative prescription of 20 years[3].

A claim is made by notice duly served on the owner[4]. Service is discussed in chapter 12. No form of notice is provided by the legislation, but it is necessary to specify the amount claimed and refer to the duty of disclosure mentioned below[5]. A suggested style of notice is given in Appendix 5 to this book.

The person entitled to claim compensation is the superior who registered the s 33 notice, or any assignee or successor of that person[6]. Since the Abolition of Feudal Tenure Act provides that a right to compensation is assigned 'by execution *and registration* of an assignation'[7], it would appear to follow that title must be completed by registration before an assignee is in a position to make a claim[8]. A prudent debtor will check the claimant's title before risking payment to the wrong person.

The debtor in the claim is the owner of the land (ie the former feu) at the time when the 'burden' was first 'breached'[9]. Liability is attracted even without completion of title, and if more than one person holds an incomplete title, the relevant 'owner' is the most recent to have acquired[10]. A statutory duty of disclosure assists in identifying the correct person[11]. If the land is owned as common property, each co-owner is jointly and severally liable and may be pursued for the full amount, subject to a right of relief from the other co-owners in proportion to the size of the *pro indiviso* share[12]. The s 35 notice must probably be served on each co-owner separately[13]. The rules may possibly be the same where, after registration of the s 33 notice, the land has come to be divided with each part in separate ownership; but no provision is made in the 2000 Act.

[1]   Abolition of Feudal Tenure etc (Scotland) Act 2000, s 35(4).
[2]   AFT(S)A 2000, s 35(5).
[3]   Prescription and Limitation (Scotland) Act 1973, s 7. The 20-year period runs from the date when the obligation first becomes enforceable – in the present case, the date of the 'breach' and not of the service of the s 35 notice: see AFT(S)A 2000, s 35(2). Compensation in respect of feuduty prescribes after only five years: see para 10.9.
[4]   AFT(S)A 2000, s 35(3).
[5]   AFT(S)A 2000, s 38.
[6]   AFT(S)A 2000, s 35(1).
[7]   AFT(S)A 2000, s 40.
[8]   A possible counter-argument is that an assignee can assign the claim in turn without first completing title. See para 9.11.
[9]   AFT(S)A 2000, ss 35(1), 39(1).
[10] AFT(S)A 2000, s 39(1). The rule is the same where compensation is being claimed in respect of feuduty. See para 10.10.
[11] AFT(S)A 2000, s 38, discussed at para 12.4.
[12] AFT(S)A 2000, s 39(2).
[13] Para 12.1. The same rule may possibly apply in the case of the s 33 notice: see para 11.7.

AMOUNT OF COMPENSATION

The compensation formula

9.15   The amount payable by way of compensation is the lesser of (i) the gain to the owner from the release of development value resulting from the 'breach' and (ii) the loss to the former superior as represented by the discount originally given in return for the imposition of the burden. But (iii) in arriving at a figure it is necessary to take into account any alternative entitlement to recover compensation[1]. Each of these factors is considered separately below.

1   Abolition of Feudal Tenure etc (Scotland) Act 2000, s 37. And see further Scottish Law Commission *Report on Abolition of the Feudal System* paras 5.41–5.47.

Owner's gain: development value

9.16   For the purposes of calculating the owner's gain it is assumed (i) that the burden continued to affect the former feu after the appointed day and (ii) that it has now been modified to the extent (but only to the extent) of permitting the activity which constituted the 'breach'. The gain is then the difference between the value of the land if it were still subject to the original burden and its (increased) value if it were subject to the burden as now notionally modified[1]. This difference is referred to in the legislation as the 'development value'[2]. In order for compensation to be due at all, the increase in value requires to be 'significant'[3].

In practice the size of any increase may depend on whether the 'burden' was the only remaining impediment to development. There may often be others. For example, the same burden, extinguished in a question with the superior, may still be enforceable by neighbours[4]; or other real burdens may exist which prevent the development; or there may be a s 75 agreement[5]; or planning permission may yet be needed. Only when the last impediment is removed will the full development value be released. It is in the owner's interests to ensure, so far as possible, that the burden, notionally modified by the 'breach', is not the last, for development value is measured 'at the time of the breach'[6]. That suggests that it may be advantageous to begin construction work before all of the consents are in place.

It need hardly be added that, in calculating the gain, no account is taken of the value of any buildings the erection of which may follow the 'breach'. The question to be determined is the value of the unimproved land, and any increase in that value following the notional modification of the burden.

1   Abolition of Feudal Tenure etc (Scotland) Act 2000, s 37(1), read with s 33(5).
2   AFT(S)A 2000, s 37(1).
3   AFT(S)A 2000, s 33(5).
4   Para 2.5.
5   Ie an agreement under the Town and Country Planning (Scotland) Act 1997, s 75.
6   AFT(S)A 2000, s 37(1).

Superior's loss: value of the discount

9.17   The former superior's loss is the discount which formed the original 'price' for the burden[1]. For, now that the 'burden' is 'modified', the 'price' turns out to have been too generous. Hence the loss. In arriving at the figure for the superior's loss, the Abolition of Feudal Tenure Act employs a formula already used by the Lands Tribunal for calculating compensation for variation and discharge of burdens[2]. Thus the loss is[3]

> such sum as will make up for any effect which the burden produced, at the time when it was imposed, in reducing the consideration then paid or made payable for the feu.

Where the discount was in the feuduty rather than in the grassum (price), the approach taken by the Lands Tribunal is to capitalise the lost income stream at current rates based on the price of two and a half per cent Consolidated Stock[4]. So, for example, if the discount in a Victorian feu was £5 and the feuduty factor (for capitalisation) is 20 at the time of the 'breach', the loss would be calculated as £100. The figure is always likely to be small. The Lands Tribunal has rejected the view that the discount should be adjusted for inflation before the capitalisation formula is applied[5]. This acknowledges the fact that feuduty itself is a poor hedge against inflation, and that to build in an inflationary element now would be to give the superior more than he would have been entitled to if the discount had never been offered. For if the £5 had, after all, been included in the original feuduty, the sum due in 2004, on the eve of feudal abolition, would still have been only £5 and it would be capitalised on the appointed day without any adjustment for inflation.

It remains an open question whether the position is different, or the same, where the discount is in the grassum[6]. There is no reported case in which depreciation was at issue. In arguing that the grassum should not be adjusted for inflation, the Scottish Law Commission pointed out that the older the burden, the more benefit the superior has had already, and hence the less the need for compensation[7]. That view is indeed the basis of the 'sunset rule', introduced by the Title Conditions (Scotland) Act 2003, which allows the ready removal of burdens which are more than 100 years old[8]. The Commission also doubted whether, in a case where the superiority had changed hands, its value was affected by the existence of the burden.

The superior's loss provides an absolute ceiling for claims under the 2000 Act[9]. Thus if there is a series of 'breaches' of the burden, so that more than one claim is made, the total compensation payable on all claims cannot exceed the loss as calculated in the manner just described.

[1]   For which see para 9.6.
[2]   Conveyancing and Feudal Reform (Scotland) Act 1970, s 1(4)(ii), replaced, after the appointed day, by the Title Conditions (Scotland) Act 2003, s 90(7)(b).
[3]   Abolition of Feudal Tenure etc (Scotland) Act 2000, s 37(2).
[4]   *Gorrie and Banks Ltd v Musselburgh Town Council* 1974 SLT (Lands Tr) 5.

5   *Manz v Butter's Trs* 1973 SLT (Lands Tr) 2.
6   Sir Crispin Agnew of Lochnaw *Variation and Discharge of Land Obligations* (1999) para 7–26.
7   Scottish Law Commission *Report on Abolition of the Feudal System* para 5.46. As was said in *Manz v Butter's Trs* 1973 SLT (Lands Tr) 2 at 5, until discharge 'the benefited proprietor has had the advantage of the land obligation'.
8   TC(S)A 2003, ss 20–24, discussed briefly at para 7.22.
9   AFT(S)A 2000, s 37(2).

Other entitlement to compensation

9.18   In arriving at the final amount due, any other entitlement of the former superior to compensation is to be 'taken into account'[1]. Normally this means deducted from the total, for the principle is that the superior is not to be paid twice[2]. But where a claim is speculative or uncertain, it falls to be valued accordingly and will be deducted from the total only at a reduced valuation. Examples of claims otherwise arising include contractual claims and claims secured by a standard security[3].

An assignee can be met by the same defences as the cedent: *assignatus utitur jure auctoris*[4]. It follows that any alternative claim available to the former superior and which, in a question with him, would have fallen to be deducted from the statutory compensation, falls to be deducted also in a question with any assignee who derives right from the former superior[5].

1   Abolition of Feudal Tenure etc (Scotland) Act 2000, s 37(3)(a).
2   Scottish Law Commission *Report on Abolition of the Feudal System* para 5.47.
3   Para 9.3.
4   K G C Reid *The Law of Property in Scotland* (1996) para 660.
5   The position is, indeed, put beyond doubt by the AFT(S)A 2000, s 37(3)(b).

Recourse to Lands Tribunal

9.19   Unless the owner of the land accepts the amount requested, the service of a notice under s 35 of the 2000 Act is likely to lead to a period of negotiation. Either party may refer the matter to the Lands Tribunal, where the burden of proof is then on the former superior (or his assignee)[1].

1   Abolition of Feudal Tenure etc (Scotland) Act 2000, s 44.

Chapter 10

Compensation (2): feuduty

INTRODUCTION

Nature of feuduty

10.1 Feuduty is the *reddendo* (periodical payment) due by a vassal to a superior under feu farm tenure, the standard tenure of modern feudalism[1]. Originally feuduty could be payable in kind rather than in money, but over time such feuduties were converted into monetary payments[2]. Sometimes the sums due were substantial[3]. In the nineteenth century, feuduty might be the only consideration for a feu, relieving the vassal of the need to borrow money for a capital payment (grassum), or there might be a combination of a modest grassum and a sizeable feuduty. Superiorities were freely traded on account of the income from feuduty and were considered safe and profitable investments. The Church of Scotland, for example, purchased large numbers of superiorities from the 1850s onwards. By 1914 some £1.18 million (£65 million in current prices) had been invested in this way by the Church, generating an annual income from feuduty of £40,000 (over £2 million in current prices)[4].

In the twentieth century the trend was for the feuduty to become smaller and the grassum larger, and the practice of imposing feuduty was discontinued altogether by statute with effect from 1 September 1974[5]. Such feuduties as remain today are usually small, whether they are recent and hence small from the start, or elderly and small due to the effects of inflation. Most feuduties are under £10 per annum, and many are under £5. Traditionally feuduty is paid in two equal instalments, on Whitsunday (28 May) and Martinmas (28 November).

[1] For feuduty, see generally J M Halliday *Conveyancing Law and Practice* vol 2 (2nd edn, 1997) paras 32–17 to 32–63; W M Gordon *Scottish Land Law* (2nd edn, 1999) paras 22–03 to 22–28.
[2] Conveyancing (Scotland) Act 1874, s 20; Conveyancing (Scotland) Act 1924, s 12.
[3] See generally R Rodger *The Transformation of Edinburgh: Land, Property and Trust in the Nineteenth Century* (2001) ch 3.
[4] R Rodger *The Transformation of Edinburgh* pp 127–141.
[5] Land Tenure Reform (Scotland) Act 1974, ss 1, 24(2).

Feuduty and over-feuduty

10.2   Feuduty is payable throughout the feudal chain. Thus the payment made by a vassal to his superior should, in theory, be matched by a payment, of a smaller amount, by the superior to *his* superior; and so on further up the feudal pyramid. From the viewpoint of the proprietor of the *dominium utile*, the superior's superior is known as the 'over-superior', and the feuduty payable to him as 'over-feuduty'. Although firm evidence is lacking, it seems that over-feuduty has often ceased to be paid in modern times. As a matter of law, however, there is little difference between feuduty and over-feuduty. Both are 'rents' for the feu, recurrent personal debts by the relevant vassal to the relevant superior; and, as will be seen, both are subject to identical rules in relation to extinction and compensation.

Cumulo feuduty and allocated feuduty

10.3   *Cumulo* feuduty arises if a feu is divided, and the division proceeds by substitution (ie by ordinary disposition) as opposed to by subinfeudation[1]. Thus suppose that a one-hectare feu is divided into five plots and each plot sold by ordinary disposition. The result, after sale, is that one vassal is replaced by five. And on the basis that the superior is not to be prejudiced by subdivision, the rule is that the five vassals are jointly and severally liable for the whole feuduty. Thus the feuduty can be claimed from any one vassal, leaving that person with the task of recovering a *pro rata* share from the others. A feuduty which may be recovered in this way is known as a *cumulo* feuduty. The result is so unwelcome to vassals that the practice grew up of informal apportionment. Thus if the *cumulo* feuduty was £20, each vassal would pay £4. Sometimes payment was made directly to the superior, but quite commonly the sums were collected first and paid as a single amount. This latter practice was particularly common in cases where a tenement was subject to a *cumulo* feuduty, the collection being carried out by the tenement manager or factor.

Over time an informal apportionment might be formalised. The *cumulo* feuduty is then said to have been 'allocated' among the subdivided parts. The effect of allocation is that each part is treated as a separate feu. Thus whereas under a *cumulo* feuduty the superior can recover the full £20 from any vassal, once the *cumulo* is allocated the superior must pursue each vassal separately for individual payments of £4, and no vassal has liability for the share of his neighbour. Naturally, the result of allocation is not always as evenly distributed as this example suggests. If one part of the feu is larger, and more valuable, than the others, the tendency will be to allocate to it a larger share of the total. Sometimes, indeed, the potential allocations are given in the dispositions which effected the initial division.

Until 1970 allocation required the agreement of the superior, who would usually require that the feuduty be increased ('augmented') to make up for the inconvenience of individual collection[2]. Under the Conveyancing and Feudal Reform (Scotland) Act 1970 it is possible for a vassal to obtain allocation merely by service of a notice on the superior, provided that there has already been an informal apportionment[3]. Allocation affects only the part owned by the vassal, and the unallocated *cumulo* remains in respect of the rest of the feu[4]. If, however, the superior challenges the amount allocated, as he is entitled to do, the Lands Tribunal will then allocate the *cumulo* on the entire feu[5].

[1]   For statutory definitions, see Conveyancing and Feudal Reform (Scotland) Act 1970, s 3(2); AFT(S)A 2000, s 16(2).
[2]   For procedure, see Conveyancing (Scotland) Act 1874, s 8 and Conveyancing (Scotland) Act 1924, s 13.
[3]   Conveyancing and Feudal Reform (Scotland) Act 1970, s 3.
[4]   CFR(S)A 1970, s 5(1).
[5]   CFR(S)A 1970, s 4.

EXTINCTION

The 1974 Act

10.4   The Land Tenure Reform (Scotland) Act 1974 came into force on 1 September 1974[1]. The first time that a feu is sold on or after that date, the feuduty is automatically extinguished ('redeemed')[2]. Compensation ('redemption money') is payable by the seller, but extinction occurs whether it is paid or not. In addition, a vassal is able to redeem feuduty at other times[3]. The rules apply to over-feuduties as they apply to feuduties[4]. Since most feus have been sold at least once since 1974, the result is that most feuduties have now been extinguished. However, unallocated *cumulos* are, for practical reasons, excluded from the legislation[5], and most feuduties surviving today probably fall into that category. Even so, fewer than 10% of all properties are thought to be subject to feuduty[6].

In a case where the superior could not be identified the practice grew up of putting the redemption money on deposit receipt in the name of the seller's and buyer's agents, against the possibility that the superior might reappear. Only once the debt had prescribed, after 20 years, could the money be released and returned to the seller[7]. The Abolition of Feudal Tenure etc (Scotland) Act 2000 reduces the period of prescription to five years, with retrospective effect, and as a result most money still held on deposit receipt can be released on the appointed day[8].

[1]   Land Tenure Reform (Scotland) Act 1974, s 24(2).
[2]   LTR(S)A 1974, s 5.
[3]   LTR(S)A 1974, s 4. See also s 6 which provides special rules for cases involving compulsory purchase.
[4]   A J McDonald *Conveyancing Manual* (6th edn, 1997) para 16.29.
[5]   LTR(S)A 1974, ss 4(7), 5(12).

6   Scottish Law Commission *Report on Abolition of the Feudal System* para 3.7.

7   Scottish Law Commission *Report on Abolition of the Feudal System* para 3.39.

8   Abolition of Feudal Tenure etc (Scotland) Act 2000, ss 57, 77(2)(a).

The 2000 Act

10.5   All remaining feuduties are extinguished on the appointed day (28 November 2004)[1]. This includes over-feuduties[2], and feuduties which were in the course of being extinguished under the 1974 Act[3]. Compensation may be claimed from the (former) vassal, as described below, but, as with the 1974 Act, extinction is not dependent on compensation being paid. No feuduty is exigible for any period after the appointed day: the end of feudalism necessarily presupposes the end of the feudal *reddendo*.

1   Abolition of Feudal Tenure etc (Scotland) Act 2000, s 7.

2   Scottish Law Commission *Report on Abolition of the Feudal System* para 3.43.

3   Scottish Law Commission *Report on Abolition of the Feudal System* paras 3.46, 3.47.

Arrears

10.6   Liability for arrears is unaffected by extinction[1]. The position is simplified in practice by the fact that the appointed day is a term day (Martinmas 2004). Thus, and on the basis that feuduty is payable in advance and not in arrears[2], no new instalment of feuduty is due on Martinmas 2004 itself[3]; and assuming that previous instalments were duly paid (the most recent being due on Whitsunday 2004), no further payment in respect of feuduty falls to be made. Any unpaid instalments, however, remain due until such time as they are lost by the short negative prescription of five years[4]. The remedy of irritancy ceased to be available on 9 June 2000[5], and from the appointed day arrears are no longer secured either on the land or on the vassal's moveables[6]. Thus arrears of feuduty become an ordinary debt, enforceable by a (personal) action for payment. One practical consequence is that a person buying land after the appointed day need have no concern with unpaid arrears. The forms for claiming compensation include a space for claiming arrears[7].

1   Abolition of Feudal Tenure etc (Scotland) Act 2000, s 13(1).

2   A state of affairs which seems taken for granted. See eg J M Halliday *Conveyancing Law and Practice* vol 2 (2nd edn, 1997) para 32–20; A J McDonald *Conveyancing Manual* (6th edn, 1997) para 16.26.

3   For no feuduty is exigible for any period after the appointed day: see AFT(S)A 2000, s 7.

4   Prescription and Limitation (Scotland) Act 1973, s 6, Sch 1, para 1(a)(iii). This provision is repealed, on the appointed day, by the AFT(S)A 2000, s 76(2), Sch 13, but it seems that the same result is achieved by the 1973 Act, Sch 1, para 1(a)(vi), (vii).

5   AFT(S)A 2000, s 53.

6   AFT(S)A 2000, s 13(2), (3). For transitional arrangements, see s 13(4).

7   See Appendix 6.

Cleansing of the Register

10.7   At any time after the appointed day the Keeper is at liberty to remove feuduty from the burdens section of title sheets[1]. But even where this is not done, an acquirer will know that, following feudal abolition, no feuduty is payable. It is assumed that the Keeper will retain a reference to the feuduty formerly due in a case where feuduty determines liability for common repairs; and such liability is of course unaffected by the extinction of feuduty itself[2].

1   The legislation makes clear that removal of feuduty is not to be treated as prejudicing a proprietor in possession, nor as allowing a claim for indemnity. See Land Registration (Scotland) Act 1979, ss 9(3B), 12(3)(cc) (inserted by the AFT(S)A 2000, s 3). By contrast with real burdens (for which see para 7.11), there is no moratorium period during which the Keeper can refuse a request to make the change.
2   Scottish Law Commission *Report on the Law of the Tenement* (Scot Law Com no 162, 1998) para 5.62.

COMPENSATION

Amount

10.8   Under the Abolition of Feudal Tenure Act the compensation payable for extinction of feuduty is calculated in the same way as the equivalent compensation under the Land Tenure Reform (Scotland) Act 1974[1]. Thus the (former) superior is entitled to payment of such sum as, if invested in 2.5% Consolidated Stock at the middle market price at the close of business last preceding the appointed day, would produce an annual sum equal to the feuduty[2]. The idea is that the income stream produced by feuduty could, if desired, be reproduced by investment of the compensation sum in government stock. With falling interest rates in the years since 1974, the sum required to replicate that income stream has risen. As a matter of practice, the amount payable as compensation is calculated by multiplying the annual feuduty by the 'feuduty factor' derived from the price of 2.5% Consolidated Stock. Currently the factor is around 21[3]. By contrast to the 1974 Act scheme, where feuduty might be redeemed on any day and hence by reference to an ever-changing feuduty factor, the 2000 Act provides for a single day of extinction and thus for a single feuduty factor. At the time of writing, the figure for that factor lay in the future.

1   See eg Land Tenure Reform (Scotland) Act 1974, s 5(4).
2   Abolition of Feudal Tenure etc (Scotland) Act 2000, s 9(1).
3   In 1974 it was around 6. At the end of the nineteenth century, superiorities were changing hands for a multiplier of around 27. See R Rodger *The Transformation of Edinburgh: Land, Property and Trust in the Nineteenth Century* (2001) p 236, figure 4.3.

The need for a claim

10.9   The main departure from the scheme of the 1974 Act is the need for a claim[1]. This acknowledges the fact that the superiority may be vacant, and prevents vassals from having to seek out superiors who, where they exist at all, have not troubled to claim feuduty in the recent past[2]. Thus compensation under the 2000 Act is due if, and only if, the former superior serves a notice on the former vassal claiming payment of a 'compensatory payment'[3]. Two years are allowed from the appointed day, after which it is too late to make a claim. Service is considered further in chapter 12. The notice must be accompanied by an explanatory note, in statutory form[4], and, if the amount due is £50 or more, by an instalment document and further explanatory note[5]. The first explanatory note is to be 'attached' to the notice and the second 'appended' to the instalment document, although it seems doubtful that any difference in meaning is intended[6]. Strictly, these words would seem to require either that the note is on the same piece of paper as the document it is explaining – as may often be conveniently done in practice – or that there is some physical connection between the two, even if only a paper clip[7].

Service constitutes the debt. If the amount due is £50 or more, the former vassal can opt to pay by instalments[8]; but except where this is done, payment is due within eight weeks[9]. By contrast with compensation under the 1974 Act, which was secured on the ground at least for a temporary period[10], the debt is personal to the former vassal and does not affect future acquirers of the land[11]. One practical consequence is that any receipt for payment – the equivalent of the feuduty redemption receipt – should be retained by the former vassal when the land is ultimately sold, and not passed on to the buyer. For the buyer has no concern with feuduty or with compensation for its extinction.

Like feuduty itself, compensation is subject to the five-year negative prescription[12]. Prescription begins to run from the date on which the debt became due[13]. If compensation is being paid in a lump sum, that is the date occurring eight weeks after the date of service. Otherwise it is the date on which the instalment in question was due.

1   In terms of the Land Tenure Reform (Scotland) Act 1974, s 5(4), compensation is due as an automatic consequence of redemption.
2   Scottish Law Commission *Report on Abolition of the Feudal System* para 3.15.
3   Abolition of Feudal Tenure etc (Scotland) Act 2000, s 8(1).
4   AFT(S)A 2000, s 8(4).
5   AFT(S)A 2000, s 10(1).
6   Indeed the Scottish Law Commission gives the rule as being that the second note is 'attached' to the document. See *Report on the Abolition of the Feudal System* para 3.25.
7   Compare the position for preservation notices where the rule is merely that there should be sent both the notice and the explanatory note. See AFT(S)A 2000, s 41(3). It seems doubtful that any difference in effect was intended, and it would be a very pedantic approach to deny effect to a notice under s 8 of the 2000 Act merely on the basis that the explanatory note was not physically 'attached'.
8   Paras 10.14, 10.15.
9   AFT(S)A 2000, s 8(5).

10 Land Tenure Reform (Scotland) Act 1974, s 5(5)–(8). To the extent that such security still survives, it is extinguished on the appointed day: see AFT(S)A 2000, s 13(2).
11 Contrast the present position, described in G L Gretton and K G C Reid *Conveyancing* (2nd edn, 1999) paras 7.22–7.24.
12 Prescription and Limitation (Scotland) Act 1973, s 6, Sch 1, para 1(aa), inserted by the AFT(S)A 2000, s 12.
13 PL(S)A 1973, s 6(3).

Creditor and debtor

10.10 A debt requires a creditor and a debtor. The debtor in a claim for compensation is the person who, immediately before the appointed day, was the vassal, while the creditor is that person's immediate superior[1]. In the normal case the parties in question are the former holder of, respectively, the *dominium utile* and the immediate *dominium directum*. In relation to an over-feuduty, however, the parties are the former holders of the relevant adjacent estates of *dominium directum*. Completion of title is not required, so that an uninfeft superior could claim against an uninfeft vassal[2]. If more than one person holds on an incomplete title, the relevant 'superior' or 'vassal' is the most recent to have acquired[3].

In a case where the *dominium utile* is held as common property, each *pro indiviso* owner is a vassal and the notice must be served separately on each[4]. Liability for the debt, however, is joint and several, and an owner who is made to pay has a right of relief against the other co-owner or co-owners proportionate to the size of the *pro indiviso* shares[5].

By contrast to the rules for preservation of real burdens, where no personal claim is involved[6], the former superior must properly identify the former vassal. This will not be difficult if feuduty has continued to be collected, but an inactive superior whose interest is reawakened by the prospect of a capitalised sum must expect to bear the burden of a certain amount of research. In most cases, a search of the registers will be sufficient. However, a vassal who was uninfeft before the appointed day, and continues to hold on an uncompleted title even after that day, is less easily detected. There may also be difficulties, in the case of *cumulo* feuduties, if payment was made by a factor or other collector rather than by the vassals themselves[7]; but a collector is placed under a statutory duty to disclose the name and address of the vassals[8].

Inevitably, some notices will be addressed to the wrong person and so will be of no effect. This is a matter requiring both perseverance and care. The former superior has only two years in which to serve a valid notice. To allow for accidents, it is as well to begin as soon after the appointed day as possible. The fact that no interest is payable is a further reason for haste. A notice which does not produce payment will need to be followed up carefully[9]. If non-payment is due to service on the wrong person, the former superior will wish to have this information promptly so that a second notice can be served within the two-year period. A person on whom a notice is wrongly served must, if a former vassal, provide the superior with such information as he has as to the name and address of the person who was vassal immediately before the appointed day[10], and this duty is reinforced by a sentence in the explanatory notes which accompany the notice[11].

1   Abolition of Feudal Tenure etc (Scotland) Act 2000, ss 8(1), 16(1) (definitions of 'superior' and 'vassal').
2   AFT(S)A 2000, s 16(1) (definitions of 'superior' and 'vassal').
3   See para 3.4 for a worked example.
4   Para 12.1.
5   AFT(S)A 2000, s 16(4)(a). In this, as in other matters, the rules parallel those governing compensation in respect of development value burdens. See para 9.14.
6   See para 11.7.
7   Para 10.3.
8   AFT(S)A 2000, s 14.
9   Strictly a notice which *did* lead to payment but which turned out to be served on the wrong person also carries risks for the former superior. For if the person who paid seeks recovery, on the basis of the *condictio debiti*, but the mistake emerges only after the two-year period has expired, the former superior might be left uncompensated. In practice the risk seems small.
10   AFT(S)A 2000, s 15, discussed at para 12.4.
11   See AFT(S)A 2000, Schs 1 and 2.

Form of notice: 'standard' feuduties

10.11   Claims in respect of *cumulo* feuduties are discussed in the next paragraph[1]. For other cases the form of notice to be used is set out in Schedule 2 to the Abolition of Feudal Tenure Act[2]. A style of completed notice is given in Appendix 6 to this book. The notice contains:

- the name and address of the former vassal;
- the name and address of the former superior;
- a request to pay a specified sum by way of compensation for the extinction of feuduty in respect of specified land; and
- a note of any arrears.

It is signed by the former superior or an agent. If payment is to be made to the agent, this must be stated, and the agent's name and address given.

1   A feuduty which was in the course of allocation on the appointed day is treated as a *cumulo* if the allocation had not yet taken effect. See Scottish Law Commission *Report on Abolition of the Feudal System* para 3.49. An allocation under the Conveyancing and Feudal Reform (Scotland) Act 1970 takes effect on the first term day occurring not less than three months after the service of the notice of allocation. See CFR(S)A 1970, s 5(5). Thus a notice of allocation served within three months of the appointed day would be ineffective.
2   Abolition of Feudal Tenure etc (Scotland) Act 2000, s 8(3).

Form of notice: *cumulo* feuduties

10.12   Unlike *cumulo* feuduty itself, liability for compensation for its extinction is not joint and several[1]. Instead the former superior must allocate the total sum among the former vassals[2] and send a separate notice to each requesting payment of the appropriate amount[3]. The former superior is directed to allocate the total 'in such proportions as are reasonable in all the circumstances'[4]. If, as usually, the feuduty was subject to an informal apportionment[5], an allocation which follows such apportionment is presumed reasonable and should in practice be attempted[6]. Otherwise the matter lies within the superior's discretion. In practice he may be expected to have regard to factors such as relative size and relative value.

The superior's discretion can be challenged[7]. It would be a defence to an action for payment that the amount allocated on a particular plot was unreasonably large. In that case the former superior would be out of pocket at least to the extent of the excess, for there seems no power to serve on the other vassals a supplementary notice seeking payment of a further sum. This emphasises the need for care in allocation in a case where no informal apportionment exists. One possible approach would be to seek the agreement of the former vassals in advance of serving the notices.

If feuduty was previously paid by a factor or other collector[8], the former superior may be uncertain as to the nature, or even the existence, of a previous apportionment. The proper course is to make inquiries of the collector, who is under a statutory duty to disclose the necessary details[9].

The form of notice to be used is set out in Schedule 1 to the 2000 Act[10], and a style of completed notice is given in Appendix 6 to this book. It follows closely the style for a notice for 'standard' feuduties, discussed in the previous paragraph, but with the addition of a table showing the names and properties of all the former vassals, and the amount each must pay as compensation.

1   Scottish Law Commission *Report on Abolition of the Feudal System* para 3.16.
2   Abolition of Feudal Tenure etc (Scotland) Act 2000, s 9(3).
3   AFT(S)A 2000, s 8(2).
4   AFT(S)A 2000, s 9(3).
5   Para 10.3.
6   AFT(S)A 2000, s 9(4).
7   Para 10.13.
8   Para 10.3.
9   AFT(S)A 2000, s 14.
10 AFT(S)A 2000, s 8(2).

Challenge to notice

10.13   The Lands Tribunal can hear challenges to preservation notices[1] but not to notices claiming compensation. In the case of a notice claiming compensation for loss of feuduty, the normal occasion of challenge is likely to be as a defence to an action for payment[2]. Various grounds of challenge are possible[3], for example that the claimant was not the superior immediately before the appointed day, that the defender was not the vassal, that the amount claimed is incorrect, or that the notice is defective, was not properly served, or was not accompanied by the explanatory note or the instalment document[4].

1   Abolition of Feudal Tenure etc (Scotland) Act 2000, s 44(1), discussed at para 11.19.
2   Scottish Law Commission *Report on Abolition of the Feudal System* para 3.41.
3   The basic position is that, for a claim to be valid, there must be compliance with the AFT(S)A 2000, s 8(1)–(4). See s 8(5).
4   In relation to the instalment document it is expressly stated (AFT(S)A 2000, s 10(1)) that, in the absence of such a document, no requirement to pay compensation arises.

PAYMENT BY INSTALMENTS

Entitlement

10.14   If, as usually, the compensation due is £50 or more[1], payment can be made by half-yearly instalments. The number of instalments allowed depends on the amount due, as follows[2]:

Compensation	Number of Instalments
£50 but not exceeding £500	5
exceeding £500 but not £1,000	10
exceeding £1,000 but not £1,500	15
exceeding £1,500	20

Thus, for large debts the former vassal has up to ten years in which to make payment.

A right to pay by instalments arises only if it is claimed. This is done by signing, dating, and returning to the former superior, within the eight weeks normally allowed for payment, the instalment document which accompanies the notice to pay[3]. Before sending out that document, the superior must have completed it to the extent of entering the number and amount of the instalments, and certain other information[4]. The form of instalment document is given in Schedule 3 to the Abolition of Feudal Tenure Act, and a completed instalment document is shown in Appendix 6 to this book.

No interest is charged on payment by instalments, but the former vassal must make a one-off payment of 10% of the total compensation[5]. This is non-refundable even if the debt is paid off early. The payment must accompany the return of the instalment document. Thus a former vassal who fails, within eight weeks, to send both the instalment document and the 10% payment loses the chance of paying by instalments and must make immediate payment of the full amount.

1   The Scottish Law Commission had proposed a threshold of £100: see *Report on Abolition of the Feudal System* para 3.24.
2   Abolition of Feudal Tenure etc (Scotland) Act 2000, s 10(4).
3   AFT(S)A 2000, s 10(2)(a). However, this cannot be done if ownership is lost on sale of the land after the instalment document is served but before it can be returned: see AFT(S)A 2000, s 10(3)(b), (5).
4   AFT(S)A 2000, s 10(1) ('a filled out document'), Sch 3.
5   AFT(S)A 2000, s 10(2)(b).

Loss of entitlement

10.15   A former vassal who elects to pay by instalments is not bound to continue on that basis but is able to pay the balance outstanding at any time[1]. The 10% additional payment is not, however, then returnable[2].

The right to pay by instalments is lost where any instalment is late by six weeks or more. The first instalment is due on the first term day after return of the instalment document. Thereafter instalments are payable at half-yearly intervals, on successive term days[3].

> *Example.* The former superior serves a notice and instalment document on 19 April 2005. The amount claimed is £714. On 2 June 2005 the former vassal claims a right to pay by instalments by returning the instalment document, duly signed, together with a cheque for £71.40 (being the non-returnable payment of 10%). The debt must then be repaid by 10 instalments of £71.40 on the following dates: 28 November 2005; 28 May 2006; 28 November 2006; 28 May 2007; 28 November 2007; 28 May 2008; 28 November 2008; 28 May 2009; 28 November 2009; and 28 May 2010. If the former vassal makes punctual payment of the instalments falling due on 28 November 2005 and 28 May 2006, but has still not paid the next instalment by the early weeks of 2007, the whole balance is immediately due and the right to pay by instalments is lost.

The right to pay by instalments is also lost if the land (ie the former feu) or any part of it is sold by the former vassal[4] – a conscious imitation of the rule of the Land Tenure Reform (Scotland) Act 1974 that feuduty is redeemed on sale[5]. The whole balance outstanding becomes due seven days after 'the former vassal ceases to have right to the land'[6]. The expression is perhaps unfortunate, for a seller 'has right' to land until such time as the purchaser chooses to register his disposition[7], and it is not clear how the former superior or vassal is to know when this occurs. Furthermore, if the purchaser elects not to register at all, the former vassal can continue to pay by instalments.

Sale *before* service of the instalment document has no effect on entitlement to pay by instalments and the former vassal can claim the right by returning the document in the usual way[8].

1   Abolition of Feudal Tenure etc (Scotland) Act 2000, s 10(4)(iii).
2   AFT(S)A 2000, s 10(2)(b).
3   AFT(S)A 2000, s 10(4).
4   AFT(S)A 2000, s 10(3)(a).
5   Land Tenure Reform (Scotland) Act 1974, s 5. This provision was not in the original Scottish Law Commission Bill but was added by the Scottish Executive, in response to the views of the Justice and Home Affairs Committee, at Stage 3. See Scottish Parliament *Official Report* 3 May 2000 cols 228–9.
6   AFT(S)A 2000, s 10(4)(ii).
7   A view reinforced by the language of Pt 3 of the 2000 Act itself: see AFT(S)A 2000, s 16(1) (definitions of 'superior' and 'vassal').
8   By AFT(S)A 2000, s 10(3) the rule only applies to sales 'on or after the date on which an instalment document is served on a former vassal'.

OTHER PERIODICAL PAYMENTS

Introduction

10.16   Like the 1974 Act scheme[1], the new scheme extends beyond feuduties to other periodical payments which are not feudal in nature. Indeed the scope of the 2000 Act is slightly wider. The forms provided under the 2000 Act for feuduty are to be modified as appropriate where they are used for other periodical payments[2].

1   Land Tenure Reform (Scotland) Act 1974, s 5(12).
2   Abolition of Feudal Tenure etc (Scotland) Act 2000, s 56(1)(b).

Blench duties

10.17   Apart from feu farm tenure, blench tenure was the only feudal tenure to survive into the twentieth century, although it was rarely encountered in practice[1]. Under blench tenure the *reddendo* is purely nominal, such as one penny Scots if asked only. Blench duties are treated by the 2000 Act in the same way as feuduties and so are extinguished on the appointed day[2]. It seems improbable that compensation will actually be claimed.

1   K G C Reid *The Law of Property in Scotland* (1996) para 67 (G L Gretton).
2   Abolition of Feudal Tenure etc (Scotland) Act 2000, s 16(1) (definition of 'feuduty').

Ground annuals

10.18   Sometimes land was sold subject to a ground annual instead of feuduty. Typically this occurred in burgage tenure or other circumstances where, for one reason or another, subinfeudation was barred. Like feuduty, ground annual is a perpetual periodical payment secured on the land. Unlike feuduty, there is no personal liability in the owner, and the creditor is not a feudal superior but merely the holder of the heritable security. Thus ground annual is not itself a form of tenure, and almost all land affected by ground annuals is held on feudal tenure.

New ground annuals were prohibited by the Land Tenure Reform (Scotland) Act 1974, and existing ground annuals can be redeemed under the scheme introduced by that Act[1]. All remaining ground annuals are swept away on the appointed day, and compensation may be claimed in the same manner as for feuduty[2].

1   Land Tenure Reform (Scotland) Act 1974, ss 2, 5(12). Nonetheless, puzzlingly, the Land Registration (Scotland) Act 1979, s 2(1)(a) provides that first registration occurs, among other events, on the grant of an interest in land by way of contract of ground annual. This provision is repealed by the Abolition of Feudal Tenure etc (Scotland) Act 2000, s 76(1), Sch 12, para 39(2)(a).
2   AFT(S)A 2000, s 56(1).

Skat

10.19   Skat is the periodical payment due to the Crown in respect of the allodial land found in Orkney and Shetland and known as udal land[1]. Skat is treated like feuduty under the 2000 Act[2], as previously under the 1974 Act[3]. Thus all remaining skat is extinguished on the appointed day, but in other respects udal land is untouched by the 2000 Act. Indeed, since the effect of that Act is to make feudal land allodial, it is possible to present the result as the assimilation of feudal land to udal land. Thus in introducing the legislation to Parliament the Minister for Justice and MSP for Orkney, Mr Jim Wallace, said that[4]:

It gives me particular pleasure to introduce a Bill that extends to the rest of Scotland the freedoms that my constituents have enjoyed for centuries.

Nonetheless, some differences remain, especially in relation to the foreshore, where udal rights are more extensive[5].

1   For udal land, see W M Gordon *Scottish Land Law* (2nd edn, 1999) paras 3–08 to 3–10; 24 *Stair Memorial Encyclopaedia* paras 307 ff.
2   Abolition of Feudal Tenure etc (Scotland) Act 2000, s 56(1).
3   Land Tenure Reform (Scotland) Act 1974, s 5(12).
4   Scottish Parliament *Official Report* 15 December 1999 col 1543.
5   Scottish Law Commission *Report on Abolition of the Feudal System* paras 7.19–7.21. See also Scottish Law Commission *Report on the Law of the Foreshore and Sea Bed*, Scot Law Com no 190, 2003, paras 4.9–4.17.

Teind, stipend and standard charge

10.20   Historically, teinds[1] were the right of the church to a tenth part of the land and industry of the laity, but today long since converted into a monetary equivalent[2].

Originally teinds were paid directly to the clergy or to religious foundations, but the pre-Reformation church introduced the practice of alienating the right to teinds to members of the laity, known as titulars. Titulars paid a proportion of the teinds collected, known as stipend, to the church, and the balance, known as free teinds, they were allowed to retain. In time the practice, and eventually the law, became for landowners to pay the stipend directly to the church and the free teinds to the titular[3]; and if, as often, the landowner acquired the right to the teinds from the titular – in other words, bought his own teinds – no payment of teinds was in fact made. Teinds were separate tenements, and did not pass with a conveyance of the land without express mention. Indeed until relatively recently, it remained common for the parts and pertinents clause of a disposition to include a reference to teinds, although this was usually the unthinking copying of a writ from a previous age.

Since 1925 stipend has been secured as a pecuniary real burden, known as standard charge, on the land from which payment falls to be made[4]. Standard charge, but not teind, is redeemed under the Land Tenure Reform (Scotland) Act 1974 in the same way as feuduty[5]. The Abolition of Feudal Tenure Act applies also to teinds[6]. As a result, all remaining payments by way of teind, stipend and standard charge are extinguished on the appointed day, but compensation may be claimed by the Church of Scotland or, as the case may be, by the teind holder[7].

---

[1]   Pronounced 'teends'. The standard work on teinds is W Buchanan *Treatise on the Law of Scotland on the subject of Teinds or Tithes* (1862). A useful modern summary can be found in W M Gordon *Scottish Land Law* (2nd edn, 1999) paras 10–50 to 10–77.

[2]   See now the Church of Scotland (Property and Endowments) Act 1925, s 16, Sch 6.

[3]   CS(PE)A 1925, ss 8(1), 12(2), 17.

[4]   CS(PE)A 1925, s 12(1).

[5]   Land Tenure Reform (Scotland) Act 1974, s 5(12). There could also be voluntary redemption of standard charge under the CS(PE)A 1925, s 12(3), (4).

[6]   Abolition of Feudal Tenure etc (Scotland) Act 2000, s 56.

[7]   This allows the repeal, by the AFT(S)A 2000, s 76(2), Sch 13, of a large number of legislative provisions. See Scottish Law Commission *Report on Abolition of the Feudal System* para 9.18.

Dry multures

10.21   Dry multures[1] are the monetary commutation of thirlage, which was an obligation to take corn from particular land to a particular mill to be ground[2]. Although described by Stair as 'the chief and most frequent servitude in Scotland'[3], thirlage is long since obsolete and is formally abolished by the 2000 Act[4]. Dry multures are treated in the same way as feuduty both by the 1974 Act[5] and by the 2000 Act[6]. Accordingly, all remaining dry multures are extinguished on the appointed day.

---

[1]   Pronounced 'mew-ters'.

[2]   D J Cusine and R R M Paisley *Servitudes and Rights of Way* (1998) paras 1.29, 3.75; W M Gordon *Scottish Land Law* (2nd edn, 1999) paras 10–78 to 10–90.

[3]   Stair II.7.15. Indeed the accounts of servitudes in the institutional writers are dominated by the subject of thirlage: see Stair II.7.15–27; Bankton II.7.38–61; Erskine II.9.18–32.

4   Abolition of Feudal Tenure etc (Scotland) Act 2000, s 55.
5   Though not by name. See W M Gordon *Scottish Land Law* para 10–90.
6   AFT(S)A 2000, s 56(1). This includes compensation in respect of commutation of thirlage under the Thirlage Act 1799.

Other perpetual periodical payments

10.22   The scheme developed for the extinction of feuduty also applies, finally, to 'any other perpetual periodical payment in respect of the tenure, occupancy or use of land or under a title condition'[1]. The phrase is copied from the Land Tenure Reform (Scotland) Act 1974[2] and is intended to encompass obligations sufficiently unusual as to have been omitted from the principal list. Examples are the Dunkeld Deanery dues and St Andrews Deanery dues collected by the Church of Scotland[3], and rent payable to the Earl of Mansfield by the Kindly Tenants of Lochmaben[4]. Rent under a lease is excluded, for all practical purposes[5], by the requirement that the payment be perpetual. And, following again the 1974 Act, there are express exclusions of payments made under a heritable security, and payments in defrayal of, or as a contribution towards, some continuing cost relating to land (for example, a service charge)[6]. A separate provision of the 2000 Act makes clear that the obligation, under the Mines and Metals Act 1592, to pay to the Crown one tenth of all gold and silver mined is a royalty and not a periodical payment[7].

1   Abolition of Feudal Tenure etc (Scotland) Act 2000, s 56(1).
2   Land Tenure Reform (Scotland) Act 1974, ss 4(7), 5(12). The phrase is similar to, but intriguingly different from, that used by the 1974 Act, s 2(1) to describe the periodical payments which are now disallowed.
3   Scottish Law Commission *Report on Abolition of the Feudal System* para 3.52.
4   Para 14.1.
5   In theory, however, a perpetual lease is possible at common law, but it would not then be a real right. See eg A McAllister *Scottish Law of Leases* (3rd edn, 2002) para 1.5.
6   AFT(S)A 2000, s 56(2).
7   AFT(S)A 2000, s 61. See further Scottish Law Commission *Report on Abolition of the Feudal System* para 3.56.

Chapter 11

Preservation notices

INTRODUCTION

Preservation notices and compensation notices

11.1 Two different types of notice are provided for by the Abolition of Feudal Tenure etc (Scotland) Act 2000. There are, in the first place, those notices which act to preserve feudal real burdens by providing for their conversion into neighbour burdens or personal real burdens. Such notices, which must always be registered in order to take effect, are referred to in this book as 'preservation notices'. They are the subject of the present chapter. Notices issued under s 33 of the 2000 Act may also be included under this head, although their purpose is to preserve, not the burden itself, but the right to claim compensation for its loss[1].

The purpose of the other type of notice, which may be termed a 'compensation notice', is to claim compensation from the former vassal in respect of the loss either of development value burdens or of feuduty. Its effect is both to constitute the debt and also to require its payment. Compensation notices are not registered and in other respects are subject to a different regime from preservation notices. They are considered more fully in chapter 12.

---

[1] The 2000 Act groups together these notices as 'any notice which is to be submitted for registration under this Act': see AFT(S)A 2000, s 41(1).

The preservation notices listed

11.2 The following is a complete list of the preservation notices provided for in the 2000 Act, and covered by this chapter:

- s 18 notice (preservation as neighbour burdens)[1];
- s 18A notice (preservation as personal pre-emption/redemption burdens)[2];
- s 18B notice (preservation as economic development burdens)[3];
- s 18C notice (preservation as health care burdens)[4];
- s 20 notice (blocking notice, preserving as neighbour burdens for a transitional period)[5];

- s 27 notice (preservation as conservation burdens)[6];
- s 27A notice (preservation as conservation burdens in favour of a third party)[7];
- s 33 notice (preservation of claim for compensation for loss of development value burdens)[8]; and
- s 65A notice (preservation of sporting rights as a separate tenement)[9].

An additional notice is provided for by s 19 of the 2000 Act as a preliminary to entering into an agreement between superior and vassal, but it is not registered and has its own rules as to service[10]. It is not considered further in this chapter.

Finally, it should be said that an agreement made under s 19, just mentioned, requires to be registered and is subject to many of the same rules as preservation notices. Much of what is said in this chapter, therefore, applies equally to such agreements.

[1]   Paras 3.4–3.16.
[2]   Paras 4.22, 4.23, and 4.26.
[3]   Paras 4.11– 4.15.
[4]   Paras 4.16–4.20.
[5]   Paras 3.28, 3.29.
[6]   Paras 4.4–4.10.
[7]   Paras 4.4–4.10.
[8]   Paras 9.8–9.11.
[9]   Paras 8.6–8.10. Sporting rights, however, may not be real burdens; and in any event they are preserved, not as real burdens, but as a separate tenement in land.
[10]   Para 3.23.

MUTUAL EXCLUSIVITY

One-for-one substitution

11.3   The manner in which feudal real burdens may be preserved under the 2000 Act is intended to avoid, so far as possible, the proliferation of enforcement rights. Thus, for the most part the, single, superior is replaced by an, equally single, enforcer – either the owner of the new benefited property (in the case of preservation as a neighbour burden) or the nominated holder (in the case of preservation as a personal real burden)[1]. There is, in short, a one-for-one substitution. It is true, of course, that in the case of a neighbour burden a later division of the benefited property might increase the number of enforcers; but, at least for divisions occurring after the appointed day, this effect is restrained by the rule in the Title Conditions (Scotland) Act 2003 that, in general, only one part of the divided whole will be treated as the benefited property[2].

The principle of one-for-one substitution is concerned with the superiority only and has no bearing on whether enforcement rights are held by third parties (co-feuars) in addition. Such third-party rights as exist will survive the appointed day[3], and the Title Conditions Act creates many new rights[4].

1 'Single' here refers to the title. There is to be only one title to enforce the burden. But that title (whether superiority or, after the appointed day, ownership of the benefited property) may itself be held by two or more people *pro indiviso*.

2 TC(S)A 2003, s 12, discussed briefly at para 7.16.

3 Para 2.5.

4 See further ch 5.

Preservation on more than one ground

11.4 Occasionally preservation is possible on more than one ground. For example, a superior which owns land within 100 metres might also be a conservation body with the option of saving the burden as a conservation burden. Or again, and much more commonly, the same superior might be able to preserve a right of pre-emption either as a neighbour burden or as a personal pre-emption burden[1]. The principle of one-for-one substitution dictates that the superior should not be allowed to do both, and the Abolition of Feudal Tenure Act so provides[2]. In cases like this, therefore, a choice falls to be made, marked by the fact of registration. The superior can opt for a neighbour burden or for a personal real burden[3]. And having registered a notice for one, the superior is disabled from registering a second notice unless the first is discharged, in the manner explained below. The same rule applies where one of the documents is an agreement under s 19 of the 2000 Act.

It need hardly be said that a superior cannot both preserve a burden and then reserve a right to compensation for its extinction under s 33 of the 2000 Act. Accordingly, the registration of a preservation notice (or s 19 agreement), unless discharged, prevents the subsequent registration of a notice under s 33[4].

1 Para 4.21.

2 Abolition of Feudal Tenure etc (Scotland) Act 2000, s 42(1). Although this provision does not apply to s 65A notices, much the same effect is achieved by the exclusion of sporting rights from the definition of 'real burden' in s 49, and hence from the possibility of using notices of any other type.

3 Or, in the unlikely event of a choice between two personal real burdens being available, for one such burden but not for both.

4 Or vice versa. See AFT(S)A 2000, s 42(1).

Choosing again: the discharge of an earlier notice

11.5 Superiors are, however, allowed to change their minds. A superior who registers a notice of one type (or a s 19 agreement) in preference to another can, by discharging the first notice (or agreement), restore the entitlement to register a second[1]. Both the discharge[2] and the new notice must, however, be registered before the appointed day.

If the property has changed hands since the original notice, it is the 'successor' who must grant the discharge[3]. In the case of a notice in respect of a personal real burden, that means the successor as superior; but the position is less clear for a notice in respect of a neighbour burden, for here there are two properties (the superiority and the nominated property) and hence the possibility of two successors. If, therefore, superiority and nominated property have fallen into different hands, the only safe course is to have the discharge executed by the owner of each[4].

There is no requirement that the granter be infeft or, apparently, in a case where there is no infeftment, that title be deduced; and indeed the provisions of the general law concerning deduction of title are inapplicable to such a discharge[5]. In some circumstances, however, and especially if the granter is a successor, a narrative of entitlement will be helpful.

Except in the case of s 33 notices, considered in the next paragraph, the 2000 Act does not give a style of discharge, but the s 33 style can be readily adapted. The following are suggested:

Style of discharge of preservation notice (personal real burdens)

I, AB, (*designation*), hereby discharge the Notice made under section (*number*) of the Abolition of Feudal Tenure etc (Scotland) Act 2000 dated (*date*) and registered in the Land Register of Scotland on (*date*) against the subjects in title number (*number*) [*or* recorded in the Register of Sasines for (*county*) on (*date*) under (*fiche and frame*)]: IN WITNESS WHEREOF

Style of discharge of preservation notice (neighbour burdens)

I, AB, (*designation*), hereby discharge the Notice made under section (*number*) of the Abolition of Feudal Tenure etc (Scotland) Act 2000 dated (*date*) and registered on (date) (in the first place) in the Land Register of Scotland against the subjects in title number (*number*) [*or* in the Register of Sasines for (*county*) under (*fiche and frame*)] and (in the second place) in the Land Register of Scotland against the subjects in title number (*number*) [*or* in the Register of Sasines for (*county*) under (*fiche and frame*)]: IN WITNESS WHEREOF

Arguably a discharge of a notice (or agreement) in respect of a neighbour burden should, like the original notice (or agreement), be registered against the nominated property as well as the feu[6]. A warrant of registration is needed in respect of registration in the Register of Sasines[7].

---

1   Abolition of Feudal Tenure etc (Scotland) Act 2000, s 42(1).
2   Other than the discharge of a s 33 notice: see AFT(S)A 2000, s 40.
3   AFT(S)A 2000, s 42(1).
4   In the style given below, the granter grants in a dual capacity, both as superior and as owner of the nominated property.

5   Conveyancing (Scotland) Act 1924, s 3. Except, however, where the superiority has changed hands, an informal narration of the granter's title would appear in the original notice.
6   Compare, under the law in force after the appointed day, the discharge of a real burden, which is registered only against the burdened property, but which the Keeper acknowledges in the title of the benefited: see the Title Conditions (Scotland) Act 2003, ss 15(1), 105.
7   The exemption given in the AFT(S)A 2000, s 41(2) in respect of the original notice does not apply.

Discharge of a s 33 notice

11.6   The right prospectively conferred by a s 33 notice, being a right to money and not to enforce a real burden, is a personal right, severed from the land. This means, for example, that the person registering the notice retains the right even if the superiority passes to other hands. But the right may itself be assigned, in which case it is the assignee who must grant the discharge[1], deducing title if the assignation is unregistered[2]. A style is given in the 2000 Act and is reproduced below[3]:

Style of discharge of s 33 notice

I, [AB], (*designation*), hereby discharge the right to claim compensation reserved by a notice dated (*date*) and registered in the Land Register of Scotland on (*date*) against the subjects in title number (*number*) [*or* recorded in the Register of Sasines for (*county*) on (*date*) under (*fiche and frame*)]: IN WITNESS WHEREOF

A warrant of registration is needed for registration in the Register of Sasines up to the appointed day but not thereafter[4].

1   For assignation of a right under a s 33 notice, see para 9.11. In practice it is difficult to see what an assignee has to gain by discharging a claim to compensation. Only the superior can register another notice.
2   Abolition of Feudal Tenure etc (Scotland) Act 2000, Sch 11.
3   AFT(S)A 2000, s 40, Sch 11.
4   That is the normal rule for deeds: see the Titles to Land Consolidation (Scotland) Act 1868, s 141 (repealed on the appointed day by the AFT(S)A 2000, s 76, Sch 13) for the position before the appointed day, and the AFT(S)A 2000, s 5 for the position thereafter. Section 41(2) of the 2000 Act, which exempts certain notices from warrants of registration even before the appointed day, applies to s 33 notices but not to their discharge.

SERVICE

Requirements

11.7   A preservation notice requires to be served on the vassal ('the person who has the estate of *dominium utile* of the land to which the burden relates')[1]. By comparison with compensation notices[2], however, the rules are relatively informal, reflecting the fact that no new obligations are being imposed and that there will be opportunity to challenge the notice in the future, including after the appointed day[3].

Service is to be by post, and ordinary post will do. The superior sends a copy both of the notice and of the explanatory note provided as part of the statutory style. If the superior is in touch with the vassal already, as for example where feuduty continues to be collected, there is no difficulty as to name or address. Otherwise[4] it is sufficient to send the notice to the feu addressed to 'The Proprietor'. The superior, therefore, is relieved of the need to make exhaustive investigations. Indeed, even where the superior knows the vassal's name it may be safer to add 'or The Proprietor' to cover the possibility of a change of ownership. If the *dominium utile* is owned as common property, it is arguable, although not certain, that separate service must be made on each vassal[5]. Thus if the vassals are Mr and Mrs Smith of 4 Main Street, Kirkcaldy, the safe practice would be to make up two separate envelopes, one addressed to Mr Smith and the other to Mrs Smith, and each containing a copy of the notice and other documentation.

Very occasionally it may not be possible to comply with even the modest requirements of the Abolition of Feudal Tenure Act. For example the feu might be a vacant plot of ground without a postal address, and the name and address of the vassal might not be discoverable by a search of the Registers or by other reasonable means. In such exceptional cases service is excused altogether[6].

1   Abolition of Feudal Tenure etc (Scotland) Act 2000, s 41(3).
2   For which see paras 12.2–12.6.
3   Scottish Law Commission *Report on Abolition of the Feudal System* para 4.66. For challenges, see paras 11.17–11.20.
4   Where the name of the vassal is 'not known': see AFT(S)A, s 41(3).
5   By AFT(S)A 2000, s 41(3), service is to be on 'the' person who has the estate of *dominium utile*, which seems to imply that, if there is more than one such person, service should be on each. For a discussion, see para 12.1, note 6.
6   AFTS(A) 2000, s 41(3).

Evidence

11.8   No checks are made on service. In particular the Keeper will not ask for evidence that service has taken place[1]. But as part of completing the notice, the superior must state either that[2]:

> The superior has sent a copy of this notice by [*specify whether by recorded delivery or registered post or by ordinary post*] on [*date of posting*] to the owner of the prospective servient tenement at [*state address*].

or that:

> It has not been reasonably practicable to send a copy of this notice to the owner of the prospective servient tenement for the following reason: [*specify the reason*].

It will be seen that there is no requirement to name the vassal.

The notice is not to be signed until the statement is in place[3], and in the case of some notices the superior must also swear or affirm before a notary public that to the best of the superior's knowledge and belief all the information contained in the notice, including the information as to service, is true[4]. The wilful swearing of a false oath is a criminal offence punishable by up to two years' imprisonment[5].

1   Abolition of Feudal Tenure etc (Scotland) Act 2000, ss 43(1), 65A(11).
2   AFT(S)A 2000, s 41(4).
3   AFT(S)A 2000, s 41(3). And see eg Sch 5, notes 6, 7.
4   See eg AFT(S)A 2000, s 18(4).
5   False Oaths (Scotland) Act 1933, s 1.

STAMP DUTY AND SDLT

Effect of the notices

11.9   A consideration of the stamp duty position requires a careful analysis of the effect of the notices. Three categories of notice may be identified.

The first comprises notices under ss 18, 20 and 27A of the Abolition of Feudal Tenure etc (Scotland) Act 2000. Here two legal events take place, simultaneously, on the appointed day. One is the extinction of the superior's right to enforce the burden[1]. The other is the creation of a new enforcement right in a person who is usually, but not always, the former superior[2]. The process, it is important to notice, is not one of transfer. This is partly because the acquirer is often the very person by whom the previous right is lost. But it is mainly because the new right is not the same as the old. On the contrary, the old right is extinguished and a new right created in its place. And an important difference, in the case of notices under ss 18 and 20, is that the new right is tied to a benefited property and can be enforced, not only by the owner, but by tenants, proper liferenters, and non-entitled spouses[3]. This is not to overlook the role played by the superior, who must after all sign and register the notice. Unlike community burdens or facility burdens[4], enforcement rights are not conferred automatically; and if the superior is inactive, no new right is created at all. But the right is created by statute and not by the will of the superior[5]. Far less is it created by the will of the vassal, who, as the person whose land is burdened, may often be hostile to the notice.

In one case only does the vassal play an active part. A s 19 agreement is signed by both superior and vassal and, on one view, is closer to a deed of conditions or other deed for the voluntary creation of real burdens than to a notice under the 2000 Act[6]. As will be seen, the difference may possibly be of significance for the purposes of stamp duty.

The second category comprises, broadly, those notices providing for the conversion of feudal burdens into personal real burdens. The notices in question are those registered under ss 18A, 18B, 18C, 27 (but not 27A[7]) and 65A of the 2000 Act. Their effect is to change, not the holder, but the burden type. On the appointed day there is transformation rather than transfer. The feudal burden becomes a conservation burden, or economic development burden, or personal real burden of some other kind. The 2000 Act uses the word 'conversion'[8], and in the case of a s 65A notice the conversion is so profound as to remove the product altogether from the class of real burdens[9]. But in all cases the holder remains the same: after the appointed day, as before, the burden is enforceable by, and only by, the (former) superior[10].

The final category comprises notices under s 33 of the 2000 Act. Rather than resulting in the creation of enforcement rights these merely preserve a contingent claim to compensation in respect of the extinction of the superior's right[11]. There can be no question of liability for stamp duty, and s 33 notices are not considered further here.

[1]   Abolition of Feudal Tenure etc (Scotland) Act 2000, s 17(1).
[2]   See eg AFT(S)A 2000, s 18(6).
[3]   Title Conditions (Scotland) Act 2003, s 8(2).
[4]   For which see, respectively, chs 5, 6.
[5]   And indeed a registered notice is not the only prerequisite for the statute to operate. See eg AFT(S)A 2000, s 18(6).
[6]   For s 19 agreements, see paras 3.17–3.23.
[7]   Section 27A notices fall into the first category, as already mentioned.
[8]   Except in s 28 in respect of conservation burdens.
[9]   Instead the real burden is converted into a separate legal tenement: see para 8.10.
[10]   See eg AFT(S)A 2000, s 18A(5).
[11]   See paras 9.2, 9.8–9.11.

Stamp duty

11.10   Stamp duty is due to be replaced by stamp duty land tax (SDLT), probably with effect from 1 December 2003[1]. It may be assumed that for the first months during which preservation notices are allowed, stamp duty will remain in force, and that it will later be replaced by SDLT. SDLT is considered in the next paragraph.

Of the charges to stamp duty listed in Schedule 13 to the Finance Act 1999 only two are of possible relevance for present purposes. Neither, however, seems likely to attract actual liability.

A fixed duty of £5 is charged on a 'conveyance or transfer of property otherwise than on sale', and 'conveyance or transfer' is given an extended meaning as 'every instrument, and every decree or order of a court or commissioners, by which any property is transferred to or vested in any person'[2]. As mentioned above, however, a notice does not effect a 'transfer'; and any 'vesting' is achieved by force of statute and not by an instrument or decree.

The same fixed duty is chargeable in respect of a 'disposition in Scotland of any property, or any right or interest in property'[3]. Since a notice is not a transfer, then it is not a 'disposition of ... property'; and it could only be a disposition of a 'right or interest in property' – the voluntary creation of a subordinate real right, in other words – if it was granted by the owner of the burdened land (ie the vassal), which it is not. An agreement under s 19, however, is executed by the owner of that land, and there is at least an argument that stamp duty is payable under this head[4].

[1]   Finance Act 2003, s 124, Sch 19. The existing charges to stamp duty are repealed by s 125(1).
[2]   Finance Act 1999, Sch 13, para 16.
[3]   Finance Act 1999, Sch 13, para 18(2).
[4]   Unlike the grant of a servitude for no consideration, no exemption is available under the Stamp Duty (Exempt Instruments) Regulations 1987, SI 1987/516, in respect of the grant of a real burden.

Stamp duty land tax

11.11   SDLT, once it comes into force, is chargeable on 'land transactions'[1]; and a 'land transaction' means any acquisition of a 'chargeable interest'[2]. A right to enforce a real burden is a 'right ... in or over land' and hence a 'chargeable interest' which is acquired on the appointed day[3]. Accordingly, the acquisition of rights as a result of preservation notices amounts to 'land transactions' and is in principle chargeable to SDLT. In practice no tax is likely to be payable. Among the transactions exempted from SDLT are those where there is no chargeable consideration[4], or in other words no consideration in money or money's worth[5]. Since superiors can register notices as of right, it is improbable that there will be payment to the vassal. A possible exception is agreements under s 19, which require the active co-operation of the vassal. SDLT would be chargeable on an *ad valorem* basis on any price paid which exceeds £60,000[6] – a figure which is most unlikely to be reached. A notice or agreement will, however, be accepted for registration only where it is accompanied by a self-certificate, in prescribed form[7], that no land transaction return is required in respect of the transaction[8].

[1]   Finance Act 2003, s 42(1).
[2]   Finance Act 2003, s 43(1).
[3]   Finance Act 2003, s 48(1)(a). The test, it should be noted, is acquisition and not transfer. It is, of course, possible to argue that, at least for notices in the second category mentioned in para 11.9, there is no change in entitlement and hence no acquisition.
[4]   Finance Act 2003, s 49, Sch 3, para 1.
[5]   Finance Act 2003, s 50, Sch 4, para 1.
[6]   Or £150,000 in the case of non-residential or mixed property. See Finance Act 2003, s 55.
[7]   Finance Act 2003, s 79(4), (5), Sch 11. At the time of writing no form had yet been prescribed.
[8]   Finance Act 2003, s 79. As to the circumstances in which a land transaction return *is* required, see ss 76, 77. They do not extend to preservation notices.

REGISTRATION

Registration before the appointed day

11.12   Subject to one minor exception noted later[1], all preservation notices must be registered before the appointed day[2]. The rule is the same for an agreement made under s 19 of the 2000 Act[3].

[1]   Para 11.16.
[2]   See eg the Abolition of Feudal Tenure etc (Scotland) Act 2000, s 18(1).
[3]   AFT(S)A 2000, s 19(1).

Exemption from warrant of registration

11.13   No warrant of registration is needed in respect of notices destined for the Register of Sasines[1]. But the requirement of a warrant remains for agreements made under s 19 of the 2000 Act.

[1]   Abolition of Feudal Tenure etc (Scotland) Act 2000, s 41(2). This anticipates the general abolition of warrants of registration after the appointed day: see AFT(S)A 2000, s 5(1).

Scrutiny at the Registers

11.14   The Abolition of Feudal Tenure Act limits pre-registration scrutiny. Notices raise novel issues which are not easily verifiable by the Keeper – such as whether the building which the title plan shows as lying within 100 metres of the feu is in fact used as a place of human habitation or resort, or whether a burden was truly imposed for the purpose of promoting economic development[1].

Some limitations apply to all notices. As already mentioned, the Keeper is not to consider whether a notice has been duly served[2]. And while he must, presumably, be satisfied that the condition listed in the notice is at any rate a real burden[3], he need not go on to determine the question of whether it is enforceable by the superior[4].

Other limitations are notice-specific. Puzzlingly, they include some matters which have no bearing on the validity of the notice itself. Under the 2000 Act the Keeper is not required to determine any of the following:

- *s 18 notice* (neighbour burdens): that the 100-metres rule is satisfied[5];
- *s 18B notice* (economic development burdens): that the burden is imposed for the purpose of promoting economic development and is enforceable by Scottish Ministers or a local authority[6];
- *s 18C notice* (health care burdens): that the burden is imposed to promote the provision of facilities for health care and is enforceable by an NHS trust or Scottish Ministers[7];

- *s 19 agreement* (neighbour burdens): that a preliminary notice was served[8];
- *s 20 notice* (blocking notice): that the description of an attempt to reach agreement under s 19 is correct, that the notice is registered within the required period (normally 42 days after the application to the Lands Tribunal), and that the grounds for a successful Tribunal application have been met[9]; and
- *s 33 notice* (right to compensation): that the burden reserved the development value of land and that the consideration for the grant in feu was significantly reduced[10].

Finally, the Keeper is not required to verify, in respect of any of the notices (or agreement), that the burden was still enforceable by the superior immediately before the appointed day[11]. This final exemption, at least, seems unnecessary unless it is supposed that the Keeper routinely has regard to events occurring after registration, or, more generally, that he is under a duty to monitor the Registers and remove rights which are no longer valid[12]. Here, as in some other places, the exemption provision seems over-extended[13].

[1]   Scottish Law Commission *Report on Abolition of the Feudal System* para 4.70.
[2]   Abolition of Feudal Tenure etc (Scotland) Act 2000, ss 43(1), 65A(11).
[3]   Except, it seems, in a case covered by the AFT(S)A 2000, s 43(2)(bb)(i), (e)(i).
[4]   AFT(S)A 2000, ss 43(2)(a), 65A(11). The distinction made here, between status as a real burden and enforceability by the superior, is difficult to draw in practice. The main reason that a condition will not be enforceable by the superior is that it is not enforceable by anyone, either because it is not a real burden in the first place, or because it has been extinguished by some event off the Register such as negative prescription.
[5]   AFT(S)A 2000, s 43(2)(b). It is to be hoped, however, that, in Land Register cases, he will at least verify that a *building* within 100 metres is disclosed by the plan.
[6]   AFT(S)A 2000, s 43(2)(bb), inserted by the Title Conditions (Scotland) Act 2003, s 114(6), Sch 13, para 8.
[7]   AFT(S)A 2000, s 43(2)(bb).
[8]   AFT(S)A 2000, 43(2)(c). Since, however, such a notice is not a condition of the validity of a s 19 agreement (see para 3.23), this limitation is unexpected.
[9]   AFT(S)A 2000, s 43(2)(d). The last of these is unrelated to the notice and has no bearing on its validity. It is not clear why it is included here.
[10]   AFT(S)A 2000, s 43(2)(e).
[11]   Or in the case of a Lands Tribunal order registered after the appointed day, immediately before the day of registration. See AFT(S)A 2000, ss 43(3), 65A(11).
[12]   As to which see the AFT(S)A 2000, s 46.
[13]   It is much longer than the version which left the Scottish Law Commission.

Invalidity

11.15 The exemption from scrutiny, just described, makes it more likely that defective notices will reach the Registers. But a notice might also be invalid on grounds not touched on by the exemption and some at least of which would be verified as a matter of course at the Land Register (although not, for the most the most part, at the Register of Sasines). These include, for example:

- a failure to follow the statutory style;
- the absence of sufficient title to the superiority or, in the case of a notice under ss 18 or 20 or s 19 agreement, to the nominated property;
- a failure to deduce title, in a case where this is required;
- the use of a notice for a condition which is not truly a real burden[1];
- an error in the description of one of the properties or in the narration of the real burdens;
- an error in the identification of the deed by which the burdens are imposed;
- the use of one notice for an originally single feu which has now been divided into two[2]; and
- an error in execution.

Nonetheless, cases of undiscovered error are likely to be rare, and not all errors will be so serious as to invalidate a notice. If, however, a notice is invalid, it is not cured by registration. That that should be true of the Register of Sasines is of course self-evident. But even in the Land Register it seems unlikely that the, often curative, effect of registration operates in the present case. This is because preservation is neither achieved by registration as such, nor even at the time of registration. In other words registration, while a necessary condition of preservation, is not a sufficient condition[3].

It follows that it cannot be assumed, as a matter of certainty, that a burden which was the subject of a preservation notice has successfully survived the abolition of the feudal system. In the future a cautious inquirer will inspect the notice as well as the entry on the Register. The difficulty should not be over-stated, however. It merely adds another example to an existing state of affairs, namely that the fact of a burden appearing on the Land Register is not, of itself, a guarantee of its continued existence. And in the future, as in the past, owners are likely to assume validity unless, most unusually, the contrary is shown.

[1]   Para 2.12.
[2]   Abolition of Feudal Tenure etc (Scotland) Act 2000, s 42(2), (3).
[3]   The curative provision of the Land Registration (Scotland) Act 1979 – s 3(1)(a) – is confined to the immediate creation of real rights. And see also LR(S)A 1979, s 3(4).

Wrongful rejection

11.16   A notice rejected by the Keeper[1] on the basis of a mistranscription, defect of execution, or similar error will usually be re-submitted with the error duly corrected. But a notice rejected on a substantive ground is in a different position. Sometimes, of course, the Keeper's objection can be met by corrective conveyancing or by other means. But if the 'error' cannot be corrected, the superior must either accept defeat or challenge the Keeper's view before the Lands Tribunal or the ordinary courts[2]. There is then a problem of timing, for even if the challenge succeeds it is unlikely to do so until after the appointed day, and by then it is too late to register the notice.

This difficulty is met by the Abolition of Feudal Tenure Act[3]. A notice (or agreement) determined by a court to be registrable may be registered after the appointed day provided it is registered within two months of the determination. The registration is treated as if it had occurred before the appointed day, with the result that the burden is deemed always to have been preserved. To avoid registrations long after the appointed day, some time limits are placed on this facility. Thus the judicial challenge must be made within a prescribed period, and the ultimate registration within a second such period. At the time of writing no periods had yet been prescribed by Scottish Ministers for this purpose[4].

[1]   For the Keeper's power of rejection, see Land Registration (Scotland) Act 1979, s 4 (Land Register) and *Macdonald v Keeper of the General Register of Sasines* 1914 SC 854 (Register of Sasines).

[2]   Land Registration (Scotland) Act 1979, s 25; *Macdonald v Keeper of the General Register of Sasines* 1914 SC 854; *Short's Tr v Keeper of the Registers of Scotland* 1996 SC (HL) 14.

[3]   Abolition of Feudal Tenure etc (Scotland) Act 2000, s 45.

[4]   The Scottish Law Commission recommended that the second period should be five years after the appointed day: see *Report on Abolition of the Feudal System* para 4.71.

CHALLENGES

Weighing the options

11.17   In the normal course of events the vassal will receive a copy of the notice before it is registered, accompanied by an explanatory note which closes with the words: 'If you think that there is a mistake in this notice or if you wish to challenge it, you are advised to contact your solicitor or other adviser'[1]. Of course it is true, as already mentioned, that preservation is not achieved by an inept notice[2]. Thus in a sense the vassal has nothing to lose by letting matters take their course. If the notice is void, the burden will fall on the appointed day, without any intervention on the part of the vassal; and if it is good, nothing can be done. Indeed as a tactical matter the vassal may not wish to alert the superior to a defect in the notice until after the appointed day, by which time it will be too late to register a replacement.

Nonetheless a vassal may be reluctant to let a bad notice go unchecked. For the very fact of its appearance on the Register affords a *prima facie* indication of validity, and is likely in practice to lead to compliance with the burden to which it relates. The vassal may therefore want the notice – and, unless there are third-party rights[3], the burden itself – removed from the Register. This can be achieved in more than one way.

[1]   See eg the Abolition of Feudal Tenure etc (Scotland) Act 2000, Sch 5.

[2]   Para 11.15.

[3]   If co-feuars have enforcement rights, these are unaffected by feudal abolition and so the burden lives on: see para 2.5. Similarly, a burden survives if it is preserved on some other ground: see para 2.10.

Rectification

11.18   Sometimes the defect in the notice is self-evident, or at least easily demonstrated. In that event the simplest course of action, in the case of Land Register titles, is to apply for rectification of the Register[1]. The 2000 Act amends the Land Registration (Scotland) Act 1979 to allow rectification, even against a proprietor in possession, of any inaccuracy arising out of 'anything done (or purportedly done) under or by virtue of any provision of the Abolition of Feudal Tenure etc (Scotland) Act 2000'[2]. A purported but invalid preservation notice could be removed under this provision. No indemnity is then payable by the Keeper to the superior[3].

Some grounds of objection are difficult to evaluate. Reasonable people may disagree, for example, about whether a burden is truly for the purposes of conservation, or of economic development, or whether it reserves development value. Quite often, therefore, the existence of a defect will not be self-evident, or, even if it is, will leave room for argument as to whether the defect is sufficiently serious as to invalidate the notice. But unless the position is reasonably clear, the Keeper is unlikely to rectify without judicial direction. If this point is reached the vassal has a choice of judicial process. One is to challenge directly the validity of the notice. The other, available only after the appointed day, is to challenge the burden itself. Only the former, however, is available for a s 33 notice[4] and only the latter for a 19 agreement[5].

[1]   Land Registration (Scotland) Act 1979, s 9.
[2]   LR(S)A 1979, s 9(3B), inserted by the Abolition of Feudal Tenure etc (Scotland) Act 2000, s 3(b).
[3]   LR(S)A 1979, s 12(3)(cc), inserted by the AFT(S) A 2000, s 3(c).
[4]   For such a notice does not preserve the burden.
[5]   For AFT(S)A 2000, s 44 is confined to notices. In practice it is hardly likely that a vassal who signed an agreement could subsequently challenge its validity, except perhaps on the ground of some defect of consent such as fraud or undue influence. But a successor might wish to make a challenge.

Challenge to notice

11.19   The Lands Tribunal has jurisdiction over preservation notices and can discharge those that it finds to be invalid[1]. A discharge takes effect on registration[2]. An application to the Lands Tribunal can be made before, as well as after, the appointed day. The burden of proving any disputed question of fact is placed on the superior (or other person relying on the notice) and not on the vassal[3].

[1]   Abolition of Feudal Tenure etc (Scotland) Act 2000, s 44(1).
[2]   AFT(S)A 2000, s 44(4). The fact that a Tribunal discharge is registrable circumvents any possible difficulty with rectification of the kind which arose in *Short's Tr v Keeper of the Registers of Scotland* 1996 SC (HL) 14. See Scottish Law Commission *Report on Abolition of the Feudal System* para 4.74.
[3]   AFT(S)A 2000, s 44(3).

Challenge to burden

11.20 Alternatively, the burden itself can be challenged. For an invalid notice means the extinction of the burden (in a question at least with the former superior) on the appointed day; and after that day it would be open to the (former) vassal to seek a declarator in appropriate terms, which could form the basis of an application for rectification of the Land Register. The Title Conditions Act extends jurisdiction from the ordinary courts to the Lands Tribunal, allowing a choice of forum[1].

1   Title Conditions (Scotland) Act 2003, s 90(1)(a)(ii).

Chapter 12

Compensation notices

Introduction

12.1 The Abolition of Feudal Tenure etc (Scotland) Act 2000 allows compensation for the extinction both of development value burdens and of feuduty[1]. In either case the compensation is due only if claimed by service, within a restricted period, of a notice – a compensation notice[2] – under, respectively, sections 8 and 35 of the 2000 Act. Identical service provisions apply in each case[3]. Service is made by the creditor (typically but not always the former superior) on the debtor (typically but not always the former vassal)[4]. Usually the notice must be accompanied by other documents, such as explanatory notes or an instalment document.

If the feu, or former feu, is owned by more than one person, there are a corresponding number of debtors, each with joint and several liability[5]. Although only a single notice is needed, it seems that separate service must be made on each debtor[6]. Thus even if, as usually, the debtors share a common address, a notice should be sent to each in a separate envelope[7]; and strictly this should be a principal notice, duly signed by the creditor, and not a mere copy[8].

[1] See, respectively, chs 9 and 10.

[2] As opposed to a preservation notice, the other type of notice provided for under the 2000 Act. See para 11.1.

[3] Abolition of Feudal Tenure etc (Scotland) Act 2000 ss 11, 36.

[4] Paras 9.14, 10.10.

[5] AFT(S)A 2000, ss 16(4), 39(2).

[6] The basic rule is that service is to be on 'the' former vassal or owner (AFT(S)A 2000, ss 11(1), 36(1)), which seems to carry the idea that, if the title is held *pro indiviso*, service must be made on each owner or vassal. That, certainly, was the view of the Scottish Law Commission: see *Report on Abolition of the Feudal System* p 191 (commentary on cl 31). And the idea that separate service might occur is brought out in ss 11(4), 36(4) which define the date on which service is made on 'a' former vassal and 'an' owner. The position is further reinforced by s 16(4)(b), which provides that *pro indiviso* vassals are treated as a single vassal *subject to s 11* – with the clear implication that for the purposes of s 11 they are to be treated separately. No part of s 16(4)(b) applies to s 36, however, but it is improbable that a different rule was intended for s 36, and indeed the true explanation of the reference to s 11 in s 16(4)(b) is probably that, in the version of the Bill produced by the Scottish Law Commission, s 11(2) did indeed have special rules for service on *pro indiviso* vassals.

[7] The Scottish Law Commission proposed otherwise – see cl 11(2)(a) of its draft Bill – but this provision was removed before the Bill was introduced to Parliament.

⁸   The requirement is to serve 'the documents in question' (s 11(1)) or 'the notice in question' (s 36(1)). Compare the rule for preservation notices in s 41(3) of the 2000 Act, where all that need be sent is 'a copy'.

Method of service

12.2   Service may be effected either personally or by post. Personal service means delivery to the debtor in person, and postal service means service by registered post or recorded delivery[1]. Thus a notice is *not* validly served if it is sent by ordinary post or pushed through the letter box.

In practice it may be assumed that notices will usually be served by recorded delivery. Like the notice itself, the envelope must contain the name of the debtor[2], and it must be addressed to (i) the debtor's place of residence, (ii) his place of business, or (iii) a postal address which he ordinarily uses[3]. If the creditor knows all three addresses, then there is a free choice. If he knows only one, then that address must be used. If the creditor knows of no current address, it is permissible to send the notice to the address which is most recently known[4]. Quite often that may be the former feu, although not all feus – a field, for example – have postal addresses. If all else fails, a search of the Register will disclose the conveyance in favour of the debtor and hence his address at that time.

1   Abolition of Feudal Tenure etc (Scotland) Act 2000, ss 11(1), 36(1).
2   AFT(S)A 2000, ss 11(1), 36(1).
3   AFT(S)A 2000, ss 11(5), 36(5).
4   AFT(S)A 2000, ss 11(5), 36(5).

Wrong address

12.3   If the address is not current, the notice will be returned by the Post Office. The creditor may then wish to try again, perhaps with a different address. But once a notice has been returned, the 2000 Act offers the alternative of service by sending or delivery to the Extractor of the Court of Session[1]. Ordinary post is sufficient. Service in this way is a means of complying with the time limits for service laid down by the 2000 Act but will not in itself lead to payment. If, however, postal service failed only because of a refusal to accept delivery, the debtor is extant and identifiable and can be pursued for the money.

1   Abolition of Feudal Tenure etc (Scotland) Act 2000, ss 11(2), 36(2).

Wrong debtor

12.4   Sometimes the notice is addressed to the wrong person. Assuming that the creditor had searched the Land or Sasine Register, this can occur only because the land has since been conveyed without completion of title by registration[1]. A notice addressed to the wrong person is of no legal effect, and must be re-done and served of new. Presumably in most cases a person on whom a notice is wrongly served will contact the creditor and dispute liability. He is encouraged to do so by the statement, in the notice or explanatory note, drawing attention to a duty to give the creditor such information as the person may have as to the identity and address of the true debtor. The duty itself is set out in the Abolition of Feudal Tenure Act[2]. No style of warning statement is given for notices under s 35 but one will be found in Appendix 5 to this book[3]. For notices under s 8 the statement appears in the explanatory note rather than in the notice itself, and statutory wording is provided[4].

[1]   Paras 9.14, 10.10.
[2]   Abolition of Feudal Tenure etc (Scotland) Act 2000, ss 15, 38.
[3]   AFT(S)A 2000, s 38 merely provides that 'the notice shall refer to that requirement for disclosure'.
[4]   AFT(S)A 2000, Schs 1, 2. The simpler version, which is in Sch 1, reads: 'If at one time you had right to the property in question but, immediately before the feudal system was abolished, you no longer had that right (because, for example, you had sold that property to someone else) then this notice has been served on you in error and no payment will be due; but you nevertheless have to provide the person who sent you the notice, if you can, with such information as you have which might enable him to identify the person who should have received notice instead of you'.

Date of service

12.5   The date of service is the date of posting or, in a case of personal service, the date of delivery[1]. This date is important both as indicating compliance with the time limits set by the 2000 Act and also as constituting the debt and fixing the time for payment[2].

[1]   Abolition of Feudal Tenure etc (Scotland) Act 2000, ss 11(4), 36(4).
[2]   Paras 9.14, 10.9.

Evidence of service

12.6   Evidence of service is likely to be at issue only if the debtor does not pay. Assuming that service was by post, the matter lies within the creditor's hands. It is sufficient evidence under the 2000 Act to produce the postal receipt accompanied by a certificate in the prescribed form and signed and dated by the creditor or his agent[1]. There is no requirement that the certificate be prepared contemporaneously with service. In the case of a notice under section 8 (feuduty) the certificate reads[2]:

> Notice under section 8(1) of the Abolition of Feudal Tenure etc (Scotland) Act 2000 requiring a compensatory payment was posted to Adam Smith, together with an instalment document and the requisite explanatory note relating to the notice, on 26 February 2005.

In a case of personal service, it is the debtor who must sign and date the certificate, in the following terms[3]:

I, Adam Smith, acknowledge receipt of a notice under section 8(1) of the Abolition of Feudal Tenure etc (Scotland) Act 2000 requiring a compensatory payment, of an instalment document and of an explanatory note relating to the notice.

Finally, if service was on the Extractor of the Court of Session, no certificate is needed, and the Extractor acknowledges receipt on a copy of the documents that were sent[4].

[1]   Abolition of Feudal Tenure etc (Scotland) Act 2000, ss 11(2), 36(2). The prescribed forms are set out, respectively, in Sch 4, Form B and Sch 10, Form B.

[2]   AFT(S)A 2000, Sch 4, Form B. Unexpectedly, both this certificate and the corresponding certificate under Form A (quoted below) omit any reference to the second explanatory note which must accompany the instalment document (see s 10(1)).

[3]   AFT(S)A 2000, Sch 4, Form A.

[4]   AFT(S)A 2000, ss 11(3), 36(3).

Chapter 13

Conveyancing after the appointed day

INTRODUCTION

13.1 This chapter considers the changes in conveyancing practice which are made necessary, after the appointed day (28 November 2004), by the Abolition of Feudal Tenure etc (Scotland) Act 2000. Most are a direct consequence of the abolition of the feudal system, although the opportunity of legislation was taken to make a number of other changes, such as the removal of warrants of registration[1]. Brief mention is also made of the Title Conditions (Scotland) Act 2003[2]. The changes range in importance from the minor to the highly significant. In this chapter they are analysed according to their effect on the creation of real rights, beginning with ownership itself and then progressing through the subordinate real rights (proper liferent, lease, standard security, real burden and servitude). A final section considers those changes which are of more general application.

[1] Para 13.17.
[2] Paras 13.15, 13.16. The treatment is selective, however, and a full consideration of the 2003 Act is beyond the scope of this book.

OWNERSHIP

Discontinuation of grants in feu

13.2 The feudal system is abolished on the appointed day[1]. To avoid the possibility that it might immediately be re-created by fresh grants in feu, the 2000 Act disallows new feudal estates in land[2]. Thus the last opportunity to register a feu disposition is immediately before the Registers close for the weekend on Friday 26 November 2004. Any feu so created will then be extinguished, not much more than 24 hours later, at the start of Sunday 28 November. It is arguable, but not certain, that a deed couched in the language of a grant in feu, and containing a *tenendas* clause, is not completely void after the appointed day but will be given effect to as a disposition.

¹   Abolition of Feudal Tenure etc (Scotland) Act 2000, s 1.
²   AFT(S)A 2000, s 2(3).

Crown grants

13.3   Grants from the Crown always proceeded by means of a feu, for a mere disposition would have left the land as allodial and its competency was uncertain¹. These doubts are removed by the 2000 Act². Once grants in feu cease to be available, a Crown grant will proceed by disposition³.

¹   Scottish Law Commission *Report on Abolition of the Feudal System* para 2.26.
²   Abolition of Feudal Tenure etc (Scotland) Act 2000, s 59.
³   Sections 63–93 of the Titles to Land Consolidation (Scotland) Act 1868, which deal with feudal Crown writs, are therefore repealed by the AFT(S)A 2000, s 76(2), Sch 13. For an explanation, see Scottish Law Commission *Report on Abolition of the Feudal System* paras 9.19, 9.20.

Transfer of ownership

13.4   In the law as it stood before the appointed day the transfer of ownership was couched largely in feudal terms. Thus the registration of a conveyance was declared to have the same effect as the granting of a conveyance followed by the registration of an instrument of sasine¹; and this deemed registration of the instrument of sasine was said to be as effective as if sasine had been given on the land itself, by symbolical delivery². Finally, registration of the conveyance also had the effect of entry with the superior – of, in other words, feudal investiture or infeftment as the new vassal³.

These provisions reflect the complexity of land transfer before the reforms of the period 1845 to 1874. In brief, transfer involved the following steps⁴:

(i)   A deed was granted which could operate either as a disposition (so that the land was held *a me de superiore meo*)⁵ or as a feu disposition (*de me*)⁶.

(ii)   Sasine was given on the land by delivery of the appropriate symbol, such as earth and stone.

(iii)   Both the deed and the ceremony were narrated in a further, notarial, deed, the instrument of sasine, which was recorded in the Register of Sasines. At this point the transferee became infeft as vassal *of the transferor*.

(iv)   Later, and sometimes much later, the transferor's superior confirmed the transfer by grant of a charter of confirmation. Immediately the transferee became infeft as the vassal *of the superior*, and the transferor, finally, dropped out of the feudal chain.

Of the three deeds employed, only the instrument of sasine could competently be registered. A conveyance could not be registered until as late as 1858.

The effect of the nineteenth-century reforms was to make steps (ii)–(iv) unnecessary. But rather than abolishing them as a formal requirement, the technique adopted by the legislation was to treat step (i) – provided that the conveyance itself was recorded – as the equivalent of the, now missing, steps (ii)–(iv). The rule in practice became simple and familiar: ownership was transferred by registration of a conveyance. But behind this familiar rule lay a deemed sasine and investiture[7].

The 2000 Act preserves the rule but abandons its feudal basis[8]. After the appointed day, as before, ownership of land is transferred by registration of a conveyance. Normally that conveyance will be a disposition, but the language of the rule is sufficiently general to allow for a conveyance by court decree (such as confirmation of executors) or by statute[9]. In the case of the Register of Sasines only[10], a transfer is also effected, as under the existing law, by the recording of a notice of title with an appropriate midcouple[11]. The provision is confined to the transfer of ownership in the strict sense, and is neutral on the issue raised by *Sharp v Thomson*[12] as to whether, as a matter of statutory interpretation, the mere delivery of a disposition defeats the subsequent crystallisation of the transferor's floating charge[13].

1   Titles to Land Consolidation (Scotland) Act 1868, s 15.
2   Infeftment Act 1845, s 1.
3   Conveyancing (Scotland) Act 1874, s 4.
4   See also para 1.22. For a fuller discussion, see K G C Reid *The Law of Property in Scotland* (1996) paras 94–107 (G L Gretton). The account presupposes the use of a conveyance *a me vel de me*.
5   From me of my superior.
6   Of me.
7   Hence the provisions referred to at the beginning of this paragraph.
8   Abolition of Feudal Tenure etc (Scotland) Act 2000, s 4.
9   It also, by s 4(2), preserves such other methods of transfer as might exist, most notably by operation of a survivorship destination.
10   In the Land Register notices of title are dispensed with and the midcouple can, in effect, be registered directly: see the Land Registration (Scotland) Act 1979, s 3(6).
11   AFT(S)A 2000, s 4(3)(a)(ii). Notarial instruments, the more cumbersome predecessor of notices of title, are formally abolished by the AFT(S)A 2000, s 76(2), Sch 13. See Scottish Law Commission *Report on Abolition of the Feudal System* paras 7.27–7.33. The main provisions affected are listed in note 76.
12   1997 SC (HL) 66.
13   For a full discussion, and proposals for reform, see Scottish Law Commission *Discussion Paper on Sharp v Thomson*, Scot Law Com DP no 114, 2001 (available on www.scotlawcom.gov.uk). The rule in *Sharp* has since been held by the Inner House in *Burnett's Tr v Grainger* 2002 SLT 699 to be confined to floating charges, but at the time of writing an appeal was due to be heard by the House of Lords. See, on *Burnett's Tr*, K G C Reid and G L Gretton *Conveyancing 2002* (2003) pp 92–97; S Wortley and D Reid 'Mind the Gap: Problems in the Transfer of Ownership' (2002) 7 SLPQ 211.

Feudal terminology: uninfeft proprietors

13.5   Feudal terminology should no longer be used in deeds drafted after the appointed day. 'Uninfeft proprietor' is perhaps the feudal term most current, infeftment signifying feudal investiture by entry with the superior[1]. A ready alternative is 'unregistered proprietor'[2].

[1]   K G C Reid *The Law of Property in Scotland* (1996) para 93 (G L Gretton).
[2]   Scottish Law Commission *Report on Abolition of the Feudal System* para 7.24.

Deduction of title

13.6 'Infeftment' is likewise removed from the statute book. So, for example, in the familiar provisions in the Conveyancing (Scotland) Act 1924, now amended, concerning deduction of title, title is to be deduced from the 'person having the last recorded title' and not from the 'person last infeft'[1]. The 2000 Act also fills a minor lacuna in the 1924 Act provisions by allowing deduction of title in a case where no title to the land had ever previously been registered[2]. This will usually be because the land was acquired by a corporation before the Register of Sasines was set up in 1617 and has continued in the same ownership ever since[3].

[1]   See in particular the Conveyancing (Scotland) Act 1924, s 4, as amended by the Abolition of Feudal Tenure etc (Scotland) Act 2000, s 76(1), Sch 12, para 15(4).
[2]   AFT(S)A 2000, s 6.
[3]   For an example involving the University of St Andrews, see *Wallace v University Court of the University of St Andrews* (1904) 6 F 1093.

Ownership of land by partnerships

13.7 Although a partnership in Scots (but not English) law is a juristic person, and so can in general hold title to property, the traditional view was that it could not sustain a feudal relationship and so could not hold feudal property[1]. Quite why this was so was never satisfactorily explained[2]. It is unlikely now to be tested by the courts, for the issue disappears with the feudal system itself. The Abolition of Feudal Tenure Act puts the matter beyond doubt. On or after the appointed day[3]

A firm may, if it has a legal personality distinct from the persons who compose it, itself own land.

Nonetheless, in view of the tendency of partnerships to dissolve on a change of membership[4], this course of action can hardly be recommended, and it will be much safer to continue the practice by which the land is held by trustees on behalf of the partnership[5].

The law of partnership is under review by the Law Commission and the Scottish Law Commission, and their final recommendations are due to be published during 2003[6]. If, as seems likely, they recommend continuity of legal personality, and if the recommendation is implemented by legislation, it may then be worth considering a change of conveyancing practice.

1   See eg Bell *Principles* s 357.
2   S C Styles 'Why can't partnerships hold heritage?' (1989) 34 JLSS 414.
3   Abolition of Feudal Tenure etc (Scotland) Act 2000, s 70.
4   Law Commission and Scottish Law Commission *Partnership Law: A Joint Consultation Paper*, Scot Law Com DP no 111 (2000; available on www.scotlawcom.gov.uk) paras 2.34–2.35; K G C Reid and G L Gretton *Conveyancing 1999* (2000) pp 44–48.
5   For partnership conveyancing, see G L Gretton and K G C Reid *Conveyancing* (2nd edn, 1999) ch 27.
6   Scottish Law Commission *Thirty-Seventh Annual Report 2002*, Scot Law Com no 189 (2003), para 3.5.

PROPER LIFERENTS

13.8   Proper liferent is to be distinguished from a liferent created by means of a trust. Only the former is a real right. In modern practice proper liferents are rare but not unknown[1]. A proper liferent is created either by direct grant (when it is known as a 'simple' liferent)[2], or by a conveyance of the land in which the liferent is reserved.

Ownership apart, proper liferent was the only real right on which sasine and infeftment required to be taken[3]. Originally this involved symbolical delivery and a charter by progress from the superior but, after the conveyancing reforms of the mid-nineteenth century, both sasine and infeftment were achieved merely by registration of the deed in which the liferent was granted or reserved[4]. The 2000 Act removes the feudal basis of the constitution of liferents while retaining the substance of the rule. Thus after the appointed day a proper liferent is created by registration, in the Land or Sasine Register, of the deed of grant or reservation[5]. Normally the real right comes into being at the time of registration, but provision is made for its postponement in the deed to a later date.

1   See, for example, the proper liferent litigated in *Stronach's Exrs v Robertson* 2002 SLT 1044.
2   W J Dobie *Liferent and Fee* (1941) p 4.
3   Para 1.27. Pre-1970 heritable securities were in the same position.
4   Para 13.4.
5   Abolition of Feudal Tenure etc (Scotland) Act 2000, s 65. In a case involving the Register of Sasines it is permissible, as under the previous law, to register instead a notice of title: see s 65(4).

LEASES

Restriction to 175 years

13.9   Residential leases have been restricted to 20 years since 1974[1]. With effect from 9 June 2000, the 2000 Act restricts all other leases to 175 years[2]. Both the period and the principle were controversial. One view was that there should be no restriction at all. Others thought that a restriction was justified if Scotland was to avoid a second feudal system by leasehold title, on the English model, but felt that the period should be longer than the 125 years recommended by the Scottish Law Commission. As introduced to Parliament, the Bill provided for 125 years, but an amendment by the Executive increased this to 175 years.

The main provision is straightforward. Whatever a lease might actually say about duration, it cannot continue for more than 175 years. So if a lease provides for a duration of, say, 150 years, the lease lasts for the full contractual term. But if the stipulated duration is 200 years, s 67(1) of the 2000 Act will override the contractual term and bring the lease to an end after 175 years.

The limitation applies only to new leases, ie to leases executed on or after the day the section came into force (9 June 2000). The 175-year limitation does not, however, apply to a lease in implement of an obligation entered into before 9 June 2000[3]. That obligation would normally be contained in a contract, but might also be contained in an existing lease (ie that lease might contain an option, typically in favour of the tenant, allowing for the renewal of the lease for a further period).

Pre-2000 long leases are unaffected, at least for the time being. The whole subject of long leases is, however, currently under consideration by the Scottish Law Commission, which may in due course recommend legislation allowing certain classes of long lease to be converted into ownership[4].

[1]   Land Tenure Reform (Scotland) Act 1974, ss 8–10.
[2]   Abolition of Feudal Tenure etc (Scotland) Act 2000, s 67. See Scottish Law Commission *Report on Abolition of the Feudal System* paras 9.40–9.42.
[3]   AFT(S)A 2000, s 67(4)(a).
[4]   Scottish Law Commission *Discussion Paper on Conversion of Long Leases*, Scot Law Com DP no 112 (2001; available on www.scotlawcom.gov.uk).

Consecutive leases

13.10   As a general rule, forced renewals are treated by the Abolition of Feudal Tenure Act as part of the original term. So if there is a lease for 99 years with an option in favour of the tenant to renew for another 99, this is treated as a lease for 198 years. Accordingly, if renewed, the lease comes to an end automatically after 175 years. The idea is to prevent the 175-year limit being avoided by a chain of consecutive leases. The position is different if, at the end of one 99-year lease, the parties *voluntarily* enter into a second lease for 99 years (there being no option stipulated for in the lease or elsewhere). In that case there are two leases and not one.

There are some exceptions. As already mentioned, the 175-year limit is not applied where there is (i) a lease entered into prior to 9 June 2000 containing an obligation to renew followed by (ii) a second lease, after 9 June 2000, in implement of that option[1]. Here it does not matter if the second lease is for more than 175 years. *A fortiori* it does not matter if the combined duration of the leases exceeds 175 years.

Section 67(4)(b) of the 2000 Act extends the exception by allowing *one* further lease. In other words if (i) a 200-year lease entered into on 5 January 2000 contains an option to renew for, say, 200 years, and (ii) that lease is then renewed on 5 January 2200 by a lease which itself contains an obligation to renew for a further 200 years, then (iii) the second renewal, due on 5 January 2400, is perfectly competent. But no third renewal is allowed. The purpose of this exception is to allow the continuation of so-called Blairgowrie leases (chains of leases each with a 99-year term) for long enough to allow legislation to be brought forward following the work of the Scottish Law Commission, mentioned earlier[2]. The chain must, however, have started prior to 9 June 2000. Thus new chains of lease are not now possible, and cannot be used as a means of avoiding the 175-year limit[3].

[1]   Abolition of Feudal Tenure etc (Scotland) Act 2000, s 67(4)(a).
[2]   Scottish Parliament *Official Report* Justice and Home Affairs Committee, 29 March 2000, col 1018 (Mr Angus MacKay MSP).
[3]   AFT(S)A 2000, s 67(2).

Tacit relocation

13.11   The 175-year limit has no effect on tacit relocation[1]. So if, after the 175-year period has run, neither party has served a notice to quit, the lease will continue from year to year by tacit relocation.

[1]   Abolition of Feudal Tenure etc (Scotland) Act 2000, s 67(3)(a).

Subleases

13.12   Subleases are also subject to the 175-year rule[1]. Indeed it could hardly be otherwise, for if the head lease lasts for only 175 years, a sublease could not have a longer duration. However, in cases where the duration of the head lease exceeds 175 years – usually because it was granted before 9 June 2000 – any sublease may also exceed 175 years, even if granted after 9 June 2000[2].

[1]   Abolition of Feudal Tenure etc (Scotland) Act 2000, s 67(5).
[2]   AFT(S)A 2000, s 67(4)(c).

STANDARD SECURITIES

Security subjects

13.13   Until the appointed day a standard security may be created over any 'interest in land'[1], defined as[2] any estate or interest in land, other than an entailed estate or any interest therein, which is capable of being owned or held as a separate interest and to which a title may be recorded in the Register of Sasines.

This definition, like many similar passages in the statute book, could not be left unchanged. For following the abolition of the feudal system there are no more estates in land, and an owner holds the land directly[3]. Nor is there any advantage in the use of 'interest in land', a relative newcomer to Scots law[4] but one which conveniently encompassed both feudal estates and Romanistic real rights. With the abolition of feudal estates, it becomes possible, and desirable, to refer to real rights directly[5].

From the appointed day, the rule is reformulated as permitting standard securities over any 'land or real right in land', and real right in land is defined as meaning[6]

any such right, other than ownership or a real burden, which is capable of being held separately and to which a title may be recorded in the Register of Sasines.

The change is of conceptual rather than of practical importance. Standard securities can be used in the same way after the appointed day as before[7]. But in the ordinary case of a security granted by an owner, the result is a real right in the land itself and not merely an encumbrance on a feudal estate.

[1]   Conveyancing and Feudal Reform (Scotland) Act 1970, s 9(2).
[2]   CFR(S)A 1970, s 9(8)(b).
[3]   Abolition of Feudal Tenure etc (Scotland) Act 2000, s 2(1).
[4]   *Kaur v Singh* 1999 SC 180 at 185H per Lord President Rodger: 'The concept itself is of no great antiquity in our law, having apparently made its first appearance in the 1970 Act and having surfaced again in the Prescription and Limitation (Scotland) Act 1973.'
[5]   The numerous occurrences of 'interest in land' in the Land Registration (Scotland) Act 1979 are not, however, replaced, pending the review of that Act currently being conducted by the Scottish Law Commission. Elsewhere, and especially in United Kingdom legislation, the very vagueness of 'interest in land' can make it a useful expression. The policy of the 2000 Act is to replace some occurrences but leave others. See Scottish Law Commission *Report on Abolition of the Feudal System* para 9.5.
[6]   Conveyancing and Feudal Reform (Scotland) Act 1970, s 9(8)(b), as amended by the Title Conditions (Scotland) Act 2003, s 128(1), Sch 14, para 4(2)(b).
[7]   A standard security may not, however, be granted over some of the new personal real burdens, namely conservation burdens, personal pre-emption burdens and personal redemption burdens. See Conveyancing and Feudal Reform (Scotland) Act 1970, s 9(2B), inserted by the TC(S)A 2003, s 128(1), Sch 14, para 4(2)(a); TC(S)A 2003, s 38(3).

Descriptions

13.14   Note 1 to Schedule 2 to the Conveyancing and Feudal Reform (Scotland) Act 1970, as originally enacted, provided that

The security subjects shall be described by means of a particular description or by reference to a description thereof as in Schedule D to the Conveyancing

(Scotland) Act 1924 or as in Schedule G to the Titles to Land Consolidation (Scotland) Act 1868.

Note 1 applies only to Sasine transactions and first registrations. Once a property is on the Land Register it is both necessary, and also sufficient, to refer to the title number[1].

In *Beneficial Bank plc v McConnachie*[2] the effect of note 1 was said to be that a particular description (either directly or by reference) was required in all standard securities. A general description would not do. Accordingly, a standard security which described a terraced house only by its postal address ('the Heritable Subjects known as 57 Longdykes Road, Prestonpans in the County of East Lothian') failed to satisfy the requirements of note 1.

This was an awkward rule, and one which did not apply to other conveyancing deeds, such as dispositions. Of course in most cases a standard security did in fact contain a particular description, usually by reference to another deed. But there was a special difficulty with tenement flats. According to *Beneficial Bank* it was sufficient, in the case of an upper flat, to give its location within the building (eg 'top flat south'); but with a flat on the ground floor it was necessary to stipulate the actual boundaries. Since in practice ground-floor flats tended to be described in the same way as other flats, the effect of *Beneficial Bank* was to make a large number of securities over ground-floor flats ineffective.

This decision, criticised at the time[3], is now superseded. The Abolition of Feudal Tenure Act substitutes, with effect from 9 June 2000, a new version of note 1 which says merely that[4]

> The security subjects shall be described sufficiently to identify them; but this note is without prejudice to any additional requirement imposed as respects any register.

The effect of this amendment is to readmit general descriptions. The reference to 'any additional requirement imposed as respects any register' makes clear that the Keeper must be satisfied with the sufficiency of the description[5]; but this is no more than the rule that applies (in Sasine transactions) to all conveyancing deeds.

An important feature of the change is that it is retrospective[6]. All standard securities are covered, even those executed and recorded before 9 June 2000. This is less surprising than it sounds. In *Beneficial Bank v Wardle*[7] rectification was allowed under s 8 of the Law Reform (Miscellaneous Provisions) (Scotland) Act 1985 in respect of a standard security in which – as the law then was – the security subjects had not been properly described. The rectification sought was to substitute a particular description for a general description. This decision suggested that wherever the description in a standard security fell short of the required standard, the error could be put right by an application for rectification under s 8. In practice this would only be required if the debtor defaulted and the loan was called up. The effect of making the 2000 Act amendment retrospective is not, therefore, to give the heritable creditor a right which could not be obtained by other means. Rather it is to save the trouble and expense of an application under s 8 of the 1985 Act.

1   Land Registration (Scotland) Rules 1980, SI 1980/1413, r 25.
2   1996 SC 119. An earlier decision, *Bennett v Beneficial Bank plc* 1995 SLT 1105, had been to the same effect.
3   See eg A J McDonald *Conveyancing Manual* (6th edn, 1997, by S Brymer, D J Cusine and R Rennie) para 8.11.
4   Abolition of Feudal Tenure etc (Scotland) Act 2000, Sch 12, para 30(23)(a).
5   *Macdonald v Keeper of the General Register of Sasines* 1914 SC 854. The directions at paras 6.66 and 6.67 of the *Registration of Title Practice Book* (2nd edn, 2000) must be taken to have been superseded by the legislative change.
6   AFT(S)A 2000, s 77(3).
7   1996 GWD 30-1825.

REAL BURDENS

13.15   Following the abolition of feudal real burdens[1], the law of non-feudal real burdens (praedial real burdens) is fundamentally re-cast by the Title Conditions (Scotland) Act 2003 in provisions which come into force on the appointed day. Some of those are discussed elsewhere in this work[2]. So far as the creation of burdens is concerned, the main changes are that:

(i)   any deed may be used and not only a conveyance or deed of conditions[3];
(ii)   the word 'real burden' is necessary, or alternatively 'community burden' or one of the other nominate burdens introduced by the 2003 Act[4];
(iii) the benefited property must be nominated and identified in the deed[5]; and
(iv)   the deed must be registered against both the benefited and the burdened properties[6].

1   Paras 2.6 ff.
2   Paras 7.2–7.6, 7.15–7.27.
3   Title Conditions (Scotland) Act 2003, s 4(1).
4   TC(S)A 2003, s 4(2)(a), (3).
5   TC(S)A 2003, s 4(2)(c)(ii).
6   TC(S)A 2003, s 4(5).

SERVITUDES

13.16   The Title Conditions Act makes some changes to the law of servitudes. From the appointed day the restrictive list of permitted servitudes[1] is abandoned in the case of servitudes created by deed[2]; but a servitude created by deed must now be registered against both the benefited property (dominant tenement) and the burdened property (servient tenement)[3]. Furthermore, it is no longer possible to create a negative servitude[4]. Instead the obligation is to be constituted as a (negative) real burden.

1   Described in R R M Paisley and D J Cusine *Servitudes and Rights of Way* (1998) ch 3.
2   Title Conditions (Scotland) Act 2003, s 76.
3   TC(S)A 2003, s 75(1).
4   TC(S)A 2003, s 79. One idea is to create a clear division between servitudes and real burdens: see Scottish Law Commission *Report on Real Burdens* paras 2.1–2.4.

CHANGES OF GENERAL APPLICATION

Abolition of warrants of registration

13.17   Warrants of registration were introduced in 1858 as part of the reforms which allowed direct registration of conveyances. They can be seen as replacing instruments of sasine, and, like such instruments, mark the assent of the grantee to registration[1]. In recent years the introduction of an application form for Sasine registrations has made the warrant of registration an unnecessary formality. It is abolished by the 2000 Act with effect from the appointed day[2]. The application form is put on a statutory basis although, at the time of writing, its content had yet to be prescribed by Scottish Ministers[3].

1   The current legislation is the Titles to Land Consolidation (Scotland) Act 1868, ss 15, 141 and the Conveyancing (Scotland) Act 1874, Sch F. All are repealed by the Abolition of Feudal Tenure etc (Scotland) Act s 76(2), Sch 13.
2   AFT(S)A 2000, s 5(1).
3   AFT(S)A 2000, s 5(2).

Right to consult titles

13.18   There is a new statutory right – in substance a real right – to consult any title deeds or searches held by others[1]. This ensures that former superiors will make titles available. The right is in addition to the clause of assignation of writs, since 1979 implied into conveyances by statute, which imposes certain obligations in relation to the delivery of deeds[2].

The right to consult is exercisable only by a person with a real right in the land in question, or with a right (such as a right under missives) to acquire such a right. The person holding the titles must 'make them available', and it would presumably be sufficient to offer the opportunity of consultation at the holder's place of business or residence. The person exercising the right must meet such cost as is involved – a statutory version of the traditional formula that deeds are sent on 'the usual borrowing terms'[3].

1   Abolition of Feudal Tenure etc (Scotland) Act 2000, s 66.
2   Land Registration (Scotland) Act 1979, s 16(1). For a discussion, see G L Gretton and K G C Reid *Conveyancing* (2nd edn, 1999) para 11.18.
3   Usual but, it seems, without precise meaning.

Chapter 14

Miscellaneous topics

KINDLY TENANTS OF LOCHMABEN

14.1 Four villages in the parish of Lochmaben in Dumfriesshire (Greenhill, Heck, Hightae, and Smallholm) contain land held under a medieval, and possibly pre-feudal, tenure known as Kindly Tenancies[1]. 'Kindly' in this context means hereditary, and the Tenancies are held in perpetuity on payment of a small rent to the Earl of Mansfield. Whether the land is feudal or allodial has never been properly determined, but for practical purposes the right of a Kindly Tenant can hardly be distinguished from ownership. Conveyancing practice is to treat Kindly Tenancies in the same way as *dominium utile*, and the Abolition of Feudal Tenure etc (Scotland) Act 2000 takes the same approach. Thus on the appointed day all Kindly Tenancies become outright ownership of the land, subject to any encumbrances, such as heritable securities, which previously affected the Tenancy[2]. Most rent has already been redeemed under the Land Tenure Reform (Scotland) Act 1974[3], but all remaining rents are extinguished on the appointed day[4], subject to the payment of compensation on the same basis as for feuduty[5].

By custom each Kindly Tenant holds, as common property, a non-exclusive right to fish for salmon in the River Annan for a stretch of some four miles[6]. This right is preserved by the 2000 Act, and is attached to the land as an inseverable pertinent[7].

[1]   For a fuller account, see Scottish Law Commission *Report on Abolition of the Feudal System* paras 8.4–8.9. And see also J Carmont 'The King's Kindlie Tenants of Lochmaben' (1909–10) 21 JR 323.
[2]   Abolition of Feudal Tenure etc (Scotland) Act 2000, s 64(1), (2). For a fuller discussion in the context of *dominium utile*, see para 1.9.
[3]   Land Tenure Reform (Scotland) Act 1974, ss 4–6.
[4]   AFT(S)A 2000, s 56.
[5]   Paras 10.8–10.15.
[6]   *Royal Four Towns Fishing Association v Assessor for Dumfriesshire* 1956 SC 379. The stretch of the River Annan in question extends from Shillahill Bridge to Smallholmburn: see the Royal Four Towns Fishing Order Confirmation Act 1965.
[7]   AFT(S)A 2000, s 64(3). For inseverable (or invariable) pertinents, see K G C Reid *The Law of Property in Scotland* (1996) para 201.

BARONY TITLES

Introduction

14.2   If a Crown grant was *in liberam baroniam*, important privileges were conferred on the vassal, including the right to hold a court, originally with quite extensive jurisdiction, and the right to the title of 'baron'[1]. Barons were members of the pre-Union Parliament. Barony titles, in the sense of land held on a grant *in liberam baroniam*, have survived into the modern period and are the subject of special treatment by the 2000 Act.

[1]   See, for example: N J M Grier 'Barony Title' (1992) 37 JLSS 306; A Bruce 'Barony Title' (1993) 38 JLSS 156; K G C Reid *The Law of Property in Scotland* (1996) para 54 (G L Gretton); J M Halliday *Conveyancing Law and Practice* vol 2 (2nd edn, 1997) para 33–49(10); Scottish Law Commission *Report on Abolition of the Feudal System* paras 2.31–2.42.

The right to hold a court

14.3   In theory, barons retain a right of both civil and criminal jurisdiction, although its scope was severely restricted by the Heritable Jurisdictions (Scotland) Act 1746. The civil jurisdiction is confined for the most part to cases with a value of under £2, while disposals in criminal cases are limited to a fine of up to £1 or confinement in the stocks for up to three hours[1]. In practice, barony courts have long since ceased to sit except, occasionally, for ceremonial purposes. They are formally abolished by the 2000 Act[2].

[1]   Heritable Jurisdictions (Scotland) Act 1746, s 17.
[2]   Abolition of Feudal Tenure etc (Scotland) Act 2000, s 63(1).

Conveyancing privileges

14.4   Certain conveyancing privileges attach to barony titles. Thus a barony can be conveyed by its general name without further specification[1]; and, contrary to the normal rule that a title is *habile* for the prescriptive acquisition of legal separate tenements (such as salmon fishings) only if the tenement is specially mentioned, a barony title is of itself sufficient[2]. These privileges, of much reduced significance today, are substantially ended once the land in question is entered on the Land Register[3]. The 2000 Act brings them to an end altogether from the appointed day[4]. Rights already acquired are, of course, unaffected.

[1]   J M Halliday *Conveyancing Law and Practice* vol 2 (2nd edn, 1997) para 33–15.
[2]   K G C Reid *The Law of Property in Scotland* (1996) para 324.
[3]   Thus positive prescription does not usually run on Land Register titles; and a disposition of a registered title could not proceed merely by general name but must include the title number: Land Registration (Scotland) Act 1979, s 4(2)(d).
[4]   Abolition of Feudal Tenure etc (Scotland) Act 2000, s 63(1), (4).

The right to the title 'baron'

14.5 A Crown vassal holding on a baronial grant may adopt the title 'baron'. The right to do so attaches to ownership of the head place or *caput* of the barony. In recent years a lucrative market has developed in baronies, in the sense of the right to the title[1]. Not uncommonly they change hands for £50,000 or more, and in December 2002 a barony was put on the market for £1 million[2]. There are thought to be between 1,000 and 2,000 baronies still surviving. A trend is for baronies to be sold with only a minimal amount of land, or even with a bare superiority. This means that instead of the *caput* being a mansion house or other substantial holding it becomes some notional piece of land, so that in substance it is separated from the land.

The Abolition of Feudal Tenure Act carries this process to its logical conclusion[3]. After the appointed day baronies are severed from land altogether. A conveyance of the land will not carry the barony. Instead the barony must be transferred by separate conveyance, in practice an assignation. This does not prevent the barony from continuing to accompany the land, provided that a separate conveyance is used for each. But it also allows the barony to be sold on its own without any of the land to which it was formerly attached. Title to a barony is completed merely by delivery of the deed, for registration is neither necessary nor competent[4], and, in the absence of a 'debtor' in the right, there can be no question of intimation. An assignation could, however, be registered in the Books of Council and Session, and also in the Register of Claims which is apparently to be set up by the Convention of the Baronage of Scotland[5].

As before, baronies will continue to pass to the heir at law in the event that the holder dies intestate[6].

1 See eg www.baronytitles.com.
2 *The Scotsman* 30 December 2002.
3 Abolition of Feudal Tenure etc (Scotland) Act 2000, s 63(2).
4 AFT(S)A 2000, s 63(2).
5 A J M Nairn 'Scottish Feudal Baronies in Reform' (2001) 69 SLG 46.
6 Succession (Scotland) Act 1964, s 37(1)(a). Baronies are incorporeal heritable property: see AFT(S)A 2000, s 63(2).

Grant of arms

14.6 The grant of arms is a matter within the discretion of the Lord Lyon[1]. Assuming, however, that arms are granted, a baron receives special additaments, most notably a red chapeau[2]. Feudal abolition does not of itself disturb this arrangement, s 63 of the 2000 Act taking care to provide that nothing in the Act is to affect the dignity of baron, including any heraldic privilege[3]. Nonetheless a change in practice has been announced by the Lord Lyon[4]. The last date on which petitions will be accepted for recognition as a baron or for baronial additaments is 30 April 2004. This is to allow the petition to be processed before the appointed day. Thereafter, while barons already holding arms with baronial additaments may continue to use them, no new grants of such additaments will be made. The result seems likely to be a fall, and possibly a substantial fall, in the value of baronies. At the time of writing, however, the position adopted by the Lord Lyon was being reconsidered.

1   In terms of the Lyon King of Arms Act 1672 (c 47) the Lord Lyon 'may give Armes to vertuous and well-deserving Persones'.
2   11 *Stair Memorial Encyclopaedia* para 1607.
3   Abolition of Feudal Tenure etc (Scotland) Act 2000, s 63(1), (4). The jurisdiction and prerogative of the Lord Lyon are expressly preserved by s 62. See Scottish Law Commission *Report on Abolition of the Feudal System* para 2.40.
4   For the full text see 2003 SLT (News) 6; K G C Reid and G L Gretton *Conveyancing 2002* (2003) p 42.

Heritable securities

14.7   Heritable securities are unaffected by the severance of the barony from the land. Thus a standard security which burdened a barony title before the appointed day will after that day burden, separately, both the land and the barony[1]. In view of the value of baronies, this may sometimes be a matter of importance.

1   Abolition of Feudal Tenure etc (Scotland) Act 2000, s 63(3). If, however, the land was *dominium directum*, it is extinguished on the appointed day by s 2(2) and only the barony is subject to the security. For a case where the barony was *not* included in the security, see *Bristol and West Building Society v Aitken Nairn WS* 1999 SLT 43.

ENTAILS

14.8   By 1825 around one half of the territorial extent of Scotland was entailed, a percentage which continued to rise for much of the century[1]. 'The expediency of tailzies', in Stair's words, was 'to preserve the memory and dignity of families'[2]. After the passing of the Rutherford Act in 1848 it became possible to disentail land by registration in the Register of Entails of an instrument of disentail authorised by the Court of Session[3]. An heir in possession could do this as of right unless he was born before the date of the entail, in which case the heir next in succession must either give consent or be compensated[4]. It ceased to be possible to create new entails after 10 August 1914[5].

Today few entails are thought to survive. Those that do are extinguished on the appointed day, to the same effect as if an instrument of disentail had been registered in the Register of Entails[6]. An heir next in succession whose consent would have been needed under the Rutherford Act can apply to the Lands Tribunal within two years for compensation on the same basis as under the previous law[7]; but since consent was needed only where the heir in possession was born before the date of the entail, and given that new entails ceased to be possible after 10 August 1914, it seems doubtful whether this provision will be ever be used.

Sir Walter Scott once sought, but failed to obtain, the position of Keeper of the Register of Entails, a sinecure carrying a salary, in 1829, of £150[8]. With the extinction of the last remaining entails, that Register is formally closed immediately before the appointed day[9].

1   Scottish Home Department *Report of the Scottish Leases Committee* (1952, Cmd 8656) para 44. For the law relating to entails, see W M Gordon *Scottish Land Law* (2nd edn, 1999) ch 18.

2   Stair III.4.33.

3   Entail Amendment Act 1848.

4   The alternative of compensation was introduced by the Entail Amendment (Scotland) Act 1875 and the Entail (Scotland) Act 1882.

5   Entail (Scotland) Act 1914.

6   Abolition of Feudal Tenure etc (Scotland) Act 2000, s 50.

7   AFT(S)A 2000, s 51.

8   Scott's journal entry for 24 January 1829 reads, in part: 'Heavy fall of snow ... The day bitter cold. I went to court and with great difficulty returnd along the slippry street ... Little but trifles to do at the court. I wrote to Lord Register and Lord Melville about the situation of Keeper of Record of Entails. I suppose they will give it me as they proposed. My hands are so coverd with Chillblains that I can hardly use a pen. My feet *ditto*.' Scott was not in fact appointed. See W E K Anderson (ed) *The Journal of Sir Walter Scott* (1972) p 572.

9   AFT(S)A 2000, s 52.

AMENDMENTS AND REPEALS

14.9   The removal of feudal concepts and terminology from the statute book has required a great deal in the way of amendments and repeals[1]. In addition, the opportunity of the 2000 Act was taken to repeal many other obsolete provisions touching on land law and conveyancing. These include provisions on teinds and stipend, Crown writs, and pre-1970 heritable securities. Among the Acts wholly repealed are the Feu-duty Act 1597, the Entail Act 1685, the Thirlage Act 1799, the Erasures in Deeds (Scotland) Act 1836, the Infeftment Act 1845, the Feudal Casualties (Scotland) Act 1914, and the Church of Scotland (Property and Endowments) (Amendment) Act 1957[2]. The existing, cumbersome, rules on service of heirs in respect of deaths prior to 10 September 1964 are replaced by concise modern provisions[3]. Provision is also made for heirs of provision of a last surviving trustee[4]. Finally, mention may be made of the repeal of the numerous provisions on pre-1970 heritable securities, and the application to such securities instead of the rules in the Conveyancing and Feudal Reform (Scotland) Act 1970 in relation to assignation, variation, discharge, and calling-up[5].

1   See eg para 13.13.

2   Abolition of Feudal Tenure etc (Scotland) Act 2000, s 76(2), Sch 13.

3   Titles to Land Consolidation (Scotland) 1868, s 26A, inserted by the AFT(S)A 2000, s 68. See further Scottish Law Commission *Report on Abolition of the Feudal System* paras 9.21, 9.22.
4   Titles to Land Consolidation (Scotland) 1868, s 26B, inserted by the AFT(S)A 2000, s 68.
5   AFT(S)A 2000, s 69. See Scottish Law Commission *Report on Abolition of the Feudal System* para 9.31.

Appendix 1

Abolition of Feudal Tenure etc (Scotland) Act 2000

2000 asp 5

(The text of the Act is stated as at 1 August 2003.)

(As well as future amendment by primary legislation, it may be noted that the Act can also be amended by a statutory instrument made under the Title Conditions (Scotland) Act 2003, s 128(4)).

The Bill for this Act of the Scottish Parliament was passed by the Parliament on 3rd May 2000 and received Royal Assent on 9th June 2000.

An Act of the Scottish Parliament to abolish the feudal system of land tenure; to abolish a related system of land tenure; to make new provision as respects the ownership of land; to make consequential provision for the extinction and recovery of feuduties and of certain other perpetual periodical payments and for the extinction by prescription of any obligation to pay redemption money under the Land Tenure Reform (Scotland) Act 1974; to make further provision as respects real burdens affecting land; to provide for the disentailment of land; to discharge all rights of irritancy held by superiors; to abolish the obligation of thirlage; to prohibit with certain exceptions the granting of leases over land for periods exceeding 175 years; to make new provision as respects conveyancing; to enable firms with separate personality to own land; and for connected purposes.

PART I
ABOLITION OF FEUDAL TENURE

1 Abolition on appointed day

The feudal system of land tenure, that is to say the entire system whereby land is held by a vassal on perpetual tenure from a superior is, on the appointed day, abolished.

2 Consequences of abolition

(1) An estate of *dominium utile* of land shall, on the appointed day, cease to exist as a feudal estate but shall forthwith become the ownership of the land and, in so far as

is consistent with the provisions of this Act, the land shall be subject to the same sub-ordinate real rights and other encumbrances as was the estate of *dominium utile*.

(2) Every other feudal estate in land shall, on that day, cease to exist.

(3) It shall, on that day, cease to be possible to create a feudal estate in land.

3 Amendment of Land Registration (Scotland) Act 1979

The Land Registration (Scotland) Act 1979 (c 33) shall be amended as follows—

    (a)   in section 4(2) (applications for registration which are not to be accepted by the Keeper of the Registers of Scotland), after paragraph (a) there shall be inserted—

"(aa) it relates in whole or in part to an interest in land which by, under or by virtue of any provision of the Abolition of Feudal Tenure etc (Scotland) Act 2000 (asp 5) is an interest which has ceased to exist;";

    (b)   in section 9 (rectification of Land Register of Scotland)—

        (i)   in subsection (3), at the beginning insert "Subject to subsection (3B) below,"; and

        (ii)   after subsection (3A) insert—

"(3B) Subject to subsection (3C) below, rectification (whether requisite or in exercise of the Keeper's discretion) to take account of, or of anything done (or purportedly done) under or by virtue of, any provision of the Abolition of Feudal Tenure etc (Scotland) Act 2000 (asp 5), other than section 4 or 65, shall, for the purposes of subsection (3) above (and of section 12(3)(cc) of this Act), be deemed not to prejudice a proprietor in possession.

(3C) For the purposes of subsection (3B) above, rectification does not include entering or reinstating in a title sheet a real burden or a condition affecting an interest in land."; and

    (c)   in section 12(3) (circumstances in which there is no entitlement to be indemnified by the Keeper), after paragraph (c) insert—

"(cc) the loss arises in consequence of—

        (i)   a rectification which; or

        (ii)   there being, in the register, an inaccuracy the rectification of which,

were there a proprietor in possession, would be deemed, by subsection (3B) of section 9 of this Act, not to prejudice that proprietor;".

PART 2
LAND TRANSFERS ETC ON AND AFTER APPOINTED DAY

4 Ownership of land

(1) Ownership of land shall pass—

    (a)   in a case where a transfer is registrable under section 2 of the Land Registration (Scotland) Act 1979 (c 33), on registration in the Land Register of Scotland;

    (b)   in any other case, on recording of a conveyance of the land in the Register of Sasines.

(2) This section is without prejudice to any other enactment, or rule of law, by or under which ownership of land may pass.

(3) In subsection (1) above—

    (a)   "conveyance" includes—

        (i)   conveyance by, or under, any enactment, rule of law or decree; and

        (ii)   a notice of title deducing title through a conveyance; and

    (b)   "registrable" and "registration" have the meanings respectively assigned to those expressions by section 1(3) of the Land Registration (Scotland) Act 1979 (c 33).

5   Form of application for recording deed in Register of Sasines

(1) Any application for the recording of a deed in the Register of Sasines shall be made by, or on behalf of, the person in whose favour the deed is granted; and it shall not be necessary to endorse on any deed a warrant of registration.

(2) The Scottish Ministers may, after consultation with the Lord President of the Court of Session, make rules—

    (a)   prescribing the form to be used for the purposes of subsection (1) above; and

    (b)   regulating the procedure relating to applications for recording.

6   Deduction of title for unregistered land etc

In respect of any land—

    (a)   a real right in which has never been registered in the Land Register of Scotland; and

    (b)   title to which has never been constituted by the recording of a deed in the Register of Sasines,

title may be deduced from any person having ownership of the land.

PART 3
FEUDUTIES

Extinction of feuduties

7   Extinction on appointed day

Without prejudice to section 13 of this Act, any feuduty which has not been extinguished before the appointed day is extinguished on that day; and accordingly no payment shall be exigible, in respect of feuduty, for that day or for any period after that day.

8   Requiring compensatory payment

(1) Where a feuduty is extinguished by section 7 of this Act, the person who was the superior in relation to the feu (that person being in the following provisions of this Part of this Act referred to as the "former superior") may, within two years after the appointed day, duly serve on the person who was the vassal in relation to the feu (that person being in those provisions referred to as the "former vassal") notice requiring that a payment specified in the notice (being a payment calculated in accordance with section 9 of this Act) be made to him by the former vassal; and any such payment is referred to in this Act as a "compensatory payment".

(2) In its application to a feuduty which was, at extinction, a *cumulo* feuduty, sub-section (1) above shall be construed as relating to separate notice being duly served on each former vassal from whom payment is sought; and in that application, notice under that subsection shall be in (or as nearly as may be in) the form, with its Appendix, contained in schedule 1 to this Act.

(3) Except in the application mentioned in subsection (2) above, notice under sub-section (1) above shall be in (or as nearly as may be in) the form contained in schedule 2 to this Act.

(4) To any notice served under subsection (1) above shall be attached a copy of the explanatory note which immediately follows, as the case may be—

  (a)   the Appendix to the form in schedule 1; or

  (b)   the form in schedule 2,

to this Act.

(5) Subject to section 10 of this Act, if subsections (1) to (4) above are complied with, then within 56 days after due service on him a former vassal shall make the compensatory payment.

(6) The reference in subsection (1) above to a notice being duly served shall be con-strued in accordance with section 11 of this Act.

9   Calculation of amount of compensatory payment

(1) In calculating the compensatory payment in respect of which notice may be served under section 8(1) of this Act, there shall first be determined the sum of money which would, if invested in two and a half per cent Consolidated Stock at the middle market price at the close of business last preceding the appointed day, pro-duce an annual sum equal to the feuduty.

(2) Unless the feuduty was, at extinction, a *cumulo* feuduty the sum so determined shall be the compensatory payment.

(3) If the feuduty was, at extinction, a *cumulo* feuduty the former superior shall, after determining that sum, allocate it among the former vassals in such proportions as are reasonable in all the circumstances; and an amount which is so allocated to a former vassal shall be the compensatory payment for that former vassal.

(4) If the feuduty was, at extinction, a *cumulo* feuduty wholly or partly apportioned among the former vassals, then for the purposes of subsection (3) above the propor-

tions of an allocation shall be presumed reasonable in so far as they accord with that apportionment.

10   Making compensatory payment by instalments

(1) Where notice under subsection (1) of section 8 of this Act requires from a former vassal a compensatory payment of not less than £50, the former superior shall serve with it a filled out document (in this section referred to as an "instalment document"), in (or as nearly as may be in) the form contained in schedule 3 to this Act, for signature and dating by the former vassal (there being appended to the document so sent a copy of the explanatory note which immediately follows that form in the schedule); and if the former superior does not do so then no requirement to make the compensatory payment shall arise under subsection (5) of that section by virtue of that notice.

(2) Subject to subsection (3) below, a former vassal on whom an instalment document is served shall obtain the option of making the compensatory payment by instalments if (and only if)—

   (a)   he signs, dates and returns the document within the period which (but for this section) is allowed for making that payment by section 8(5) of this Act; and

   (b)   when so returning the document, he pays to the former superior an amount equivalent to one tenth of the compensatory payment (being an amount thus payable in addition to the compensatory payment and irrespective of how or when the compensatory payment is subsequently made).

(3) If on or after the date on which an instalment document is served on a former vassal he ceases by virtue of a sale, or transfer for valuable consideration, to have right to the land in respect of which the feuduty was payable or any part of that land (that land or any part of it being in this section referred to as "the land") then—

   (a)   where he has obtained the option mentioned in subsection (2) above, he shall lose that option; and

   (b)   where he has not obtained that option, he shall lose the right to obtain it.

(4) Where the option of making the compensatory payment by instalments is obtained, those instalments shall be equal instalments payable where—

   (a)   the compensatory payment is £500 or less, on each of the five;

   (b)   it is more than £500 but not more than £1,000, on each of the ten;

   (c)   it is more than £1,000 but not more than £1,500, on each of the fifteen; and

   (d)   it is more than £1,500, on each of the twenty,

term days of Whitsunday or Martinmas which then next follow; except that—

   (i)   in a case where any such instalment remains unpaid for forty-two days after falling due, the outstanding balance of the entire compensatory payment shall immediately fall due;

(ii)   in a case where, by virtue of subsection (3)(a) above, the option is lost, that outstanding balance shall fall due on the seventh day after the day on which the former vassal ceases to have right to the land; and

(iii)   in any other case, the former vassal may pay that outstanding balance at any time.

(5) In a case where, by virtue of subsection (3)(b) above, the right to obtain the option of making the compensatory payment by instalments is lost, section 8(5) of this Act shall apply accordingly.

11   Service under section 8(1)

(1) Due service under section 8(1) of this Act is effected by delivering the documents in question to the former vassal or by sending them by registered post, or the recorded delivery service, addressed to him at an appropriate place.

(2) An acknowledgement, signed by the former vassal, which conforms to Form A of schedule 4 to this Act, or as the case may be a certificate which conforms to Form B of that schedule and is accompanied by the postal receipt, shall be sufficient evidence of such due service; and if the packet containing the documents in question is, under subsection (1) above, sent by post but is returned to the former superior with an intimation that it could not be delivered, the packet may be delivered or sent by post, with that intimation, to the Extractor of the Court of Session, the delivering or sending to the Extractor being taken to be equivalent to the service of those documents on the former vassal.

(3) For the purposes of subsection (2) above, an acknowledgement of receipt by the Extractor on a copy of those documents shall be sufficient evidence of their receipt by him.

(4) The date on which notice under section 8(1) of this Act is served on a former vassal is the date of delivery, or as the case may be of posting, in compliance with subsection (1) or (2) above.

(5) A reference in this section to an "appropriate place" is, for any former vassal, to be construed as a reference to—

(a)   his place of residence;

(b)   his place of business; or

(c)   a postal address which he ordinarily uses,

or, if none of those is known at the time of delivery or posting, as a reference to whatever place is at that time his most recently known place of residence or place of business or postal address which he ordinarily used.

12   Extinction by prescription of requirement to make compensatory payment

In Schedule 1 to the Prescription and Limitation (Scotland) Act 1973 (c 52) (which specifies obligations affected by prescriptive periods of five years under section 6 of that Act)—

(a) in paragraph 1, after sub-paragraph (a) there shall be inserted—

"(aa) to any obligation to make a compensatory payment ("compensatory payment" being construed in accordance with section 8(1) of the Abolition of Feudal Tenure etc (Scotland) Act 2000 (asp 5), including that section as read with section 56 of that Act);"; and

(b) in paragraph 2(e), after the words "paragraph 1(a)" there shall be inserted "or (aa)".

Arrears

13 Arrears of feuduty etc

(1) Feuduty shall continue to be exigible for any period before the appointed day; and if (in so far as so exigible) it has not fallen due before that day, it shall fall due on that day.

(2) On the appointed day feuduty shall cease to constitute a *debitum fundi* as shall any amount secured, in favour of a superior, by virtue of section 5 of the Land Tenure Reform (Scotland) Act 1974 (c 38) (redemption on transfer of land).

(3) The superior's hypothec is, on the appointed day, abolished.

(4) Subsections (2) and (3) above are without prejudice to any—

(a) action—

(i) founded on a *debitum fundi* or superior's hypothec; and

(ii) commenced before the appointed day; or

(b) right or preference—

(i) so founded; and

(ii) claimed in a sequestration, or in some other process in which there is ranking, commenced before that day.

Disclosure

14 Duty of collecting third party to disclose information

For the purposes of section 8(1) of this Act, a superior (or, on or after the appointed day, a former superior) who receives, or has at any time received, from a third party an amount collected in respect of feuduty from and remitted to the superior (or former superior) on behalf of a vassal (or, on or after the appointed day, a former vassal) may require the third party to disclose the identity and address of the vassal (or former vassal) and, in the case of remission as a part of a feuduty, the amount so collected from the vassal (or former vassal); and the third party shall, in so far as it is practicable for him to do so, forthwith comply with that requirement.

15 Duty to disclose identity etc of former vassal

Where the former superior purports duly to serve notice under section 8(1) of this Act but the person on whom it is served, being a person who had right to the feu before the appointed day, is not the former vassal because, immediately before the appointed day, some other person and not he had right to the feu, he shall forthwith disclose to the former superior—

(a) the identity and address of that other person; or

(b) (if he cannot do that) such other information as he has which might enable the former superior to discover that identity and address.

Interpretation

16 Interpretation of Part 3

(1) In this Part of this Act, unless the context otherwise requires—

"compensatory payment" shall be construed in accordance with section 8(1) of this Act;

"feuduty" includes blench duty;

"superior", in relation to a feu, means the person who, immediately before the appointed day, has right to the immediate superiority, whether or not he has completed title (and if more than one person comes within that description, then the person who has most recently acquired such right); and "former superior" shall be construed in accordance with section 8(1) of this Act; and

"vassal", in relation to a feu, means the person who, immediately before the appointed day, has right to the feu, whether or not he has completed title (and if more than one person comes within that description, then the person who has most recently acquired such right); and "former vassal" shall be construed in accordance with section 8(1) of this Act.

(2) Where a feu comprises parts each held by a separate vassal, being parts upon which feuduty has not been allocated, the whole of any feuduty exigible in respect of the parts so held is in this Part of this Act referred to as a "*cumulo* feuduty"; and any reference in this Part of this Act to a feu is to be construed, in relation to the parts so held, as a reference to those parts collectively.

(3) Any reference in this Part of this Act to a feu is to be construed as including a reference to any part of a feu if it is a part upon which feuduty has been allocated.

(4) Where, immediately before the appointed day a feu, or any part of a feu, is held by two or more vassals as common property—

(a) they shall be severally liable to make any compensatory payment (but as between, or as the case may be among, themselves they shall be liable in the proportions in which they hold the feu); and

(b) subject to section 11 of this Act they shall together be treated for the purposes of this Act as being a single vassal.

PART 4
REAL BURDENS

Extinction of superior's rights

17   Extinction of superior's rights

(1) Subject to sections 18 to 18C, 19, 20, 27, 27A, 28, 28A and 60 of this Act and to sections 52 to 56 (which make provision as to common schemes, facility burdens and service burdens) and 63 (which makes provision as to manager burdens) of the Title Conditions (Scotland) Act 2003 (asp 9)—

    (a)   a real burden which, immediately before the appointed day, is enforceable by, and only by, a superior shall on that day be extinguished; and

    (b)   any other real burden shall, on and after that day, not be enforceable by a former superior other than in that person's capacity as owner of land or as holder of a conservation burden, health care burden or economic development burden.

(2) Subject to subsection (3) below and to the provision made by section 20 of this Act for there to be a transitional period during which a real burden shall yet be enforceable—

    (a)   on or after the appointed day, no proceedings for such enforcement shall be commenced;

    (b)   any proceedings already commenced for such enforcement shall be deemed to have been abandoned on that day and may, without further process and without any requirement that full judicial expenses shall have been paid by the pursuer, be dismissed accordingly; and

    (c)   any decree or interlocutor already pronounced in proceedings for such enforcement shall be deemed to have been reduced, or as the case may be recalled, on that day.

(3) Subsection (2) above shall not affect any proceedings, decree or interlocutor in relation to—

    (a)   a right of irritancy held by a superior;

    (aa)   a right of enforcement held by virtue of any of the provisions mentioned in subsection (1) above; or

    (b)   a right to recover damages or to the payment of money.

Reallotment etc

18   Reallotment of real burden by nomination of new dominant tenement

(1) Without prejudice to sections 18A to 18C of this Act, where—

    (a)   a feudal estate of *dominium utile* of land is subject to a real burden enforceable by a superior of the feu or which would be so enforceable were the person in question to complete title to the *dominium directum*; and

(b)   at least one of the conditions set out in subsection (7) below is met,

the superior may, before the appointed day, prospectively nominate other land (being land of which he has the right to the sole *dominium utile* or sole allodial ownership), or any part of that other land, as a dominant tenement by duly executing and registering a notice in, or as nearly as may be in, the form contained in schedule 5 to this Act.

(2) The notice shall—

(a)   set out the title of the superior;

(b)   describe, sufficiently to enable identification by reference to the Ordnance Map, both the land the *dominium utile* of which is subject to the real burden (or any part of that land) and the land (or part) nominated;

(c)   specify which of the conditions set out in subsection (7) below is (or are) met;

(d)   set out the terms of the real burden; and

(e)   set out the terms of any counter-obligation to the real burden if it is a counter-obligation enforceable against the superior.

(3) For the purposes of subsection (1) above a notice is duly registered only when registered against both tenements described in pursuance of subsection (2)(b) above.

(4) Before submitting any notice for registration under this section, the superior shall swear or affirm before a notary public that to the best of the knowledge and belief of the superior all the information contained in the notice is true.

(5) For the purposes of subsection (4) above, if the superior is—

(a)   an individual unable by reason of legal disability, or incapacity, to swear or affirm as mentioned in that subsection, then a legal representative of the superior may swear or affirm;

(b)   not an individual, then any person authorised to sign documents on its behalf may swear or affirm;

and any reference in that subsection to a superior shall be construed accordingly.

(6) Subject to subsection (6A) below, if subsections (1) to (5) above are complied with and immediately before the appointed day the real burden is still enforceable by the superior (or by his successor) or would be so enforceable, or still so enforceable, were the person in question to complete title to the *dominium directum* then, on that day—

(a)   the land (or part) nominated shall become a dominant tenement; and

(b)   the land the *dominium utile* of which was subject to the real burden (or if part only of that land is described in pursuance of subsection (2)(b) above, that part) shall be the servient tenement.

(6A) Such compliance as is mentioned in subsection (6) above shall not be effective to preserve any right to enforce a manager burden ("manager burden" being construed in accordance with section 63(1) of the Title Conditions (Scotland) Act 2003 (asp 9)).

(7) The conditions are—

    (a)   that the land which by virtue of this section would become the dominant tenement has on it a permanent building which is in use wholly or mainly as a place of human—

        (i)   habitation; or

        (ii)   resort

and that building is, at some point, within one hundred metres (measuring along a horizontal plane) of the land which would be the servient tenement;

    (b)   that the real burden comprises—

        (i)   a right (other than any sporting rights, as defined by section 65A(9) of this Act) to enter, or otherwise make use of, the servient tenement; or

        (ii)   a right of pre-emption or of redemption; or

    (c)   that the land which by virtue of this section would become the dominant tenement comprises—

        (i)   minerals; or

        (ii)   salmon fishings or some other incorporeal property,

and it is apparent from the terms of the real burden that it was created for the benefit of such land.

(8) This section is subject to sections 41 and 42 of this Act.

18A   Personal pre-emption burdens and personal redemption burdens

(1) Without prejudice to section 18 of this Act, where a feudal estate of *dominium utile* of land is subject to a real burden which comprises a right of pre-emption or redemption and is enforceable by a superior of the feu or would be so enforceable were the person in question to complete title to the *dominium directum* the superior may, before the appointed day, by duly executing and registering against the *dominium utile* a notice in, or as nearly as may be in, the form contained in schedule 5A to this Act, prospectively convert that burden into a personal pre-emption burden or as the case may be into a personal redemption burden.

(2) The notice shall—

    (a)   set out the title of the superior;

    (b)   describe, sufficiently to enable identification by reference to the Ordnance Map, the land the *dominium utile* of which is subject to the real burden (or any part of that land);

    (c)   set out the terms of the real burden; and

    (d)   set out the terms of any counter-obligation to the real burden if it is a counter-obligation enforceable against the superior.

(3) Before submitting any notice for registration under this section, the superior shall swear or affirm as is mentioned in subsection (4) of section 18 of this Act.

(4) Subsection (5) of that section applies for the purposes of subsection (3) above as it applies for the purposes of subsection (4) of that section.

(5) If subsections (1) to (3) above are, with subsection (4) of that section, complied with and immediately before the appointed day the real burden is still enforceable by the superior (or his successor) or would be so enforceable, or still so enforceable, were the person in question to complete title to the *dominium directum* then, on that day—

    (a)   the real burden shall be converted into a real burden in favour of that person, to be known as a "personal pre-emption burden" or as the case may be as a "personal redemption burden"; and

    (b)   the land the *dominium utile* of which was subject to the real burden (or if part only of that land is described in pursuance of subsection (2)(b) above, that part) shall become the servient tenement.

(6) Title to enforce the burden against the land to which the notice relates shall be subject to any such counter-obligation as was set out by virtue of subsection (2)(d) above.

(7) The right to a personal pre-emption burden or personal redemption burden may be assigned or otherwise transferred to any person; and any such assignation or transfer shall take effect on registration.

(8) Where the holder of a personal pre-emption burden or personal redemption burden does not have a completed title—

    (a)   title may be completed by the holder registering a notice of title; or

    (b)   without completing title, the holder may grant a deed—

        (i)   assigning the right to; or

        (ii)   discharging, in whole or in part,

the burden; but unless the deed is one to which section 15(3) of the Land Registration (Scotland) Act 1979 (c 33) (circumstances where unnecessary to deduce title) applies, it shall be necessary, in the deed, to deduce title to the burden through the midcouples linking the holder to the person who had the last completed title.

(9) This section is subject to sections 41 and 42 of this Act.

18B   Conversion into economic development burden

(1) Without prejudice to section 18 of this Act, where a feudal estate of *dominium utile* of land is subject to a real burden which is imposed for the purpose of promoting economic development and is enforceable by the Scottish Ministers or a local authority, being in either case the superior of the feu, or would be so enforceable were the Scottish Ministers or as the case may be the local authority to complete title to the *dominium directum*, the superior may, before the appointed day, by duly executing and registering against the *dominium utile* a notice in, or as nearly as may be

in, the form contained in schedule 5B to this Act, prospectively convert that burden into an economic development burden.

(2) The notice shall—

(a)   set out the title of the superior;

(b)   describe, sufficiently to enable identification by reference to the Ordnance Map, the land the *dominium utile* of which is subject to the real burden (or any part of that land);

(c)   set out the terms of the real burden;

(d)   set out the terms of any counter-obligation to the real burden if it is a counter-obligation enforceable against the superior; and

(e)   state that the burden was imposed for the purpose of promoting economic development and provide information in support of that statement.

(3) If subsections (1) and (2) above are complied with and immediately before the appointed day the real burden is still enforceable by the superior or would be so enforceable were the Scottish Ministers or as the case may be the local authority to complete title to the *dominium directum* then on that day the real burden shall be converted into an economic development burden and on and after that day the Scottish Ministers or, as the case may be, the authority, shall—

(a)   have title to enforce the burden against the land to which the notice relates; and

(b)   be presumed to have an interest to enforce it.

(4) Title to enforce the burden against the land to which the notice relates shall be subject to any such counter-obligation as was set out by virtue of subsection (2)(d) above.

(5) This section is subject to sections 41 and 42 of this Act.

18C   Conversion into health care burden

(1) Without prejudice to section 18 of this Act, where a feudal estate of *dominium utile* of land is subject to a real burden which is imposed for the purpose of promoting the provision of facilities for health care and is enforceable by a National Health Service trust or the Scottish Ministers, being in either case the superior of the feu, or would be so enforceable were the trust or as the case may be the Scottish Ministers to complete title to the *dominium directum*, the superior may, before the appointed day, by duly executing and registering against the *dominium utile* a notice in, or as nearly as may be in, the form contained in schedule 5C to this Act, prospectively convert that burden into a health care burden.

(2) The notice shall—

(a)   set out the title of the superior;

(b)   describe, sufficiently to enable identification by reference to the Ordnance Map, the land the *dominium utile* of which is subject to the real burden (or any part of that land);

(c)   set out the terms of the real burden;

(d)   set out the terms of any counter-obligation to the real burden if it is a counter-obligation enforceable against the superior; and

(e)   state that the burden was imposed for the purpose of promoting the provision of facilities for health care and provide information in support of that statement.

(3) If subsections (1) and (2) are complied with and immediately before the appointed day the real burden is still enforceable by the superior or would be so enforceable were the trust or as the case may be the Scottish Ministers to complete title to the *dominium directum* then on that day the real burden shall be converted into a health care burden and on and after that day the trust or, as the case may be, the Scottish Ministers, shall—

(a)   have title to enforce the burden against the land to which the notice in question relates; and

(b)   be presumed to have an interest to enforce it.

(4) Title to enforce the burden against the land to which the notice relates shall be subject to any such counter-obligation as was set out by virtue of subsection (2)(d) above.

(5) In subsections (1) and (2) above, "facilities for health care" includes facilities ancillary to health care; as for example (but without prejudice to that generality) accommodation for staff employed to provide health care.

(6) This section is subject to sections 41 and 42 of this Act.

19   Reallotment of real burden by agreement

(1) Where a feudal estate of *dominium utile* of land is subject to a real burden enforceable by a superior of the feu or which would be so enforceable were the person in question to complete title to the *dominium directum* the superior may, before the appointed day—

(a)   serve notice in, or as nearly as may be in, the form contained in schedule 6 to this Act, on the person who has right to the feu that he seeks to enter into an agreement with that person under this section prospectively nominating other land (being land of which the superior has right to the sole *dominium utile* or sole allodial ownership), or any part of that other land, as a dominant tenement;

(b)   enter into such an agreement with that person; and

(c)   duly register that agreement;

but if they think fit they may, by the agreement, modify the real burden or any counter-obligation to the real burden if it is a counter-obligation enforceable against the superior (or both the real burden and any such counter-obligation).

(2) The notice shall—

(a)   set out the title of the superior;

(b)   describe both the land the *dominium utile* of which is subject to the real burden (or any part of that land) and the land (or part) nominated;

(c)   set out the terms of the real burden; and

(d)   set out the terms of any such counter-obligation as is mentioned in subsection (1) above.

(3) An agreement such as is mentioned in paragraph (b) of subsection (1) above shall be a written agreement—

(a)   which expressly states that it is made under this section; and

(b)   which includes all the information, other than that relating to service, required to be set out in completing the notice the form of which is contained in schedule 6 to this Act.

(4) For the purposes of subsection (1)(c) above an agreement is duly registered only when registered against both tenements described in pursuance of subsection (2)(b) above.

(5) If subsections (1)(b) and (c), (3) and (4) above are complied with and immediately before the appointed day the real burden is still enforceable by the superior (or by his successor) or would be so enforceable, or still so enforceable, were the person in question to complete title to the *dominium directum* then on that day—

(a)   the land (or part) nominated shall become a dominant tenement; and

(b)   the land the *dominium utile* of which was subject to the real burden (or if part only of that land is described in pursuance of subsection (2)(b) above, that part) shall be the servient tenement.

(6) A person may enter into an agreement under this section even if he has not completed title to the *dominium utile* of the land subject to the real burden, or as the case may be title to the *dominium directum* of that land or to the *dominium utile* of the land nominated (or, if the land nominated is allodial land, to the land nominated), provided that, in any case to which section 15(3) of the Land Registration (Scotland) Act 1979 (c 33) (simplification of deeds relating to registered interests) does not apply, he deduces title, in the agreement, from the person who appears in the Register of Sasines as having the last recorded title to the interest in question.

(7) This section is subject to section 42 of this Act.

20   Reallotment of real burden by order of Lands Tribunal

(1) Where but for paragraph (b) of subsection (1) of section 18 of this Act a superior could proceed under that subsection prospectively to nominate land (in this section referred to as the "prospective dominant tenement") he may, provided that he has first, in pursuance of section 19 of this Act, attempted to reach agreement as respects the real burden in question with the person who has right to the feu, apply to the Lands Tribunal for an order under subsection (7) of this section; but such an application is competent only if made before the appointed day.

(2) An applicant under subsection (1) above shall include in his application a description of the requisite attempt to reach agreement.

(3) After sending or delivering to the Lands Tribunal an application under subsection (1) above, the superior may, within—

    (a)   42 days; or

    (b)   such longer period of days (being a period which ends before the appointed day) as the Lands Tribunal may allow if it is satisfied that there is good cause for so allowing,

duly execute and register a notice in, or as nearly as may be in, the form contained in schedule 7 to this Act; and section 17(1) of this Act shall have no effect as regards a real burden in respect of which such notice has been so executed and registered.

(4) The notice shall—

    (a)   set out the title of the superior;

    (b)   describe, sufficiently to enable identification by reference to the Ordnance Map, both the land the *dominium utile* of which is subject to the real burden (or any part of that land) and the prospective dominant tenement;

    (c)   set out the terms of the real burden; and

    (d)   set out the terms of any counter-obligation to the real burden if it is a counter-obligation enforceable against the superior.

(5) For the purposes of this section, a notice is duly registered only when registered against both tenements described in pursuance of subsection (4)(b) above; and if it is so registered and immediately before the appointed day—

    (a)   the real burden is still enforceable by the superior (or by his successor) or would be so enforceable, or still so enforceable, were the person in question to complete title to the *dominium directum*; and

    (b)   no order under subsection (7) below has been registered under subsection (11) below in respect of the application,

then on that day the prospective dominant tenement shall, for the transitional period, become the dominant tenement and the land the *dominium utile* of which is subject to the real burden (or, if part only of that land is described under paragraph (b) of subsection (4) above, that part) shall, for the transitional period, be the servient tenement.

(6) The reference in subsection (5) above to the transitional period is to the period beginning on the appointed day and ending on—

    (a)   the day on which an order under subsection (7) below is registered under subsection (11) below in respect of the application; or

    (b)   if no such order is so registered, such day later than the appointed day as the Scottish Ministers may by order specify (that later day being in this Act referred to as the "specified day").

(7) If, on an application under subsection (1) above as respects which a notice has been duly registered—

    (a)   the Lands Tribunal is satisfied that, were the real burden to be extinguished, there would be material detriment to the value or enjoyment of

the applicant's ownership (taking him to have ownership) of the dominant tenement, the Tribunal may order that, subject to subsection (9) of
this section—

> (i)   if the order can be and is registered before the appointed day, then
> on that day the prospective dominant tenement shall become the
> dominant tenement and the land the *dominium utile* of which is
> subject to the real burden (or, if part only of that land is described
> under paragraph (b) of subsection (4) above, that part) shall be the
> servient tenement; or

> (ii)   the dominant tenement for the transitional period shall, after that
> period, continue to be the dominant tenement and the servient ten-
> ement for the transitional period shall, after that period, continue to
> be the servient tenement;

> (b)   *(repealed by the Title Conditions (Scotland) Act 2003, s 114(6), Sch 13,
> paras 1, 4(b)(ii))*

(8) Where in respect of the application—

> (a)   an order under paragraph (a) of subsection (7) above is registered—

> > (i)   before the appointed day and immediately before that day the real
> > burden is still enforceable by the superior (or by his successor) or
> > would be so enforceable, or still so enforceable, were the person in
> > question to complete title to the *dominium directum*, then on that
> > day; or

> > (ii)   on or after the appointed day and immediately before the day of
> > registration the real burden is still enforceable by the former supe-
> > rior (or by his successor) or would be so enforceable, or still so
> > enforceable, as mentioned in sub-paragraph (i) above, then on the
> > day of registration,

the prospective dominant tenement shall become the dominant tenement and
the land the *dominium utile* of which was subject to the real burden (or, if part
only of that land is described under paragraph (b) of subsection (4) above, that
part) shall be the servient tenement;

> (b)   *(repealed by the Title Conditions (Scotland) Act 2003, s 128(2), Sch 15)*

> (c)   *(repealed by the Title Conditions (Scotland) Act 2003, s 128(2), Sch 15)*

(9) An order under subsection (7)(a) above may modify the real burden or any
counter-obligation to the real burden if it is a counter-obligation enforceable against
the applicant (or both the real burden and any such counter-obligation).

(10) The decision of the Lands Tribunal on an application under subsection (1)
above shall be final.

(11) An order under subsection (7) above shall forthwith be extracted and registered
by the Lands Tribunal against both tenements described in pursuance of subsection
(4)(b) above; and the expenses of registration shall be borne by the applicant.

(12) Subsections (2) and (3) of section 17 of this Act shall apply in relation to real
burdens extinguished or rendered unenforceable by virtue of this section as they

apply in relation to real burdens extinguished or so rendered by subsection (1) of that section with the substitution, if the extinction or rendering is after the appointed day, for each reference in them to that day, of a reference to the day which ends the transitional period.

(13) A person opposing an application made under subsection (1) above incurs no liability, unless in the opinion of the Lands Tribunal his actings are vexatious or frivolous, in respect of expenses incurred by the applicant.

(14) This section is subject to sections 41 and 42 of this Act.

(15) Before submitting any notice for registration under this section, the superior shall swear or affirm before a notary public that to the best of the knowledge and belief of the superior all the information contained in the notice is true.

(16) For the purposes of subsection (15) above, if the superior is—

    (a)   an individual unable by reason of legal disability, or incapacity, to swear or affirm as mentioned in that subsection, then a legal representative of the superior may swear or affirm;

    (b)   not an individual, then any person authorised to sign documents on its behalf may swear or affirm;

and the references in that subsection to the superior shall be construed accordingly.

21 Manner of dealing with application under section 20

(1) On receiving an application under section 20 of this Act the Lands Tribunal shall give such notice of that application, whether by way of advertisement or otherwise, as may be prescribed for the purposes of that section by the Scottish Ministers by rules under section 3 of the Lands Tribunal Act 1949 (c 42) to any person who has right to the feu which is subject to the real burden in question and, if the Lands Tribunal thinks fit, to any other person.

(2) Any person who, whether or not he has received notice under subsection (1) above, has right to the feu which is subject to the real burden in question (or as the case may be has right to the servient tenement) or is affected by that real burden or by its proposed reallotment shall be entitled, within such time as may be so prescribed, to oppose or make representations in relation to the application; and the Lands Tribunal shall allow any such person, and may allow any other person who appears to it to be affected by that real burden or by its proposed reallotment, to be heard in relation to the application.

(3) Without prejudice to subsections (1) and (2) above, the Scottish Ministers may, in rules under the said section 3, make special provision in relation to any matter pertaining to proceedings in applications under section 20 of this Act (or in any class of such applications).

22 Amendment of Tribunals and Inquiries Act 1992

In section 11 (proceedings in relation to which there is no appeal from the decision of the Lands Tribunal) of the Tribunals and Inquiries Act 1992 (c 53), in subsection (2)—

(a)   the words after "in relation to" shall be paragraph (a); and

(b)   after that paragraph there shall be inserted

"; or

(b)   proceedings under section 20 of the Abolition of Feudal Tenure etc (Scotland) Act 2000 (asp 5) (reallotment of real burden)".

23   *(repealed by the Title Conditions (Scotland) Act 2003, s 128(2), Sch 15)*

24   Interest to enforce real burden

Sections 18 to 20 of this Act are without prejudice to any requirement that a dominant proprietor have an interest to enforce a real burden (and such interest shall not be presumed).

25   Counter-obligations on reallotment

Where a real burden is reallotted under section 18, 19 or 20 of this Act or under section 56 or 63 of the Title Conditions (Scotland) Act 2003 (asp 9) (which make provision, respectively, as to facility burdens and service burdens and as to manager burdens), the right to enforce the burden shall be subject to any counter-obligation (modified as the case may be by the agreement or by the order of the Lands Tribunal) enforceable against the superior immediately before reallotment is effected.

Conservation burdens

26   *(repealed by the Title Conditions (Scotland) Act 2003, s 128(2), Sch 15)*

27   Notice preserving right to enforce conservation burden

(1)   Where a conservation body has, or the Scottish Ministers have, the right as superior to enforce a real burden of the class described in subsection (2) below or would have that right were it or they to complete title to the *dominium directum*, it or they may, before the appointed day, preserve for the benefit of the public the right to enforce the burden in question after that day by executing and registering against the *dominium utile* of the land subject to the burden a notice in, or as nearly as may be in, the form contained in schedule 8 to this Act; and, without prejudice to section 27A(1) of this Act, any burden as respects which such a right is so preserved shall, on and after the appointed day, be known as a "conservation burden".

(2)   The class is those real burdens which are enforceable against a feudal estate of *dominium utile* of land for the purpose of preserving, or protecting—

(a)   the architectural or historical characteristics of the land; or

(b)   any other special characteristics of the land (including, without prejudice to the generality of this paragraph, a special characteristic derived from the flora, fauna or general appearance of the land).

(3)   The notice shall—

(a)   state that the superior is a conservation body by virtue of section 38 of the Title Conditions (Scotland) Act 2003 (asp 9) (which makes provision generally as respects conservation burdens) or that the superior is the Scottish Ministers;

(b)   set out the title of the superior;

(c)   describe, sufficiently to enable identification by reference to the Ordnance Map, the land subject to the real burden (or any part of that land);

(d)   set out the terms of the real burden;

(e)   set out the terms of any counter-obligation to the real burden if it is a counter-obligation enforceable against the superior.

(4)   This section is subject to sections 41 and 42 of this Act.

27A   Nomination of conservation body or Scottish Ministers to have title to enforce conservation burden

(1)   Where a person other than a conservation body or the Scottish Ministers has the right as superior to enforce a real burden of the class described in section 27(2) of this Act or would have that right were he to complete title to the *dominium directum*, he may, subject to subsection (2) below, before the appointed day nominate for the benefit of the public, by executing and registering against the *dominium utile* of the land subject to the burden a notice in, or as nearly as may be in, the form contained in schedule 8A to this Act, a conservation body or the Scottish Ministers to have title on or after that day to enforce the burden against that land; and, without prejudice to section 27(1) of this Act, any burden as respects which such title to enforce is by virtue of this subsection so obtained shall, on and after the appointed day, be known as a "conservation burden".

(2)   Subsection (1) above applies only where the consent of the nominee to being so nominated is obtained—

(a)   in a case where sending a copy of the notice, in compliance with section 41(3) of this Act, is reasonably practicable, before that copy is so sent; and

(b)   in any other case, before the notice is executed.

(3)   The notice shall—

(a)   state that the nominee is a conservation body (identifying it) or the Scottish Ministers, as the case may be; and

(b)   do as mentioned in paragraphs (b) to (e) of section 27(3) of this Act.

(4)   This section is subject to sections 41 and 42 of this Act except that, in the application of subsection (1)(i) of section 42 for the purposes of this subsection, such discharge as is mentioned in that subsection shall be taken to require the consent of the nominated person.

28   Enforcement of conservation burden

(1)   If a notice has been executed and registered in accordance with section 27 of this Act and, immediately before the appointed day, the burden to which the notice relates

is still enforceable by the conservation body or the Scottish Ministers as superior or would be so enforceable, or still so enforceable, were the body in question or they to complete title to the *dominium directum* then, on and after the appointed day, the conservation body or as the case may be the Scottish Ministers shall—

(a)   subject to any counter-obligation, have title to enforce the burden against the land to which the notice in question relates; and

(b)   be presumed to have an interest to enforce that burden.

(2) The references in subsection (1) above to—

(a)   the conservation body include references to—

(i)   any conservation body which is; or

(ii)   the Scottish Ministers where they are,

its successor as superior;

(b)   the Scottish Ministers include references to a conservation body which is their successor as superior.

28A   Effect of section 27A nomination

If a notice has been executed and registered in accordance with section 27A of this Act and, immediately before the appointed day, the burden to which the notice relates is still enforceable by the nominating person as superior (or by such person as is his successor) or would be so enforceable, or still so enforceable, were the person in question to complete title to the *dominium directum* then, on and after the appointed day, the conservation body or as the case may be the Scottish Ministers shall—

(a)   subject to any counter-obligation, have title to enforce the burden against the land to which the notice in question relates; and

(b)   be presumed to have an interest to enforce that burden.

29   *(repealed by the Title Conditions (Scotland) Act 2003, s 128(2), Sch 15)*

30   *(repealed by the Title Conditions (Scotland) Act 2003, s 128(2), Sch 15)*

31   *(repealed by the Title Conditions (Scotland) Act 2003, s 128(2), Sch 15)*

32   *(repealed by the Title Conditions (Scotland) Act 2003, s 128(2), Sch 15)*

Compensation

33   Notice reserving right to claim compensation where land subject to development value burden

(1) Where—

(a)   before the appointed day, land was feued subject to a real burden enforceable by a superior (or so enforceable if the person in question were to complete title to the *dominium directum*) which reserved for the superior the benefit (whether wholly or in part) of any development value of the land (such a real burden being referred to in this Part of this Act as a "development value burden"); and

(b)   either—

    (i)   the consideration paid, or payable, under the grant in feu was significantly lower than it would have been had the feu not been subject to the real burden; or

    (ii)   no consideration was paid, or payable, under the grant in feu,

the superior may, before that day, reserve the right to claim (in accordance with section 35 of this Act) compensation by executing and registering against the *dominium utile* of the land subject to the burden a notice in, or as nearly as may be in, the form contained in schedule 9 to this Act.

(2) A notice under this section shall—

(a)   set out the title of the superior;

(b)   describe, sufficiently to enable identification by reference to the Ordnance Map, the land the *dominium utile* of which is subject to the development value burden;

(c)   set out the terms of the burden;

(d)   state that the burden reserves development value and set out any information relevant to that statement;

(e)   set out, to the best of the superior's knowledge and belief, the amount by which the consideration was reduced because of the imposition of the burden; and

(f)   state that the superior reserves the right to claim compensation in accordance with section 35 of this Act.

(3) Before submitting any notice for registration under this section, the superior shall swear or affirm before a notary public that to the best of the knowledge and belief of the superior all the information contained in the notice is true.

(4) For the purposes of subsection (3) above, if the superior is—

(a)   an individual unable by reason of legal disability, or incapacity, to swear or affirm as mentioned in that subsection, then a legal representative of the superior may swear or affirm;

(b)   not an individual, then any person authorised to sign documents on its behalf may swear or affirm;

and any reference in that subsection to a superior shall be construed accordingly.

(5) In this Part of this Act, "development value" (except in the expression "development value burden") means any significant increase in the value of the land arising as a result of the land becoming free to be used, or dealt with, in some way not permitted under the grant in feu.

(6) This section is subject to sections 41 and 42 of this Act.

34   Transmissibility of right to claim compensation

A right to claim compensation reserved in accordance with section 33 of this Act is transmissible.

35   Claiming compensation

(1) Where the conditions mentioned in subsection (2) below are satisfied, any person who has, by or by virtue of a notice executed and registered in accordance with section 33 of this Act, a reserved right to claim compensation shall be entitled, subject to any order under section 44(2) of this Act, to compensation from the person who is the owner.

(2) The conditions are that—

   (a)   the real burden set out in the notice was, immediately before the appointed day, enforceable by the superior or would have been so enforceable immediately before that day had the person in question completed title to the *dominium directum*;

   (b)   on that day the burden, or as the case may be any right (or right on completion of title) of the superior to enforce the burden, was extinguished, or rendered unenforceable, by section 17(1) of this Act; and

   (c)   at any time—

      (i)   during the period of five years ending immediately before the appointed day, there was a breach of the burden; or

      (ii)   during the period of twenty years beginning with the appointed day, there was an occurrence, which, but for the burden becoming extinct, or unenforceable, as mentioned in paragraph (b) above, would have been a breach of the burden.

(3) Where a person is entitled, by virtue of subsection (1) above, to compensation, he shall make any claim for such compensation by notice in writing duly served on the owner; and any such notice shall specify, in accordance with section 37 of this Act, the amount of compensation claimed.

(4) Where, in relation to a claim made under subsection (3) above, the condition mentioned in—

   (a)   sub-paragraph (i) of subsection (2)(c) above applies, any such claim may not be made more than three years after the appointed day;

   (b)   sub-paragraph (ii) of subsection (2)(c) above applies, any such claim may not be made more than three years after the date of the occurrence.

(5) For the purposes of this section, if a breach, or occurrence, such as is mentioned in subsection (2)(c) above is continuing, the breach or, as the case may be, occurrence shall be taken to occur when it first happens.

(6) The reference in subsection (3) above to a notice being duly served shall be construed in accordance with section 36 of this Act.

36   Service under section 35(3)

(1) Due service under section 35(3) of this Act is effected by delivering the notice in question to the owner or by sending it by registered post, or the recorded delivery service, addressed to him at an appropriate place.

(2) An acknowledgement, signed by the owner, which conforms to Form A of schedule 10 to this Act, or as the case may be a certificate which conforms to Form B of that schedule and is accompanied by the postal receipt, shall be sufficient evidence of such due service; and if the notice in question is, under subsection (1) above, sent by post but is returned to the person who is entitled to compensation with an intimation that it could not be delivered, the notice may be delivered or sent by post, with that intimation, to the Extractor of the Court of Session, the delivery or sending to the Extractor being taken to be equivalent to the service of that notice on the owner.

(3) For the purposes of subsection (2) above, an acknowledgement of receipt by the Extractor on a copy of that notice shall be sufficient evidence of its receipt by him.

(4) The date on which notice under section 35(3) of this Act is served on an owner is the date of delivery, or as the case may be of posting, in compliance with subsection (1) or (2) above.

(5) A reference in this section to an "appropriate place" is, for any owner, to be construed as a reference to—

   (a)   his place of residence;

   (b)   his place of business; or

   (c)   a postal address which he ordinarily uses,

or, if none of those is known at the time of delivery or posting, as a reference to whatever place is at that time his most recently known place of residence or place of business or postal address which he ordinarily used.

37   Amount of compensation

(1) The amount of any compensation payable on a claim made under section 35(3) of this Act shall, subject to subsections (2) and (3) below, be such sum as represents, at the time of the breach or occurrence in question, any development value which would have accrued to the owner had the burden been modified to the extent necessary to permit the land to be used, or dealt with, in the way that constituted the breach or, as the case may be, occurrence on which the claim is based.

(2) The amount payable as compensation (or, where more than one claim is made in relation to the same development value burden, the total compensation payable) under subsection (1) above shall not exceed such sum as will make up for any effect which the burden produced, at the time when it was imposed, in reducing the consideration then paid or made payable for the feu.

(3) In assessing for the purposes of subsection (1) above an amount of compensation payable—

   (a)   any entitlement of the claimant to recover any part of the development value of the land subject to the development value burden shall be taken into account; and

(b) a claimant to whom the reserved right was assigned or otherwise transferred shall be entitled to no greater sum than the former superior would have been had there been no such assignation or transfer.

(4) The reference in subsection (1) above to a burden shall, in relation to an occurrence, be construed as a reference to the burden which would have been breached but for its becoming, by section 17(1) of this Act, extinct or unenforceable.

38   Duty to disclose identity of owner

Where a person ("the claimant") purports duly to serve notice under section 35(3) of this Act and the person on whom it is served, being a person who had right, before the time of the breach (or, as the case may be, occurrence) founded on by the claimant, to the *dominium utile* (or the ownership) of the land, is not the owner, that person shall forthwith disclose to the claimant—

(a) the identity and address of the owner; or

(b) (if he cannot do that) such other information as he has that might enable the claimant to discover the identity and address;

and the notice shall refer to that requirement for disclosure.

39   The expression "owner" for purposes of sections 35 to 38

(1) In sections 35 to 38 of this Act, "owner" means the person who, at the time of the breach or, as the case may be, occurrence, mentioned in section 35(2)(c) of this Act, has right to—

(a) the *dominium utile*; or

(b) the ownership,

of the land which, immediately before the appointed day, was subject to the development value burden, whether or not he has completed title; and if more than one person comes within that description, then the owner is the person who has most recently acquired such right.

(2) Where the land in question is held by two or more such owners as common property, they shall be severally liable to make any compensatory payment (but as between, or as the case may be among, themselves they shall be liable in the proportions in which they hold the land).

40   Assignation, discharge, or restriction, of reserved right to claim compensation

A reserved right to claim, in accordance with section 35 of this Act, compensation may be—

(a) assigned, whether wholly or to such extent (expressed as a percentage of each claim which may come to be made) as may be specified in the assignation; or

(b)   discharged or restricted,

by execution and registration of an assignation, or as the case may be a discharge, or restriction, in the form, or as nearly as may be in the form, contained in schedule 11 to this Act.

Miscellaneous

41   Notices: pre-registration requirements etc

(1) This section applies in relation to any notice which is to be submitted for registration under this Act.

(2) It shall not be necessary to endorse on the notice a warrant of registration.

(3) Except where it is not reasonably practicable to do so, a superior shall, before he executes the notice, send by post to the person who has the estate of *dominium utile* of the land to which the burden relates (addressed to "The Proprietor" where the name of that person is not known) a copy of—

(a)   the notice; and

(b)   the explanatory note set out in whichever schedule to this Act relates to the notice.

(4) A superior shall, in the notice, state either—

(a)   that a copy of the notice has been sent in accordance with subsection (3) above; or

(b)   that it was not reasonably practicable for such a copy to be sent.

42   Further provision as respects sections 18 to 20, 27 and 33

(1) Where—

(a)   a notice relating to a real burden has been registered under section 18, 18A, 18B, 18C, 20, 27, 27A or 33 of this Act; or

(b)   an agreement relating to a real burden has been registered under section 19 of this Act,

against the *dominium utile* of any land which is subject to the burden, it shall not be competent to register under any of those sections against that *dominium utile* another such notice or agreement relating to the same real burden; but nothing in this subsection shall prevent registration where—

(i)   the discharge of any earlier such notice has been registered by the person who registered that notice (or by his successor); or

(ii)   as the case may be, the discharge of any earlier such agreement has been registered, jointly, by the parties to that agreement (or by their successors).

(2) Where the *dominium utile* of any land comprises parts each held by a separate vassal, each part shall be taken to be a separate feudal estate of *dominium utile*.

(3) Where more than one feudal estate of *dominium utile* is subject to the same real burden enforceable by a superior of the feu, he shall, if he wishes to execute and register a notice under section 18, 18A, 18B, 18C, 20, 27, 27A or 33 of this Act against those feudal estates in respect of that real burden, require to do so against each separately.

(4) Where a feudal estate of *dominium utile* is subject to more than one real burden enforceable by a superior of the feu, he may if he wishes to—

    (a)   execute and register a notice under section 18, 18A, 18B, 18C, 20, 27, 27A or 33 of this Act against that feudal estate in respect of those real burdens, do so by a single notice; or

    (b)   enter into and register an agreement under section 19 of this Act against that feudal estate in respect of those real burdens, do so by a single agreement.

(5) Nothing in this Part requires registration against land prospectively nominated as a dominant tenement but outwith Scotland.

43   Notices and agreements under certain sections: extent of Keeper's duty

(1) In relation to any notice submitted for registration under section 18, 18A, 18B, 18C, 20, 27, 27A or 33 of this Act, the Keeper of the Registers of Scotland shall not be required to determine whether the superior has complied with the terms of section 41(3) of this Act.

(2) In relation to any notice, or as the case may be any agreement, submitted for registration under—

    (a)   section 18, 18A, 18B, 18C, 19, 20, 27, 27A or 33 of this Act, the Keeper shall not be required to determine whether, for the purposes of subsection (1) of the section in question, a real burden is enforceable by a superior;

    (b)   section 18 of this Act, the Keeper shall not be required to determine, where, in pursuance of subsection (2)(c) of that section, the condition specified is that mentioned in subsection (7)(a) of that section, whether the terms of that condition are satisfied;

  (bb)   section 18B or 18C of this Act, the Keeper shall not be required to determine whether—

        (i)   the requirements of subsection (1) of the section in question are satisfied; or

       (ii)   the statement made in pursuance of subsection (2)(e) of the section in question is correct;

    (c)   paragraph (c) of subsection (1) of section 19 of this Act, the Keeper shall not be required to determine whether the requirements of paragraph (a) of that subsection are satisfied;

    (d)   section 20 of this Act, the Keeper shall not be required to determine—

        (i)   whether the description provided in pursuance of subsection (2) of that section is correct;

> (ii)   whether the notice has been executed, and is being registered, timeously; or
>
> (iii)   any matter as to which the Lands Tribunal must be satisfied before making an order under that section;

(e)   section 33 of this Act, the Keeper shall not be required to determine whether—

> (i)   the requirements of subsection (1)(a) and (b) of that section are satisfied; or
>
> (ii)   the statements made or information provided, in pursuance of subsection (2)(d) or (e) of that section, are correct.

(3) The Keeper shall not be required to determine—

(a)   for the purposes of section 18(6), 18A(5), 18B(3), 18C(3), 19(5), 20(5) or (8)(a)(i), 28, 28A or 60(1) of this Act, whether immediately before the appointed day a real burden is, or is still, enforceable, or by whom; or

(b)   for the purposes of subsection (8)(a)(ii) of section 20 of this Act, whether immediately before the day of registration of an order of the Lands Tribunal under subsection (7) of that section a real burden is, or is still, enforceable, or by whom.

44   Referral to Lands Tribunal of notice dispute

(1) Any dispute arising in relation to a notice registered under this Act may be referred to the Lands Tribunal; and, in determining the dispute, the Tribunal may make such order as it thinks fit discharging or, to such extent as may be specified in the order, restricting the notice in question.

(2) Any dispute arising in relation to a claim made under section 35(3) of this Act may be referred to the Lands Tribunal; and, in determining the dispute, the Tribunal may make such order as it thinks fit (including an order fixing the amount of any compensation payable under the claim in question).

(3) In any referral under subsection (1) or (2) above, the burden of proving any disputed question of fact shall be on the person relying on the notice or, as the case may be, making the claim.

(4) An extract of any order made under subsection (1) or (2) above may be registered and the order shall take effect as respects third parties on such registration.

45   Circumstances where certain notices may be registered after appointed day

(1) Subject to subsection (2) below, where—

(a)   a notice submitted, before the appointed day, for registration under this Act, or an agreement so submitted for registration under section 19 of this Act, is rejected by the Keeper of the Registers of Scotland; but

(b)   a court or the Lands Tribunal then determines that the notice or agreement is registrable, the notice or agreement may, if not registered before the appointed day, be registered—

  (i)   within two months after the determination is made; but

  (ii) before such date after the appointed day as the Scottish Ministers may by order prescribe,

and any notice or agreement registered under this subsection on or after the appointed day shall be treated as if it had been registered before that day.

(2) For the purposes of subsection (1) above, the application to the court, or to the Lands Tribunal, which has resulted in the determination shall require to have been made within such period as the Scottish Ministers may by order prescribe.

(3) In subsection (1)(b) above, "court" means any court having jurisdiction in questions of heritable right or title.

46   Duties of Keeper: amendments relating to the extinction of certain real burdens

(1) The Keeper of the Registers of Scotland shall not be required to remove from the Land Register of Scotland a real burden extinguished by section 17(1)(a) of this Act unless—

  (a)   subject to subsection (3) below, he is requested to do so in an application for registration or rectification; or

  (b)   he is, under section 9(1) of the Land Registration (Scotland) Act 1979 (c 33) (rectification of the register), ordered, subject to subsection (3) below, to do so by the court or the Lands Tribunal;

and no such request or order shall be competent during a period which commences with the appointed day and is of such number of years as the Scottish Ministers may by order prescribe.

(2) During the period mentioned in subsection (1) above a real burden, notwithstanding that it has been so extinguished, may at the discretion of the Keeper, for the purposes of section 6(1)(e) of that Act of 1979 (entering subsisting real right in title sheet), be taken to subsist; but this subsection is without prejudice to subsection (3) below.

(3) The Keeper shall not, before the date mentioned in subsection (4) below, remove from the Land Register of Scotland a real burden which is the subject of a notice or agreement in respect of which application had been made for a determination by—

  (a)   a court; or

  (b)   the Lands Tribunal,

under section 45(1)(b) of this Act.

(4) The date is whichever is the earlier of—

  (a)   that two months after the final decision on the application; and

  (b)   that prescribed under section 45(1)(ii) of this Act.

47   Extinction of counter-obligation

Without prejudice to any other way in which a counter-obligation to a real burden may be extinguished, any such counter-obligation is extinguished on the extinction of the real burden.

48   No implication as to dominant tenement where real burden created in grant in feu

Where a real burden is created (or has at any time been created) in a grant in feu, the superior having the *dominium utile*, or allodial ownership, of land (the "superior's land") in the vicinity of the land feued, no implication shall thereby arise that the superior's land is a dominant tenement.

Interpretation

49   Interpretation of Part 4

In this Part of this Act, unless the context otherwise requires—

> "conservation body" means a body prescribed by order under section 38(4) of the Title Conditions (Scotland) Act 2003 (asp 9);

> "conservation burden" shall be construed in accordance with sections 27(1) and 27A(1) of this Act;

> "development value burden" and "development value" shall be construed in accordance with section 33 of this Act;

> "economic development burden" shall be construed in accordance with section 18B(3) of this Act;

> "health care burden" shall be construed in accordance with section 18C(3) of this Act;

> "local authority" means a council constituted under section 2 of the Local Government etc (Scotland) Act 1994 (c 39);

> "notary public" includes any person duly authorised by the law of the country (other than Scotland) in which the swearing or affirmation takes place to administer oaths or receive affirmations in that other country;

> "personal pre-emption burden" and "personal redemption burden" shall be construed in accordance with section 18A(5) of this Act;

> "real burden"—

>> (a)   includes—

>>> (i)   a right of pre-emption;

>>> (ii)   a right of redemption; or

>>> (iii)   *(repealed by the Title Conditions (Scotland) Act 2003, s 128(2), Sch 15)*

>> provided that it is constituted as a real burden; but

>> (b)   does not include a pecuniary real burden or sporting rights (as defined by section 65A(9) of this Act);

"registering" means registering an interest in land (or information relating to such an interest) in the Land Register of Scotland or, as the case may be, recording a document in the Register of Sasines; and cognate expressions shall be construed accordingly; and

"superior" means a person who has right to the immediate superiority or to any over-superiority, whether or not he has completed title (and if more than one person comes within either of those descriptions then, in relation to that description, the person who has most recently acquired such right) and "former superior" shall be construed accordingly.

PART 5
ENTAILS

50   Disentailment on appointed day

(1) Land which, immediately before the appointed day, is held under an entail is disentailed on that day.

(2) Section 32 of the Entail Amendment Act 1848 (c 36) (which makes provision as respects an instrument of disentail executed and recorded under that Act) shall apply to the effect of disentailment by subsection (1) above as that section applies to the effect of such an instrument so executed and recorded.

51   Compensation for expectancy or interest of apparent or other nearest heir in an entailed estate

(1) Where, immediately before the appointed day—

(a)   land is held under an entail; and

(b)   the consent of a person who is an apparent or other nearest heir is required to any petition for authority of the court for the purpose of presenting an instrument of disentail,

the valuation of any expectancy or interest of the person, which on his refusal to give such consent would fall, before the appointed day, to be ascertained under section 13 of the Entail (Scotland) Act 1882 (c 53) may, within two years after the appointed day, be referred by him to, and determined by, the Lands Tribunal.

(2) The Tribunal shall direct that any sum ascertained by them in a valuation by virtue of subsection (1) above shall be secured on the land, for the benefit of the person, in such manner as they think fit.

52   Closure of Register of Entails

The Keeper of the Registers of Scotland shall, immediately before the appointed day, close the Register of Entails; and as soon as is practicable thereafter, he shall transmit that register to the Keeper of the Records of Scotland for preservation.

PART 6
MISCELLANEOUS

Discharge of certain rights and extinction of certain obligations and payments

53   Discharge of rights of irritancy

(1) All rights of irritancy held by a superior are, on the day on which this section comes into force, discharged; and on that day any proceedings already commenced to enforce any such right shall be deemed abandoned and may, without further process and without any requirement that full judicial expenses shall have been paid by the pursuer, be dismissed accordingly.

(2) Subsection (1) above shall not affect any cause in which final decree (that is to say, any decree or interlocutor which disposes of the cause and is not subject to appeal or review) is granted before the coming into force of this section.

54   Extinction of superior's rights and obligations *qua* superior

(1) Subject to section 13, to Part 4, and to sections 60(1) and 65A, of this Act, a right or obligation which, immediately before the appointed day, is enforceable by, or as the case may be against, a superior *qua* superior (including, without prejudice to that generality, sporting rights as defined by subsection (9) of that section 65A) shall, on that day, be extinguished.

(2) Subject to subsection (3) below—

   (a)   on or after the appointed day, no proceedings for such enforcement shall be commenced;

   (b)   any proceedings already commenced for such enforcement shall be deemed to have been abandoned on that day and may, without further process and without any requirement that full judicial expenses shall have been paid by the pursuer, be dismissed accordingly; and

   (c)   any decree, or interlocutor, already pronounced in proceedings for such enforcement shall be deemed to have been reduced, or as the case may be recalled, on that day.

(3) Subsection (2) above shall not affect any proceedings, decree or interlocutor in relation to—

   (a)   a right of irritancy held by a superior;

   (aa) a right of enforcement held by virtue of section 13, 33, 60(1) or 65A of this Act; or

   (b)   a right to recover damages or to the payment of money.

55   Abolition of thirlage

Any obligation of thirlage which has not been extinguished before the appointed day is extinguished on that day.

56   Extinction etc of certain payments analogous to feuduty

(1) The provisions of Part 3 of this Act shall apply as regards ground annual, skat, teind, stipend, standard charge, dry multures (including compensation payable in respect of commutation pursuant to the Thirlage Act 1799 (c 55)) and, subject to the exceptions mentioned in subsection (2) below, as regards any other perpetual periodical payment in respect of the tenure, occupancy or use of land or under a title condition, as those provisions apply as regards feuduty; but for the purposes of that application—

(a)   references in the provisions to "vassal" and "superior" shall be construed as references to, respectively, the payer and the recipient of the ground annual, skat, teind, stipend, standard charge, dry multures or other payment in question ("former vassal" and "former superior" being construed accordingly); and

(b)   a form (and its explanatory note) contained in a schedule to this Act shall be modified so as to accord with the kind of payment to which it relates.

(2) The exceptions are any payments—

(a)   in defrayal of, or as a contribution towards, some continuing cost related to land; or

(b)   made under a heritable security.

(3) The definition of "title condition" in section 122(1) of the Title Conditions (Scotland) Act 2003 (asp 9) shall apply for the purposes of this section as that definition applies for the purposes of that Act.

(4) Nothing in subsections (1) to (3) above shall be taken to prejudice the tenure, occupancy or use of land.

57   Extinction by prescription of obligation to pay redemption money for feuduty, ground annual etc

Notwithstanding the terms of Schedule 1 to the Prescription and Limitation (Scotland) Act 1973 (c 52) (which defines obligations affected by prescriptive periods of five years), any obligation under section 5 (redemption of feuduty, ground annual etc on transfer for valuable consideration) or 6 (redemption of feuduty, ground annual etc on compulsory acquisition) of the Land Tenure Reform (Scotland) Act 1974 (c 38) to pay redemption money is an obligation to which section 6 of that Act of 1973 (extinction of obligation by prescriptive period of five years) applies; and for the purposes of that application, the reference in subsection (1) of section 6 of that Act of 1973 to the "appropriate date" is a reference to the date of redemption within the meaning of—

(a)   except in the case mentioned in paragraph (b) below, section 5 (read, as the case may be, with section 6(2)(a)); or

(b)   in the case of an obligation arising out of the acquisition of land by means of a general vesting declaration, section 6(4),

of that Act of 1974.

The Crown, the Lord Lyon and Barony

58   Crown application

(1) This Act binds the Crown and accordingly such provision as is made by section 2 of this Act as respects feudal estates of *dominium* shall apply to the superiority of the Prince and Steward of Scotland and to the ultimate superiority of the Crown; but nothing in this Act shall be taken to supersede or impair any power exercisable by Her Majesty by virtue of Her prerogative.

(2) Without prejudice to the generality of subsection (1) above, in that subsection—

    (a)   Her Majesty's prerogative includes the prerogative of honour; and

    (b)   "any power exercisable by Her Majesty by virtue of Her prerogative" includes—

        (i)   prerogative rights as respects ownerless or unclaimed property; and

        (ii)   the *regalia majora.*

59   Crown may sell or otherwise dispose of land by disposition

It shall be competent for the Crown, in selling or otherwise disposing of any land, to do so by granting a disposition of that land.

60   Preserved right of Crown to maritime burdens

(1) Where, immediately before the appointed day, the Crown has the right as superior to enforce a real burden against part of the sea bed or part of the foreshore, then, on and after that day, the Crown shall—

    (a)   subject to any counter-obligation, have title to enforce; and

    (b)   be presumed to have an interest to enforce,

the burden; and any burden as respects which the Crown has such title and interest shall, on and after the appointed day, be known as a "maritime burden".

(2) *(repealed by the Title Conditions (Scotland) Act 2003, s 128(2), Sch 15)*

(3) For the purposes of this section—

    "sea bed" means the bed of the territorial sea adjacent to Scotland; and

    "territorial sea" includes any tidal waters.

(4) In this section, "real burden" has the same meaning as in Part 4 of this Act.

61   Mines of gold and silver

The periodical payment to the Crown, in respect of the produce of a mine which by the Royal Mines Act 1424 (c 12) belongs to the Crown, of an amount which is not fixed but is calculated as a proportion of that produce is not—

    (a)   a payment to the Crown *qua* superior for the purposes of section 54 of this Act;

(b) a perpetual periodical payment for the purposes of section 56 of this Act; or

(c) a feuduty for the purposes of Part 3 of this Act.

62 Jurisdiction and prerogative of Lord Lyon

Nothing in this Act shall be taken to supersede or impair the jurisdiction or prerogative of the Lord Lyon King of Arms.

63 Baronies and other dignities and offices

(1) Any jurisdiction of, and any conveyancing privilege incidental to, barony shall on the appointed day cease to exist; but nothing in this Act affects the dignity of baron or any other dignity or office (whether or not of feudal origin).

(2) When, by this Act, an estate held in barony ceases to exist as a feudal estate, the dignity of baron, though retained, shall not attach to the land; and on and after the appointed day any such dignity shall be, and shall be transferable only as, incorporeal heritable property (and shall not be an interest in land for the purposes of the Land Registration (Scotland) Act 1979 (c 33) or a right as respects which a deed can be recorded in the Register of Sasines).

(3) Where there is registered, before the appointed day, a heritable security over an estate to which is attached the dignity of baron, the security shall on and after that day (until discharge) affect—

(a) in the case of an estate of *dominium utile*, both the dignity of baron and the land; and

(b) in any other case, the dignity of baron.

(4) In this section—

"conveyancing privilege" includes any privilege in relation to prescription;

"dignity" includes any quality or precedence associated with, and any heraldic privilege incidental to, a dignity; and

"registered" has the same meaning as in Part 4 of this Act.

Kindly Tenants of Lochmaben

64 Abolition of Kindly Tenancies

(1) The system of land tenure whereby the persons known as the Kindly Tenants of Lochmaben hold land on perpetual tenure without requiring to procure infeftment is, on the appointed day, abolished.

(2) On the appointed day the interest of a Kindly Tenant shall forthwith become the ownership of the land (which shall be taken to include any right of salmon fishing inseverable from the kindly tenancy); and, in so far as is consistent with the provisions of this Act, the land shall be subject to the same subordinate real rights and other encumbrances as was the kindly tenancy.

(3) A right of salmon fishing inseverable from a kindly tenancy shall on and after the appointed day be inseverable from the ownership of the land in question.

Miscellaneous

65   Creation of proper liferent

(1) A proper liferent over land is created—

    (a)   in a case where the right is registrable under section 2 of the Land Registration (Scotland) Act 1979 (c 33)—

        (i)   (unless the deed granting or reserving the right makes provision for some later date) on registration; or

        (ii)   (where provision is made for such a date and the right has been registered) on that date; or

    (b)   in any other case—

        (i)   (unless the deed granting or reserving the right makes provision for some later date) on recording of the deed in the Register of Sasines; or

        (ii)   (where provision is made for such a date and such deed has been so recorded) on that date.

(2) This section is without prejudice to any other enactment, or rule of law, by or under which a proper liferent over land may be created.

(3) In subsection (1)(a) above, "registrable" and "registration" have the meanings respectively assigned to those expressions by section 1(3) of the Land Registration (Scotland) Act 1979 (c 33).

(4) The references, in subsection (1)(b) above, to a deed being recorded include references to a notice of title deducing title through a deed being recorded.

65A   Sporting rights

(1) Where a feudal estate of *dominium utile* of land is subject to sporting rights which are enforceable by a superior of the feu or which would be so enforceable were the person in question to complete title to the *dominium directum* the superior may, before the appointed day, by duly executing and registering against the *dominium utile* a notice in, or as nearly as may be in, the form contained in schedule 11A to this Act, prospectively convert those rights into a tenement in land.

(2) The notice shall—

    (a)   set out the title of the superior;

    (b)   describe, sufficiently to enable identification by reference to the Ordnance Map, the land the *dominium utile* of which is subject to the sporting rights (or any part of that land);

    (c)   describe those rights; and

    (d)   set out the terms of any counter-obligation to those rights if it is a counter-obligation enforceable against the superior.

(3) Before submitting any notice for registration under this section, the superior shall swear or affirm as is mentioned in subsection (4) of section 18 of this Act.

(4) Subsection (5) of that section applies for the purposes of subsection (3) above as it applies for the purposes of subsection (4) of that section.

(5) If subsections (1) to (3) above are, with subsection (4) of that section, complied with and immediately before the appointed day the sporting rights are still enforceable by the superior (or his successor) or would be so enforceable, or still so enforceable, were the person in question to complete title to the *dominium directum* then, on that day, the sporting rights shall be converted into a tenement in land.

(6) No greater, or more exclusive, sporting rights shall be enforceable by virtue of such conversion than were (or would have been) enforceable as mentioned in subsection (5) above.

(7) Where the *dominium utile* comprises parts each held by a separate vassal, each part shall be taken to be a separate feudal estate of *dominium utile*.

(8) Where sporting rights become, under subsection (5) above, a tenement in land, the right to enforce those rights shall be subject to any counter-obligation enforceable against the superior immediately before the appointed day; and section 47 of this Act shall apply in relation to any counter-obligation to sporting rights as it applies in relation to any counter-obligation to a real burden.

(9) In this section, "sporting rights" means a right of fishing or game.

(10) This section is subject to section 41 of this Act.

(11) Subsections (1) and (2)(a) of section 43 of this Act apply in relation to a notice submitted for registration under this section as they apply in relation to a notice so submitted under any of the provisions mentioned in those subsections; and paragraph (a) of subsection (3) of that section applies in relation to a determination for the purposes of subsection (5) of this section as it applies in relation to a determination for the purposes of any of the provisions mentioned in that paragraph.

(12) Subsections (1), (3) and (4) of section 46 of this Act apply in relation to sporting rights extinguished by virtue of section 54 of this Act as they apply in relation to a real burden extinguished by section 17(1)(a) of this Act.

66 Obligation to make title deeds and searches available

A possessor of title deeds or searches which relate to any land shall make them available to a person who has (or is entitled to acquire) a real right in the land, on all necessary occasions when the person so requests, at the person's expense.

67 Prohibition on leases for periods of more than 175 years

(1) Notwithstanding any provision to the contrary in any lease, no lease of land executed on or after the coming into force of this section (in this section referred to as the "commencement date") may continue for a period of more than 175 years; and any such lease which is still subsisting at the end of that period shall, by virtue of this subsection, be terminated forthwith.

(2) If a lease of land so executed includes provision (however expressed) requiring the landlord or the tenant to renew the lease then the duration of any such renewed lease shall be added to the duration of the original lease for the purposes of reckoning the period mentioned in subsection (1) above.

(3) Nothing in subsection (1) above shall prevent—

    (a)   any lease being continued by tacit relocation; or

    (b)   the duration of any lease being extended by, under or by virtue of any enactment.

(4) Subsections (1) and (2) above do not apply—

    (a)   to a lease executed on or after the commencement date in implement of an obligation entered into before that date;

    (b)   to a lease executed after the commencement date in implement of an obligation contained in a lease such as is mentioned in paragraph (a) above; or

    (c)   where—

        (i)   a lease for a period of more than 175 years has been executed before the commencement date; or

        (ii)   a lease such as is mentioned in paragraph (a) or (b) above is executed on or after that date,

to a sub-lease executed on or after that date of the whole, or part, of the land subject to the lease in question.

(5) For the purposes of this section "lease" includes sub-lease.

68   Certain applications to Sheriff of Chancery

After section 26 of the Titles to Land Consolidation (Scotland) Act 1868 (c 101) there shall be inserted—

"26A   Application for declarator of succession as heir in general or to specified lands

On an application being made by any person having an interest, the Sheriff of Chancery may, if satisfied that—

    (a)   such deceased person as may be specified in the application died before 10th September 1964 and that person either—

        (i)   was domiciled in Scotland at the date of his death; or

        (ii)   was the owner of lands situated in Scotland to which the application relates; and

    (b)   the applicant, or as the case may be such person as may be specified in the application, has succeeded as heir to that deceased, and is either—

        (i)   heir in general; or

        (ii)   heir to such lands as may be specified in the application, grant declarator that the applicant, or as the case may be such person as may be specified in the declarator, is the heir in general or heir to the lands so specified.

26B   Application for declarator of succession as heir to last surviving trustee under a trust

On an application being made under this section, the Sheriff of Chancery may, if satisfied that—

(a)   such deceased person as may be specified in the application was the last surviving trustee named in, or assumed under, a trust;

(b)   the trust provides for the heir of such last surviving trustee to be a trustee;

(c)   either—

    (i)   the trust is governed by the law of Scotland; or

    (ii)   lands subject to the trust and to which the application relates are situated in Scotland; and

(d)   the applicant has succeeded as heir to the deceased,

grant declarator that the applicant is the heir of the deceased and accordingly is a trustee under the trust.

26C   Construction of reference to service of heir

A reference in any enactment or deed to a decree of service of heir (however expressed) shall include a reference to a declarator granted under section 26A or 26B of this Act.".

69   Application of 1970 Act to earlier forms of heritable security

(1) Sections 14 to 30 of the Conveyancing and Feudal Reform (Scotland) Act 1970 (c 35) (which provisions relate to the assignation, variation, discharge and calling-up etc of standard securities) shall apply (with the substitution of the word "heritable" for "standard" and subject to such other modifications as may be necessary) as respects any heritable security granted before 29th November 1970 as those provisions apply as respects a standard security.

(2) For the purposes of the said sections 14 to 30 (as modified by, or by virtue of, subsection (1) above), "heritable security" shall, with the modification mentioned in subsection (3) below, include a pecuniary real burden but shall not include a security constituted by *ex facie* absolute disposition.

(3) The modification is that the reference to the date in subsection (1) above shall be disregarded.

70   Ownership of land by a firm

A firm may, if it has a legal personality distinct from the persons who compose it, itself own land.

PART 7
GENERAL

71   The appointed day

The Scottish Ministers may, for the purposes of this Act, by order appoint a day (in this Act referred to as the "appointed day"), being a day which—

    (a)   falls not less than six months after the order is made; and

    (b)   is one or other of the terms of Whitsunday and Martinmas.

72   Interpretation

In this Act, unless the context otherwise requires—

    "land" includes all subjects of heritable property which, before the appointed day, are, or of their nature might be, held of a superior according to feudal tenure;

    "Lands Tribunal" means Lands Tribunal for Scotland; and

    "the specified day" and "the transitional period" shall be construed in accordance with section 20(6) of this Act.

73   Feudal terms in enactments and documents: construction after abolition of feudal system

(1) Where a term or expression, which before the appointed day would ordinarily, or in the context in which it is used, depend for its meaning on there being a feudal system of land tenure, requires to be construed, in relation to any period from that day onwards—

    (a)   in an enactment (other than this Act) passed before that day;

    (b)   in an enactment contained in subordinate legislation made before that day;

    (c)   in a document executed before that day; or

    (d)   in the Land Register of Scotland or in—

        (i)   a land certificate;

        (ii)   a charge certificate; or

        (iii)   an office copy,

issued, whether or not before that day, under the Land Registration (Scotland) Act 1979 (c 33),

then in so far as the context admits, where the term or expression is, or contains, a reference to—

    (i)   the *dominium utile* of the land, that reference shall be construed either as a reference to the land or as a reference to the ownership of that land;

    (ii)   an estate in land, that reference shall be construed as a reference to a right in land and as including ownership of land;

(iii) a vassal in relation to land, that reference shall be construed as a reference to the owner of the land;

(iv) feuing, that reference shall be construed as a reference to disponing;

(v) a feu disposition, that reference shall be construed as a reference to a disposition;

(vi) taking infeftment, that reference shall be construed as a reference to completing title,

analogous terms and expressions being construed accordingly.

(2) On and after the appointed day, any reference—

(a) in any document executed before that day; or

(b) in the Land Register of Scotland or in any certificate or copy such as is mentioned in subsection (1)(d) above (whenever issued),

to a superior shall, where that reference requires to be construed in relation to a real burden which a person is entitled, by virtue of section 18, 18A, 18B, 18C, 19, 20, 28, 28A or 60 of this Act or section 56 of the Title Conditions (Scotland) Act 2003 (asp 9) (facility burdens and service burdens), to enforce on and after that day, be construed as a reference to that person.

(2A) In construing, after the appointed day and in relation to a right enforceable on or after that day, a document, or entry in the Land Register, which—

(a) sets out the terms of a real burden; and

(b) is not a document or entry references in which require to be construed as mentioned in subsection (2) above,

any provision of the document or entry to the effect that a person other than the person entitled to enforce the burden may waive compliance with, or mitigate or otherwise vary a condition of, the burden shall be disregarded.

(3) Subsection (1) above is without prejudice to section 76 of, and schedules 12 and 13 to, this Act or to any order made under subsection (3) of that section.

(4) In subsection (1) above—

(a) in paragraph (a), "enactment" includes a local and personal or private Act; and

(b) in paragraph (b), "subordinate legislation" has the same meaning as in the Interpretation Act 1978 (c 30) (but includes subordinate legislation made under an Act of the Scottish Parliament).

74 Orders, regulations and rules

(1) Any power of the Scottish Ministers under this Act to make orders, regulations or rules shall be exercisable by statutory instrument; and a statutory instrument containing any such orders, regulations or rules, other than an order under section 71, 76(3) or 77(4), shall be subject to annulment in pursuance of a resolution of the Scottish Parliament.

(2) A statutory instrument containing an order under section 76(3) of this Act shall not be made unless a draft of the instrument has been—

  (a) laid before; and

  (b) approved by a resolution of,

the Scottish Parliament.

75   Saving for contractual rights

(1) As respects any land granted in feu before the appointed day, nothing in this Act shall affect any right (other than a right to feuduty) included in the grant in so far as that right is contractual as between the parties to the grant (or, as the case may be, as between one of them and a person to whom any such right is assigned).

(2) In construing the expression "parties to the grant" in subsection (1) above, any enactment or rule of law whereby investiture is deemed renewed when the parties change shall be disregarded.

76   Minor and consequential amendments, repeals and power to amend or repeal enactments

(1) Schedule 12 to this Act, which contains minor amendments and amendments consequential upon the provisions of this Act, shall have effect.

(2) The enactments mentioned in schedule 13 to this Act are hereby repealed to the extent specified in the second column of that schedule.

(3) The Scottish Ministers may by order make such further amendments or repeals, in such enactments as may be specified in the order, as appear to them to be necessary or expedient in consequence of any provision of this Act.

(4) In this section "enactment" has the same meaning as in section 73(1)(a) of this Act.

77   Short title and commencement

(1) This Act—

  (a) may be cited as the Abolition of Feudal Tenure etc (Scotland) Act 2000; and

  (b) subject to subsections (2) and (4) below, comes into force on Royal Assent.

(2) There shall come into force on the appointed day—

  (a) sections 1 and 2, 4 to 13, 32, 35 to 37, 46, 50 and 51, 54 to 57, 59 to 61, 64, 65, 66, 68 to 70, 73, 75 and 76(1) (except in so far as relating to paragraph 30(23)(a) of schedule 12) and (2);

  (b) schedules 1 to 3;

  (c) subject to paragraph 46(3) of schedule 12, that schedule, except paragraph 30(23)(a); and

  (d) schedule 13.

(3) Note 1 to Schedule 2 to the Conveyancing and Feudal Reform (Scotland) Act 1970 (c 35) shall be deemed to have been originally enacted as amended by the said paragraph 30(23)(a).

(4) There shall come into force on such day as the Scottish Ministers may by order appoint—

  (a)   sections 17 to 31, 33, 34, 38 to 45, 47 to 49, 63 and 65A;

  (b)   schedules 5 to 11;

  (c)   *(repealed by the Title Conditions (Scotland) Act 2003, s 128(2), Sch 15)*

  (d)   *(repealed by the Title Conditions (Scotland) Act 2003, s 128(2), Sch 15)*

and different days may be so appointed for different provisions.

SCHEDULE I
Form of Notice Requiring Compensatory Payment etc: *Cumulo* Feuduty

(introduced by section 8(2))

"NOTICE UNDER SECTION 8(1) OF THE ABOLITION OF FEUDAL TENURE ETC (SCOTLAND) ACT 2000 (*CUMULO* FEUDUTY)

To: [*name and address of former vassal*].

This notice is sent by [*name and address of former superior*]. You are required to pay the sum of £ [*amount*] as a compensatory payment for the extinction of the *cumulo* feuduty of £ [*amount*] per annum due in respect of [*give sufficient identification of the land in respect of which the cumulo feuduty was due*].

The attached appendix shows the total sum due as compensation for the extinction of the feuduty and the compensatory payment due by each owner.

(If arrears of the feuduty are also sought, then add:

You are also required to pay the sum of £ [*amount*] as arrears of the feuduty.)

Signed: [*signature either of the former superior or of his agent; and if an agent signs he should put the word* "Agent" *after his signature*]

Date:

(If payment is to be made to an agent of the former superior then add:

Payment should be made to: [*name and address of agent*].)".

Appendix referred to in the Notice:

Total compensation payable is £ [*amount*], allocated as follows:

Owner (*see note for completion 1*)	Property (*see note for completion 2*)	Compensatory payment (*see note for completion 3*)

Explanatory Note

(This explanation, and the "Notes for completion of the Appendix" which immediately follows it, have no legal effect)

The feudal system was abolished on [*insert date of abolition*]. By this notice your former feudal superior is claiming compensation from you for the extinction of the *cumulo* feuduty which affected your property. A *cumulo* feuduty is one which affects two or more properties in separate ownership. This notice must have been sent within two years after the date of abolition.

The appendix sets out the total sum due as compensation for the extinction of the *cumulo* feuduty and divides that sum among the owners of the affected properties.

The total compensation payable is that sum which would, if invested in 2?% Consolidated Stock at the middle market price at the close of business last preceding the date of abolition, produce an annual sum equal to the *cumulo* feuduty. In practice the sum is arrived at by multiplying the feuduty by a factor known as the "compensation factor". This factor is [*insert factor*].

If the amount of the compensatory payment allocated to you is £50 or more you can choose to pay the sum due by instalments. You may do this by signing, dating and returning, within eight weeks, the enclosed instalment document.

If, having received the instalment document, you sell, or transfer for valuable consideration, the property or any part of it you will lose the option of paying by instalments.

Unless you are paying by instalments you must pay the compensatory payment allocated to you within eight weeks.

Your former feudal superior may also be claiming arrears of feuduty for the period before the date of abolition.

If at one time you had right to the property in question but, immediately before the feudal system was abolished, you no longer had that right (because, for example, you had sold that property to someone else) then this notice has been served on you in error and no payment will be due; but you nevertheless have to provide the person who sent you the notice, if you can, with such information as you have which might enable him to identify the person who should have received notice instead of you.

If you think that the amount required from you is not due for that or any other reason, you are advised to consult your solicitor or other adviser.

Notes for completion of the Appendix

1   Insert the name of each owner.

2   Give sufficient identification of each part of the land held in separate ownership (including, where appropriate, the postal address) which was subject to the *cumulo* feuduty.

3   Insert the amount of the compensation allocated to each owner.

SCHEDULE 2
Form of Notice Requiring Compensatory Payment etc: Ordinary Case

(introduced by section 8(3))

"NOTICE UNDER SECTION 8(1) OF THE ABOLITION OF FEUDAL TENURE ETC (SCOTLAND) ACT 2000 (ORDINARY CASE)

To: [*name and address of former vassal*].

This notice is sent by [*name and address of former superior*]. You are required to pay the sum of £ [*amount*] as a compensatory payment for the extinction of the feuduty of £ [*amount*] per annum due in respect of [*give sufficient identification of the land in respect of which the feuduty was due*].

(*If arrears of the feuduty are also sought, then add:*

You are also required to pay the sum of £ [*amount*] as arrears of the feuduty.)

Signed: [*signature either of the former superior or of his agent; and if an agent signs he should put the word* "Agent" *after his signature*]

Date:

(*If payment is to be made to an agent of the former superior then add:*

Payment should be made to: [*name and address of agent*].)".

Explanatory Note

(This explanation has no legal effect)

The feudal system was abolished on [*insert date of abolition*]. By this notice your former feudal superior is claiming compensation from you for the extinction of the feuduty which affected your property. This notice must have been sent within two years after the date of abolition.

The compensatory payment is that sum which would, if invested in 2?% Consolidated Stock at the middle market price at the close of business last preceding the date of abolition, produce an annual sum equal to the feuduty. In practice the sum is arrived at by multiplying the feuduty by a factor known as the "compensation factor". This factor is [*insert factor*].

If the compensatory payment is £50 or more you can choose to pay the sum by instalments. You may do this by signing, dating and returning, within eight weeks, the enclosed instalment document.

If, having received the instalment document, you sell, or transfer for valuable consideration, the property or any part of it you will lose the option of paying by instalments.

Unless you are paying by instalments you must pay the compensatory payment within eight weeks.

Your former feudal superior may also be claiming arrears of feuduty for the period before the date of abolition.

If at one time you had right to the property in question but, immediately before the feudal system was abolished, you no longer had that right (because, for example, you had transferred that property to someone else) then this notice has been served on you in error and no payment will be due in terms of the notice; but you nevertheless have to provide the person who sent you the notice, if you can, with such information as you have which might enable him to identify the person who ostensibly (that is to say, disregarding questions such as whether the feuduty has already been redeemed in the case of a transfer by conveyance for valuable consideration) should have received notice instead of you.

If you think that the amount required from you is not due for whatever reason, you are advised to consult your solicitor or other adviser.

SCHEDULE 3
Form of Instalment Document

(introduced by section 10(1))

"INSTALMENT DOCUMENT

To: [*name and address of former superior or of his agent*].

I [*name and address of former vassal*] opt to make the compensatory payment of £ [*amount*] due under the notice dated [*date*] by [*number of instalments: see note for completion*] equal half-yearly instalments of £ [*amount*] on 28 May and 28 November each year, commencing on [28 May *or* 28 November] [*year*].

I enclose payment of £ [*amount*] as an amount payable in addition to the compensatory payment.

Signed:

Date: .".

Explanatory Note

(This explanation has no legal effect)

You can choose to pay by instalments by signing, dating and returning this form within eight weeks, but if you do so you must enclose the additional amount (10% over and above the compensatory payment) mentioned in this notice.

The compensatory payment will be payable in 5, 10, 15, or 20 equal instalments (depending on the total amount). The first payment will be made at the first term day of Whitsunday (28 May) and Martinmas (28 November) which follows the return of the instalment document. Payments will be due half-yearly thereafter on 28 May and 28 November until payment in full has been made.

If you fail to pay an instalment within 42 days after the day on which it is due, the whole balance of the compensatory payment will be due at once.

If, having chosen to pay by instalments, you sell, or transfer for valuable consideration, the property or any part of it the whole balance of the compensatory payment will be due seven days after the sale or transfer.

If, after you receive this document, you sell, or so transfer, the property or any part of it without having signed, dated and returned this form, you will lose the right to obtain the option to pay by instalments and the entire compensatory payment will be payable in accordance with the notice which accompanied this document.

If you have difficulty in making the compensatory payment you may be able to make arrangements with your former superior different from those you would obtain by signing, dating and completing this form; but that is a matter on which you are advised to consult your solicitor or other adviser without delay.

Note for completion of the form by the former superior

(This note has no legal effect)

Insert the number of instalments in accordance with the following table:

Compensatory Payment	Number of Instalments
£50 but not exceeding £500	5
exceeding £500 but not exceeding £1,000	10
exceeding £1,000 but not exceeding £1,500	15
exceeding £1,500	20

SCHEDULE 4
Procedures as to Service Under Section 8(1)

(introduced by section 11(2))

FORM A

"I, [*name of former vassal*], acknowledge receipt of a notice under section 8(1) of the Abolition of Feudal Tenure etc (Scotland) Act 2000 requiring a compensatory payment [*add if applicable,* of an instalment document] and of an explanatory note relating to the notice.

Signed: [*signature of former vassal*]

Date: .".

FORM B

"Notice under section 8(1) of the Abolition of Feudal Tenure etc (Scotland) Act 2000 requiring a compensatory payment was posted to [*name of former vassal*], together with [*add if applicable* an instalment document and] the requisite explanatory note relating to the notice, on [*date*].

Signature: [*signature either of the former superior or of his agent; and if an agent signs he should put the word "Agent" after his signature*]

Date: .".

SCHEDULE 5
Form of Notice Prospectively Nominating Dominant Tenement

(introduced by section 18(1))

"NOTICE PROSPECTIVELY NOMINATING DOMINANT TENEMENT

Superior:
(see note for completion 1)

Description of land which is to be the servient tenement:
(see note for completion 2)

Description of land nominated as dominant tenement:
(see note for completion 2)

Specification of condition met:
(see note for completion 3)

Terms of real burden:
(see note for completion 4)

Any counter-obligation:
(see note for completion 4)

Title to the superiority:
(see note for completion 5)

Title to land nominated as dominant tenement:
(see note for completion 5)

Service:
(see note for completion 6)

I swear [*or* affirm] that the information contained in the notice is, to the best of my knowledge and belief, true.

Signature of superior:
(see note for completion 7)

Signature of notary public:

Date: .".

Explanatory Note

(This explanation has no legal effect)

This notice is sent by your feudal superior, who is also a neighbour. In this notice your property (or some part of it) is referred to (prospectively) as the "servient tenement" and neighbouring property belonging to the superior is referred to (again prospectively) as the "dominant tenement".

By this notice the feudal superior asserts that at present the use of your property is subject to certain burdens and conditions enforceable by him and claims the right to continue to enforce the burdens and conditions, not as superior but in his capacity of owner of neighbouring property. The notice, if it is registered in the Land Register or Register of Sasines under section 18 of the Abolition of Feudal Tenure etc (Scotland) Act 2000, will allow him and his successors, as such owners, to enforce the burdens and conditions after the feudal system is abolished (which will be shortly).

Normally, for the notice to be valid, there must, on the dominant tenement, be a permanent building which is within 100 metres of the servient tenement. That building must be in use as a place of human habitation or of human resort. However, the presence of a building is not required if the burden gives a right to enter or otherwise make use of the servient tenement, or if it gives a right of pre-emption or redemption, or if the dominant tenement comprises, and the real burden was created for the benefit of, minerals, salmon fishings or some other incorporeal property.

If you think that there is a mistake in this notice or if you wish to challenge it, you are advised to contact your solicitor or other adviser.

Notes for completion of the notice

(These notes have no legal effect)

1   Insert name and address of superior.

2   Describe the land in a way that is sufficient to enable the Keeper to identify it by reference to the Ordnance Map. Where the title to the land has been registered in the Land Register the description should refer to the title number of the land or of the larger subjects of which the land forms part. Otherwise it should normally refer to and identify a deed recorded in a specified division of the Register of Sasines.

3   Insert one or more of the following:

> "The dominant tenement has on it a [*specify type of building*] at [*specify address of building*] which is within 100 metres of the servient tenement.";

> "The real burden comprises a right to enter, or otherwise make use of, the servient tenement.";

> "The real burden comprises a right of [*specify pre-emption or redemption (or both)*].".

> "The dominant tenement comprises, and (as is apparent from the terms of the real burden) that burden was created for the benefit of, [*specify minerals or salmon fishings or some other incorporeal property*].".

4   Specify by reference to the appropriate Register the deed or deeds in which the real burden or counter-obligation was imposed. Set out the real burden or counter-obligation in full or refer to the deed in such a way as to identify the real burden or counter-obligation.

5   Where the title has been registered in the Land Register of Scotland and the superior is—

> (a)   registered as proprietor, specify the title number;

> (b)   not registered as proprietor, specify the title number and set out the mid-couples or links between the person last registered and the superior so as sufficiently to identify them.

Where the title has not been registered in the Land Register and the superior—

> (a)   has a recorded title, specify by reference to the Register of Sasines the deed constituting the immediate title;

> (b)   does not have a recorded title, either—

> > (i)   specify by reference to the Register of Sasines the deed constituting the immediate title of the person with the last recorded title and set out the midcouples or links between that person and the superior so as sufficiently to identify them; or

> > (ii)   if there is no such deed, specify the nature of the superior's title.

6   Do not complete until a copy of the notice has been sent to the owner of the prospective servient tenement (except in a case where this is not reasonably practicable). Then insert whichever is applicable of the following:

"The superior has sent a copy of this notice by [*specify whether by recorded delivery or registered post or by ordinary post*] on [*date of posting*] to the owner of the prospective servient tenement at [*state address*]."; or

"It has not been reasonably practicable to send a copy of this notice to the owner of the prospective servient tenement for the following reason: [*specify the reason*].".

7   The superior should not swear or affirm, or sign, until a copy of the notice has been sent (or otherwise) as mentioned in note 6. Before signing the superior should swear or affirm before a notary public (or, if the notice is being completed outwith Scotland, before a person duly authorised under the local law to administer oaths or receive affirmations) that, to the best of the superior's knowledge and belief, all the information contained in the notice is true. The notary public should also sign. Swearing or affirming a statement which is known to be false or which is believed not to be true is a criminal offence under the False Oaths (Scotland) Act 1933. Normally the superior should swear or affirm, and sign, personally. If, however, the superior is legally disabled or incapable (for example, because of mental disorder) his legal representative should swear or affirm and sign. If the superior is not an individual (for example, if it is a company) a person entitled by law to sign formal documents on its behalf should swear or affirm and sign.

SCHEDULE 5A
Form of Notice Prospectively Converting Real Burden into Personal Pre-Emption Burden or Personal Redemption Burden

(introduced by section 18A(1))

"NOTICE PROSPECTIVELY CONVERTING REAL BURDEN INTO PERSONAL PRE-EMPTION BURDEN OR PERSONAL REDEMPTION BURDEN

Superior:

(see note for completion 1)

Description of land which is to be servient tenement:

(see note for completion 2)

Terms of real burden:

(see note for completion 3)

Any counter obligation:

(see note for completion 3)

Title to the superiority:

(see note for completion 4)

Service:

(see note for completion 5)

I swear [*or* affirm] that the information contained in the notice is, to the best of my knowledge and belief, true.

Signature of superior:

(see note for completion 6)

Signature of notary public:

Date: .”

Explanatory Note

(This explanation has no legal effect)

This notice is sent by your feudal superior. In this notice your property (or some part of it) is referred to (prospectively) as the "servient tenement".

By this notice the feudal superior asserts that at present your property is subject to a right of pre-emption [*or* of redemption] enforceable by him and claims the right to continue to enforce it not as superior but in a personal capacity. The notice, if it is registered in the Land Register or Register of Sasines under section 18A of the Abolition of Feudal Tenure etc (Scotland) Act 2000, will allow him to enforce the right after the feudal system is abolished (which will be shortly).

If you think that there is a mistake in this notice or if you wish to challenge it, you are advised to contact your solicitor or other adviser.

Notes for completion of the notice

(These notes have no legal effect)

1   Insert name and address of superior.

2   Describe the land in a way that is sufficient to enable the Keeper to identify it by reference to the Ordnance Map. Where the title to the land has been registered in the Land Register the description should refer to the title number of the land or of the larger subjects of which the land forms part. Otherwise it should normally refer to and identify a deed recorded in a specified division of the Register of Sasines.

3   Specify by reference to the appropriate Register the deed or deeds in which the real burden or counter-obligation was imposed. Set out the real burden or counter-obligation in full or refer to the deed in such a way as to identify the real burden or counter-obligation.

4   Where the title has been registered in the Land Register of Scotland and the superior is—

    (a)   registered as proprietor, specify the title number;

    (b)   not so registered, specify the title number and set out the midcouples or links between the person last registered and the superior so as sufficiently to identify them.

Where the title has not been registered in the Land Register and the superior—

(a)   has a recorded title, specify by reference to the Register of Sasines the deed constituting the immediate title;

(b)   does not have a recorded title, either—

   (i)   specify by reference to the Register of Sasines the deed constituting the immediate title of the person with the last recorded title and set out the midcouples or links between that person and the superior so as sufficiently to identify them; or

   (ii)   if there is no such deed, specify the nature of the superior's title.

5   Do not complete until a copy of the notice has been sent to the owner of the prospective servient tenement (except in a case where this is not reasonably practicable). Then insert whichever is applicable of the following:

"The superior has sent a copy of this notice by [*specify whether by recorded delivery or registered post or by ordinary post*] on [*date of posting*] to the owner of the prospective servient tenement at [*state address*]."; or

"It has not been reasonably practicable to send a copy of this notice to the owner of the prospective servient tenement for the following reason: [*specify the reason*]".

6   The superior should not swear or affirm, or sign, until a copy of the notice has been sent (or otherwise) as mentioned in note 5. Before signing, the superior should swear or affirm before a notary public (or, if the notice is being completed outwith Scotland, before a person duly authorised under the local law to administer oaths or receive affirmations) that, to the best of the superior's knowledge and belief, all the information contained in the notice is true. The notary public should also sign. Swearing or affirming a statement which is known to be false or which is believed not to be true is a criminal offence under the False Oaths (Scotland) Act 1933. Normally the superior should swear or affirm, and sign, personally. If, however, the superior is legally disabled or incapable (for example, because of mental disorder) his legal representative should swear or affirm and sign. If the superior is not an individual (for example, if it is a company) a person entitled by law to sign formal documents on its behalf should swear or affirm and sign.

SCHEDULE 5B
Form of Notice Prospectively Converting Real Burden into Economic Development Burden

(introduced by section 18B(1))

"NOTICE PROSPECTIVELY CONVERTING REAL BURDEN INTO ECONOMIC DEVELOPMENT BURDEN

Superior:

(see note for completion 1)

Description of land which is to be servient tenement:

(see note for completion 2)

Terms of real burden:

(see note for completion 3)

Statement that purpose was to promote economic development:

(with supporting evidence: see note for completion 3)

Any counter obligation:

(see note for completion 3)

Title to the superiority:

(see note for completion 4)

Service:

(see note for completion 5)

Signature on behalf of superior:

Date: ”

Explanatory Note

(This explanation has no legal effect)

This notice is sent by your feudal superior; that is to say by [the Scottish Ministers] or [*specify local authority*].

By this notice the feudal superior asserts that at present your property is subject to a real burden enforceable by the superior and claims both the right to continue to enforce it, not as superior but in a personal capacity, and that the real burden is for the purpose of promoting economic development. The notice, if it is registered in the Land Register or Register of Sasines under section 18B of the Abolition of Feudal Tenure etc (Scotland) Act 2000, will allow the superior to enforce that right after the feudal system is abolished (which will be shortly).

If you think that there is a mistake in this notice or if you wish to challenge it, you are advised to contact your solicitor or other adviser.

Notes for completion of the notice

(These notes have no legal effect)

1   Insert "the Scottish Ministers" or as the case may be the name and address of the local authority.

2   Describe the land in a way that is sufficient to enable the Keeper to identify it by reference to the Ordnance Map. Where the title to the land has been registered in the Land Register the description should refer to the title number of the land or of the

larger subjects of which the land forms part. Otherwise it should normally refer to and identify a deed recorded in a specified division of the Register of Sasines.

3 Specify by reference to the appropriate Register the deed or deeds in which the real burden or counter-obligation was imposed. Set out the terms of the real burden, or as the case may be the terms of the counter-obligation, in full or refer to the deed in such a way as to identify the real burden or counter-obligation. Provide the statement specified and set out any information which supports it.

4 Where the title has been registered in the Land Register of Scotland and the superior is—

(a)   registered as proprietor, specify the title number;

(b)   not so registered, specify the title number and set out the midcouples or links between the person last registered and the superior so as sufficiently to identify them.

Where the title has not been registered in the Land Register and the superior—

(a)   has a recorded title, specify by reference to the Register of Sasines the deed constituting the immediate title;

(b)   does not have a recorded title, either—

(i)   specify by reference to the Register of Sasines the deed constituting the immediate title of the person with the last recorded title and set out the midcouples or links between that person and the superior so as sufficiently to identify them; or

(ii)   if there is no such deed, specify the nature of the superior's title.

5 Do not complete until a copy of the notice has been sent to the owner of the prospective servient tenement (except in a case where such sending is not reasonably practicable). Then insert whichever is applicable of the following:

"The superior has sent a copy of this notice by [*specify whether by recorded delivery or registered post or by ordinary post*] on [*date of posting*] to the owner of the prospective servient tenement at [*state address*]."; or

"It has not been reasonably practicable to send a copy of this notice to the owner of the prospective servient tenement and the reason is that: [*specify the reason*].".

SCHEDULE 5C
Form of Notice Prospectively Converting Real Burden into Health Care Burden

(introduced by section 18C(1))

"NOTICE PROSPECTIVELY CONVERTING REAL BURDEN INTO HEALTH CARE BURDEN

Superior:

(see note for completion 1)

Description of land which is to be servient tenement:

(see note for completion 2)

Terms of real burden:

(see note for completion 3)

Statement that purpose was to promote the provision of facilities for health care:

(with supporting evidence: see note for completion 3)

Any counter obligation:

(see note for completion 3)

Title to the superiority:

(see note for completion 4)

Service:

(see note for completion 5)

Signature on behalf of superior:

Date: ."

Explanatory Note

(This explanation has no legal effect)

This notice is sent by your feudal superior; that is to say by [the Scottish Ministers] *or* [*specify National Health Service trust*].

By this notice the feudal superior asserts that at present your property is subject to a real burden enforceable by the superior and claims both the right to continue to enforce it, not as superior but in a personal capacity, and that the real burden is for the purpose of promoting the provision of facilities for health care. The notice, if it is registered in the Land Register or Register of Sasines under section 18C of the Abolition of Feudal Tenure etc (Scotland) Act 2000, will allow the superior to enforce that right after the feudal system is abolished (which will be shortly).

If you think that there is a mistake in this notice or if you wish to challenge it, you are advised to contact your solicitor or other adviser.

Notes for completion of the notice

(These notes have no legal effect)

1   Insert "the Scottish Ministers" or as the case may be the name and address of the National Health Service trust.

2   Describe the land in a way that is sufficient to enable the Keeper to identify it by reference to the Ordnance Map. Where the title to the land has been registered in the Land Register the description should refer to the title number of the land or of the

larger subjects of which the land forms part. Otherwise it should normally refer to and identify a deed recorded in a specified division of the Register of Sasines.

3   Specify by reference to the appropriate Register the deed or deeds in which the real burden or counter-obligation was imposed. Set out the terms of the real burden, or as the case may be the terms of the counter-obligation, in full or refer to the deed in such a way as to identify the real burden or counter-obligation. Provide the statement specified and set out any information which supports it.

4   Where the title has been registered in the Land Register of Scotland and the superior is—

   (a)   registered as proprietor, specify the title number;

   (b)   not so registered, specify the title number and set out the midcouples or links between the person last registered and the superior so as sufficiently to identify them.

Where the title has not been registered in the Land Register and the superior—

   (a)   has a recorded title, specify by reference to the Register of Sasines the deed constituting the immediate title;

   (b)   does not have a recorded title, either—

      (i)   specify by reference to the Register of Sasines the deed constituting the immediate title of the person with the last recorded title and set out the midcouples or links between that person and the superior so as sufficiently to identify them; or

      (ii)   if there is no such deed, specify the nature of the superior's title.

5   Do not complete until a copy of the notice has been sent to the owner of the prospective servient tenement (except in a case where such sending is not reasonably practicable). Then insert whichever is applicable of the following:

"The superior has sent a copy of this notice by [*specify whether by recorded delivery or registered post or by ordinary post*] on [*date of posting*] to the owner of the prospective servient tenement at [*state address*]."; or

"It has not been reasonably practicable to send a copy of this notice to the owner of the prospective servient tenement and the reason is that: [*specify the reason*].".

SCHEDULE 6
Form of Notice Seeking Agreement to the Prospective Nomination of a Dominant Tenement

(introduced by section 19(1)(a))

"NOTICE SEEKING AGREEMENT TO PROSPECTIVE NOMINATION OF DOMINANT TENEMENT

Superior:
(see note for completion 1)

Person who has the feudal estate of *dominium utile*:
(see note for completion 2)

Description of land which, if agreement is reached and the agreement is registered, shall be the prospective servient tenement:

Description of land which, if agreement is reached and the agreement is registered, shall be the prospective dominant tenement:

Terms of real burden:
(see note for completion 3)

Any counter-obligation:
(see note for completion 3)

Title to the superiority:
(see note for completion 4)

Title to land which would be the prospective dominant tenement:
(see note for completion 4)

Service:
(see note for completion 5)

Signature of superior:

Date: .".

Explanatory Note

(This explanation has no legal effect)

This notice is sent by your feudal superior. In this notice your property (or some part of it) is referred to (prospectively) as the "servient tenement" and property belonging to the superior is referred to (again prospectively) as the "dominant tenement".

By this notice the feudal superior asserts that at present the use of your property is subject to certain burdens and conditions enforceable by him. He wishes to be able to continue to enforce the burdens and conditions, not as superior but in his capacity of owner of the prospective dominant tenement. If you agree and if the agreement is registered in the Land Register or Register of Sasines under section 19 of the Abolition of Feudal Tenure etc (Scotland) Act 2000, he and his successors, as such owners, will be able to enforce the burdens and conditions after the feudal system is abolished (which will be shortly).

In the absence of agreement the superior may yet be able to enforce the burdens and conditions provided that he can meet certain statutory conditions or if he applies to the Lands Tribunal for Scotland and the Tribunal grants an appropriate order on being satisfied by him that there would be substantial loss or disadvantage to him as owner of the prospective dominant tenement were the real burden to be extinguished or to cease to be enforceable by him.

If the superior does apply to the Tribunal you may oppose the application and in doing so may be eligible for Legal Aid. You would not ordinarily have to meet the superior's expenses. You are advised to consult your solicitor or other adviser if you wish to consider opposing the application or if you are uncertain about what is said in this notice.

Notes for completion of the notice

(These notes have no legal effect)

1 Insert name and address of superior.

2 Insert name and address of person who has the feudal estate of *dominium utile.*

3 Specify by reference to the appropriate Register the deed or deeds in which the real burden or counter-obligation was imposed. Set out the real burden or counter-obligation in full or refer to the deed in such a way as to identify the real burden or counter-obligation. You may if you wish propose and set out a modification to either the real burden or to the counter-obligation (or modifications to both).

4 Where the title has been registered in the Land Register of Scotland and the superior is—

    (a) registered as proprietor, specify the title number;

    (b) not registered as proprietor, specify the title number and set out the mid-couples or links between the person last registered and the superior so as sufficiently to identify them.

Where the title has not been registered in the Land Register and the superior—

    (a) has a recorded title, specify by reference to the Register of Sasines the deed constituting the immediate title;

    (b) does not have a recorded title, either—

        (i) specify by reference to the Register of Sasines the deed constituting the immediate title of the person with the last recorded title and set out the midcouples or links between that person and the superior so as sufficiently to identify them; or

        (ii) if there is no such deed, specify the nature of the superior's title.

5 Do not complete until a copy of the notice has been delivered or sent to the person with right to the feu. Then insert the following:

    "The superior has served this notice by [*specify whether by delivery, by recorded delivery, by registered post or by ordinary post*] on [*date of posting*] to the person with right to the feu at [*state address*]."

The notice should not be signed until a copy of it has been so delivered or sent.

SCHEDULE 7
Form of Notice Intimating Application to Lands Tribunal Under Section 20(1)

(introduced by section 20(3))

"NOTICE INTIMATING APPLICATION TO LANDS TRIBUNAL UNDER SECTION 20(1) OF THE ABOLITION OF FEUDAL TENURE ETC (SCOTLAND) ACT 2000

Superior:
(see note for completion 1)

Description of land which is the prospective servient tenement:
(see note for completion 2)

Description of land which is the prospective dominant tenement:
(see note for completion 2)

Terms of real burden:
(see note for completion 3)

Any counter-obligation:
(see note for completion 3)

Title to the superiority:
(see note for completion 4)

Title to the *dominium utile* of the prospective dominant tenement:
(see note for completion 4)

Terms of description given, in application to Lands Tribunal, of attempt to reach agreement:
(see note for completion 5)

Service:
(see note for completion 6)

I swear [*or* affirm] that the information contained in the notice is, to the best of my knowledge and belief, true.

Signature of superior:
(see note for completion 7)

Signature of notary public:

Date: .".

Explanatory Note

(This explanation has no legal effect)

This notice is sent by your feudal superior. In this notice your property (or some part of it) is referred to as the "prospective servient tenement" and the superior's property is referred to as the "prospective dominant tenement".

At present the use of your property is subject to certain burdens and conditions enforceable by the feudal superior. The feudal system is shortly to be abolished. The feudal superior cannot satisfy any of the conditions in section 18(7) of the Abolition of Feudal Tenure etc (Scotland) Act 2000 but is applying to the Lands Tribunal for Scotland to be allowed the right to continue to enforce the burdens and conditions, not as superior but in his capacity of owner of the prospective dominant tenement. The Lands Tribunal's order, if it is registered in the Land Register or Register of Sasines under section 20 of the 2000 Act, would allow him and his successors, as such owners, to enforce the burdens and conditions after the feudal system is abolished. He claims that there would be substantial loss or disadvantage to him as owner of the prospective dominant tenement were the real burden to be extinguished or no longer to be enforceable by him.

You may oppose his application to the Tribunal and in doing so may be eligible for Legal Aid. You would not ordinarily have to meet the superior's expenses. You are advised to consult your solicitor or other adviser if you wish to consider opposing the application or if you think that there is a mistake in this notice.

The effect of the superior registering this notice will be that the burdens and conditions to which the notice relates will continue to be burdens and conditions (though, after the feudal system is abolished, non-feudal burdens and conditions) until the order made by the Lands Tribunal in respect of the application is registered as mentioned above unless the order is registered before the feudal system is abolished in which case until the feudal system is abolished (or, if there is no such registration at all, until a date specified by the Scottish Ministers) at which time the burdens and conditions would either be saved as non-feudal burdens and conditions or would be extinguished because the superior had been unsuccessful in his application.

Notes for completion of the notice

(These notes have no legal effect)

1   Insert name and address of superior.

2   Describe the land in a way that is sufficient to enable the Keeper to identify it by reference to the Ordnance Map. Where the title to the land has been registered in the Land Register the description should refer to the relevant title number of the land or of the larger subjects of which the land forms part. Otherwise it should normally refer to and identify a deed recorded in a specified division of the Register of Sasines.

3   Specify by reference to the Register the deed or deeds in which the real burden or counter-obligation was imposed. Set out the real burden or counter-obligation in full or so as sufficiently to identify it.

4   The superiority referred to in the box "Title to the superiority" is the superiority of land which comprises the prospective servient tenement.

Where the title—

    (a)   has been registered in the Land Register and the applicant is infeft, specify the title number or if he is uninfeft specify the title number and set out the midcouples or links between the person last infeft and the applicant in such terms as are sufficient to identify them;

(b)   has not been registered in the Land Register and the applicant is infeft, specify by reference to the Register the deed constituting the title or if he is uninfeft specify the deed constituting the title of the person last infeft and the date of recording and set out the midcouples or links as in paragraph (a).

5   Set out in full the description which was, in pursuance of section 20(2) of the Abolition of Feudal Tenure etc (Scotland) Act 2000, included in the application.

6   Insert either: "The applicant has sent a copy of this notice by [*specify recorded delivery mail or registered post*] to the owner of the prospective servient tenement at [*specify the address of the prospective servient tenement, or the place of residence or place of business, or the most recently known place of residence or place of business, of the owner of the servient tenement*]." or "It has not been reasonably practicable to serve a copy of this notice on the owner of the prospective servient tenement for the following reasons: [*specify the reasons*].".

7   The superior should not swear or affirm, or sign, until a copy of the notice has been sent (or otherwise) as mentioned in note 6. Before signing the superior should swear or affirm before a notary public (or, if the notice is being completed outwith Scotland, before a person duly authorised under the local law to administer oaths or receive affirmations) that, to the best of the superior's knowledge and belief, all the information contained in the notice is true. The notary public should also sign. Swearing or affirming a statement which is known to be false or which is believed not to be true is a criminal offence under the False Oaths (Scotland) Act 1933. Normally the superior should swear or affirm, and sign, personally. If, however, the superior is legally disabled or incapable (for example, because of mental disorder) his legal representative should swear or affirm and sign. If the superior is not an individual (for example, if it is a company) a person entitled by law to sign formal documents on its behalf should swear or affirm and sign.

SCHEDULE 8
Form of Notice Preserving Conservation Body's or Scottish Ministers' Right to Real Burden

(introduced by section 27(1))

"NOTICE PRESERVING CONSERVATION BODY'S OR SCOTTISH MINISTERS' RIGHT TO REAL BURDEN

Superior (being a conservation body or the Scottish Ministers):
(see note for completion 1)

Description of land subject to the real burden:
(see note for completion 2)

Terms of real burden:
(see note for completion 3)

Any counter-obligation:
(see note for completion 3)

Title to the superiority:
(see note for completion 4)

Service:
(see note for completion 5)

Signature of superior:
(see note for completion 6)

Signature of witness:

Name and address of witness:

Date: .".

Explanatory Note

(This explanation has no legal effect)

This notice is sent by your feudal superior.

At present the use of your property is subject to certain burdens and conditions enforceable by the feudal superior. The feudal system is shortly to be abolished. [By the regulations mentioned in the notice, the Scottish Ministers have prescribed that your superior should be a conservation body. Such a body is entitled to enforce certain real burdens (referred to prospectively as "conservation burdens").] *or* [The feudal superior is the Scottish Ministers and it is intended that they shall enforce certain real burdens (referred to prospectively as "conservation burdens")] These are burdens which have been imposed in the public interest for the preservation or protection either of architectural or historic characteristics of land or of some other special characteristic of land derived from the flora, fauna, or general appearance of the land. By this notice [the conservation body is] [the Scottish Ministers are] claiming the right to continue to enforce a conservation burden, not as superior but [in its capacity as a conservation body] [in their capacity as the Scottish Ministers]. The notice, if it is registered in the Land Register of Scotland or recorded in the Register of Sasines under section 27 of the Abolition of Feudal Tenure etc (Scotland) Act 2000, will allow the burden and conditions to be so enforced after the feudal system has been abolished.

If you think that there is a mistake in this notice or if you wish to challenge it, you are advised to consult your solicitor or other adviser.

Notes for completion of the notice

(These notes have no legal effect)

1   In the case of a conservation body, insert the year and number of the relevant statutory instrument and the name and address of that body.

2　Describe the land in a way that is sufficient to enable the Keeper to identify it by reference to the Ordnance Map. Where the title to the land has been registered in the Land Register the description should refer to the title number of the land or of the larger subjects of which the land forms part. Otherwise it should normally refer to and identify a deed recorded in a specified division of the Register of Sasines.

3　Specify by reference to the appropriate Register the deed or deeds in which the real burden or counter-obligation was imposed. Set out the real burden or counter-obligation in full or refer to the deed in such a way as to identify the real burden or counter-obligation.

4　Where the title has been registered in the Land Register of Scotland and the superior is—

    (a)　infeft, specify the title number;

    (b)　uninfeft, specify the title number and set out the midcouples or links between the person last infeft and the superior so as sufficiently to identify them.

Where the title has not been registered in the Land Register and the superior—

    (a)　has a recorded title, specify by reference to the Register of Sasines the deed constituting the immediate title;

    (b)　does not have a recorded title, either—

        (i)　specify by reference to the Register of Sasines the deed constituting the immediate title of the person last infeft and set out the midcouples or links between the person last infeft and the superior so as sufficiently to identify them; or

        (ii)　if there is no such deed, specify the nature of the superior's title.

5　Do not complete until a copy of the notice has been sent to the owner of the land subject to the burden (except in a case where this is not reasonably practicable). Then insert whichever is applicable of the following:

    "The superior has sent a copy of this notice by [*specify whether by recorded delivery or registered post or by ordinary post*] on [*date of posting*] to the owner of the land subject to the real burden at [*state address*]."; or

    "It has not been reasonably practicable to send a copy of this notice to the owner of the land subject to the real burden for the following reason: [*specify the reason*].".

6　The notice should not be signed until a copy of it has been sent (or otherwise) as mentioned in note 5. The conservation body or the Scottish Ministers should sign.

SCHEDULE 8A
Form of Notice Nominating Conservation Body or Scottish Ministers to Have Title to Enforce Real Burden

(introduced by section 27A(1))

"NOTICE NOMINATING CONSERVATION BODY OR SCOTTISH MINISTERS TO HAVE TITLE TO ENFORCE REAL BURDEN

Superior:

Nominee (being a conservation body or the Scottish Ministers):

(see note for completion 1)

Description of land subject to the real burden:

(see note for completion 2)

Terms of real burden:

(see note for completion 3)

Any counter-obligation:

(see note for completion 3)

Title to the superiority:

(see notes for completion 4 and 5)

Service:

(see note for completion 6)

Signature of superior:	**Signature of consenting nominee:**
(see note for completion 7)	*(see note for completion 8)*
Signature of superior's witness:	**Signature of nominee's witness:**
Name and address of witness:	**Name and address of witness:**

Date: "

Explanatory note

(This explanation has no legal effect)

This notice is sent by your feudal superior.

At present the use of your property is subject to certain burdens and conditions enforceable by the feudal superior. The feudal system is shortly to be abolished. The feudal superior intends to nominate a conservation body or the Scottish Ministers to have title to enforce certain of those burdens (referred to prospectively as "conservation burdens") when he ceases to have such title. These are burdens which have been imposed in the public interest for the preservation or protection either of architectural or historic characteristics of land or of some other special characteristic of land derived from the flora, fauna or general appearance of the land. By virtue of this notice the nominee would have the right to enforce a conservation burden in the capacity of conservation body or of the Scottish Ministers, as the case may be. The notice, if it is registered in the Land Register of Scotland or recorded in the Register of Sasines under section 27A of the Abolition of Feudal Tenure etc (Scotland) Act 2000, will allow the burden to be so enforced after the feudal system has been abolished.

If you think there is a mistake in this notice or if you wish to challenge it, you are advised to consult your solicitor or other adviser.

Notes for completion of the notice

(These notes have no legal effect)

1   In the case of a conservation body, insert the year and number of the relevant statutory instrument and the name and address of that body.

2   Describe the land in a way that is sufficient to enable the Keeper to identify it by reference to the Ordnance Map. Where the title to the land has been registered in the Land Register the description should refer to the title number of the land or of the larger subjects of which the land forms part. Otherwise it should normally refer to and identify a deed recorded in a specified division of the Register of Sasines.

3   Specify by reference to the appropriate Register the deed or deeds in which the real burden or counter-obligation was imposed. Set out the real burden or counter-obligation in full or refer to the deed in such a way as to identify the real burden or counter-obligation.

4   Where the title has been registered in the Land Register of Scotland and the superior is—

    (a)   infeft, specify the title number;

    (b)   uninfeft, specify the title number and set out the midcouples or links between the person last infeft and the superior so as sufficiently to identify them.

5   Where the title has not been registered in the Land Register and the superior—

    (a)   has a recorded title, specify by reference to the Register of Sasines the deed constituting the immediate title;

    (b)   does not have a recorded title, either—

        (i)   specify by reference to the Register of Sasines the deed constituting the immediate title of the person last infeft and set out the midcouples or links between the person last infeft and the superior so as sufficiently to identify them; or

(ii)   if there is no such deed, specify the nature of the superior's title.

6   Do not complete until a copy of the notice has been sent to the owner of the land subject to the burden (except in a case where this is not reasonably practicable). Then insert whichever is applicable of the following:

"The superior has sent a copy of this notice by [*specify whether by recorded delivery or registered post or by ordinary post*] on [*date of posting*] to the owner of the land subject to the real burden at [*state address*]."; or

"It has not been reasonably practicable to send a copy of this notice to the owner of the land subject to the real burden for the following reason: [*specify the reason*]."

7   The notice should not be signed by the superior until a copy of it has been sent (or otherwise) as mentioned in note 6.

8   The nominee should sign, so as to indicate consent, before that copy is sent (or otherwise) as so mentioned.

SCHEDULE 9
Form of Notice Reserving Right to Compensation in Respect of Extinction of Development Value Burden

(introduced by section 33(1))

"NOTICE RESERVING RIGHT TO COMPENSATION IN RESPECT OF EXTINCTION OF DEVELOPMENT VALUE BURDEN

Superior:
(see note for completion 1)

Description of land (or part) subject to the real burden:
(see note for completion 2)

Terms of real burden:
(see note for completion 3)

Statement that burden reserves development value:
(see note for completion 4)

Title to the superiority:
(see note for completion 5)

Details of feu grant:
(see note for completion 6)

Amount by which consideration reduced:
(see note for completion 7)

Service:
(see note for completion 8)

By this notice I [A B] (*superior*) reserve the right to claim compensation in respect of the extinction of the development value burden(s) set out in this form.

I swear [*or* affirm] that the information contained in the notice is, to the best of my knowledge and belief, true.

Signature of superior:
(see note for completion 9)

Signature of notary public:

Date: .".

Explanatory Note

(This explanation has no legal effect)

This notice is sent by your feudal superior.

The feudal system is shortly to be abolished. By this notice the feudal superior is claiming that your property is subject to a development value burden. He is reserving the right to claim compensation for the loss of the burden. Compensation so claimed is payable if either during the five year period ending on [*insert date of appointed day*] or during the twenty year period starting on that date something happens which, had the feudal system not been abolished, would have been a breach of the burden.

A development value burden is a special type of real burden designed to reserve for the superior the benefit of any increase in the value of the land arising from the land being freed to be used or dealt with in a way prohibited by the burden. Burdens of this type were typically inserted in feudal grants where the superior gave away land, or sold it very cheaply, on condition that it was used only for some charitable or community purposes (for example, for use only as a community hall or sports field).

For the superior to be entitled to reserve the right to claim compensation, the burden must have led to the price paid for your property when it was first sold by the superior being significantly lower than it would otherwise have been.

This notice will be registered in the Land Register of Scotland, or recorded in the Register of Sasines, under section 33 of the Abolition of Feudal Tenure etc (Scotland) Act 2000.

If you think that there is a mistake in this notice or if you wish to challenge it, you are advised to consult your solicitor or other adviser.

Notes for completion of notice

(These notes have no legal effect)

1   Insert name and address of superior.

2   Describe the land in a way that is sufficient to enable the Keeper to identify it by reference to the Ordnance Map. Where the title to the land has been registered in the Land Register the description should refer to the title number of the land or of the larger subjects of which the land forms part. Otherwise it should normally refer to and identify a deed recorded in a specified division of the Register of Sasines.

3   Specify by reference to the appropriate Register the deed or deeds in which the development value burden was imposed. Set out the burden in full or refer to the deed in such a way as to identify the burden. If the notice is used to reserve rights in relation to more than one development value burden, details of each burden should be set out separately, in numbered paragraphs.

4   State that the burden reserves the development value. Section 33(5) of the Abolition of Feudal Tenure etc (Scotland) Act 2000 defines "development value" as "any significant increase in the value of the land arising as a result of the land becoming free to be used, or dealt with, in some way not permitted under the grant in feu". Set out any information (additional to that provided in the other boxes) which supports that statement.

5   Where the title has been registered in the Land Register of Scotland and the superior is—

   (a)   infeft, specify the title number;

   (b)   uninfeft, specify the title number and set out the midcouples or links between the person last infeft and the superior so as sufficiently to identify them.

Where the title has not been registered in the Land Register and the superior—

   (a)   has a recorded title, specify by reference to the Register of Sasines the deed constituting the immediate title;

   (b)   does not have a recorded title, either—

      (i)   specify by reference to the Register of Sasines the deed constituting the immediate title of the person last infeft and set out the midcouples or links between the person last infeft and the superior so as sufficiently to identify them; or

      (ii)   if there is no such deed, specify the nature of the superior's title.

6   Specify by reference to the appropriate Register the writ granting the relevant land in feu.

7   State the amount by which the consideration was reduced because of the imposition of the burden. (If the notice relates to more than one burden, the amounts should be shown separately for each burden.) The statement should be made to the best of the superior's knowledge and belief.

8   Do not complete until a copy of the notice has been sent to the owner of the land subject to the burden (except in a case where this is not reasonably practicable). Then insert whichever is applicable of the following:

   "The superior has sent a copy of this notice by [*specify whether by recorded delivery or registered post or by ordinary post*] on [*date of posting*] to the owner of the land subject to the burden at [*state address*]."; or

"It has not been reasonably practicable to send a copy of this notice to the owner of the land subject to the burden for the following reason: [*specify the reason*].".

9   The superior should not swear or affirm, or sign, until a copy of the notice has been sent (or otherwise) as mentioned in note 8. Before signing the superior should swear or affirm before a notary public (or, if the notice is being completed outwith Scotland, before a person duly authorised under the local law to administer oaths or receive affirmations) that, to the best of the superior's knowledge and belief, all the information contained in the notice is true. The notary public should also sign. Swearing or affirming a statement which is known to be false or which is believed not to be true is a criminal offence under the False Oaths (Scotland) Act 1933. Normally the superior should swear or affirm, and sign, personally. If, however, the superior is legally disabled or incapable (for example, because of mental disorder) his legal representative should swear or affirm and sign. If the superior is not an individual (for example, if it is a company) a person entitled by law to sign formal documents on its behalf should swear or affirm and sign.

SCHEDULE 10
Procedures as to Service Under Section 35(3)

(introduced by section 36(2))

FORM A

"I [*name of owner*] acknowledge receipt of a notice under section 35(3) of the Abolition of Feudal Tenure etc (Scotland) Act 2000 claiming compensation of [*amount*].

Signed: [*signature of owner*]

Date: .".

FORM B

"Notice under section 35(3) of the Abolition of Feudal Tenure etc (Scotland) Act 2000 claiming compensation was posted to [*name of owner*] on [*date*].

Signature: [*signature either of the owner or his agent; and if an agent signs he should put the word "Agent" after his signature*]

Date: .".

SCHEDULE 11
Form of Assignation, Discharge or Restriction of Reserved Right to Claim Compensation

(introduced by section 40)

"ASSIGNATION [*OR* DISCHARGE *OR* RESTRICTION] OF RESERVED RIGHT TO CLAIM COMPENSATION

I, [A B] (*designation*), hereby [assign to C D (*designation*)] *or* [discharge] the right to claim compensation reserved by a notice dated (*specify date*) and [recorded in the Register of Sasines for (*specify county*) on (*specify date*) under (*specify fiche and frame*) *or* registered in the Land Register of Scotland on (*specify date*) against the subjects in title number (*specify number*)] [*add if applicable* but only to the extent of (*specify percentage*) of each claim which may come to be made] *or* [*add if applicable* but only to the extent of (*specify restriction*) *or* but only in relation to (*specify restriction*)]. [*Where the person assigning or as the case may be discharging or restricting the right to claim compensation is not registered as having that right, add a note setting out the midcouples or links between that person and the person last so registered so as sufficiently to identify them.*]".

(*Execute in accordance with section 3 of the Requirements of Writing (Scotland) Act 1995.*)

SCHEDULE 11A
Form of Notice Prospectively Converting Sporting Rights into Tenement in Land

(introduced by section 65A(1))

"NOTICE PROSPECTIVELY CONVERTING SPORTING RIGHTS INTO TENEMENT IN LAND

Superior:

(see note for completion 1)

Description of land subject to sporting rights:

(see note for completion 2)

Description of sporting rights:

(see note for completion 3)

Any counter-obligation:

(see note for completion 3)

Title to the superiority:

(see note for completion 4)

Service:

(see note for completion 5)

I swear [*or* affirm] that the information contained in this notice is, to the best of my knowledge and belief, true.

Signature of superior:

(see note for completion 6)

Signature of notary public:

Date: ."

Explanatory note

(This explanation has no legal effect)

This notice is sent by your feudal superior.

By it the feudal superior asserts that at present your property is subject to certain sporting rights (that is to say, to rights of fishing or game) enforceable by him as superior and he seeks to continue to enjoy those rights on a different basis: that is to say, as a tenement in land.

The notice, if it is registered in the Land Register of Scotland or recorded in the Register of Sasines under section 65A of the Abolition of Feudal Tenure etc (Scotland) Act 2000, will have that effect when (shortly) the feudal system is abolished.

If you think there is a mistake in this notice or if you wish to challenge it, you are advised to consult your solicitor or other adviser.

Notes for completion of the notice

(These notes have no legal effect)

1   Insert name and address of superior.

2   Describe the land in a way that is sufficient to enable the Keeper to identify it by reference to the Ordnance Map. Where the title to the land has been registered in the Land Register the description should refer to the title number of the land or of the larger subjects of which the land forms part. Otherwise it should normally refer to and identify a deed recorded in a specified division of the Register of Sasines.

3   Specify by reference to the appropriate Register the deed or deeds in which the sporting rights were reserved or the counter-obligation was imposed. Describe the sporting rights or set out the counter-obligation in full or refer to the deed in such a way as to identify those rights or that counter-obligation.

4   Where the title has been registered in the Land Register of Scotland and the superior is—

    (a)   infeft, specify the title number;

    (b)   uninfeft, specify the title number and set out the midcouples or links between the person last infeft and the superior so as sufficiently to identify them.

Where the title has not been registered in the Land Register and the superior—

    (a)   has a recorded title, specify by reference to the Register of Sasines the deed constituting the immediate title;

    (b)   does not have a recorded title, either—

        (i)   specify by reference to the Register of Sasines the deed constituting the immediate title of the person last infeft and set out the midcouples or links between the person last infeft and the superior so as sufficiently to identify them; or

        (ii)   if there is no such deed, specify the nature of the superior's title.

5   Do not complete until a copy of the notice has been sent to the owner of the land subject to the sporting rights (except in a case where this is not reasonably practicable). Then insert whichever is applicable of the following:

The superior has sent a copy of this notice by [*specify whether by recorded delivery or registered post or by ordinary post*] on [*date of posting*] to the owner of the land subject to the sporting rights at [*state address*]".; or

"It has not been reasonably practicable to send a copy of this notice to the owner of the land subject to the sporting rights for the following reason: [*specify the reason*]".

6   The notice should not be signed by the superior until a copy of it has been sent (or otherwise) as mentioned in note 5. Before signing, the superior should swear or affirm before a notary public (or, if the notice is being completed outwith Scotland, before a person duly authorised under the local law to administer oaths or receive affirmations) that, to the best of the superior's knowledge and belief, all the information contained in the notice is true. The notary public should also sign. Swearing or affirming a statement which is known to be false or which is believed not to be true is a criminal offence under the False Oaths (Scotland) Act 1933. Normally the superior should swear or affirm, and sign, personally. If, however, the superior is legally disabled or incapable (for example, because of mental disorder) his legal representative should swear or affirm and sign. If the superior is not an individual (for example, if it is a company) a person entitled by law to sign formal documents on its behalf should swear or affirm and sign.

(Schedules 12 and 13, being concerned with amendments and repeals,
are omitted from this book)

Appendix 2

Title Conditions (Scotland) Act 2003

2003 asp 9

(This appendix contains extracts from Part 4 only. The text of the Act is stated as at 1 August 2003.)

(As well as future amendment by primary legislation, it may be noted that the Act can also be amended by statutory instrument made under s 128(4).)

The Bill for this Act of the Scottish Parliament was passed by the Parliament on 26th February 2003 and received Royal Assent on 3rd April 2003

An Act of the Scottish Parliament to make further provision as respects real burdens, servitudes and certain other obligations affecting land; to amend the law relating to the ranking of standard securities; and for connected purposes.

PART 4
TRANSITIONAL: IMPLIED RIGHTS OF ENFORCEMENT

Extinction of implied rights of enforcement

49 Extinction

(1) Any rule of law whereby land may be the benefited property, in relation to a real burden, by implication (that is to say, without being nominated in the constitutive deed as the benefited property and without being so nominated in any deed into which the constitutive deed is incorporated) shall cease to have effect on the appointed day and a real burden shall not, on and after that day, be enforceable by virtue of such rule; but this subsection is subject to subsection (2) below.

(2) In relation to a benefited property as respects which, on the appointed day, it is competent (taking such rule of law as is mentioned in subsection (1) above still to be in effect) to register a notice of preservation or of converted servitude, subsection (1) above shall apply with the substitution, for the reference to the appointed day, of a reference to the day immediately following the expiry of the period of ten years beginning with the appointed day.

[ss 50 and 51 omitted from this book]

New implied rights of enforcement

52　Common schemes: general

(1)　Where real burdens are imposed under a common scheme and the deed by which they are imposed on any unit, being a deed registered before the appointed day, expressly refers to the common scheme or is so worded that the existence of the common scheme is to be implied (or a constitutive deed incorporated into that deed so refers or is so worded) then, subject to subsection (2) below, any unit subject to the common scheme by virtue of—

    (a)　that deed; or

    (b)　any other deed so registered,

shall be a benefited property in relation to the real burdens.

(2)　Subsection (1) above applies only in so far as no provision to the contrary is impliedly (as for example by reservation of a right to vary or waive the real burdens) or expressly made in the deed mentioned in paragraph (a) of that subsection (or in any such constitutive deed as is mentioned in that subsection).

(3)　This section confers no right of pre-emption, redemption or reversion.

(4)　This section is subject to sections 57(1) and 122(2)(ii) of this Act.

53　Common schemes: related properties

(1)　Where real burdens are imposed under a common scheme, the deed by which they are imposed on any unit comprised within a group of related properties being a deed registered before the appointed day, then all units comprised within that group and subject to the common scheme (whether or not by virtue of a deed registered before the appointed day) shall be benefited properties in relation to the real burdens.

(2)　Whether properties are related properties for the purposes of subsection (1) above is to be inferred from all the circumstances; and without prejudice to the generality of this subsection, circumstances giving rise to such an inference might include—

    (a)　the convenience of managing the properties together because they share—

        (i)　some common feature; or

        (ii)　an obligation for common maintenance of some facility;

    (b)　there being shared ownership of common property;

    (c)　their being subject to the common scheme by virtue of the same deed of conditions; or

    (d)　the properties each being a flat in the same tenement.

(3)　This section confers no right of pre-emption, redemption or reversion.

(4)　This section is subject to sections 57 and 122(2)(ii) of this Act.

54   Sheltered housing

(1) Where by a deed (or deeds) registered before the appointed day real burdens are imposed under a common scheme on all the units in a sheltered or retirement housing development or on all such units except a unit which is used in some special way, each unit shall be a benefited property in relation to the real burdens.

(2) Subsection (1) above is subject to section 122(2)(ii) of this Act.

(3) In this section, "sheltered or retirement housing development" means a group of dwelling-houses which, having regard to their design, size and other features, are particularly suitable for occupation by elderly people (or by people who are disabled or infirm or in some other way vulnerable) and which, for the purposes of such occupation, are provided with facilities substantially different from those of ordinary dwelling-houses.

(4) Any real burden which regulates the use, maintenance, reinstatement or management—

   (a)   of—

      (i)   a facility; or

      (ii)   a service,

   which is one of those which make a sheltered or retirement housing development particularly suitable for such occupation as is mentioned in subsection (3) above; or

   (b)   of any other facility if it is a facility such as is mentioned in that subsection,

is in this section referred to as a "core burden".

(5) In relation to a sheltered or retirement housing development—

   (a)   section 28 of this Act applies with the following modifications—

      (i)   in subsection (1), the reference to the owners of a majority of the units in a community shall, for the purposes of paragraphs (b) and (c) of that subsection, be construed as a reference to the owners of at least two thirds of the units in the development; and

      (ii)   in paragraph (c) of subsection (2), the reference to varying or discharging shall be construed as a reference only to varying and that to community burdens as a reference only to real burdens which are not core burdens (the words "Without prejudice to the generality of subsection (1)(b) above," which begin the subsection being, for the purposes of that modification, disregarded except in so far as they give meaning to the words "the powers mentioned there" which immediately follow them);

   (b)   section 33 of this Act, in relation to core burdens, applies with the following modifications—

      (i)   in subsection (1), the reference to varying or discharging shall, in relation to a deed granted in accordance with subsection (2) of the section, be construed as a reference only to varying; and

> (ii) in subsection (2)(a) the reference to the owners of a majority of the units shall be construed as a reference to the owners of at least two thirds of the units of the development; and

(c) no real burden relating to a restriction as to any person's age may be varied or discharged by virtue of section 33(2) of this Act.

(6) This section confers no right of pre-emption, redemption or reversion and is subject to section 57 of this Act.

[s 55 omitted from this book]

56 Facility burdens and service burdens

(1) Where by a deed registered before the appointed day—

(a) a facility burden is imposed on land, then—

> (i) any land to which the facility is (and is intended to be) of benefit; and

> (ii) the heritable property which constitutes the facility,

shall be benefited properties in relation to the facility burden;

(b) a service burden is imposed on land, then any land to which the services are provided shall be a benefited property in relation to the service burden.

(2) Subsection (1) above is subject to section 57 of this Act; and in paragraph (a) of that subsection "facility burden" does not include a manager burden.

57 Further provisions as respects rights of enforcement

(1) Nothing in sections 52 to 56 revives a right of enforcement waived or otherwise lost as at the day immediately preceding the appointed day.

(2) Where there is a common scheme, and a deed, had it nominated and identified a benefited property, would have imposed under that scheme the real burdens whose terms the deed sets out, the deed shall, for the purposes of sections 25 and 53 to 56 of this Act, be deemed so to have imposed them.

(3) Sections 53 to 56 do not confer a right of enforcement in respect of anything done, or omitted to be done, in contravention of the terms of a real burden before the appointed day.

58 Duty of Keeper to enter on title sheet statement concerning enforcement rights

The Keeper of the Registers of Scotland—

(a) during that period of ten years which commences with the appointed day, may; and

(b) after the expiry of that period, shall,

where satisfied that a real burden subsists by virtue of any of sections 52 to 56 of this Act or section 60 of the 2000 Act (preserved right of Crown to maritime burdens), enter on the title sheet of the burdened property—

    (i)   a statement that the real burden subsists by virtue of the section in question; and

    (ii)   where there is sufficient information to enable the Keeper to describe the benefited property, a description of that property,

and where there is that sufficient information the Keeper shall enter that statement on the title sheet of the benefited property also, together with a description of the burdened property.

Appendix 3

Notices for preservation as neighbour burdens

SECTION 18 NOTICE

See further paras 3.4–3.16. The form of notice is set out in Schedule 5 to the Abolition of Feudal Tenure etc (Scotland) Act 2000, and the notes to that schedule should be consulted for further guidance.

NOTICE PROSPECTIVELY NOMINATING DOMINANT TENEMENT

Superior: James Alexander Macfarlane 47 Church Lane Lanark ML11 6LH
Description of land which is to be the servient tenement: 47A Church Lane, Lanark registered in the Land Register under title number LAN 57312.
Description of land nominated as dominant tenement: 47 Church Lane, Lanark, being the subjects described in Disposition by Andrew Rennie in favour of Catherine Anne Smith dated 9 September 1912 and recorded in the Division of the General Register of Sasines for the County of Lanark on 15 September 1912, under exception of the subjects registered in the Land Register under title number LAN 57312.
Specification of condition met: The dominant tenement has on it a house at 47 Church Lane, Lanark which is within 100 metres of the servient tenement[1].

continued

[1]   For alternatives to the 100-metres rule, see paras 3.8–3.12 and the Abolition of Feudal Tenure etc (Scotland) Act 2000, Sch 5, note 3.

Terms of real burdens:

The real burdens set out in Feu Disposition by Robert Campbell Wilson in favour of Norman Adams and Serena Joanna Knowles or Adams dated 12 February 1958 and recorded in the said Division of the General Register of Sasines on 19 February 1958, but excluding burdens (fourth), (sixth) and (fourteenth)[2].

Any counter-obligation:

None.

Title to the superiority:

Disposition by Robert Campbell Wilson in favour of James Alexander Macfarlane dated 4 September 1980 and recorded in the said Division of the General Register of Sasines on 30 September 1980.

Title to land nominated as dominant tenement:

The said Disposition by Robert Campbell Wilson in favour of James Alexander Macfarlane[3].

Service:

The superior has sent a copy of this notice by recorded delivery on 8 December 2003 to the owner of the prospective servient tenement at 47A Church Lane, Lanark ML11 6LH[4].

I swear that the information contained in the notice is, to the best of my knowledge and belief, true.

Signature of superior[5]:

Signature of notary public:

Date:

No warrant of registration is needed[6].

On service the notice must be accompanied by the explanatory note set out in Schedule 5 to the 2000 Act. This may be reproduced at the end of the notice or, if preferred, on a separate piece of paper. The note is as follows:

---

[2] Alternatively, the terms of the burdens can be given in full, as in the style of the blocking (s 20) notice below. But it is still necessary to refer to the deed by which the burdens were imposed.

[3] For other possibilities, see AFT(S)A 2000, Sch 5, note 5, and also other notices in Appendices 3 and 4 to this book.

[4] For other possibilities, see AFT(S)A 2000, Sch 5, note 6. For service see paras 11.7, 11.8.

[5] Normally the superior must sign personally: see para 3.13.

[6] AFT(S)A 2000, s 41(2).

Explanatory Note

This notice is sent to you by your feudal superior, who is also a neighbour. In this notice your property (or some part of it) is referred to (prospectively) as the 'servient tenement' and neighbouring property belonging to the superior is referred to (again prospectively) as the 'dominant tenement'.

By this notice the feudal superior asserts that at present the use of your property is subject to certain burdens and conditions enforceable by him and claims the right to continue to enforce the burdens and conditions, not as superior but in his capacity of owner of neighbouring property. The notice, if it is registered in the Land Register or Register of Sasines under section 18 of the Abolition of Feudal Tenure etc (Scotland) Act 2000, will allow him and his successors, as such owners, to enforce the burdens and conditions after the feudal system is abolished (which will be shortly).

Normally, for the notice to be valid, there must, on the dominant tenement, be a permanent building which is within 100 metres of the servient tenement. That building must be in use as a place of human habitation or of human resort. However, the presence of a building is not required if the burden gives a right to enter or otherwise make use of the servient tenement, or if it gives a right of pre-emption or redemption, or if the dominant tenement comprises, and the real burden was created for the benefit of, minerals, salmon fishings or some other incorporeal property.

If you think that there is a mistake in this notice or if you wish to challenge it, you are advised to contact your solicitor or other adviser.

SECTION 19 NOTICE

See further para 3.23. The form of notice is set out in Schedule 6 to the Abolition of Feudal Tenure etc (Scotland) Act 2000, and the notes to that schedule should be consulted for further guidance.

NOTICE SEEKING AGREEMENT TO PROSPECTIVE NOMINATION OF DOMINANT TENEMENT

Superior: Frederick Alastair Buchanan and William Archibald Macpherson as Trustees of the late James Robert Macpherson[1]   95 Charlotte Square   Edinburgh EH3 6DP
Person who has the feudal estate of *dominium utile*:   Margaret Ann Leven   Early Cottage   Kinlethan   Inverness-shire IV51 6LH
Description of land which, if agreement is reached and the agreement is registered, shall be the prospective servient tenement[2]:   Early Cottage   Kinlethan   Inverness-shire IV51 6LH
Description of land which, if agreement is reached and the agreement is registered, shall be the prospective dominant tenement: Craigmore House   Kinlethan   Inverness-shire IV51 6LK

continued

---

[1] See para 3.14 for the case where the superiors are trustees.

[2] By contrast with notices which are to be registered, there is no need to give a conveyancing description.

Terms of real burdens:

The following burdens contained in Feu Disposition by James Robert Macpherson in favour of Alan Muir dated 9 February 1952 and recorded in the Division of the General Register of Sasines for the County of Inverness on 15 February 1952:

(1) 'The said cottage shall be used as a dwellinghouse for one family only and for no other purpose.'

(2) 'No buildings, structures or others shall be erected on the said subjects without the consent of me and my successors.'

Suggested modification[3]: In burden (2) for 'me and my successors' substitute 'the proprietors for the time being of Craigmore House, Kinlethan'.

Any counter-obligation:

None.

Title to the superiority:

Last recorded title: Notice of Title in favour of Andrew Renton Macpherson, James Leslie and Frederick Alastair Buchanan as Trustees of the late James Robert Macpherson dated 14 March 1978 and recorded in the said Division of the General Register of Sasines on 2 April 1978.

Midcouple: Deed of Assumption and Conveyance by James Leslie and Frederick Alastair Buchanan in favour of Frederick Alastair Buchanan and William Archibald Macpherson dated 24 July and 10 August 1991 and registered in the Books of Council and Session on 14 September 1991[4].

Title to land which would be the prospective dominant tenement:

Last recorded title: the said Notice of Title in favour of Andrew Renton Macpherson, James Leslie and Frederick Alastair Buchanan as Trustees of the late James Robert Macpherson.

Midcouple: the said Deed of Assumption and Conveyance by James Leslie and Frederick Alastair Buchanan in favour of Frederick Alastair Buchanan and William Archibald Macpherson.

Service:

The superior has served this notice by delivery on 24 January 2004 to the person with right to the feu at Early Cottage, Kinlethan, Inverness-shire[5].

continued

[3]   Since an agreement requires the consent of the vassal, provision is made for the superior to propose modifications: see the Abolition of Feudal Tenure etc (Scotland) Act 2000, s 19(1), Sch 6, note 3. In the example give, the modification suggested would in any event be implied by the AFT(S)A 2000, s 73(2), and is included only for neatness.

[4]   This assumes that the superiors are uninfeft. For other possibilities, see AFT(S)A 2000, Sch 6, note 4, and also other notices in Appendices 3 and 4 to this book.

[5]   For other possibilities, see AFT(S)A 2000, Sch 6, note 5. Unlike other notices, mere delivery is sufficient.

Signature of superior[6]:

Date:

On service the notice must be accompanied by the explanatory note set out in Schedule 6 to the 2000 Act[7]. This may be reproduced at the end of the notice or, if preferred, on a separate piece of paper. The note is as follows:

Explanatory Note

This notice is sent by your feudal superior. In this notice your property (or some part of it) is referred to (prospectively) as the 'servient tenement' and property belonging to the superior is referred to (again prospectively) as the 'dominant tenement'.

By this notice the feudal superior asserts that at present the use of your property is subject to certain burdens and conditions enforceable by him. He wishes to be able to continue to enforce the burdens and conditions, not as superior but in his capacity of owner of the prospective dominant tenement. If you agree and if the agreement is registered in the Land Register or Register of Sasines under section 19 of the Abolition of Feudal Tenure etc (Scotland) Act 2000, he and his successors, as such owners, will be able to enforce the burdens and conditions after the feudal system is abolished (which will be shortly).

In the absence of agreement the superior may yet be able to enforce the burdens and conditions provided that he can meet certain statutory conditions or if he applies to the Lands Tribunal for Scotland and the Tribunal grants an appropriate order on being satisfied by him that there would be substantial loss or disadvantage[8] to him as owner of the prospective dominant tenement were the real burden to be extinguished or to cease to be enforceable by him.

If the superior does apply to the Tribunal you may oppose the application and in doing so may be eligible for Legal Aid. You would not ordinarily have to meet the superior's expenses. You are advised to consult your solicitor or other adviser if you wish to consider opposing the application or if you are uncertain about what is said in this notice.

---

[6] Notarial execution is not required.
[7] Or so at least it is assumed: see para 3.23.
[8] In fact the test to be applied by the Lands Tribunal has been changed from 'substantial loss or disadvantage' to 'material detriment to the value or enjoyment' of ownership: see the Title Conditions (Scotland) Act 2003, s 114(6), Sch 13, para 4(b); but the prescribed form of explanatory note had not, at the time of writing, been altered.

BLOCKING NOTICE (S 20)

See further paras 3.28 and 3.29. The form of notice is set out in Schedule 7 to the Abolition of Feudal Tenure etc (Scotland) Act 2000, and the notes to that schedule should be consulted for further guidance.

NOTICE INTIMATING APPLICATION TO LANDS TRIBUNAL UNDER SECTION 20(I) OF THE ABOLITION OF FEUDAL TENURE ETC (SCOTLAND) ACT 2000

Superior:

Frederick Alastair Buchanan and William Archibald Macpherson as Trustees of the late James Robert Macpherson[1]

95 Charlotte Square

Edinburgh EH3 6DP

Description of land which is the prospective servient tenement:

Early Cottage, Kinlethan, Inverness-shire described in Feu Disposition by James Robert Macpherson in favour of Alan Muir dated 9 February 1952 and recorded in the Division of the General Register of Sasines for the County of Inverness on 15 February 1952.

Description of land which is the prospective dominant tenement:

Craigmore House, Kinlethan, Inverness-shire being the subjects outlined in red on the plan annexed and signed as relative hereto and being part and portion of the subjects in the County of Inverness described in Disposition by Roderick Alasdair Macdonald in favour of Sir Malcolm Rose-Innes dated 7 December 1920 and recorded in the said Division of the General Register of Sasines on 12 December 1920[2].

Terms of real burdens:

The following burdens contained in the said Feu Disposition by James Robert Macpherson in favour of Alan Muir:

(1) 'The said cottage shall be used as a dwellinghouse for one family only and for no other purpose.'

(2) 'No buildings, structures or others shall be erected on the said subjects without the consent of me and my successors[3].'

---

continued

[1]   See para 3.14 for the case where the superiors are trustees.

[2]   The legislation does not expressly contemplate the use of a plan. But in order to satisfy the duty (Abolition of Feudal Tenure etc (Scotland) Act 2000, Sch 7, note 2) to 'describe the land in a way that is sufficient to enable the Keeper to identify it by reference to the Ordnance Map' a plan may be unavoidable or at least highly convenient. This would be so where, for example, there have been so many break-offs from the estate title that it would be wearisome to list them, or where only part of the land still held by the superior is being nominated as the dominant tenement.

[3]   Alternatively, the burdens can be incorporated by reference to the deed, as in the style of a s 18 notice above.

Any counter-obligation:

None.

Title to the superiority:

Last recorded title: Notice of Title in favour of Andrew Renton Macpherson, James Leslie and Frederick Alastair Buchanan as Trustees of the late James Robert Macpherson dated 14 March 1978 and recorded in the said Division of the General Register of Sasines on 2 April 1978.

Midcouple: Deed of Assumption and Conveyance by James Leslie and Frederick Alastair Buchanan in favour of Frederick Alastair Buchanan and William Archibald Macpherson dated 24 July and 10 August 1991 and registered in the Books of Council and Session on 14 September 1991[4].

Title to the *dominium utile* of the prospective dominant tenement:

Last recorded title: the said Notice of Title in favour of Andrew Renton Macpherson, James Leslie and Frederick Alastair Buchanan as Trustees of the late James Robert Macpherson.

Midcouple: the said Deed of Assumption and Conveyance by James Leslie and Frederick Alastair Buchanan in favour of Frederick Alastair Buchanan and William Archibald Macpherson.

Terms of description given, in application to Lands Tribunal, of attempt to reach agreement:

A notice under the Abolition of Feudal Tenure etc (Scotland) Act 2000, s 19 was served on 24 January 2004 on Margaret Ann Leven, Early Cottage, Kinlethan, Inverness-shire IV51 6LH, as the person who has right to the feu. Mrs Leven indicated by letter to the superiors dated 15 March 2004 that she was unwilling to enter into an agreement under s 19[5].

Service:

The applicant[6] has sent a copy of this notice by recorded delivery on 16 June 2004[7] to the owner of the prospective servient tenement at Early Cottage, Kinlethan, Inverness–shire.

---

continued

---

[4]   This assumes that the superiors are uninfeft. For other possibilities, see AFT(S)A 2000, Sch 7, note 4, and also other notices in Appendices 3 and 4 to this book.

[5]   This must set out in full the account given in the Lands Tribunal application: see AFT(S)A 2000, Sch 7, note 5. See further para 3.26.

[6]   At this point the statutory form uses the (undefined) term 'applicant' rather than, as in the rest of the form, 'superior'.

[7]   Strictly (and presumably by accident) the statutory wording does not require mention of the date: see AFT(S)A 2000, Sch 7, para 6.

We swear that the information contained in the notice is, to the best of our knowledge and belief, true.

Signature of superior[8]:

Signature of notary public:

Date:

No warrant of registration is needed[9].

On service the notice must be accompanied by the explanatory note set out in Schedule 7 to the 2000 Act. This may be reproduced at the end of the notice or, if preferred, on a separate piece of paper. The note is as follows:

Explanatory Note

This notice is sent by your feudal superior. In this notice your property (or some part of it) is referred to as the 'prospective servient tenement' and the superior's property is referred to as the 'prospective dominant tenement'.

At present the use of your property is subject to certain burdens and conditions enforceable by the feudal superior. The feudal system is shortly to be abolished. The feudal superior cannot satisfy any of the conditions in section 18(7) of the Abolition of Feudal Tenure etc (Scotland) Act 2000 but is applying to the Lands Tribunal for Scotland to be allowed the right to continue to enforce the burdens and conditions, not as superior but in his capacity of owner of the prospective dominant tenement. The Lands Tribunal's order, if it is registered in the Land Register or Register of Sasines under section 20 of the 2000 Act, would allow him and his successors, as such owners, to enforce the burdens and conditions after the feudal system is abolished. He claims that there would be substantial loss or disadvantage[10] to him as owner of the prospective dominant tenement were the real burden to be extinguished or no longer to be enforceable by him.

You may oppose his application to the Tribunal and in doing so may be eligible for Legal Aid. You would not ordinarily have to meet the superior's expenses. You are

---

8   Both superiors must separately swear or affirm and sign the notice. See para 3.29.
9   AFT(S)A 2000, s 41(2).
10 In fact the test to be applied by the Lands Tribunal has been changed from 'substantial loss or disadvantage' to 'material detriment to the value or enjoyment' of ownership: see the Title Conditions (Scotland) Act 2003, s 114(6), Sch 13, para 4(b); but the prescribed form of explanatory note had not, at the time of writing, been altered.

advised to consult your solicitor or other adviser if you wish to consider opposing the application or if you think that there is a mistake in this notice.

The effect of the superior registering this notice will be that the burdens and conditions to which the notice relates will continue to be burdens and conditions (though, after the feudal system is abolished, non-feudal burdens and conditions) until the order made by the Lands Tribunal in respect of the application is registered as mentioned above unless the order is registered before the feudal system is abolished in which case until the feudal system is abolished (or, if there is no such registration at all, until a date specified by the Scottish Ministers) at which time the burdens and conditions would either be saved as non-feudal burdens and conditions or would be extinguished because the superior had been unsuccessful in his application[11].

---

[11]   This mis-states the effect of the notice in a case where an order of the Tribunal refusing the application is registered before the appointed day. See para 3.33.

Appendix 4

Notices for preservation as personal real burdens

NOTICE FOR PRESERVATION AS A CONSERVATION BURDEN

See further paras 4.4–4.10. Two forms of notice are provided, in Schedules 8 and 8A to the Abolition of Feudal Tenure etc (Scotland) Act 2000, for use respectively where (i) the superior is itself a conservation body or Scottish Ministers, and (ii) where the superior, not being a conservation body or Scottish Ministers, nominates a conservation body or Scottish Ministers to be the holder of the conservation burden. The forms are almost identical and only that set out in Schedule 8 is given below. The notes to the schedule should be consulted for further guidance.

NOTICE PRESERVING CONSERVATION BODY'S OR SCOTTISH MINISTERS' RIGHT TO REAL BURDEN

Superior (being a conservation body or the Scottish Ministers):
SSI 2003/928[1]
Hilary Jane Smith, Jennifer Angela Brown and Michael John Sinclair as Trustees of the Grange Preservation Trust[2]
14 Hill Place
Aberdeen AB4 1RU
Description of land subject to the real burdens:
19 Hill Street, Aberdeen registered in the Land Register under title number ABN 23471.

continued

---

[1]   It is necessary to give the year and number of the statutory instrument made under the Title Conditions (Scotland) Act 2003, s 38(4) in virtue of which the superior is a conservation body. At the time of writing no statutory instrument had yet been made.

[2]   In cases involving trusts, it is the trustees who are treated as the conservation body: see TC(S)A 2003, s 38(6). For completion of forms in respect of trustees, see para 3.14.

Terms of real burdens:

The real burdens set out in Feu Disposition by Hilary Jane Smith, Jennifer Angela Brown and Michael John Sinclair as Trustees of the Grange Preservation Trust in favour of Richard Owen Ruddock and Kylie Olga Gunn dated 3 February 1997 and registered in the Land Register on 23 February 1997 under title number ABN 23471[3].

Any counter-obligation:

The following obligation contained in the said Feu Disposition by Hilary Jane Smith, Jennifer Angela Brown and Michael John Sinclair as Trustees foresaid in favour of Richard Owen Ruddock and Kylie Olga Gunn:

'And insofar as it is in our power, and on payment foresaid, we undertake to source and supply the necessary materials'.

Title to the superiority:

Disposition by Rialto Concrete Limited in favour of Hilary Jane Smith, Jennifer Angela Brown and Michael John Sinclair as Trustees of the Grange Preservation Trust dated 12 November 1993 and recorded in the Division of the General Register of Sasines for the County of Aberdeen on 24 March 1994[4].

Service:

The superior has sent a copy of this notice by recorded delivery on 22 January 2004 to the owner of the land subject to the real burdens at 19 Hill Street, Aberdeen AB4 1RX[5].

Signature of superior[6]:

Signature of witness:

Name and address of witness:

Date:

On service the notice must be accompanied by the explanatory note set out in Schedule 8 to the 2000 Act. This may be reproduced at the end of the notice or, if preferred, on a separate piece of paper. The note is as follows[7]:

[3]   Alternatively, the terms of the burdens can be given in full, as is done in respect of the counter-obligation.

[4]   For other possibilities, see the Abolition of Feudal Tenure etc (Scotland) Act 2000, Sch 8, note 4, and also other notices in Appendices 3 and 4 to this book.

[5]   For other possibilities, see AFT(S)A 2000, Sch 8, note 5. For service see paras 11.7, 11.8.

[6]   It is *probably* sufficient for an agent to sign on behalf of the superiors: see para 4.9.

[7]   The version given below presupposes that the superior is a conservation body. Where the superior is Scottish Ministers the wording is slightly different.

Explanatory Note

This notice is sent by your feudal superior.

At present the use of your property is subject to certain burdens and conditions enforceable by the feudal superior. The feudal system is shortly to be abolished. By the regulations mentioned in the notice, the Scottish Ministers have prescribed that your superior should be a conservation body. Such a body is entitled to enforce certain real burdens (referred to prospectively as 'conservation burdens'). These are burdens which have been imposed in the public interest for the preservation or protection either of architectural or historic characteristics of land or of some other special characteristic of land derived from the flora, fauna, or general appearance of the land. By this notice the conservation body is claiming the right to continue to enforce a conservation burden, not as superior but in its capacity as a conservation body. The notice, if it is registered in the Land Register of Scotland or recorded in the Register of Sasines under section 27 of the Abolition of Feudal Tenure etc (Scotland) Act 2000, will allow the burden and conditions to be so enforced after the feudal system has been abolished.

If you think that there is a mistake in this notice or if you wish to challenge it, you are advised to consult your solicitor or other adviser.

NOTICE FOR PRESERVATION AS AN ECONOMIC DEVELOPMENT BURDEN

See further paras 4.11–4.15. The form of notice is set out in Schedule 5B to the Abolition of Feudal Tenure etc (Scotland) Act 2000[1], and the notes to that schedule should be consulted for further guidance.

NOTICE PROSPECTIVELY CONVERTING REAL BURDEN INTO ECONOMIC DEVELOPMENT BURDEN

Superior:
Dundee City Council
21 City Square
Dundee DD1 3BY
Description of land which is to be servient tenement:
That land lying to the south of India Street, Dundee and extending to 1.73 hectares described in Feu Disposition by City of Dundee District Council in favour of Tayside Brick Company Limited dated 14 June 1978 and recorded in the Division of the General Register of Sasines for the County of Angus 17 July 1978.
Terms of real burden:
The following burden contained in the said Feu Disposition by City of Dundee District Council in favour of Tayside Brick Company Limited:
'The building erected as aforesaid shall be used in all time coming for the manufacture of bricks or for such other manufacturing purposes as shall be agreed to by us and our successors'[2].
Statement that purpose was to promote economic development:
The purpose of the burden was to promote economic development. The use of the property for manufacturing purposes provides employment and generates income. It is of material importance for the local economy.
Any counter-obligation:
None.

continued

---

[1]   As inserted by the Title Conditions (Scotland) Act 2003, s 114(6), Sch 13, para 16.
[2]   Alternatively, the burdens can be incorporated by reference to the deed, as in the style of notice for preservation of a conservation burden, above.

Title to the superiority:

Last recorded title: Disposition by Grantham Steelworks Limited in favour of City of Dundee District Council dated 14 October 1976 and recorded in the said Division of the General Register of Sasines on 10 November 1976.

Midcouple: The Local Authorities (Property Transfer) (Scotland) Order 1995, SI 1995/2499[3].

Service:

The superior has sent a copy of this notice by recorded delivery on 12 March 2004 to the owner of the prospective servient tenement at 112 India Street, Dundee[4].

Signature on behalf of superior[5]:

Date:

No warrant of registration is needed[6].

On service the notice must be accompanied by the explanatory note set out in Schedule 5B to the 2000 Act. This may be reproduced at the end of the notice or, if preferred, on a separate piece of paper. The note is as follows[7]:

Explanatory Note

This notice is sent by your feudal superior; that is to say by Dundee City Council.

By this notice the feudal superior asserts that at present your property is subject to a real burden enforceable by the superior and claims both the right to continue to enforce it, not as superior but in a personal capacity, and that the real burden is for the purpose of promoting economic development. The notice, if it is registered in the Land Register or Register of Sasines under section 18B of the Abolition of Feudal Tenure etc (Scotland) Act 2000, will allow the superior to enforce that right after the feudal system is abolished (which will be shortly).

If you think that there is a mistake in this notice or if you wish to challenge it, you are advised to contact your solicitor or other adviser.

---

[3]   For other possibilities, see the Abolition of Feudal Tenure etc (Scotland) Act 2000, Sch 5B, note 4, and also other notices in Appendices 3 and 4 to this book.

[4]   For other possibilities, see AFT(S)A 2000, Sch 5B, note 5. For service see paras 11.7, 11.8.

[5]   For execution, see para 4.14.

[6]   AFT(S)A 2000, s 41(2).

[7]   The version given below presupposes that the superior is a local authority. Where the superior is Scottish Ministers the wording is slightly different.

NOTICE FOR PRESERVATION AS A HEALTH CARE BURDEN

See further paras 4.16–4.20. The form of notice is set out in Schedule 5C to the Abolition of Feudal Tenure etc (Scotland) Act 2000[1], and the notes to that schedule should be consulted for further guidance.

NOTICE PROSPECTIVELY CONVERTING REAL BURDEN INTO HEALTH CARE BURDEN

Superior:
Strathspey National Health Service Trust
Focus House
Grantown-on-Spey
PH26 3GH
Description of land which is to be servient tenement:
Nether House, Grantown-on-Spey described in Feu Disposition by Strathspey National Health Service Trust in favour of Leisure Developments Limited dated 14 April 1999 and recorded in the Division of the General Register of Sasines for the County of Moray on 2 May 1999.
Terms of real burden:
The following burden contained in the said Feu Disposition by Strathspey National Health Service Trust in favour of Leisure Developments Limited:
'The subjects shall be used as residential accommodation for nurses and for no other purpose'[2].
Statement that purpose was to promote the provision of facilities for health care:
The effect of the burden is to ensure the availability of low-cost accommodation for nurses working at Grantown-on-Spey Hospital. Accordingly, its purpose was to promote the provision of facilities for health care.
Any counter-obligation:
None.

continued

---

[1]   As inserted by the Title Conditions (Scotland) Act 2003, s 114(6), Sch 13, para 16.
[2]   Alternatively, the burdens can be incorporated by reference to the deed, as in the style of notice for preservation of a conservation burden, above.

Title to the superiority:
Disposition by Thomas Alan Wright as Executor of the late Janice Freedman in favour of the Strathspey National Health Service Trust dated 12 November 1997 and recorded in the said Division of the General Register of Sasines on 29 November 1997[3].
Service:
The superior has sent a copy of this notice by recorded delivery on 10 February 2004 to the owner of the prospective servient tenement at Nether House, Grantown-on-Spey PH26 3BG[4].
Signature on behalf of superior[5]:
Date:

No warrant of registration is needed[6].

On service the notice must be accompanied by the explanatory note set out in Schedule 5C to the 2000 Act. This may be reproduced at the end of the notice or, if preferred, on a separate piece of paper. The note is as follows[7]:

Explanatory Note

This notice is sent by your feudal superior; that is to say by the Strathspey National Health Service Trust.

By this notice the feudal superior asserts that at present your property is subject to a real burden enforceable by the superior and claims both the right to continue to enforce it, not as superior but in a personal capacity, and that the real burden is for the purpose of promoting the provision of facilities for health care. The notice, if it is registered in the Land Register or Register of Sasines under section 18C of the Abolition of Feudal Tenure etc (Scotland) Act 2000, will allow the superior to enforce that right after the feudal system is abolished (which will be shortly).

If you think that there is a mistake in this notice or if you wish to challenge it, you are advised to contact your solicitor or other adviser.

---

[3]   For other possibilities, see the Abolition of Feudal Tenure etc (Scotland) Act 2000, Sch 5C, note 4, and also other notices in Appendices 3 and 4 to this book.

[4]   For other possibilities, see AFT(S)A 2000, Sch 5C, note 5. For service see paras 11.7, 11.8.

[5]   For execution, see para 4.19.

[6]   AFT(S)A 2000, s 41(2).

[7]   The version given below presupposes that the superior is an NHS Trust. Where the superior is Scottish Ministers the wording is slightly different.

NOTICE FOR PRESERVATION AS A PERSONAL PRE-EMPTION BURDEN

See further paras 4.21–4.23. The form of notice is set out in Schedule 5A to the Abolition of Feudal Tenure etc (Scotland) Act 2000[1]. The notes to that schedule should be consulted for further guidance. The same form may also be used for preservation as a personal redemption burden[2].

NOTICE PROSPECTIVELY CONVERTING REAL BURDEN INTO PERSONAL PRE-EMPTION BURDEN

Superior:
George Henry Wilson
Sylent House
Tynbraic
Argyllshire PA33 2LH
Description of land which is to be servient tenement:
4 The Strand, Tynbraic described in Feu Contract between Archibald James Renwick and Norman Duncan Campbell dated 13 April 1943 and recorded in the Division of the General Register of Sasines for the County of Argyll on 19 April 1943.
Terms of real burden:
Burden (sixth) set out in the said Feu Contract between Archibald James Renwick and Norman Duncan Campbell[3].
Any counter-obligation:
None.
Title to the superiority:
Disposition by Robert Cameron Mactaggart in favour of George Henry Wilson dated 15 July 1984 and recorded in the said Division of the General Register of Sasines on 19 July 1984[4].

continued

---

[1] As inserted by the Title Conditions (Scotland) Act 2003, s 114(6), Sch 13, para 16.
[2] For which see para 4.26.
[3] Alternatively, the terms of the burden can be given in full, as is done, for example, in respect of the notice for preservation as a health care burden, above.
[4] For other possibilities, see the Abolition of Feudal Tenure etc (Scotland) Act 2000, Sch 5A, note 4, and also other notices in Appendices 3 and 4 to this book.

> **Service:**
>
> The superior has sent a copy of this notice by recorded delivery on 12 May 2004 to the owner of the prospective servient tenement at 4 The Strand, Tynbraic, Argyllshire PA33 6ND[5].
>
> ---
>
> I affirm that the information contained in the notice is, to the best of my knowledge and belief, true.
>
> **Signature of superior[6]:**
>
> **Signature of notary public:**
>
> **Date:**

No warrant of registration is needed[7].

On service the notice must be accompanied by the explanatory note set out in Schedule 5A to the 2000 Act. This may be reproduced at the end of the notice or, if preferred, on a separate piece of paper. The note is as follows:

Explanatory Note

This notice is sent by your feudal superior. In this notice your property (or some part of it) is referred to (prospectively) as the 'servient tenement'.

By this notice the feudal superior asserts that at present your property is subject to a right of pre-emption enforceable by him and claims the right to continue to enforce it not as superior but in a personal capacity. The notice, if it is registered in the Land Register or Register of Sasines under section 18A of the Abolition of Feudal Tenure etc (Scotland) Act 2000, will allow him to enforce the right after the feudal system is abolished (which will be shortly).

If you think that there is a mistake in this notice or if you wish to challenge it, you are advised to contact your solicitor or other adviser.

---

[5]   For other possibilities, see AFT(S)A 2000, Sch 5A, note 5. For service see paras 11.7, 11.8.
[6]   Normally the superior must sign personally: see para 4.22.
[7]   AFT(S)A 2000, s 41(2).

Appendix 5

Notices for compensation for development value burdens

SECTION 33 NOTICE

See further paras 9.4–9.11. The form of notice is set out in Schedule 9 to the Abolition of Feudal Tenure etc (Scotland) Act 2000, and the notes to that schedule should be consulted for further guidance.

NOTICE RESERVING RIGHT TO COMPENSATION IN RESPECT OF
EXTINCTION OF DEVELOPMENT VALUE BURDEN

Superior:
William Redfern Arnott
Fenwick House
Dornal
Dumfriesshire DG5 2RF
Description of land (or part) subject to the real burden:
Dornal Community Centre, Dornal registered in the Land Register under title number DMF 3431.
Terms of real burden:
The following burden contained in Feu Disposition by William Redfern Arnott in favour of Murray Campbell Robertson, Raymond Alastair Wood and Margaret Anne Bennett dated 15 December 1981 and recorded in the Division of the General Register of Sasines for the County of Dumfries on 6 January 1982:
'The said subjects shall be used in all time coming as a community centre for the inhabitants of Dornal and for no other purpose'[1].

continued

[1] If there is more than one development value burden, each must be set out separately in numbered paragraphs: see the Abolition of Feudal Tenure etc (Scotland) Act 2000, Sch 9, note 3.

Statement that burden reserves development value:

The value of the land would be significantly increased if the burden were to be removed by a minute of waiver by the superior and the land made free for development. Hence the burden reserves development value to the superior[2].

Title to the superiority:

Disposition by William Redfern Arnott and Bruce Ronald Rankine, as Trustees of the late William Arthur Arnott, in favour of William Redfern Arnott dated 14 May 1980 and recorded in the said Division of the General Register of Sasines on 27 May 1980[3].

Details of feu grant:

The said Feu Disposition by William Redfern Arnott in favour of Murray Campbell Robertson, Raymond Alastair Wood and Margaret Anne Bennett.

Amount by which consideration reduced:

£7,000[4].

Service:

The superior has sent a copy of this notice by recorded delivery on 3 March 2004 to the owner of the land subject to the burden at 240 Irish Street, Dumfries DG1 5LF[5].

By this notice I, William Redfern Arnott, reserve the right to claim compensation in respect of the extinction of the development value burden set out in this form.

I swear that the information contained in the notice is, to the best of my knowledge and belief, true.

Signature of superior[6]:

Signature of notary public:

Date:

If, as in the example above, the (*dominium utile* of the) land subject to the burden is recorded in the Land Register, the notice should be registered there[7]. Otherwise it falls to be recorded in the Register of Sasines. No warrant of registration is needed[8].

---

[2]   See para 9.5.

[3]   For other possibilities, see AFT(S)A 2000, Sch 9, note 5, and also the notices in Appendices 3 and 4 to this book.

[4]   See para 9.6. Only the actual figure need be stated. Unlike the statement as to reservation of development value, no further explanation is required. See AFT(S)A 2000, Sch 9, note 7.

[5]   For other possibilities, see AFT(S)A 2000, Sch 9, note 8. For service see paras 11.7, 11.8.

[6]   Normally the superior must sign personally: see para 9.9.

[7]   Land Registration (Scotland) Act 1979, s 2(4)(c).

[8]   AFT(S)A 2000, s 41(2).

On service the notice must be accompanied by the explanatory note set out in Schedule 9 to the 2000 Act. This may be reproduced at the end of the notice or, if preferred, on a separate piece of paper. The note is as follows:

Explanatory Note

This notice is sent by your feudal superior.

The feudal system is shortly to be abolished. By this notice the feudal superior is claiming that your property is subject to a development value burden. He is reserving the right to claim compensation for the loss of the burden. Compensation so claimed is payable if either during the five-year period ending on 28 November 2004 or during the twenty-year period starting on that date something happens which, had the feudal system not been abolished, would have been a breach of the burden.

A development value burden is a special type of real burden designed to reserve for the superior the benefit of any increase in the value of the land arising from the land being freed to be used or dealt with in a way prohibited by the burden. Burdens of this type were typically inserted in feudal grants where the superior gave away land, or sold it very cheaply, on condition that it was used only for some charitable or community purposes (for example, for use only as a community hall or sports field).

For the superior to be entitled to reserve the right to claim compensation, the burden must have led to the price paid for your property when it was first sold by the superior being significantly lower than it would otherwise have been.

This notice will be registered in the Land Register of Scotland, or recorded in the Register of Sasines, under section 33 of the Abolition of Feudal Tenure etc (Scotland) Act 2000.

If you think that there is a mistake in this notice or if you wish to challenge it, you are advised to consult your solicitor or other adviser.

SECTION 35 NOTICE

See further paras 9.12–9.19. No statutory form is provided although some guidance is given as to content[1]. The following is just one of the ways in which a notice could be drafted. It seeks to inform the owner by including much more than the minimal information required by the Abolition of Feudal Tenure etc (Scotland) Act 2000. This seems especially important given that no provision is made for an explanatory note.

NOTICE CLAIMING COMPENSATION IN RESPECT OF EXTINCTION OF DEVELOPMENT VALUE BURDEN

To: Newstone Developments Limited, 362 High Street, Dumfries DG1 2HL.

This notice is sent by William Redfern Arnott, Fenwick House, Dornal, Dumfriesshire DG5 2RF in terms of section 35 of the Abolition of Feudal Tenure etc (Scotland) Act 2000. It follows an earlier notice, made under section 33 of that Act, which was dated 10 March 2004 and registered in the Land Register of Scotland on 17 March 2004.

In the earlier notice I reserved the right to claim compensation in respect of the extinction of a development value burden which affected the property known as Dornal Community Centre, Dornal registered in the Land Register under title number DMF 3431 and now owned by you. My right to enforce the burden was extinguished on 28 November 2004 as part of the abolition of the feudal system of land tenure. The burden provided that the property 'shall be used in all time coming as a community centre for the inhabitants of Dornal and for no other purpose'.

The community centre having now been demolished and sixteen houses erected in its place, the use of the property no longer complies with the burden. The burden, had it still existed, would thus have breached. Accordingly I claim compensation from you in terms of section 35 of the Act.

The amount of the compensation due is the lesser of (i) the development value accruing to you by a notional modification of the burden so as to allow the breach and (ii) such sum as will make up for the effect which the burden produced, at the time it was imposed, in reducing the consideration paid for the property. I estimate figure (ii) at £7,000[2]. I estimate figure (i) as substantially in excess of £7,000. **Accordingly, I hereby claim payment from you of the sum of £7,000.**

---

[1]   Para 9.14.

[2]   This is the figure used in the s 33 notice without any allowance being made for inflation. As to whether such an allowance is due, see para 9.17.

If you previously owned the property but no longer did so at the time of the breach mentioned above, then this notice has been served on you in error and no payment is due. But you must give me such information as you have as to the name and address of the owner at that time[3].

Signed:

Date:

---

[3]   Abolition of Feudal Tenure etc (Scotland) Act 2000, s 38. A s 35 notice must mention this requirement of disclosure.

Appendix 6

Notices for compensation for feuduty

NOTICE FOR STANDARD FEUDUTIES

See further para 10.11. A feuduty is 'standard' in the sense meant here if it is not an unallocated *cumulo*. The form of notice is set out in Schedule 2 to the Abolition of Feudal Tenure etc (Scotland) Act 2000. It includes an explanatory note which should probably[1] be on the same piece of paper.

NOTICE UNDER SECTION 8(1) OF THE ABOLITION OF FEUDAL TENURE ETC (SCOTLAND) ACT 2000 (ORDINARY CASE)

To: Sarah Angela Brown, 14 Bridge Street, Nairn IV12 2NT.

This notice is sent by Crossfield Insurance Limited, 114 Old Edinburgh Road, Perth PH2 3LN. You are required to pay the sum of £87.36 as a compensatory payment for the extinction of the feuduty of £3.80 per annum due in respect of 14 Bridge Street, Nairn.

You are also required to pay the sum of £1.90 as arrears of the feuduty[2].

Signed:

     Agent[3]

Date:

Payment should be made to: McNair & Co, 3 Mill Road, Perth PH1 3JT[4].

---

[1] Para 10.9.
[2] If feuduty has been regularly paid, no arrears will be due: see para 10.6.
[3] If an agent signs on behalf of the superior, as is permitted, it is necessary to add the word 'agent'.
[4] Insert only if payment is not to be made directly to the former superior.

Explanatory Note

The feudal system was abolished on 28 November 2004. By this notice your former feudal superior is claiming compensation from you for the extinction of the feuduty which affected your property. This notice must have been sent within two years after the date of abolition.

The compensatory payment is that sum which would, if invested in 2½% Consolidated Stock at the middle market price at the close of business last preceding the date of abolition, produce an annual sum equal to the feuduty. In practice the sum is arrived at by multiplying the feuduty by a factor known as the 'compensation factor'. This factor is [*insert factor*].

If the compensatory payment is £50 or more you can choose to pay the sum by instalments. You may do this by signing, dating and returning, within eight weeks, the enclosed instalment document.

If, having received the instalment document, you sell, or transfer for valuable consideration, the property or any part of it you will lose the option of paying by instalments.

Unless you are paying by instalments you must pay the compensatory payment within eight weeks.

Your former feudal superior may also be claiming arrears of feuduty for the period before the date of abolition.

If at one time you had right to the property in question but, immediately before the feudal system was abolished, you no longer had that right (because, for example, you had transferred that property to someone else) then this notice has been served on you in error and no payment will be due in terms of the notice; but you nevertheless have to provide the person who sent you the notice, if you can, with such information as you have which might enable him to identify the person who ostensibly (that is to say, disregarding questions such as whether the feuduty has already been redeemed in the case of a transfer by conveyance for valuable consideration) should have received notice instead of you.

If you think that the amount required from you is not due for whatever reason, you are advised to consult your solicitor or other adviser.

NOTICE FOR *CUMULO* FEUDUTIES

See further para 10.12. The form of notice is set out in Schedule 1 to the Abolition of Feudal Tenure etc (Scotland) Act 2000. It includes an explanatory notice which should probably[1] be on the same piece of paper. The notes to the schedule should be consulted for further guidance.

NOTICE UNDER SECTION 8(1) OF THE ABOLITION OF FEUDAL TENURE ETC (SCOTLAND) ACT 2000 (*CUMULO* FEUDUTY)

To: Mr and Mrs J R Macdonald[2], 2nd floor south, 7 Holm Street, Glasgow G3 2LQ.

This notice is sent by Westview Property Company Limited, 14 East Clyde Street, Glasgow G2 1TP. You are required to pay the sum of £81.70 as a compensatory payment for the extinction of the *cumulo* feuduty of £31.30 per annum due in respect of the tenement 5, 7, and 9 Holm Street, Glasgow.

The attached appendix shows the total sum due as compensation for the extinction of the feuduty and the compensatory payment due by each owner[3].

Signed:

Agent[4]

Date:

Payment should be made to: Burns & Murray, 14 Gray Street, Glasgow G3 1RT[5].

---

[1] Para 10.9.
[2] The notice must be served separately on each of Mr Macdonald and Mrs Macdonald: see para 12.1.
[3] If arrears are due, they should be claimed here, as in the style for standard feuduty.
[4] If an agent signs on behalf of the superior, as is permitted, it is necessary to add the word 'agent'.
[5] Insert only if payment is not to be made directly to the former superior.

Appendix referred to in the Notice:

Total compensation payable is £672.94, allocated as follows:

Owner	Property	Compensatory payment
Janice Smith	5 Holm Street	£91.37
Bruce Laing and Irene Shepherd	9 Holm Street	£91.37
Jean Williamson	1st floor north, 7 Holm Street	£81.70
J Leven	1st floor south, 7 Holm Street	£81.70
R Singh	2nd floor north, 7 Holm Street	£81.70
Mr and Mrs J R Macdonald[6]	2nd floor south, 7 Holm Street	£81.70
Suzanne Jordan	3rd floor north, 7 Holm Street	£81.70
R Mactaggart	3rd floor south, 7 Holm Street	£81.70

Explanatory Note

The feudal system was abolished on 28 November 2004. By this notice your former feudal superior is claiming compensation from you for the extinction of the *cumulo* feuduty which affected your property. A *cumulo* feuduty is one which affects two or more properties in separate ownership. This notice must have been sent within two years after the date of abolition.

The appendix sets out the total sum due as compensation for the extinction of the *cumulo* feuduty and divides that sum among the owners of the affected properties.

The total compensation payable is that sum which would, if invested in 2½% Consolidated Stock at the middle market price at the close of business last preceding the date of abolition, produce an annual sum equal to the *cumulo* feuduty. In practice the sum is arrived at by multiplying the feuduty by a factor known as the 'compensation factor'. This factor is [*insert factor*].

If the amount of the compensatory payment allocated to you is £50 or more you can choose to pay the sum due by instalments. You may do this by signing, dating and returning, within eight weeks, the enclosed instalment document.

---

[6]   It is necessary to include the person at whom the notice is directed.

If, having received the instalment document, you sell, or transfer for valuable consideration, the property or any part of it you will lose the option of paying by instalments.

Unless you are paying by instalments you must pay the compensatory payment allocated to you within eight weeks.

Your former feudal superior may also be claiming arrears of feuduty for the period before the date of abolition.

If at one time you had right to the property in question but, immediately before the feudal system was abolished, you no longer had that right (because, for example, you had sold that property to someone else) then this notice has been served on you in error and no payment will be due; but you nevertheless have to provide the person who sent you the notice, if you can, with such information as you have which might enable him to identify the person who should have received notice instead of you.

If you think that the amount required from you is not due for that or any other reason, you are advised to consult your solicitor or other adviser.

INSTALMENT DOCUMENT

See further paras 10.14 and 10.15. The form of notice is set out in Schedule 3 to the Abolition of Feudal Tenure etc (Scotland) Act 2000. It includes an explanatory note which should probably[1] be on the same piece of paper.

INSTALMENT DOCUMENT

To: Burns & Murray, 14 Gray Street, Glasgow G3 1RT.

We, Mr and Mrs J R Macdonald, 2nd floor south, 7 Holm Street, Glasgow G3 2LQ, opt to make the compensatory payment of £81.70 due under the notice dated 5 July 2005 by five equal half-yearly instalments of £16.34 on 28 May and 28 November each year, commencing on 28 November 2005.

We enclose payment of £8.17 as an amount payable in addition to the compensatory payment[2].

Signed[3]:

Date:

Explanatory Note

You can choose to pay by instalments by signing, dating and returning this form within eight weeks, but if you do so you must enclose the additional amount (10% over and above the compensatory payment) mentioned in this notice.

The compensatory payment will be payable in 5, 10, 15, or 20 equal instalments (depending on the total amount). The first payment will be made at the first term day of Whitsunday (28 May) or Martinmas (28 November) which follows the return of

---

[1]   Para 10.9.

[2]   This is a non-returnable deposit of 10%: see para 10.14.

[3]   To be left blank for the signature of the former vassal. If, as here, the property is owned in common, it is thought that both *pro indiviso* owners must sign.

the instalment document. Payments will be due half-yearly thereafter on 28 May and 28 November until payment in full has been made.

If you fail to pay an instalment within 42 days after the day on which it is due, the whole balance of the compensatory payment will be due at once.

If, having chosen to pay by instalments, you sell, or transfer for valuable consideration, the property or any part of it the whole balance of the compensatory payment will be due seven days after the sale or transfer.

If, after you receive this document, you sell, or so transfer, the property or any part of it without having signed, dated and returned this form, you will lose the right to obtain the option to pay by instalments and the entire compensatory payment will be payable in accordance with the notice which accompanied this document.

If you have difficulty in making the compensatory payment you may be able to make arrangements with your former superior different from those you would obtain by signing, dating and completing this form; but that is a matter on which you are advised to consult your solicitor or other adviser without delay.

Index